I Was a Dancer

Jacques d'Amboise

I Was a Dancer

A MEMOIR

ALFRED A. KNOPF  NEW YORK · 2011

This Is a Borzoi Book
Published by Alfred A. Knopf
Copyright © 2011 by Jacques d'Amboise
All rights reserved. Published in the United States by Alfred A. Knopf,
 a division of Random House, Inc., New York, and in Canada by
Random House of Canada Limited, Toronto.
www.aaknopf.com

Knopf, Borzoi Books, and the colophon are registered trademarks
of Random House, Inc.

Grateful acknowledgment is made to the following for permission to
reprint previously published material:

Judy Collins: Lyrics from "The Other Side of My World" and
"Rosebud's Song," music and lyrics by Judy Collins. Reprinted by
permission of the author.

Nicholas Jenkins: Excerpt from the poem "Patton" and the entire poem
"Vaudeville" by Lincoln Kirstein, copyright © 2011 by the New York
Public Library (Astor, Lenox and Tilden Foundations). Reprinted by
permission of Nicholas Jenkins, Literary Executor of the Copyrights and
Papers of Lincoln Kirstein.

Library of Congress Cataloging-in-Publication Data
D'Amboise, Jacques, {date}
I was a dancer / by Jacques d'Amboise.
p.   cm.
Includes index.
ISBN 978-1-4000-4234-0
 1. D'Amboise, Jacques, {date}   2. Dancers—United States—Biography.
3. New York City Ballet.   I. Title.
GV1785.D23A3 2011
792.8028092—dc22
{B}   2010045356

Front-of-jacket photograph © John Dominis/Time Life Pictures/Getty Images
Back-of-jacket photographs: (top right) John Dominus/Time Life
Pictures/Getty Images; (center right) © Martha Swope; (lower right) John
Dominus/Time Life Pictures/Getty Images; (all others) Carolyn George
Jacket Design by Jason Booher

Manufactured in the United States of America
First Edition

Contents

Illustrations

All images without a photo credit are courtesy of the author.

Acknowledgments

This book exists because of:

1. Vicky Wilson—at a dinner table she said, "Hey! I'm with Knopf . . . We would be interested in publishing a book by you on your life."
2. Kay Gayner—fingers at a computer, ears to listen, voice to ask questions, patience to make it through my garrulousness, shared her brilliance to aid me in everything.
3. The skills given so generously by Kyle Goodman, Malcolm St. Clair, and Tamara Tweedy.
4. Carmen Johnson—whose beauty is matched by her intellect.
5. Vicky—again, who is to be thanked or blamed depending on the reader's judgment.

Prologue

In my early twenties, I was approached to write a book about my life as a dancer. I thought, "Ridiculous! I haven't lived yet." However, over the next fifty years, I kept diaries, collected materials, and occasionally dabbled, writing little essays of an autobiographical nature. Ingredients were being stored for future use.

In 1999, I took close to seven months off to backpack the length of the Appalachian Trail with my son George. It was an exhilarating adventure. The first six weeks (Maine and New Hampshire) were brutal, but soon we became walking machines, easily knocking off twenty miles a day, while lugging a backpack up and down the rocky terrain. From north to south, through the fourteen states we traversed, and staged forty dance events. I invented an Appalachian hiking dance for those events, teaching more than fifteen thousand people. During the more than five million steps it takes to hike the Appalachian Trail, I spent a lot of time listening to voices in my head. A recurring one urged, "Jacques, stop delaying! Finish your hike and finish your book! It's ready to be baked!" Well, it took over a decade to prepare and serve these pages.

Anecdotal and episodic, this book is a buffet of stories about the experiences and relationships that shaped me as a person, dancer, and teacher. Seasoned with tales of friendships and collaborations with great artists, celebrities, and individuals, these stories weave a tapestry. I trust you will read them and as a result come to believe, as I do, in the importance of the arts and their value to the development of our humanity and culture. Who am I? I'm a man, an American, a father, a teacher, but most of all, I am a person who knows how the arts can change lives, because they transformed mine. I was a dancer.

I Was a Dancer

The Boss

My father would tell us, "She thinks she's Sarah Bernhardt, the queen of the theater, putting on airs." My mother relished the comparison, ignoring the slur Pop intended. She did resemble photographs of the great actress, and acted the part as well. "She's so bossy, we should call her the Boss!" The family agreed and adopted the nickname, but soon transformed it into a term of affection. When that happened, my father went back to calling her Georgiana.

Christened Georgiana d'Amboise, she grew up to be a determined woman—tiny (four foot nine), sturdy, shapely, and volcanic with energy. Her hair was thick, chocolate brown, and her matching eyes danced. "Oh, I had such hair," she boasted, "hanging down below my knees!" I imagined her as a young girl in Canada with her mother and four sisters singing French Canadian folk songs, lined up in a row as they rhythmically combed one another's hair—the feminine version of a line of paddling canoers.

Pop claimed 1900 as the year of his birth. My mother claimed the same year, though when asked, she declared, with her irrefutable logic, "Your father's a year older than me."

Georgiana's father, David Bergeron d'Amboise, married Marie Pelletier, and I believe that out of the children born to them, nine survived. Their farm was in Île Vert, in the province of Quebec.

In Canada, winters were brutal. One of my mother's chores sent her out into the freezing cold with an ice pick to chip frozen herring from the barrels stored outside their farmhouse. "Those fish kept us alive," she would announce dramatically. After chores were done, the family played board games, and Marie read to them by the light of oil lamps and the fireplace. "We read them all, the French books—Victor Hugo, Alexandre Dumas, Voltaire—Camille! Oh, how I loved Camille!—and books describing the life of the French court, *l'histoire de France,* and Château d'Amboise!" They read stories from the Bible and tales from the lives of saints, wallowing in the gory deaths of Christian martyrs, replete with miracles and sacrifices. Nothing subtle about the

My mother, Georgiana d'Amboise, ca. 1918

way my mother retold and embellished her favorites: "Oh, poor Saint Bernadette Soubirous,* she had tuberculosis of the knees and was in agony, but she crawled on her poor knees every day to wash the feet of the sick and minister to the dying in hospice. She was so good, the Virgin came for her!" I never knew what that meant, "the Virgin came for her," but it sounded impressive. "When Bernadette died, she went directly to heaven, and her body smelled of perfume. But Henry the Eighth and King Herod of Judea had *horrible* deaths for their sins! They both died the same way—eaten from the inside out!" Then the punch line, "They say that when Henry the Eighth was dying, he smelled so bad, no one could go near him."[†]

The high point of drear midwinter was the joy of Réveillon! Before Mass on Christmas Eve, families would bundle into sleighs to visit one another's homes, bearing gifts of food and drink—a pot of beans, smoked fish, preserves, jellies, baked goodies, and wine (Clos des Mouches was a favorite of the d'Amboises). Then everyone gathered for Midnight Mass and Communion, and since it was the custom to fast before receiving Communion, when the final "*Ite, missa est*"[‡] was sung, the congregation, their stomachs growling with anticipation, dashed to various people's homes for an orgy of eating and drinking. Laughter, joy, and bonhomie resounded into the wee hours.

A family farm in Île Verte, Province of Quebec, meant short

* Bernadette Soubirous, who died at the age of thirty-five in 1879 and was canonized in 1933, reportedly saw apparitions of Our Lady at Lourdes. In fact, she did suffer from tuberculosis of the bones.

† There was always some truth to Boss's cautionary tales. King Herod, the bloodthirsty Judean ruler who reputedly tried to kill the infant Jesus, died an excruciating death, probably brought on by kidney disease and finished off by gangrene. Henry VIII died of a variety of illnesses, and his body lay swelling in his bed for some days before embalming, while his court figured out the best way to break the news of his death.

‡ "Go, you are sent forth" could be a good idiomatic translation of "*Ite, missa est.*"

summers, and endless labor. David would work the farm, get Marie pregnant, bring in the harvest, and then disappear into the woods for the winter, to work with a crew of lumberjacks, cutting trees, trimming logs and sliding them down to rest on top of the frozen river. When spring came, the ice would break, the logs would fall into the water, and the lumberjacks would shepherd them down to the mills. The most dangerous part of the job was breaking up logjams; in those days, the average life span of a lumberjack was forty years. Overwhelming was the relief and joy of the family when David returned in the spring. At home, he would likely soon find a new baby along

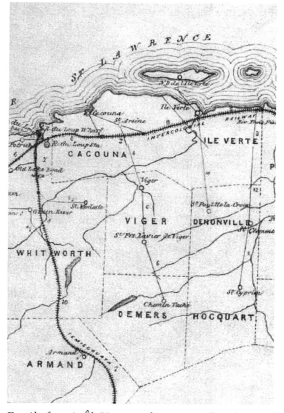

Family farm in Île Verte, in the province of Quebec

with the spring buds, and the cycle would start again, declaring, as the Chilean poet Pablo Neruda put it, "I want to do with you what spring does with the cherry trees."

My mother often recounted to me vivid stories about her parents, Marie and David, and growing up in Canada.

DAVID D'AMBOISE'S FIGHT WITH THE DEVIL

"Your grandfather, *mon père*—his name was David—was riding his calèche*—it's like a small buggy—from our farmhouse to go to town.

---

* Commonly used in Quebec, a calèche is a two-wheeled, horse-drawn vehicle with a driver's seat on the splashboard.

It was fall, a cold morning, and a long way, maybe ten miles in the forest, before you came to anything. There were a few farms along the rutted dirt track through thickets of trees, a tunnel in the great, dark forest of Canada.

"He was about halfway there when suddenly his seat jerked back. A big man had leaped from the forest and landed behind him on the calèche. A black man! 'I'm here to ride with you!' the man announced. Terrified, *mon père* struggled with the horse, which was kicking, rearing, and twisting about. Yelling, David ordered, 'Get off, get off!' The man threw his arms around David's neck, choking him, and they began a terrible fight, buffeting each other and finally rolling off the back of the calèche onto the ground. The horse fled down the road, leaving the two of them punching and clutching in the dirt.

"Now, Jacques, remember, your grandfather worked in the woods with ax and saw. He was not tall, but he was powerful and strong. Soon, he began to get the better of the other and managed to wrest himself away from the terrible embrace. Then, he delivered the black man such a wallop that it knocked him down. My father took this opportunity to turn and run down the road as fast as his feet could carry him, imagining he heard pounding footsteps behind him. Sweating and panting, he prayed to Our Lady for help. Oh, how happy he was when he saw the horse and calèche waiting for him around a bend in the road. He leaped on and galloped off toward town with seconds to spare, never daring to look back.

"When he arrived, he gasped out his story, and in minutes, a group of townspeople grabbed their guns and followed him back to deal with the stranger. No one had ever seen a black man before. When they reached the clearing where the fight had taken place, there was no one there! The black man had disappeared without a trace, and no one saw him in the days and weeks that followed.

"Oh, but your grandfather was the talk of all the province. 'Have you heard? David d'Amboise had a fight with the DEVIL!' "

La Grosse de Castonguey

"Now, I will tell you a story of a terrible thing that happened to our family:

"The French Canadians in Île Verte have a custom. If anyone asks for shelter, we provide it, as it is many miles between farms. In those days, big families and few beds meant no one had their own room, except maybe the Maman and Papa, but a traveler could always count on shelter. A blanket would be placed on the floor near the hearth or stove, and an extra place set at the dinner table. No one was turned away.

"There was an awful woman named La Grosse de Castonguey. Everyone was afraid of her. She was big—that's what 'La Grosse' means—but how big, nobody knew, because she hid herself under piles of clothes. She wore several dresses, with many petticoats underneath, one on top of the other. Even her mouth was big, and missing teeth. The few she had were big, yellow, and rotten. She never washed, smelled bad, and her greasy hair was tangled. And she stole. She had sewn cloth bags or pouches among her petticoats, and if you weren't watching her every move with a hawk's eye, she would pick up anything lying around, slip it through a slit in her outside dress, and drop it into one of those bags. No one wanted her in their home, but if she came around, they didn't dare refuse. La Grosse was most frightening at night.

"At bedtime, it was the custom for families to kneel together and say the Rosary (five sets of ten Hail Marys each), and during the prayers, La Grosse would screech out her own prayers, her little piggy eyes gleeful when she saw how her words shocked us:

THE FAMILY PRAYER	CASTONGUEY'S PRAYER
Hail Mary, full of grace,	*Hail Mary, full of grace,*
The Lord is with thee.	*You had a son and*
Blessed art thou amongst women,	*So did I,*
And blessed is the fruit	*Yours was crucified,*
Of thy womb, Jesus.	*Mine was hung.*

"The families had to listen to this, every Hail Mary, through the entire Rosary!

"One morning, my father had taken us into town in the calèche, leaving Maman alone at home with my two sisters, Adèle and Emélia. They were young, maybe seven or eight, and were playing down near the gate in front of our house, not far from the dirt road leading into town. Way down that road, they spotted La Grosse coming, and quickly ran into the house to tell Maman, *'La Grosse de Castonguey! Elle revient!'* Oh, my mother was frightened. She did not know what to do. 'Tell her I'm not here, no one is at home!' she said. 'If La Grosse wants a place to stay, tell her she has to go to the next farm.' Maman shut the door and hid.

"La Grosse arrived at the gate, all sweaty and hot. Her belongings were wrapped up in pieces of cloth, knotted into bundles, and she had one in each of her hands. Putting them down in front of the gate, she announced to Adèle and Emélia, 'Tell your mother I'm staying here tonight.'

" 'Maman's not home,' Adèle said. *(Now, Jacques, they were lying, but sometimes, there is such a thing as a good lie.)*

" 'I am tired, and I want to stay here,' La Grosse demanded.

" 'Go away, go away! Go to the next house,' Adèle and Emélia chorused.

"La Grosse seized the gate and shook it. 'No, it is too far, and it is late. I want to stay here, so let me in!' Feisty Adèle, she was tiny, but she was brave and mischievous. She started to dance and wiggle her behind, mocking La Grosse, and she made up a song right on the spot, *'Go away, Castonguey,* plein poux, plein poux [lots of lice], *take your* poux, *and go away, Castonguey, Castonguey!'*

"Emélia, who was generally shy and frightened, got caught up in the game too. As they wiggled their po-pos and sang Adèle's song, they picked up dirt and stones, and ran to the gate to hurl them at La Grosse.

"Oh, she roared with rage and began to run her hands through her hair and fling them at the girls, making strange movements with her fingers, 'You *vers de terre*!' she screeched, 'you say to me, *"plein poux,"* but it is YOU who are *plein poux,* and I say it to you!' She directed her strange movements to the girls and began making awful sounds and words, words they had never heard before. And then, she seized her bundles and strode off angrily down the road. You could hear her bellowing, even after she had disappeared. Adèle and Emélia stood at the gate, laughing and mocking her, silly girls.

"Adèle and Emélia could not wait for the rest of the family to come home so they could regale us with tales of their adventure. That night, around the table, they told us over and over again, about La Grosse at the gate and how brave they were, chasing her off, and how Maman was hiding behind the door. Oh, they acted it all out! Adèle especially loved performing all the roles, mimicking La Grosse, and we all laughed as she tried to recreate the strange sounds and movements La Grosse had made. At bedtime, reciting the Rosary, we all thanked the good little Jesus that La Grosse de Castonguey was not kneeling next to us.

"In the wee hours of the morning, we were awakened by Adèle and Emélia, wailing and crying, screeching and scratching. When Maman looked to see what was wrong, she found their bodies covered in bites. It wasn't until she looked under the folds in the seams of their night-shirts that she discovered the culprits. Rows and rows of lice and fleas, bibbits—*poux!*—crawling there. Now, my Maman hated dirt and vermin! She kept a spotless house scrubbing all the time, washing everything. She ordered the whole family to search their bedclothes and mattresses. Everything was shaken out and the whole house searched for bibbits. But only Adèle and Emélia had been infested.

"Maman scrubbed and cleaned Adèle and Emélia, and she put the infested nightshirts in a pot of hot soap and water to soak. At last, we all went back to bed to try to sleep, Adèle and Emélia wearing a pair of clean nightshirts—my mother always had a few extra. No sooner had we gone to sleep than it happened again! Adèle and Emélia awoke, scratching and crying, and there, all along the seams of their new nightshirts were the *poux,* thick and fat. Mysteriously, they were the only ones being tormented; nobody else in the family had one *poux!*

"How frightened we were! We all assembled near the stove in the kitchen. Maman threw the infested nightshirts in the fire to burn and wrapped Adèle and Emélia in blankets. Then we all knelt and began saying the Rosary over and over again, until dawn. We were so tired.

"The sun had barely come up when we heard clatter and the clanging of bells from the outside. We rushed out, to see a man known through-out the county pulling up to the gate. Everyone recognized the sound of his bell and knew it was shopping time when they heard it. Every month or so, he came around, a thin bony man with a black beard. He was *le propriéteur* of a store that moved on wheels. His poor, tired horses pulled an enormous wagon—every inch, inside and out, covered and stuffed with things to buy. You could get everything!—needles, thread, bolts of cloth, pots, pans, skillets, assorted tools. He had herbs and different elixirs and medicine to cure anything that made you sick. There were oils for cooking, as well as perfumes, colognes, soaps, kerosene, vinegar, and you could buy beans and peas, grains, powders, dried mushrooms, and fruits such as prunes, apricots, and raisins.

"We dashed to his wagon and started telling him about the curse on Adèle and Emélia, and what an awful night we had had. 'What can we do? What can we do?' It's like today, Jacques, when you have bronchitis and you go to see the man at the drugstore and ask him, 'Have you anything to stop this coughing?'

"Well, sure enough, the peddler said, 'Ahhhh, I know exactly what to do,' and slowly he got off his wagon. He wore big leather boots, without socks, even in winter, and Maman never could understand why, as his wagon was well stocked with all sorts of woolies. But we gathered around to listen to him. 'You must follow my directions perfectly, or it will be very bad for you.' We were quiet as mice.

" 'There are three things you must do.' We were all ears. '*First,* you must take your biggest pot, fill it with kerosene, and then throw into it every needle, scissors, knife, pin, razor—all the sharp things, the cutting things you have. Leave out only your big fork and biggest knife. *Second,*' he paused, we held our breath, 'you must put the pot on the fire and bring it to a boil. When it is bubbling and hot, you are ready for the third. Now! The *third* is this,' at this point none of us dared blink, 'stand over the pot and stab into the hot kerosene with the big fork, then slice into it with the big knife, stabbing and slicing, stabbing and slicing, over and over again, in every direction, fork and knife, fork and knife. And as you do this, you must say exactly: "LA GROSSE DE CASTONGUEY, COME AND GET YOUR *POUX!*" '

" 'Say this over and over as you stab and cut. Do not stop or rest for anything! It could be hours, it could be all through the day, maybe even through the night, but you must never stop. She will come. I promise you, *she will come.*'

"We, all of us, rushed to collect the ingredients, but he stopped us.

" 'Wait! There is more!'

" 'When she comes, do not let her enter the doorway of the house! Make her stay outside and do not stop stabbing and slicing. She will beg you to stop, she will cry for mercy. Now, you must change the words you say. You must begin to say:

" ' "Take *back* your *poux,* take *back* your *poux!*" '

" 'She will stand at the doorway and beg you to let her in. DO NOT GIVE IN! Keep stabbing, cutting, and saying "TAKE *BACK* YOUR *POUX.*" '

" 'Soon she will cry out, "I take it back, I take it back!" Only then can you stop. The spell will be broken, but there is still danger. Make her go away! Threaten to kill her, she *must* leave. Do not let her enter your house! Not one step can she take across your threshold or everything will be lost, and it will be very bad for you.'

"We did exactly as he said.

"When the kerosene was boiling, Maman started slicing and jabbing with the big fork and knife, all of us sitting around, chanting with her: 'La Grosse de Castonguey, come and get your *poux*! La Grosse de Castonguey, come and get your *poux*!'

"Before the hour was up, Maman was exhausted. My father took over without breaking the rhythm, and so it continued. When one would tire, the other would take over.

"It could have gone on all night and longer, but a little after midday, coming from way down the road, you could hear her howling, 'Stop it, you're killing me, stop it!'

"It was Maman's turn at the pot, but she never looked up, just clenched her jaw and kept stabbing and slicing.

"La Grosse burst through our gate. Her clothes were a mess, and she was panting and red-faced. She came up to our doorway. Her cheeks were twitching and her awful mouth grimaced. 'Stop cutting me, stop cutting me, you're hurting me! Mercy, mercy! Let me in, let me in!' We stood frozen and couldn't move our feet. Even my father, as strong as he was, was afraid to move.

"But Maman never looked up from the pot. Stabbing and slashing, she changed her words, and said,

" 'Take back your *poux*, take back your *poux*!'

" 'Let me in first, and I'll do what you say!' La Grosse whined.

"We were so frightened, we thought we would faint. But Marie Pelletier d'Amboise never faltered, stabbing and slicing until she finally heard La Grosse scream out, 'Stop, all right! I take it back, I take it back!'

"It was like the end of a storm. Black clouds blew away and our legs were free to move. In a second, our fears were stilled. La Grosse seemed different, smaller, like a pricked balloon. She stood with tears streaming down her face, bitter, her head bent. My father, shotgun in hand, said to her, '*Va-t'en!* Go away! Never let your shadow cross our door. If I see you, I will kill you!' "

In the late nineteenth century, conditions must have been dreadful in northeast Canada, as masses of French Canadians migrated to the U.S.

To this day, French Canadian names pepper the states of northern New England.

Around 1908, my mother's family left their little farm in Île Verte and joined a group emigrating to Lewiston, Maine. My mother was eight years old. She told me that all the boys in the family had already left home by then; when they reached twelve or thirteen years old, they found work as bonded laborers on more prosperous farms.

David and Marie must have migrated to Lewiston with just the girls—Alexina, Emélia, Adèle, Georgiana, and Jeanne. ("You would have loved our sister Jeanne. She was the best of all of us—but she died young.") The girls' lives were knit together. They grew up, married, and clustered in Lewiston, which was 90 percent French Canadian. I had relatives all over town.

I never knew David, but I remember my grandmother Marie as an old lady, lying ill in a bedroom on the second floor of Emélia's house in Lewiston. I toddled up the stairs to peer at her, then, giggling, bounced on my butt back down.

I knew of my uncles only from snippets of family gossip. One uncle did visit Lewiston from time to time, dapperly dressed, smoking Havana cigars, and driving a Cadillac. He was THE GANGSTER ("Nobody knows what he does. He hangs out with a bad crowd. Someday he'll die of a bullet!"). Another uncle was THE SAILOR ("Oh, we never see him, he's always at sea! He could be drowned, and we'd never know it!"). Then there was THE SOLDIER ("Oh, our poor brother, his lungs were scarred by mustard gas in World War I. That awful army! They took everything from him, even his breath!"). The last of the quartet, THE ORDINARY, escaped the hyperbole ("He lives in Massachusetts somewhere with his family. You have cousins there").

LOVE AND INCOMPATIBILITY

My mother did not finish elementary school. At twelve, she started working in the shoe factories of Maine, and later found employment as a cleaning girl in the fancy hotels in the White Mountains of New Hampshire, or at bed-and-breakfasts on the coast of Maine. She was never without work.

My father, Andrew Patrick Ahearn, was born in Boston of Irish immigrants from Loughrea, Galway. His father, Joseph Ahearn, worked as a hostler,* a cabbie, picking up fares with a horse and carriage. His mother's name was Mary Gavin, and that's all I know about either of them. My father told me nothing. He spoke as if his life started after high school, when he found employment with the Associated Press as a telegraph operator. Soon, he was assigned to the *Lewiston Journal* in Maine.

One summer, while eating lunch in a restaurant at Old Orchard Beach on the coast of Maine, Andy, the dashing, six-foot Irishman, espied the tiny, vivacious waitress, Georgiana. He was smitten; so was she. "Your father was

Boss on a rock while hiking in the White Mountains in New Hampshire, 1917

so stylish, always dressed well, and he had such beautiful hands, with long, elegant fingers!" As it turned out, stylish clothes and slender fingers were not enough. Boss and Pop were essentially incompatible.

A brilliant activity director, my mother would tackle a problem by deciding what she and everyone else should do, and without qualms coerced all to execute her commands. Endlessly busy, she disliked seeing anyone unoccupied. "I can do it myself, and I *will* . . . but you should be doing it with me. So get up!" Frugal, she would take my father's paycheck, put aside money for rent and utilities, and then, with the few dollars remaining, go to the markets and shop for food bargains, creating menus for a week out of beans, tough cuts of meat, beet tops, and cabbage leaves.

Looking up past the bloodstained apron of the butcher, she'd charm him, "Oh, those beautiful bones and scraps! Don't throw them away! Put them here in my shopping bag." Food most people would discard, my mother turned into wonderful menus. Delicacies streamed from her kitchen—pâtés and preserves and elaborate meals of half a dozen courses. Leftovers were used for stuffing the next day's entrée. We were never hungry and ate magnificently.

My mother often sang as she worked, French Canadian songs, raucously and off-key. When she did sleep or catnap—which she could do

* One who takes care of horses.

My father, Staten Island, 1939

anywhere, at a moment's notice—the snorts and sounds that issued from her gaping mouth rivaled the groans of the sinking *Titanic.* First, the crash, a ripping sound, then gushing air snorting out of vents, followed by howls, screams, screeches of panic, the blast of klaxons, splashes of falling bodies, and finally, silent, empty calm. Her avalanches of sound, interspersed with acres of dead silence and no breathing, was monumental theater. We would watch her sleeping, wondering, "Is she dead?" Then from her tiny body and the cavern of her mouth would blast an explosion, a pride of maddened lions roaring in their sinuses. Awestruck, we'd burst into laughter, amazed by the magnitude and force of her.

Our home was spotlessly clean. The laundry, sun-and-wind-dried on outdoor clotheslines, was hand-ironed. She was a superb seamstress, designing and making our clothes. Her handiwork was everywhere—bedspreads, curtains, quilts, rugs, and tablecloths—and her gardens, both flowers and vegetables, were nurtured and pampered in their beds. She knew of plants, herbs, mushrooms, and wild edible things, and had tremendous belief that hard work and determination could make all things possible. I always thought that the Boss could take the whole family into the Canadian woods naked in midwinter, and see to it that we all came out by the end of the season fatter and dressed in stylish furs.

Pop believed in making a deal, a contract. "Be on time. Work for your employer the eight or ten hours, whatever you agreed on. Avoid overtime. At the end of the day, leave." If Pop had an hour lunch break and ate in fifteen minutes, he'd boast, "I just go into the men's room, sit on the toilet, and read the paper for forty-five minutes. Then, I go back to work. Not a minute earlier." He thought of himself as a hard and honest worker, a blue-collar worker, and he took pride in that, because "your ordinary man is the salt of the earth. Do you think Henry the Fifth could have won the Battle of Agincourt without his yeomen?" His philosophy evolved into: "Find a job, not too demanding, with a decent wage. Do your honest best for the agreed-upon hours of work—

FRENCH-CANADIAN SPREAD

CRETON RECIPE

1½ lbs ground lean pork
1 lb ground veal
½ lb of ground panne. In English
   it's call Leaflard
¾ cup of water
3 good size onions

1 teaspoon of salt
1 pinch of pepper
1 bay leave
½ teaspoon of clove
¼ teaspoon of cinnamon

Mix pork, veal and panne.
Ground once more all together.
In a large kettle, add water and the
   mix meat all mix with the leaflard.
Add bay leave stirring well on high
   flame until it is boiling. Lower the
   flame still stirring.
Add onions, salt, pepper
   then lower the heat on a slow heat.
Cook until well done, something like

2 hours stirring off and on,
   then add clove, cinnamon.
Cook slowly for 10 or 15 minutes.
Have small bowls and fill them, let
   cool. Then keep in the ice box,
   until it is cold.
It will keep for months. Put a cover
   on the bowls.
(Good luck)

French-Canadian Spread recipe—delicious, and fattening

then relax, read, listen to music, smoke a good cigar, and, most of all, get in a little fishing."

His lack of ambition defined the fishing: I never knew him to catch one. Yet the tales! "Why, right next to me, this little old fellow was reeling them in right and left! Those fish were flopping all over the place, and by God! Do you know what the rascal was using for bait? Bagels!"

What a great storyteller—Pop had the Irish gift for palaver. Among the happiest times of my childhood are memories of my father putting me to bed at sleep time. He would embrace me in his arms and stroke my forehead, as he filled my imagination with his concocted tales. He could make stories up on the spot—a mixture of Irish tales from his own youth, items from the daily newspaper embellished, and, usually, tales with a moral—stories of Peck's Bad Boy (the Dennis the Menace or Bart Simpson of his day). Pop could weave a brilliant yarn. "Your mother told me you didn't finish your dinner. Reminds me of Peck's Bad Boy and the stomachache." Then he would invent such a tale that you'd be tempted not to eat again the next night, claiming stomachache, in hopes of hearing chapter two. He'd end his stories by whispering, "*Couche, couche,*" which roughly translates to cuddle, hide, sort of a way of tucking me in.

While my mother snored away, he rose at four-thirty or five in the morning to be at work by six, and occasionally, I would wake up to have breakfast with him. "I'm going to make you an Egg Trudy sandwich! It'll be so good, you'll be sucking on your teeth the rest of the day." He would take a piece of white bread, spread it with mayonnaise, press in a slice of raw onion, cover it with a fried egg, top it with another slice of white bread, and press it down tight. It was delicious! Every once in a while, on Sundays after Mass, I would have him to myself. "Let's go get a haircut," he'd suggest, really an excuse to stop by the local ice cream parlor for hot fudge sundaes. He savored the sundaes as much as I did.

As a telegraph operator, Pop was at the top of his trade. Telegraph operators took great pride in their work, and they competed—how fast they could decipher and tap out Morse code. Just as on our phones we recognize a familiar voice, he could recognize the name of the sender on his telegraph from the pattern and style of the clicks received. At family dinners he often tapped on the table as he ate. I wonder today, was he secretly complaining? "Will you sit down, woman, and stop talking!" Dot, dot, dot-dash-dot, dot dot. Music was another passion. We had an old Victrola that you would wind up to play records. Delibes's *Coppélia,* Gounod's "Ave Maria," Strauss waltzes, and various opera arias competed with the radio's classical music stations. Pop read voraciously, especially newspapers, reading dozens front to back.

On Sunday mornings, I would share the paper with him: me, sprawled on the floor with the comics, a drawing pad, and crayons, inventing cartoons; him, reading the news with his feet on a stool, a cigar in his mouth, and arias surging from the radio—his idea of heaven. He would announce to the room, "Your mother is lucky to have me. I'm not your ordinary Irishman. I don't drink, I give my full paycheck to my wife every week, and I'm home, not out gallivanting with other women."

Boss would walk in, see my father sitting in his chair. "Andy, stop smoking that awful cigar, put down that newspaper, and help me move this table." Or bed. Or bureau. When she wasn't managing the household and our lives, she re-choreographed the placement of furniture. It was never-ending. She'd say, "Oh, Andrew, why are you sitting around, stinking up the house with your dirty cigar? Come and help me hang the curtains." He'd say, "Woman, can't I have a bit of peace and quiet on my one day off?" as he got up to do as he was told.

THE GREAT DEPRESSION — DEDHAM TO NEW YORK

In Dedham, Massachusetts, a suburb of Boston, I was born at midnight, July 27, 1934, making a quartet of siblings, in age spaced roughly three years apart. My brother John was the eldest, close to ten years old, followed by Patrick, six, and my sister, Madeleine, about three. We lived in a dollhouse, its garden crammed with flowers. "Traffic stopped when they passed our house!" Boss, boasting, would recall, "People would ooh and ahh, the flowers were so beautiful . . . I was happy there."

While our nation struggled through the Great Depression, my father snagged a great job working for a rich man—personal telegraph operator for Old Joe Kennedy, father to John, our future president. To the amazement and envy of out-of-work neighbors, Pop not only had a posh job but *owned* the brand-new Ford he used for his commute. Pop drove to Cape Cod and the Kennedy compound at Hyannis Port, where he received and passed on financial data for Old Joe, dotting and dashing off stock orders from his cubicle in the basement of the main house. Senator Ted Kennedy told me he remembered as a boy the telegraph operators in the basement of their summer home. Come fall, we all piled into the Ford, waved goodbye to the neighbors, and drove off to Florida. While New England froze, my father worked in shirtsleeves at the Kennedys' Palm Beach haven.

On these seasonal trips to Florida, my mother, behind the wheel, would put pillows under her bottom to get herself high enough to see over the steering wheel. She would roll down the window, stick out her left elbow, drape her right hand on the wheel, and stretch her toes down to the gas pedal. She tried to avoid having the pedal anywhere else but flat against the floor. My father would sit in the passenger seat next to her, jaws clenched, clutching his seat. "For the love of God, slow down! You'll kill us all." Rarely, she would allow him to drive. When he did, he would clutch the steering wheel with both hands, holding on for

Palm Beach, February 1935; my father, my brother Pat, my mother, my sister, and me

dear life, hunch himself down in the seat, thrust his head forward to stare at the road through the windshield, and try not to blink. If the speed limit said twenty miles an hour, he would go ten. Or five. "Andrew, will you move! Hurry up or it will take us a month to get to Palm Beach!" Then, "Slowpoke! We'll be *dead* before we get there."

My brother John told me about an incident that happened once on the drive from Dedham to Florida.

THE CAR STORY

There are sections in the state of Georgia where the land is flat and the earth red. We were driving on a dusty road cutting through this sanguine landscape, traveling south.

On the far horizon, another road bisected our route. The intersection made a thin, rusty cross on the crust of Georgia. As we barreled along, my father spotted a farmer's pickup truck approaching the intersection from the east. "Slow down, Georgiana! There's a truck up ahead." "I see it," she answered, stepping harder on the gas pedal. My father approached hysteria. "My God! You're going to hit him! Slow down!" Boss's jaw jutted. "Woman, for the love of God!" he screamed, "WE'LL ALL BE DEAD!"

We beat the pickup truck through the intersection by 99 percent of our car's length, not enough to avoid having our rear bumper caught by the front bumper of the truck. Our car spun several times while somehow continuing, eventually coming to rest in the center of the road some fifty yards south of the intersection. The truck, too, had spun a bit, but, seemingly little affected, came to rest straddling the middle of the intersection, with its front grille facing us. My mother, behind the wheel, staring straight ahead, announced to the windshield, "Aw, shucks, that man was going too fast!"

You could hear my father's teeth grinding. Slowly, he opened the passenger door, got out, walked to the back of our car, and stood, staring at our bumper. On one side of our vehicle, it had been ripped loose, but it remained attached on the other, so it stuck out of the rear end of the car like a spear—a shiny steel rod quivering from our backside, aggressive and challenging, like a narwhal's horn. The truck driver opened the door of his truck and climbed down. A beefy monster of a man, his fists clenched, face swollen with the flush of fury, he stomped toward my father. My siblings, watching from our car's back window, saw big trouble. Oblivious, my father continued to stare at the back of our car. Then, Pop seized the tip of the bumper, dug his feet into the dirt, and bent the steel bar back into its original place. It must have weighed a thousand pounds!!! According to John, the truck driver stopped in his tracks, stood for several moments, goggle-eyed, and then, as air vents from a bladder, diminished, he quietly turned around, slipped back into his truck, and drove off. Unaware, Pop returned to the passenger seat, slammed his door shut, sat for several moments in silence, then grunted, "Drive on, Georgiana."

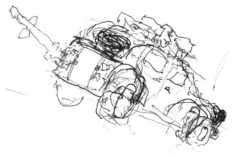

My mother always said how she loved it down in Florida, with the hot sun and the orange groves. She luxuriated in it, though she always worried about her barefoot children getting bitten by a snake.

Unfortunately, technology blew in like a South Florida hurricane, bringing telephone and teletype to replace the telegraph. Come winter, back in Dedham, my depressed father joined the unemployed.

Soon, orders came from Boss. "Andrew, we're going to New York. That's where there's work, and that's where the arts are." There was no arguing, so Pop followed her lead; he sold whatever he could (including the Ford), and we packed our belongings and boarded the train to New York City.

New York is an intimidating, expensive city; we crowded into a few rooms in an awful apartment shared with cockroaches. In the morning, they were using our toothbrushes before us! Pop couldn't get a job for love or money and walked the streets trying to find one. Boss managed to feed and care for us as she watched our meager savings drip away. When Pop came home and sat down, she would harp, "Go out and see if you can find some work. Around here, you're good for nothing!"

When he was not around, she never complained about him to us. "Your father is working hard. Your father's a good man." On the other hand, he always complained about her to us: "Your mother will never be satisfied. She always wants more! She's crazy and she'll drive us all crazy." I believe he loved her deeply, but he chose to play the patient and long-suffering receiver of abuse. For a man who took such pride in work, being unemployed and having to endure a wife who berated him brought him to the edge. Finally, in 1939, we were evicted, deposited on the sidewalk with our baggage. No car, no luck, and no apartment, we found ourselves homeless in New York City. I was five, Madeleine close to eight, Pat was ten, John, thirteen.

The nuns in a convent just off Washington Square Park gave us shelter. My sister and I slept on army cots in the cellar, straddling the furnace. The cellar door led out to a back alley and a metal fire escape led up one flight to a back-door entrance to the convent. My mother and father, with my two brothers, must have slept upstairs.

Our homelessness didn't last too long, a couple of summer months. Then things brightened—a position opened up on Wall Street for a telegraph operator, my father got the job, and we were out of the basement and into the sunlight, out of Manhattan and across the bay to Staten Island, where housing was cheaper and the Boss could have another garden.

My cot stage right, my sister's stage left, the furnace up front center

Staten Island is divided by a railroad line that runs through its center like a spine. The terminal at its head is in a town called St. George. Its tail, the end of the line, is in the town of Tottenville. We ended up there, renting a tiny two-story clapboard house. To get to work, my father had a long commute. Mornings, he trained it up the spine to St. George, then took the ferry across to Manhattan's Wall Street. Nights, the reverse. It was some two hours each way.

A boisterous five-year-old, I loved Staten Island, a place of farmlands and forests, marshlands and beaches. Near Tottenville, there was a creek that was a feeder to the bay. Its waters were full of killies (tadpoles) that I would capture and use as bait for fishing. I'd put a bit of bread in a glass jar and half submerge it sideways in the waters at the edge of the creek. When enough killies went for the bread and collected in the jar, I'd capture them by quickly lifting the jar. The creek ran parallel to the railroad tracks, flanked by unkempt hedges of honeysuckle. That's where I used to go to meet my first love. She was towheaded, tan, barefoot, and wearing a dress of delicate, pale pastels. I think she was four. I would run there and wait till she would wander down, or sometimes, she'd be there waiting for me. We would stand and stare at each other. I never said a word; neither did she. We just stared. She would watch me as I went to get the killies in the bottle, and then we would stare some more. Why is it called puppy love? I dreamed of her constantly. Dante had his Beatrice; I had mine.

Our five-room house had a backyard that opened into a wooded area, wild and overgrown. Some three hundred yards through those woods, hay-covered fields opened up and a dirt path sloped through it, past an old, collapsing barn whose giant doors gaped open on rusty hinges. It was Sunday afternoon after Mass, and I was on my way down the dirt path, following the sound of voices in the distance. My brothers, John and Pat, with their buddies, were playing football in an open field at the bottom of the slope. A man came out of the barn and gestured to me, "Hey, come here a minute. I've got something for you." I went over. "You want to make some money?" he said. "I got some pennies for you." And he backed out of the sun into the shadows of the barn. "Come in here. I got something for you." I remember the smell of hot hay and the sounds of buzzing insects and birds. Just inside the doorway, half in the shadows, half in sunlight, I heard him say, "You're a good boy. I'll give you a penny if you touch it." I had never seen an erection. It was big and red and scary. I squeaked out, "I have to meet my brothers." He was nervous and agitated. I was terrified. "Ah, come on. I'll give you a nickel if you touch it." I ran.

Fled—to my brothers—and blurted out about the Big Red Thing. In seconds, John and his whole football team dashed to the barn. The man was gone. I felt guilty and embarrassed, as if I'd done something wrong, and silently said prayers of thanks that he had escaped a beating, imagining what my brother and his gang would have done had they found him.

Still, in my memory, Staten Island was idyllic. My sister whispered ghost stories in the dark from her bed in the room we shared. Fabulous thunderstorms barreled through, punctuated by stunning cracks of lightning. I used to sit on the floor with my feet stuck out of the kitchen door, soaking them in the pouring rain, and marvel at the ferocity of storms. Inside the doorway, the dry part of me would be slurping the most delicious beefsteak tomatoes, their red juices dripping down my chin. While Boss cooked supper, I played with pots and pans in a makeshift tent she had constructed with sheets draped over the kitchen table. After dinner, when Boss finished cleaning up, she would reverse the oilcloth that covered the table to reveal an elaborate, colorful game map she'd drawn on the underside. It was her invention, a version of Monopoly before the game existed. Rolling dice, we played with varied colored buttons for pieces. Our recreation was the radio, and the Boss's game.

When I was six, she enrolled my sister, Madeleine, in ballet classes, supposedly for her health, as she had almost died from a bout of typhus fever that year. Boss had sniffed out a Miss Jones, who taught dance in St. George, and every Saturday we would take the train, me in the front car gazing out the rounded window and dreaming of how thrilling my father's commute must be. It was over an hour from Tottenville to St. George, one way. Lucky Pop got to do this every morning! Plus, the ferry ride to Wall Street! Then the whole thing back again at night!

While my sister was doing her pliés, the Boss would seize the opportunity to go shopping in the Big City of St. George. A ball of restless energy, she ran from one shop to the other, dragging me along, looking for bargains. A buzzing blender of thrift and industry, she made and sold hats and clothes for other people, did their laundry for a fee—and socked away the cash. By the end of two years of steady work and careful saving, we had a nest egg and even had wheels—a secondhand car—a Studebaker.

Old Joe Kennedy had been several years ahead of Wall Street, but the big firms caught up and phased out their telegraph operators. Uh-oh. Out of work again. Poor Pop!

Boss saw the whole thing as an opportunity. We would move "back to Manhattan, where the arts are."

So, "Goodbye clapboard house and Tottenville, hello again, Manhattan!"

We packed up, took the ferry in, and settled in a grungy, tiny apartment in Washington Heights. My father sought any kind of employment. He repaired watches for a while, even picked up work as a gravedigger—but there was never enough money. Our funds depleted, we sold the Studebaker. My sister and I enrolled at the nearest Catholic school—Incarnation, on 175th Street. The nuns had a punishment for disruptive boys: "Take your books and go sit with the girls on their side of the room!"—it was meant to humiliate the boys. I loved it! The girls were nicer, smarter, and passed me the answers to test questions. I spent a lot of time there. I discovered my first fan club when the nuns called on me to recite a poem, "Barbara Frietchie," by John Greenleaf Whittier, in front of the class. Standing, trembling and eager, I squawked out the poem:

> *Up from the meadows, rich with corn,*
> *Clear in the cool September morn,*
> *The clustered spires of Frederick stand,*
> *Green-walled by the hills of Maryland . . .*

Due to the applause of the clique of girls around me, I won first prize, and became a lifelong lover of poetry (and women).

Hooray! Pop nabbed a job as an elevator operator at Columbia Presbyterian Hospital. A full-time job within walking distance! Confident we were on an upward track, we moved to a more spacious apartment on 163rd Street and St. Nicholas Avenue. A five-block walk to work for Pop, and one block for me to the nearest elementary school, Saint Rose of Lima, at 164th Street.

We lived at 1061 St. Nicholas Avenue, in a six-story building, and called our fourth-floor apartment "the Railroad," its six rooms coupling like cars of a train along one side of the building's central court. The building looked optimistic, receiving a great deal of sunlight on its white-and-pink stone façade.

Washington Heights

It is the narrowest part of Manhattan Island. On the southeastern side, looking down from wild foliage-covered cliffs, is the Harlem River. At the southern end of the cliffs, at around 162nd Street, nestles the Morris-Jumel Mansion, where Madame Jumel and her husband, Aaron Burr, lived after the American Revolution. It served as George Washington's headquarters during the Battle of Harlem Heights, and it was also battle turf for me and my friends in our imaginary games, Continentals bayoneting Redcoats and Hessians in hand-to-hand.

Washington Heights was once a suburb, a transition between earlier farms and the encroaching city proper. The years 1942–1950 saw a population explosion. During and after World War II, all of Washington Heights became multinational and multicultural. Working-class families seethed and bubbled on my block—Hispanic, Dutch, Polish, German, Jewish, Italian, and Irish American. African Americans were moving north from Harlem and filling in the area east of Amsterdam Avenue. Asians were rare. The first Asian I remember seeing, besides stereotypes in the movies, was at Presbyterian Hospital on 168th Street. My father was running the elevator and a young Asian man got on. Pop delivered him to his floor, and when the door closed, my father winked and whispered, "A Japanese spy . . ." My breath stopped. It was less than six months after Pearl Harbor, and I believed him.

My block had St. Nicholas Avenue at one end and Broadway at the other, and was centered between two rivers. From the tree-covered cliff edge overlooking the Harlem River to the east, walk west a couple of blocks, cross Amsterdam Avenue, and you're on St. Nicholas. Continue through the block, cross Broadway, and walk two more streets, and you're at Riverside Park, with its forested hill leading down to the parkway, railroad tracks, and the Hudson River.

We called the area around Riverside Park "Jewtown." Children of Jewish immigrants—the second generation having improved their lot—had moved from Lower East Side tenements to the sun-filled,

My oldest friend since the age of eight, Jimmy Comiskey, ca. 1951

spacious, and airy apartments that overlooked the Hudson River. In turn, their children, the third generation—grown, educated, and involved in a variety of professions—were leaving their apartments and moving to the suburbs.

In urban life, a city block equals a rural village. Through the eyes of a child, streets seem wide, buildings high, cellars deep. I would walk 163rd Street from St. Nicholas to Broadway and think I'd gone half a mile. People were identified by the block they lived on, and familiarity and gossip abounded. Many blocks were marked by the gangs that claimed them—the Famwoods around 164th Street, the Victory Boys further up. On our block, we had two gangs—the Guerillas and the Panthers—that served as feeders for a third gang, bigger and older, the Vampires. Besides church and school, our playground centered around our apartments and street—life lived in and out of them. No air conditioning—on hot summer days we slept on fire escapes, rooftops, or went down to Riverside Drive and laid on the grass, while the adults sat on the park benches, gossiping and snoozing.

My closest peers and mentors at the time were, first of all, Jimmy Comiskey. Jimmy was a scholar, an intellectual, a bookworm. History, religion, arts, philosophy, the esoteric, occult, and macabre were his passions. We would meet in Jimmy's book-filled room, our intellectual clubhouse, and tell stories. A plan was hatched to acquire a complete set of the *Encyclopædia Britannica.* How? Steal them. We would need a front man—Johnny "Golden" (aka John Wanamaker) was recruited—why? With his slender build, blond hair, and baby-faced blue-eyed puss, he was innocence itself. No one would suspect him for a second-story man. At our neighborhood branch of the New York Public Library, Johnny would purloin from the bookshelf the "A" volume, and toss it out the window. Jimmy and I, with our coats spread à la fireman's safety net, would catch the book. To avoid an excessive gap in the library's shelf, volume "B" would be spirited from another branch in the same manner. And so on, through twenty-six branches in the city of New York.

My other pal was Abie Grossfeld, a superb athlete with a droll sense of humor. His cousin was the postman, a big leather sack on his shoul-

Demonstrating with Abie the differences between ballet and gymnastics on TV, early 1950s

der, delivering the mail in our block. Abie introduced me to gymnastics, and I countered with ballet.* I took him to the School of American Ballet to watch class and rehearsal. "That's Balanchine," I said, pointing, "he's the greatest teacher of them all." "Who's that?" Abie pointed to the pianist. "Oh, that's Stravinsky," I said importantly. "Oh?" said Abie, "who's Stravinsky?" "Oh, he's great! Like Beethoven, only today!" "Who's Beethoven?" Abie asked. I never knew if he was kidding or not.

My other street pals went on to careers as marines, firemen, police, priests, and crooks. One guy ran a big porno center on Forty-second Street. Several times in later years, I would be walking down Forty-second Street in Manhattan, when Mitch would pop out of his porno park and say, "Hey, Jock! Come on in," and give me tokens. He had a fancy Mercedes parked in the no-parking zone in front of his emporium.

There were no artistic types on my block, only Herbie Khaury, a goofy teenager with long hair who played a ukulele. Soon, he transformed himself into a TV star, Tiny Tim, strumming the same ukulele.

---

* In later life, he represented the United States, competing in two Olympics and then coaching five more Olympic teams, the 1984 team winning the gold. In the summer of 2008, he was inducted into the Olympic Hall of Fame.

At that time the neighborhood was still dotted with wood-framed single-family houses and old factories, most of the latter abandoned and decaying. The most dramatic was a run-down ice house on 169th Street and Audubon Avenue. Before refrigerators, people kept perishables in wooden iceboxes, their double walls filled with sawdust for insulation. For less than a dollar, you could purchase a block of ice from an ice truck, wrap it in burlap, lug it home, and install it in the icebox. To save money in the winter, you covered your butter and eggs and kept them on the windowsill.

The ice house had flourished some decades before. Now, mostly ruins, it was our haunted house, and Jimmy and I loved it. Five stories high, it loomed in dark brown wood and concrete, its windows black pigeonhole tunnels that stared out, unblinking. Gaping holes pock-marked its sides. The lower-story windows were boarded up, but we would pry one open and crawl in. The roof leaked. Rain and snow were gradually dissolving the place and the air was permeated with the moldy, pungent smell of rot, wet sawdust, and ammonia. The cavernous spaces, lit by us with candles and flashlights, would become our playground. It was deserted, except for a creepy guy who would sometimes shamble out of the shadows. He dragged his legs and couldn't move fast, but we sure did when we spotted him. He carried an ice hook. Jimmy and I speculated—perhaps he was a homeless derelict, or a security guard hired to keep out vandals. Or was he the aged foreman of the ice house, crushed under a slab of ice years ago, today a restless ghost?

Somewhere between 153rd and 158th streets, near Riverside Drive, Jimmy told me there had been an old lady who sat on the porch of a dilapidated wooden house located in a large crater devoid of greenery, just dirt. "It looked like a meteor crater." The old lady screamed invectives and curses and threw stones at Jimmy and his crony, Martin Shevlan, as they walked by. Kindergartners, they were already fearless, wild adventurers. They threw stones back at her. Jimmy believes that the house she lived in was the last vestige of John James Audubon's farm, one that originally encompassed most of the area down to the Hudson River. The farm was called Minnie's Land, after Audubon's wife. Within six months, both old lady and house were gone, and an apartment complex was built in its place. Probably they still exist as part of the rubble and landfill, dumped there to form a foundation for the new building.

The Hudson—a great stretch of swirling currents, always moving, always unpredictable. In summer, under the George Washington Bridge, the daring older boys went swimming. Winters were cold enough that the ponds in the parks would freeze over and become public skating rinks. Under the George Washington, near the Little Red Lighthouse, giant slabs of ice would form, shrinking the almost-mile-wide river flow to the width of some hundred yards. We would jump from one ice slab to another to try and reach the water that flowed freely in the middle, and throw snowballs to the ice forming on the New Jersey side. Occasionally, a giant chunk of ice would break apart and kids who started on a slab of ice at 178th Street would end up floating south to around Twenty-fifth Street, some six miles down. This gave the harbor police plenty to do.

The rail tracks bordering the Hudson, with their iron trestles bridging the tracks, became for us the battle deck of a frigate. Dueling with fate as well as pirates, I would run along the trestle, a sailor at home on the upper spars of a clipper ship. On the tracks, my buddies and I would play tag, tempting death as we jumped over the electrified third rail. Occasionally, we were pursued by railroad dicks. We baited them to a fury, scurrying up and down the trestles like miniature spider men and easily flipping over the bordering chain-link fences up and out of their reach. Big, mean, and brandishing clubs, often drunk, these guys weren't fooling. They were thugs and not interested in complaining to our mothers.

In the museums of the neighborhood, our street life carried on indoors, to more elegant settings.

There was Fort Tryon Park and the Cloisters, a world-class repository of medieval art, where we challenged one another to swordfights on the battlements, were chased by the guards, *and,* I believe, knew every item in the building better than the curators.

There was the block of museums at 155th Street and Broadway, the most mysterious being the Museum of the American Indian. Filled with sad-looking fetal-like mummies, shrunken heads, little shrunken men, evil-looking gold idols, and Pacific Northwest totem poles, it was wonderful, better than any horror movie, because it was real.*

Next to the Museum of the American Indian, the Hispanic Society of

---

* Established by the Heye Foundation and world-class, today much of the collection is in the National Museum of the American Indian in Washington, D.C.

America, a museum devoted to Iberian culture, shared the compound (conquistadors still threatening Native Americans). In its courtyard stands a giant bronze statue of the Spanish national hero El Cid on horseback. Checking, in our pilfered encyclopedias, we learned who El Cid was, and adopted him into our boyhood pantheon.

Also in this museum group stood (and still stands today) the American Academy of Arts and Letters—a massive building, closed to us, impregnable. We actually managed to climb up its sides to the roof in an attempt to break in. Fifty years later, I was installed as an honorary member of the Academy, welcomed through the front door on a red carpet and offered a glass of champagne. There are ways into a building other than the roof or cellar.

Across the street from the museum plaza complex, Jimmy and I had a secret hangout—the Episcopal Church of the Intercession's graveyard, an old, nineteenth-century City of the Dead, whose narrow streets we walked, peering into tombs filled with coffin niches and mausoleums, some of whose doors had broken down with age, others sealed with concrete. Names of Civil War heroes and officers are chiseled in stone. John Jacob Astor and his family are sleeping there, as are Audubon, and Clement Clarke Moore, who wrote "'Twas the Night Before Christmas." It is Manhattan's version of London's Highgate Cemetery. Our cemetery was intersected by Broadway, dividing it into two halves. The best was the west part. It was the spookiest, eerie even in sunlight, but thrilling in the rain. We would don our Bulldog Drummond raincoats, and, parroting the opening lines of the popular radio hero, intone, *Out of the fog and into the night walked Bulldog Drummond,*" then enter an open mausoleum, slouch on the ground in what we imagined was bone dust, and tell each other ghost stories.

CROSSING AMSTERDAM

In our apartment house on the sixth floor lived an Irish American family, the Sullivans. They all shared the same pale skin, susceptible to sunburn and freckles. The father and mother were big and boisterous, and I felt that their slaps on the back and hearty good wishes to everyone camouflaged a hidden frustration. They smelled of alcohol, made me uncomfortable, and I avoided them whenever possible. The family included a slew of boys—at least three—and a sweet, little grandmother, who we called Old Mrs. Sullivan. She was frail, and years of labor had bent her into the shape of a question mark.

Old Mrs. Sullivan may have been in her sixties, but stooped, with white hair and wrinkles, she looked at least a hundred—Methuselah's wife. She wore cheap-looking flowered housedresses that hung at odds with the torqued shape of her body. She rolled her nylon stockings down, making doughnuts around her ankles. Her shins were covered with ulcerated, running sores and anything touching them must have caused agony. In the elevator, on the street, or in the stairwell, she was always struggling with grocery bags. Those Sullivans ate a lot. Quite often, when the elevator went on the blink, she dragged those bags up all six flights. I imagined she did all the shopping, cooking, and house-cleaning for those voracious boys. Slave labor at the Sullivans'.

My mother never missed an opportunity to couple sympathy for Old Mrs. Sullivan's labors with a moral lesson for me: "Jacques, don't you be like those boys. They never lift a finger to help their poor grandmother. She's a saint, working for them day and night. They're all lazy good-for-nothings."

The front windows of our apartment looked out on 163rd Street. How I loved to play the wild games of the street. Ranging the entire length of the block, I would lead my gang, leaping up and down stoops, dodging and twisting in rough play, howling with laughter and glee, with much ripping of shirts and clothes. If harnessed, the energy we expended in our play could have kept the lights on all night in every building on the block.

Early evenings in the midst of our horseplay, an explosive sound would freeze me. "Jacques, Jacques!" It was the Boss, leaning out of our fourth-floor window and waving at me. She was the shortest mother on the block, and the loudest.

"Geezus, fellas, it's my mother." I would yell up to her, "Boss, can't I play more?" Like a blast from a trumpet, her answer would come. "No! Come up for supper now." And I would dash off. "Gotta go. See you later, fellas."

Summoned by the Boss, one day I careened around the corner and—whoops!—almost collided with Old Mrs. Sullivan. She was staggering, weaving as she struggled to carry about six or eight bottles of milk packed into a pair of shopping bags. In those days, milk came in glass bottles, and they were heavy. The milkman would deliver them to the store, where you could buy a bottle, or two, or ten—as many as you could afford and heft. Under the weight of the milk, Mrs. Sullivan listed side to side. She lowered her bags to the sidewalk and slumped against the side of the building.

Streaking by her, I called back, "Hi, Mrs. Sullivan—need any help?"

"Oh, yes, yes," she panted. That stopped me up short. "I have to get to the hospital and can't carry these bags upstairs. Could you put them under the stairwell for me? I'll take them up when I get back." So I grab the milk, put it under the staircase, and scoot back, while she continues to hold up the building.

"I'll help you to the hospital," I say, figuring she looks really sick, and it's only four or five blocks to Columbia Presbyterian. I could take her and be back in fifteen minutes. Doing a good turn like that, I'd get credit with the Boss, and, according to the nuns, credit with Jesus in heaven. So I give Mrs. Sullivan my arm, and we inch and shuffle up the block. Uh-oh! This was going to take more than fifteen minutes.

"How're you doing, Mrs. Sullivan? How are the boys? All that milk sure looked heavy to carry. You must be very strong," I jabber nonstop, until she stops on the corner of 164th Street and says, "This way," and angles east off St. Nicholas toward Amsterdam Avenue. "Stop. Mrs. Sullivan, where are we going? Presbyterian Hospital's up that way." Then she spoke the doomsday words: "Oh no, I'm going to Mother Cabrini, the Catholic hospital across Amsterdam Avenue."

Amsterdam Avenue was a demarcation line. West of Amsterdam was predominately white. On the east side of Amsterdam Avenue, the blacks lived, filling the apartments and creating a neighborhood of their own. No one from our side ever crossed to the other, and I never saw a black person walk through our block. "Don't go over there, they'll get you," we told each other, adding, "If any of those black guys come to our block, we're gonna get them." No one ever defined what "get" meant.

Mrs. Sullivan led me, dragging my feet, across Amsterdam Avenue to the black block. I, head down, watched my heart pulsating through my shirt. Every symptom of fear I had ever imagined or read about— weak knees, shortness of breath, sweating, and trembling—worked as a team to quiver me. She clutched my arm, and I froze a big grin on my face as we arrived on *their* block.

It was like my block, but everybody on it was black. Children of every age played the same games we played in the street—ring-a-levio and Johnny Chase the White Horse. Stoops were filled with teenagers, mothers, and children. Others were leaning out of windows or sitting on fire escapes, gossiping. We shuffled down the block. People stopped and stared. In the middle of the block, I spied the Cabrini Hospital emergency entrance. *I* sped up, dragging Mrs. Sullivan.

"Where you going?" a voice came from somewhere. "Oh, I'm just taking her to the hospital," I squeaked to the air. "She has to go to the hospital." And I thought to myself, "They're not going to *get* me, because I'm with her, protected by this little old lady. She's better than St. Christopher."

Some of those black bodies were stirring on the stoop and moving in. I was stuck in an anxiety nightmare, and I wasn't even asleep. It seemed we had performed a thousand slow-motion steps just to get to the middle of this average-sized block. I tried to keep my eye on the sanctuary: the emergency entrance.

Phew! We made it to the hospital and safety. Mrs. Sullivan unclutched me and latched on to a nun in a starched white habit, and I slipped back into real time.

"I'll just wait for her," I announced.

I calculated that after they finished treating her, Mrs. Sullivan would escort me back across Amsterdam, and with her protection I would survive the trip. All I would have to bear was the wrath of the Boss for showing up so late for dinner.

Then thunder struck. "We may have to keep her overnight. Better go home." I stared up into the face under the white habit. She smelled of baby powder. Her little pink mouth had opened and pronounced a death sentence. My heart kicked my ribs, and my left arm went numb. I was going to die before supper! One way or another—by heart attack or mob beating. An inner voice advised, "You're on your own now. Just walk back the way you came. Keep smiling. Don't look at anybody. Don't act afraid. Just walk, be ready to run."

I reentered the time warp and watched myself walk out the door. On the Stage of Death, under the glare of a "follow spot," I tried to walk a straight line down the street, step by step, attempting to look preoccupied, counting. One, two, three, four . . . eighteen, nineteen, twenty . . .

"Hey, you!" a voice shouted. A big black guy walked over, followed by several of his cronies. I froze, legs twitching, going nowhere. "Yeah, what?" my dry throat croaked. He's wearing white Keds, blue jeans, and a white polo shirt. For some reason, to my terrified eyes, black muscles seemed bigger than white ones. He looked like a truck!

"That old lady you with—she your mother, grandmother?" I stared at this black shadow with white eyeballs. His big white teeth had a space in the middle. "No! No! She's just a neighbor, a friend, I just walked her over." My excuses squeaked out plaintively. "She had to go to the hospital. It was an emergency. I'm going back to my block now."

His gang clustered around me, hemming me in. "She got those awful-looking legs. Man, people go there, they don't come out. The hospital's a place to go to die."

Then a girl's voice pops out of the bunch. "Shut your mouth, Joe. That ain't no way to talk—you're scaring him. It ain't that bad." A fat girl with a shiny face steps in front of Joe and blares at him. "Back off! *I'm* talking to him now!" She was right in Joe's face, and she knew how to give orders. She'd be great in the military. Then she turns and beams at me. "I got a grandma like that, but she dead now. We're sure sorry about that little old lady friend of yours. Maybe she'll come out alive, and if you ain't around here to take her home, we'll see she gets back all right." I nod repeatedly as I back through the group and try to keep my quivering under control, but near Amsterdam Avenue I run like a crazed cheetah. I never knew what happened to the milk. A week or so later Mrs. Sullivan showed up around the block.

MADAME SEDA

Within a year of our move from Staten Island, the Boss found a ballet school on 181st Street. She came to get me. It was Saturday, and I was seven, ferociously playing stoop ball with my gang. "Jacques, I am taking your sister to her ballet class. You are to come with me." Madeleine was clutching her ballet bag, smirking.

"Ah, Boss, do I have to go?"

"Of course, and you will love it." Determined, she grabbed my hand and, clutching Madeleine, led us to Madame Seda's Dance Academy. It was close to a half-hour walk.

I protested, "Boss, I want to play with the fellas. I don't want to sit around watching her stupid ballet class."

"Oh, Jacques, you don't know what you're talking about. Ballet is wonderful. It's magical and very hard to do. Great men in ballet can jump way up high in the air."

"How high?"

Her finger stabbed at a nearby fire escape twelve feet over our heads. "Oh, they can jump so high, they could reach that." In her mind, a dancer leaped in the air and finger-touched the bottom of the fire escape. *I looked up, effortlessly leaped the twelve feet, and landed on top of the fire escape!*

"And when they jump, they seem to float, and when they land on the ground again, there's no noise."

> Five ragamuffin boys—predators—close in on the last holdout, arms waving like antennae, feet drumming, an orchestra of ants converging on their victim. Squeals and pants, raucous orders: "You get him on this side! I'll get him from over here." In a second, he'd be pinned to the curb. Suddenly, he leaps, floating in slow motion over their upraised heads. He looks down, waves to them, and lands lightly on the other side of the street. Mouths drop open in amazement.
>
> "Safe!" he yelps with a triumphant laugh.

Daydreaming on my way to 181st Street, I win every game played by my gang with my amazing leaps.

At Seda's, there were about ten little girls dressed in pink wispy skirts, clutching a wooden bar set up in the middle of the room, my sister, looking skinny and awkward, among them. The pink girls were doing strange contortions and complicated exercises. My mother said Madeleine was the best. I didn't see any difference. I was squirming with boredom at the edge of a bench, sharing the only sitting space in the room with half a dozen mothers, their eyes riveted on their rosy angels, mine glazing over.

Madame Seda. Only a little taller than the Boss, black hair tied in a bun, and wearing a blood-red skirt, she gave orders to the angels. *"Tendu rond de jambe dégagé!"* I kept thinking, "Gypsy. She's a Gypsy, and doing Gypsy talk."

As the class progressed, I would fidget and diabolically make irritating little noises. Clicks, fart sounds, burps. Adjacent to the bench was a box that held rosin nuggets, hardened crystals of pine sap. I saw gold, gold that I could crunch under my foot, making gold dust and delicious sounds of cracks and crackles.

"All right, little brother, if you've got so much energy, get up and do these jumps." Madame Seda crooked a finger at me. "Hurry up now. Up! See if you can jump as high as the girls."

Ah, a challenge. A test from the Gypsy. A willing marionette, I jerked to my feet and moved to the center of the room.

"You have to start in fifth position, right foot in front." She propped me, my knees to the side, right heel against left big toe.

"Now leap in the air and change your feet so when you land, your left foot is in front." I hurled myself into the air, legs akimbo, made the switch, and somehow managed to land on my feet.

"Oh, you did it! Good. That's called a changement. Now do thirty-two of them, without a stop!"

Ah, the test gets tougher. All those girls, a benchful of mothers, and the Boss watching. Yikes, thirty-two! I bounded, uncontrolled like a pogo stick, frantically switching feet thirty-two times . . . *flying . . .*

Madame Seda's eyes danced like anthracite coals, "Oh, that was wonderful! Wasn't it, girls?" and leading them in doubtful and reluctant applause. "I've never seen any boy jump as high as you. Next week, if you are quiet during class, I'll let you join the girls for the changements." She added a Gypsy threat: "Better practice till then."

I must have done 100,000 changements in my living room over the next seven days. My mother and sister corrected my form, my brothers got out of the house as quickly as they could, and my father struggled to read the paper, smoking his cigar and trying to ignore it all. The next Saturday, on the walk up to 181st Street, I did changements on every street crossing. Even Boss grew impatient. "Enough now. Enough. We'll never get there."

Back on the bench, I sat unmoving, inwardly racehorse ready. Then it came. "All right, everyone, thirty-two changements. We're waiting for you, Jacques." I was up and in fifth position, ready to go before she blinked, and after the thirty-two with the girls, another thirty-two— solo. I didn't volunteer to do the extra.

"Do it again while you're tired, and jump even higher." *Clever Gypsy manipulator.*

"Fantastic! Dear Jacques, wonderful!" She gave me a big hug. *Seductive Gypsy. Then the bait:* "But . . . after you come down from those enormous leaps, you've got to learn how to land. You must take the beginning of class. That's where we learn the pliés [graceful knee bends] that teach you how to alight from a jump without making a sound."

Another week and 100,000 pliés later, outfitted in black tights and white T-shirt, I stood next to my sister and did the beginning of class at the barre, endured the middle sitting quietly on the bench, and joined the girls for the changements at the end.

A few weeks later, Seda closed the trap.

"You jump so high, and you are landing so beautifully using the plié, but you look awful in the air, flailing your arms about. You've got to take all of class and learn how to do port des bras and épaulement [beautiful carriage of the arms and hands], and all the other exercises to make you powerful and elegant." Seda had me hooked.

An exceptional teacher got this bored child interested in ballet. She challenged me to a test, complimented me on my effort, and immediately issued a new

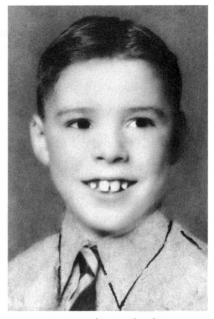

How innocent at the age of eight

challenge. The Boss was part of this conspiracy and, enlisting my sister as coach, kept me engaged, rehearsing and practicing between Seda's once-a-week classes. Boss upped the ante by creating a performing element—our living room was the stage, my father and brothers the unwilling audience, and I the center of attention. Heaven. I loved performing.

> Shoosh, shoosh, shoosh. Pirouettes, twenty or thirty, and I perch on the ball of one foot, pausing, "Should I continue for another twenty?" A circular blur of eyes from the stunned audience as I toss off another twenty or a hundred spins. "This is an entrechat dix!" I announce. Oohs and ahs from the upturned faces of my gang. The whirling and beating of my feet propels me twenty feet in the air.

I stare out the school window at St. Rose's, crossing the sky, grand jeté-ing from one cloud to another while Sister Carmelita chalks multiplication tables on the blackboard.

Among Madame Seda's bevy of girls, I was the only boy, and I loved my classes. Then, spring, and school was out. It was the middle of June

1942, and my mother announced to Madame Seda imperiously, "We won't be here for the summer course. I am taking my children to visit my relatives in Maine." She then added, as though conferring a big favor, "You can hold our place for September."

"Madame," Seda said, "your daughter and son are very talented. But I will not hold a place for them." My mother was in SHOCK! Then Seda did an unbelievably modest and generous thing. She wrote on a piece of paper: Fifty-ninth Street and Madison Avenue, George Balanchine's School of American Ballet.

"Take them here in September. This is where they should be. There are better teachers than I."

I didn't think of ballet during that summer. In Maine, I played with my cousins, clamming, fishing, eating lobster, playing cards, reading books, and staining my teeth with blueberries.

September came. I was eight, and, back in New York City, the School of American Ballet awaited.

When Madame Seda said, "There are better teachers than I," she sent me to a crucible, a laboratory of theater and dance that would shape and influence the performing arts in this country for the rest of the century. There, I would plié, changement, and pirouette my heart out, guided by some of the greatest artists and innovators residing in New York City, most of them from pre-Soviet Russia, role models who demanded the best of their students.

SAB

The primary teacher for children at the School of American Ballet (SAB) was gentle Kyra Blank. She was impeccable—not a scuff on her ballet shoes, and when she demonstrated a turn, a pirouette in slow motion, her skirt floated in the air, to return to rest smoothly, a few beats after, her feet had landed in a perfect fifth position. The skirt echoed the movement, settling a beat later. I stared, mesmerized at the beauty of her—the soft, white skin, black hair and eyes. She smelled beautiful and her soft voice rose only when, in utter frustration, she had to correct this awkward student, "Jacques, feefth, feefth!" I loved her, but my amorous hopes deflated when I learned from gossip in the men's dressing room that she was married to a guy named Vladimir Dimitriev. Don Driver, a charismatic and manic extrovert, who relished prancing nude atop the bench between the lockers, genitals flaunting at eye level, informed me, "Oh, Dimitriev? He used to be director of the school, but no one's ever seen him." My eyes avoided the gyrating genitalia and focused on Don's tattoo, a Technicolor dragon that twitched on the calf of his leg. "But Dimitriev's gone. Kirstein got rid of him, planted him somewhere in Connecticut."

The founder of the school, Lincoln Kirstein, was this immense shadow dashing around the halls, occasionally sticking his head in the doorway of class for a peek.

At Madame Seda's school, my sister was the best dancer, by far. At SAB, the classes were filled with her equals, and a star among them was a long-limbed teenager named Tanaquil LeClercq. Everyone knew Tanny was special. Before Tanny, George Balanchine had drawn inspiration from a chain of dancers: Tamara Geva, Alexandra Danilova, Tamara Toumanova, Irina Baronova, Vera Zorina, Marie-Jeanne, and Maria Tallchief. All of them were short, fast, virtuoso dancers. Tanny was different. She was elongated and stretched out, and fascinating to watch, an elegant praying mantis, but in no way predatory. Balanchine's aesthetic changed with Tanny. She was to become the new prototype for his ideal dancer—long neck, small head, and mile-long limbs.

Kyra Blank teaching at SAB, 1957

"She's too skinny!" the Boss would announce to Tanny's mother, Edith LeClercq. "She should eat more!" Boss always had something to say to the cabal of ballet mothers. Presided over by Edith, they would sit and gossip in the hall outside the studios during their children's ballet classes, the Boss moving among them like a ferret.

It was from Edith that the Boss found out about the King-Coit School, an after-school program run by two little old ladies in a town house they owned together. They were prim Victorians, and created a place where kindergarten play and games were taken to a sophisticated performing-arts level. Tanny was enrolled, and I don't know how the Boss swung it, but she had Madeleine and me enrolled as well, on scholarships. The town house teemed with activity—plays, recitals, poetry readings, dramatic recitations, costume making, anything in the performing arts that tickled Miss King and Miss Coit's fancy. Over the course of some six months, we performed in little vignettes, variety shows, all forgotten by me—with one exception. In that recital, I played a sailor dancing a hornpipe with two belles. The teenage Tanny was on the same program, but the star was a plump little girl, a pasty-faced dumpling with red pouty lips, who recited a poem. Her voice,

Dancing a hoedown, 1943

strident and ear-scraping, would cut through an Alaskan oil slick faster than carbolic acid. That voice is so ingrained in the memories of King-Coit alumni that, fifty years later, I could pick up the phone, call Tanny, and, mimicking THE VOICE, screech, *"Eat little bird and think no more of sorrow!"* and Tanny would immediately parrot the next line, *"I'll feed you every day at this time!"* Then, amid laughter, she would quip, "Are you soliciting me for an invitation to dinner?"

Hanging around SAB, Boss queried the other mothers, "Where can I find a great acting teacher for my children?" Eventually, she zeroed in on Theodore Komisarjevsky, reputed to have been a superb actor and noted director in Moscow. He was eking out a living in New York City, teaching and coaching. After ballet class, Madeleine and I would rush to his studio. For a few dollars a lesson, he had my sister and me—he claimed, "the only children I teach"—memorize, speak, and perform for him excerpts from Shakespeare's *A Midsummer Night's Dream.* Weekends in our living room, my sister and I would rehearse. *"Through the forest have I gone, but Athenian found I none . . ."* I didn't know what I was saying, but the Boss relished her power as coach and director. In "Pyramus and Thisbe," she would stand between Madeleine and me, playing the wall, arm extended, fingers spread to form the chink, *"I see a voice! Now will I to the chink to spy an I can hear my Thisby's face."*

The School of American Ballet had been my home for less than a year when Balanchine snared me for the role of Puck in a production of *A Midsummer Night's Dream.* The Boss went into paroxysms of joy.

In rehearsals for *Midsummer,* I couldn't take my eyes off Balanchine's nose. He was plagued by a nervous twitch, sniffing continually, his mouth playing second fiddle to the nose. Cigarettes moved from fingers to mouth to ashtray, nonstop. He was this nice man with dark hair. His words were hard to understand, but he conveyed whatever movement he wanted by demonstrating. Kindly and unthreatening, he was clear, precise, and gentle in his directions, no waste of time, and no coddling. Until then, he had been a vague figure to me. I'd stand still watching Balanchine dash from one rehearsal room to another, usually followed by Lincoln Kirstein. When I'd see Lincoln coming like a locomotive, I'd dash to get out of the way.

Meanwhile, Boss demonstrated her own artfulness. "I'll make Jacques's costume!" she announced to Balanchine. Out of the itchiest wool conceivable, she created a milk-chocolate-brown unitard, appliquéd with patches of beige. Clusters of grapes and red berries were strategically placed, and one sprig of berries adorned my backside in lieu of a tail. Two little gold horns sprouted from my head, held by a claustrophobic, choking elastic band around my chin. I carried pan-pipes sprayed with gold leaf that rubbed off on my fingers, and for the performance, the Boss made up my face with painted vines and leaves that, when I began to sweat, melted down my cheeks.

I seem to recall that *A Midsummer Night's Dream* premiered. As far as I can remember, there was one performance only, in a garden on an outdoor stage. As Puck, I Pied-Pipered six woodland nymphs (Tanny among them). More than sixty years later, I still remember Balanchine's steps—one, a kind of jump in the air, while kicking my feet behind me like a gamboling colt, and on landing, wiggling my bottom while playing my pipes. Bronchitis hit me the day of the performance, and Lincoln paid for a limousine to pick me up in Washington Heights and deliver me to the performance. It was grand.

Soon, Boss had tracked down a music teacher for us, Pietro Yon. I never knew if it was true or a dramatic embellishment, but the Boss claimed he had been the chief organist for His Holiness the Pope at St. Peter's in Rome, had escaped Mussolini, and was now in charge of music at Manhattan's St. Patrick's Cathedral. Maestro Yon taught theory and composition to music luminaries, and he lived in a very elegant place on Central Park West—I think it may have been the Dakota apartments. One of his compositions, a Christmas song, "Gesù Bambino" (The infant Jesus), is popular to this day.

Madeleine and I were there when my mother first laid siege to him.

Knock, knock, knock, knock. Mr. Yon opened the door. He was a classic and elegant gentleman, old-school Italian. Tiny, with a little paunch, he wore a vest with a gold watch and chain looped to a pocket. The Boss, at the doorway, accusatory in her heavy French accent, inquired, "Are you Mr. Yon?"

"Yes, Madame, I am."

"The great teacher of music?"

"Well, I don't know how great I am, Madame, but yes, I do teach music. Come in. What can I do for you?"

Boss crossed the threshold, entered his living room. He was a goner. My sister and I, hand in hand, followed, gaping at the beautiful rugs, tapestries, and the antique piano of rich, dark wood.

"I want my daughter, Madeleine, to have piano lessons. How much does it cost?"

"Madame, I do not take children for lessons."

"Oh. Well. If you *did* take children, how much would you charge?"

"Madame, I do not take children. But my fee is fifteen dollars an hour." (This was 1943, so his fee would be upward of three hundred dollars an hour today.) My mother turned white and staggered back. She hit the wall. Her hand clutched her throat, and she croaked, "So much!"

Poor, embarrassed Mr. Yon stood there speechless, as the Boss, gathering up her forces and leaping back into the breach, continued, "Well, for my daughter, how much for *half* an hour?"

"Madame, I do not take children . . . but if I *were* to do half an hour, it would be half of fifteen dollars."

"Well," my mother said. "We will see. I think I can afford that. When can Madeleine start?"

Maestro Yon stood there in awe of her audacity and determination, his small brown eyes darting, seeking an escape, as he temporized, and finally saying to my sister, "Come over to the piano." Madeleine shuffled over. "Sit next to me on the piano bench, and put your thumb here. It's called middle C." He stretched her fingers to see how far they could reach, and then had her play two or three notes. After a few moments of silence, moved by the angel of pity, Maestro Pietro Yon sighed, and capitulated. "Well, let us try it for a lesson or two."

Triumphant, Boss arranged for Madeleine to have a lesson once a week and promised to pay the seven dollars and fifty cents after each lesson. Then, as we were leaving, she turned back to deliver the coup de grâce: "Oh, do you mind if Madeleine's little brother, Jacques, sits on the edge of the bench to learn along with his sister?" Poor Mr. Yon! He must have been so intrigued by her brashness and willpower—or completely numbed by her persistence. Without a whimper, he acquiesced.

A week later, we had our first lesson. We barely touched the piano; instead he taught us how to conduct 2/4, 4/4, 3/4, and 5/4 time, and how to write time signatures on a musical staff. When the lesson was over, my mother, who had sat in the living room beaming throughout, announced, "Dear Mr. Yon, I did not bring your fee with me, but I will bring it first thing in the morning." The week before, she had saved up about ten dollars, making hats and selling them on street corners. At home, she put seven dollars and fifty cents in an envelope, and with her remaining two dollars and fifty cents she bought a chicken, stuffed it with chestnuts, made a sauce to go with it, and garnished and wrapped it beautifully. The next morning, she left the envelope with the money and the chicken on his doorstep with the following note: "I have worked all week to get the money for these lessons, and next week will have to work just as hard again to get the money for your big fee. I hope you like the chicken."

Next week, when our second lesson came to a close, the Boss produced an envelope, heavy with coins, and proceeded to count them out on the piano, laboriously stacking quarters, dimes, nickels, and pennies—seven dollars and fifty cents. After watching this woman do her act, Mr. Yon scraped the coins back into the envelope, bowed, and, handing it back to my mother, pronounced elegantly, "Madame, forget the fee, but please, keep me in chickens."

Mr. Yon was fattened, not just with chickens but with stuffed flank steaks, crown roasts, marinated fish, pâtés, and pies. She even left him a bottle of homemade wine. Awful.

Pop managed to get a secondhand—out-of-tune—upright piano for our apartment, and Boss insisted that my sister and I spend at least twenty minutes to a half hour every night practicing.

Boss could be so charming—her English, with heaping spoonfuls of

French Canadian accent, could disarm anyone. She believed without question that she was right, and that the process of striving was its own reward; if she didn't sell a hat, the fact that she had worked so hard to make such a beautiful object was enough in itself. If things did not work out for her, it was not because she held back one iota of effort.

She tried to get Komisarjevsky to forfeit his fees, but lost that bout, so our acting lessons terminated within the year. The piano lessons continued for three years.

I think it was late spring of 1943 that I did Puck . . . Pearl Harbor had been bombed by the Japanese December 7, 1941. During the war, my father worked in a factory that made ball bearings for gyroscopes at Sperry Works. My mother busied herself hanging black shades on all the windows—to hide any luminosity from airplanes flying over—and teaching us to close them when we heard air raid signals. We were instructed to find a place in the house structurally sound (usually a doorframe), stand in it, and wait. Don't light candles, in case the building gets hit by a bomb—a still-flickering candle flame could start a conflagration. In the streets, we all collected tinfoil from discarded cigarette packs along the sidewalk curbs and in trash bins to donate at collection sites—the bits of tinfoil, released from airplanes, deflected enemy radar. During those tumultuous years, little changed at the ballet. Pliés, tendus, and class continued. SAB remained a peaceful and sane place, though Balanchine, busy with myriad projects, was rarely around. Lincoln had disappeared. I noticed the dearth of adult male dancers in the locker room (so many had gone off to war).

From the cabal at SAB, Boss learned of a Czechoslovakian dance teacher, Vaslav Swoboda, and the Swoboda-Yurieva school of ballet (Yurieva was his wife). Rumor had it that Swoboda had been in the corps of Diaghilev's Ballets Russes. All the ballet mothers were in love with him. The Boss was smitten—"He has the demeanor of a prince noble!" My sister remembered, "He was the most beautiful man I ever saw, until I saw Lew Christensen."

Deciding we would be better off studying with Swoboda, Boss switched us from SAB. I took to Swoboda immediately, and he to me. A handsome man with broad shoulders and gorgeous muscles, Swoboda was, indeed, grand, his carriage and use of arms and hands—épaulement—mesmerizing. Madame Yurieva, a tough taskmaster and strict disciplinarian, was not heavy with charm. I tried to keep out of her sight.

Brother Pat was roped in too, and started taking the adult beginner classes. He mopped the floors at the studio in exchange for our scholarships. Boss even coerced Pop to come in the evenings to help clean and close up the studio.

As there were no other boys my age in the children's classes, I shared Swoboda's dressing room, and I would play in there alone before and after ballet classes. There were high lockers that flanked a bench that ran down the center of the room. Like a monkey, I loved to climb from the bench to the top of the lockers, and up there discovered a real sword with a round, silvery hand guard. When you bent and released the blade, it would snap and whistle. One day, Swoboda surprised me, stabbing at the lockers in my underwear. He laughed and told me it was his "épée."

I loved his classes, especially the folk dances—mazurkas and czardas—in one, we would chassé in a circle, leaning into the center and slapping our behinds. However, Swoboda seemed to lose energy before our eyes. His teaching became less rigorous; challenges vanished.

Boss realized that our technique was slipping, and decided to switch back to SAB. In a dramatic scene, she announced to the horn-rimmed glasses of Swoboda's secretary, Viola, and to assorted mothers sitting around, "This is their last class! My children have lost their technique here, so we are leaving! I'm taking them back to SAB."

In the dressing room after class, Swoboda shook my hand, and handed me a goodbye gift, the épée. Overwhelmed, I thanked him and thanked him, until he shushed me. "I want you to have it. I'll never use it anymore." Not long after we left, he died of esophageal cancer.

THE NOVENA

"Mary has promised us that if we do a Novena and request a favor from God, she will intercede with Jesus on our behalf, and what son could refuse his mother?" Sister Carmelita stared at my fourth-grade class as she imparted this momentous truth. "The Blessed Virgin Mary, Mother of God, will be your advocate, a direct voice to Jesus."

She had a lined face, and her white habit pressed the folds of her skin into pudgy wrinkles and trumpet cheeks. In my memory, she was short, so she must have been truly diminutive, because most of her students were under four feet tall. I don't ever recall a smile, but when she was angry, she flamed a shiny pink.

At this moment, however, her expression was benign. "If you want the ear of God, the best way to reach Him is through prayer. The Dominican Order is especially dedicated to the veneration of the Mother of God. To honor Mary, we use one of the great forms of prayer, the Rosary Novena." Her voice charged with excitement. "Today, we will learn what a Novena is and how to do it."

A rustle of excitement rose from the class. Some forty or more boys and girls sat at their desks, divided (as was common), the girls to the right along the wall near the closets, the boys to the left, next to the windows.

"It takes nine weeks to do a full Novena," Sister Carmelita continued, "and there are three tasks to complete. *First,* you must go to confession and confess your sins, receive absolution, and do the penance imposed by the priest. Only then, when your soul is clean, will you be worthy to receive Jesus into your body." She paused, then printed in chalk on the chalkboard, "CLEAN YOUR SOUL!" "*Second,*" she continued, "Mass and Communion once a week. For nine weeks, the Body and Blood of Jesus enters you, and transforms and fills you with goodness." "NINE WEEKS" joined "CLEAN YOUR SOUL!" "*Third,* at the beginning of each day, you must kneel down and say five decades of the Rosary. Then, at night, before you go to sleep, on your knees, recite it again, three times in a row. Do not skip. Do not cut any of the prayers short. You cannot cheat. GOD WILL KNOW!"

A knowing smirk spread across her face as she made eye contact with all of us at once. Not a sound. Every one of us stared back at Sister Carmelita.

"GOD WILL KNOW." I imagined His Presence, the All-Seeing Eye, probing my throat, stomach, heart, brain, and spreading and displaying the viscera of my very thoughts across a big white table. The light so bright. Everything exposed. No shadows possible.

"GOD WILL KNOW" joined "CLEAN YOUR SOUL!" and "NINE WEEKS" on the blackboard. Her chalk screeched bitterly as she wrote the words.

Sister Carmelita wandered among us, and as her voice continued its hypnotic cadence, her white robes swished in rhythm.

"If you have any idle time during the weeks, send your thoughts heavenward to Little Jesus and His Mother. That way, you will keep your mind pure. You will transform yourself into a vessel of God, and His grace will fill you. At the end of the nine weeks, the Novena will be complete, and you can make your request to Jesus."

Arriving back at the chalkboard, she clutched the crucifix hanging from the beads of her rosary, and, standing under "GOD WILL KNOW," imparted in a hushed voice, "You can be sure His Mother will be whispering in His ear, telling Him to give you what you want."

I was so excited. Repetition enthralled, rules to follow, the challenge thrilled me. My imagination leapfrogged, kneeling, praying the Rosary, taking Communion, as my delighted mind envisioned my soul gleaming with cleanliness, eliciting smiles from the All-Seeing Eye. And a luminous, foglike essence of grace perfumed, filling my heart, lungs, and stomach.

I was impetuous, already on my feet. One half of me was looking at my hand in the air, the other half hearing my voice stammer the question. "Sister, can you ask for anything? Sister Carmelita. Anything? I mean . . . no matter what?"

"Of course, anything," she nodded to me in approval. (She had caught a fish.) "Remember, this is a promise from the Blessed Virgin Mary. You will receive your wish . . . provided it is good for you."

I sat down, my mind reeling with the possibilities of *Anything*. Much later, I came to realize that she had cleverly slipped in an escape clause at the end of that sentence, the " . . . provided it is *good* for you."

Sister Carmelita tilted her head slightly to the right. "Remember, children, when you formulate your request, be careful of Pride," her finger waggled, a gentle coach warning us of pitfalls. "It's the most dangerous of sins, thinking you're special, better than the others, the sin of Pride. Lucifer was guilty of it. Swollen and puffed up with his own importance, he envied the goodness and power of God. This sin caused his downfall. God threw him out of Heaven, and he tumbled down to Hell. Into the Great Emptiness he fell, screaming all the way, but no one heard him."

I didn't start the Novena right away, because I hadn't zeroed in on what was the *Anything* I wanted from Jesus. So I hurried home to question the Boss. "Do you know about the Novena?"

"Of course, the Novena. I know all about it. You must go to Mass and receive Communion every day for nine weeks, and then you must say the Rosary nine times in a row, morning, noon, and night."

She always exaggerated.

"Boss, it's only once a week that I have to go to Mass and Communion, and it's only in the morning and at night that I have to say the Rosary, and it's only three times. That's what Sister Carmelita said."

"Well, the French nuns in Montreal taught me differently. Better."

"Sister Carmelita said if I did it, Jesus would give me any wish I picked."

"Well, I don't know about what Sister Carmelita said, but I've been saying the Novena all my life, and I know how to do it. Nine, that's how many times you say the Rosary, not three. Besides, it doesn't hurt to do more. Doing more is good for you, and you only get your wish if it is good for you." (She knew the escape clause.)

I was nine and a half and, back at SAB, already attending the intermediate class, where many of the students were adults, hoping to become performing artists. Once you start to perform, the ANXIETY DREAMS begin. A typical one:

> The Overture's playing, and in your dressing room you can't get into your tights, or can't find your costume or dancing shoes.

But *before* you become a performer, you have the GLORY DREAMS. A recurring one for me:

> In an assemblé (a vigorous leap, the legs glued together and to one side), I would cross the entire room in slow motion. Floating, soaring, landing feather-light. Then, I'd take off again and in one grand jeté (legs in a split, arms flung skyward), I would cross Central Park.

I fed on these delicious GLORY DREAMS, night after night, then replayed and embellished them in daydreams. Then it came to me. I knew what favor I wanted Mary to ask her Son to impart. "Jesus, help me to fly."

Sister Carmelita's version of the Novena was discarded for the Boss's Montreal version—and play it safe, throw in a few extra Rosaries here and there—plus work on the flying costume.

Black tights, white socks coming up to below the knee, black ballet shoes, a black long-sleeved shirt. Tights and shirt held at the waist with a shiny black leather belt. A Lone Ranger mask, purchased at a local five-and-dime store, added a sinister touch. The Boss had acquired a

In a grand jeté. Drawing by David Levine, 1985

new oilcloth for the kitchen table, a royal-blue one. With the shiny surface up, spilled foods could easily be wiped clean. The discarded oilcloth, I pilfered from the garbage can. Its underside was off-white, and marked with the designs for Boss's button game.

Late at night, I took the Boss's sewing scissors and shaped the rectangular oilcloth into a batlike cape with a neck hole cut on one edge, so I could stick my head through. That way the cape would drape off my shoulders and down my back. Neat. How I pranced and swirled in front of the bathroom mirror, posturing and delighting in my creation. The off-white with its button-game pattern on the lining of the cape dramatically highlighted the silhouette of my costume, black mask and all.

The hardest was to make the sword. Swoboda's sword was an icon that I kept in my bedroom closet, but it was adult length and dragged on the floor behind me when I put it in my belt, so I made my own. I found an old broomstick on the street and, using gloves and several dishcloths to protect my hand, heated red hot the tip of a pencil-sized piece of iron over the kitchen stove. I used the red-hot tip to burn a hole through one end of the broomstick. This in-depth branding required multiple ministrations. The heated tip would cool quickly, and it took several days of sneaking into the kitchen in the wee hours to heat the iron and drive the hole through the handle.

I then used a pair of pliers to unbend a wire coat hanger. I threaded the coat hanger through the hole in my broomstick. Then I opened up my copy of *The Three Musketeers* and replicated the illustration of the hand guard on d'Artagnan's sword. It took several hours of trial and error, but it worked. Many late nights were devoted to whittling the broomstick down to a smaller length and flattened blade with a sharpened point. I collected the shavings on spread-out newspapers, bundled them up, and stuffed them into my schoolbag, to be shed in the morning in the street-corner waste bin. Prisoners of war discarding soil from their tunnel-dug escape routes were no more furtive than I. By the sixth week, I was ready. The seventh, eighth, and ninth dragged. Nine weeks seemed a year. But I had a Contract with God.

Midnight on the last day in the ninth week found me kneeling on the roof of our apartment house. I was costumed up, my beautiful sword painted silver and stuck through my belt. I was praying through the final nine Rosaries, not rushing. Each one was portentous, bringing me closer to the great moment when Jesus would let me fly. Apostles' Creed, Our Father, five Hail Marys, Our Father, then repeated Hail Marys in a circle around the beads until you end up back where you started. At last! "I'm ready, Jesus."

I went to the edge of the roof and jumped.

And fell . . .

Only two stories . . . to the roof of the adjoining building (Jesus really was watching out for me). Had I gone off any of the other three sides, a six-story drop would have awaited me.

I was knocked out. Coming out of it after how many minutes? a few? ten? twenty? half an hour? One whole side of my leg was scraped, knee to hip. My costume was shredded, my ankles and knees throbbing so badly that I was sure they were broken. My sword shattered.

The fall was probably some twenty-five to thirty feet. Lucifer's fall was much farther. I crawled up onto my aching knees. "Forgive me, Jesus, I'm so sorry. It was not right for me to fly. I'm not worthy. I was too proud. I had the sin of pride. IT WAS NOT GOOD FOR ME."

The d'Artagnan's wire hand guard on my sword was flattened. I tried to stand, but my ankle did not support me. Broken? Maybe just a sprain. Glory Dreams vanished. My concern was, "How can I get off the roof?"

I had imagined I would fly, batlike, through the night sky, soar around my neighborhood for a while, then alight gently back where I started, and so I had propped open the door to my roof, to welcome my return. But now, I found myself on another roof!

Chastened and dejected, I limped over to the door to the stairwell. Horrors! Locked!

"Oh, please Jesus, don't let them find me here in the morning." It would be worse than being caught naked in the subway. My costume seemed stupid, the splintered sword a travesty, my cape, pathetic, and me, battered—all because of the sin of Pride.

Crawling off the roof by descending a ladder to the top floor's out-door fire escape, I zigzagged down several levels of metal stairs, limping past the open windows of sleeping families. Most perilous was the ten-foot drop from the lowest level of the fire escape to the ground! What a nightmare! Terrified, I hung by my fingertips from the final rung of the raised ladder, said another prayer, and let go. This time, I was certain I would break both ankles.

Not so bad. I was okay. "Oh, thank you, Jesus, thank you!"

Yikes! The alley door to my apartment building was locked! I sat down and cried. They would find me in the alley in the morning, unable to move, exposed by bright morning sun, my ankle a swollen balloon.

Then, right in front of my eyes lay the half-open casement window to the coal bin in the basement of my building. Inside, the piles of coal were packed right up to the window's edge. I saw how I could squeeze through the window, roll down a hill of coal to the floor, then wend my way through and out of the cellar, up the stairs, and to bed. Hooray!

Black with coal dust when I emerged from the basement, I left smudges on the stairs all the way up to our fourth-floor apartment. It took me two hours to clean the filth off, bandage the scrapes, and wash away the coal dust rimming the bathtub. I could hear Boss snoring as I cleaned away the evidence. No spy could have done better. The cape and the shards of d'Artagnan's sword were on the roof of the building next door, abandoned.

Now I had to hide my ripped and blackened costume. I threw it out the window.

Folds twisting, swirling downward, bat wings fluttering away in darkness. Lucifer, on his way down to the abyss. (See Appendix.)

Laughing John lost his smile and his weight, but kept his life, 1945

Madeleine and I, this time with Pat, were taking daily ballet classes every day at SAB. My eldest brother, John, escaped my mother's dream of having "cultured children," but into horror. Having been drafted into the U.S. Army, he ended up in Okinawa, in mopping-up operations against the entrenched Japanese. John left home a good-natured, pudgy boy with buckteeth. After Armistice Day in 1945, he returned to us, bone thin, his skin green. Once, at the dinner table, I accidentally dropped a fork, and the sound had John on his feet, screaming. For months after, I whispered around him. Pop returned to running the elevator at Columbia Presbyterian Hospital.

NUNS

Nuns! Their outfits made them magical. Their actions seemed malevolent. Their bodies hidden, breastless, hands always under their habits, fiddling with their rosaries. What were they doing? Their ears were covered, bandaged tightly as if they had head injuries, and their stiff, hooded headdresses prevented peripheral vision. Still, they had super hearing and somehow could see sideways and behind. Magic. They lived in a mysterious, impenetrable fortress called the convent. We never saw them use the bathroom at school, so the fortress was the only possible place they could have relieved themselves. I never thought about the fact that they were women, until someone said that they were, and then I thought, "What do they do with their hair?" Jimmy Comiskey told me they shaved their heads, or had crew cuts, like marines, and they wore gold wedding rings that Jesus had given them. Christ had women in His Special Forces, and was married to them!

Sometimes they punished our infractions by beating the palms of our hands with a ruler. Other punishments stressed humiliation—having to sit with the girls if you were a boy or vice versa; being sent to the chalkboard to write continuously, "I am a liar," or "I am sorry I misbehaved." When the chalkboard was filled, you erased and started over.

School ended at three o'clock, when the bell rang for freedom. We would all wait for Sister's "Dismissed!" then grab our schoolbooks and flee. Boss had given me orders: "You don't have a second to spare!" I would run home, grab an apple and the four nickels that waited on the table, put my tights and ballet shoes in my practice bag, guzzle a glass of milk, and head for the subway. One nickel got me to Columbus Circle at Fifty-ninth Street by three thirty p.m. A second nickel was for the Fifty-ninth Street crosstown bus to Madison Avenue. (I could save that nickel by running across the park, which I often did, leaping to touch the leaves of overhead trees all the way.) My hand would be on the ballet barre by four o'clock, as we began our pliés. There were some twenty girls and two other boys in my class—Eddie Villella, a year or so younger, and Paul, a year older, I think his last name was Mackowitz. Eddie would go on to join the New York City Ballet and thrill audiences for decades. Paul dropped out before we reached our teens. Rumor was, he had a short career as a banker before being arrested for embezzlement.

Class was an hour long. After, I would dawdle and fool around in the locker room, wrestling with Eddie, being a bully, and sometimes peeking in to watch the professional dancers at their evening class. Eventually, I'd eat my apple on the subway and be home by seven p.m. Boss would be in the kitchen cooking. I'd hand her my sweaty dance clothes and head out to join my buddies on the block until she bellowed, "Dinner!" from the window.

None of my pals ever questioned where I went after school. Till one day!

The bell rang, and we waited for Sister Carmelita's "Dismissed!" Instead, we got a barked order: "Stand up." We rose. "Face the back of the room." We turned. "Don't move." We froze. Then she softly addressed the backs of our heads. "As punishment for your rowdiness, you will stand in silence until I dismiss you." Nobody breathed; the ticking of the clock sounded its sledgehammer. Sister Carmelita wrote, and the scratching of her pen hurt your eyeballs. She'd turn a page, and it sounded like an avalanche. I was going to miss ballet class!

After half an hour, Sister Carmelita uttered sweetly, "Dismissed." Those two softly worded syllables, dripping with false gentleness, sent us all, cowed, pussyfooting out of the room. I shambled home.

When the Boss found out why I had missed my class, she announced, grim-faced, "I will speak to the principal, Sister Mathilda." She spoke with such determination and assuredness—power! It was not that she had any thought of a challenge, of throwing down the gauntlet, or creating a conflict with Sister Mathilda. It was just a fact of nature; Boss would solve the problem. She put on her coat and headed straight to the fortress. And was back within an hour.

"I spoke with the principal and explained that you cannot miss your ballet class. You may be punished in other ways, but you must be released from school at the three o'clock bell . . . and you will be."

The potential repercussions of this solution never crossed my mind. Within a week, my class got punished again. The three o'clock bell rang, Carmelita's order came: "Stand up. Face the back of the room. Don't move. Oh, yes, Ahearn, you have my permission to leave. Ahearn has a ballet class. His mother says he has to go." Titters, sidelong glances, and some openmouthed amazed stares.

The candy store, 1941

Though Zeus's thunderbolt had never caused more devastation, I put up a good front. Grinning frozenly and bobbing like a marionette, I collected my schoolbags, croaked a "Thank you, Sister," and zoomed out the door.

Though I was relieved to make my ballet class and not infuriate the Boss, I would have to face everyone—my pals, the girls, the whole school—when I returned.

I got the apple and the nickels, did the subway trip, took class, headed back, and at seven o'clock came out of the subway not far from Dave's Candy Store on the corner of 163rd Street to find eight or ten of the guys lurking. Dave's was a hangout. I drank my first egg cream there. A glass with chocolate syrup, seltzer, and a little milk. Where the label "egg" came from was a mystery. The store had a telephone booth, heavily used as few families on the block had a private phone.*

Right away the guys challenged me. "Hey, Jock. What the hell is all this stuff about ballet? You taking dancing lessons?" Farel, one of the toughs, added, "You a sissy? A queer?"

---

* In 2008, while I was watching the Russian dancers from the Kirov perform at City Center, a lady in the row in front of me turned around. "Excuse me," she ventured. "I'm Irene Rosner David. I know you're Jacques d'Amboise, but you used to be Ahearn. My dad was Dave and had the candy store on your block. He always spoke of you and your dancing, followed your career." I begged her for a photo. Two came within a week.

Dave and his candy store, 1941

I just told the truth. "It's great! It's so hard. And there's this guy, Eglevsky, who jumps up in the air and stays there for a while. He's got all these muscles. His thighs are as big around as your chest. And he does this step called a sauté. It's a jump. Here, I'll show you." I put my practice bag on the sidewalk, stood in fifth position to one side of it, leaped in the air—moving sideways over my bag—and landed on the other side. Then I said, "That's only a few feet. Eglevsky goes much higher and moves seven or eight feet. Here, you want to try it?"

I had them all doing it, contorting to get into fifth position and jumping over my practice bag. Then I put down soda bottles, assorted jackets, and caps, and choreographed them sautéing in concert, all over the sidewalk. Except Farel.

"You all look like a bunch of spastics," he mumbled. "I ain't doing any of that queer shit."

We ignored him and went on to tours and entrechats, with an incredulous Dave standing in the doorway of his candy store.

I never again had trouble from my pals about taking ballet lessons. As time went on, I would demonstrate, and they would try the latest steps I had learned, and I would keep them up-to-date with how many pirouettes I could do. They accepted my ballet classes, and their acceptance percolated throughout St. Rose's School.

I don't remember much truck with Farel. He kept away from me and I from him.

Until I turned fifteen.

BALLET SOCIETY YEARS

Lincoln Kirstein was to be seared several times trying to create ballet companies, and encountered disaster trying to create a resident ballet company at the Metropolitan Opera. In 1946, he decided to hell with trying to curry favor with the public, and he formed the Ballet Society, a group of American aristocrats (meaning members of the moneyed class) to commission performances in New York—evenings of ballet to be performed in rented spaces. In the public announcement that circulated among the New York elite, Lincoln promised "completely new reper- tory, consisting of ballets, ballet-opera and other lyric forms . . . [with] the planned collaboration of independent easel-painters, progressive choreographers and musicians, employing the full use of avant-garde ideas, methods, and materials."* In mid-September, Ballet Society was born, and the first ballet at the birth was *The Spellbound Child*, with music by Ravel.

Balanchine wanted me to play the young boy in Ravel's mini-opera *L'Enfant et les Sortilèges*. It was to be called *The Spellbound Child*, and an ecstatic Boss escorted me to the first rehearsal. I was to *be* that Child. In the course of rehearsals, I discovered the action in *L'Enfant* centers on a child and the magical, dreamlike adventures he conjures. A hodge- podge of moving furniture, ticking clocks, threatening math numbers (the "Arithmetic" dance), flirting cats, croaking frogs (my brother Pat, recently renamed Paul, was a frog). These assorted creatures appear and dance to Ravel's sumptuous music. Learning the role of the Child, I was terrified. There were many consultations among Lincoln, Balanchine, Leon Barzin, the conductor, and various unknown people, talking about me, staring at me. I didn't know it then, but they were deciding whether to go with a dancing lead (me) accompanied by a boy soprano singing from the orchestra pit, or with the boy soprano singing onstage, but not dancing. Just simple staging. I lost out to the voice. His name was Joseph Connolly, and he was sweet and scared, like I was. Relieved, I became his understudy. In case laryngitis struck or he croaked, I would perform his stage movements while an adult female soprano sang from the pit. Every performance, I sat watching from the audience, in the chilly and drafty Central High School of Needle Trades auditorium on Twenty-fourth Street.

* Anatole Chujoy, *The New York City Ballet* (Knopf, 1953). For both background and factual information regarding Balanchine, Kirstein, and the creation of the School of American Ballet and the companies that sprang from it, I am indebted primar- ily to Anatole Chujoy and Bernard Taper for Chujoy's *The New York City Ballet* and Taper's *Balanchine: A Biography* (1984 edition), along with Debra Hickenlooper Sowell's *The Christensen Brothers: An American Dance Epic* (1998)—highly readable and thoroughly enjoyable accounts. The many conversations with Lincoln, Lew, his brother Willam, and Balanchine himself, I recorded in my diaries.

I liked the "Arithmetic" section the best. The rest of *L'Enfant* has faded from memory, and I blame the second ballet on the program for overwhelming my imagination.* To this day, on any dance program, *The Four Temperaments* (we called it *Four T's*) will not be eclipsed. Balanchine's realization of Hindemith's music—his choreography, the dancers, costumes, lighting, and scenery—still haunt me. I can even conjure up the scent of the high school auditorium, dank and blended with the intoxicating heated air generated by the stage lights and the aroma of sweat and rosin.

I was a mouth-gaping, unblinking twelve-year-old watching that ballet—the Sanguinic section, with Nicholas Magallanes lifting Mary Ellen Moylan in a series of slow-motion waves in a circle; the Choleric section, with Tanny flaying her mile-long limbs in a circle, reminding me of the Boss's eggbeater whipping up heavy cream; as Melancholic, the pantherish Bill Dollar was all amorphous softness. But Todd Bolender took the crown. In the Phlegmatic section, he stole the show. Among the many great artists who have subsequently danced this role, none can touch Todd's slinky, feline magic. His face, covered in pale white makeup, was bisected by a giant painted slash of a mouth, drawn with one side curling downward in a sneer and the other upward in a smirk. A lavender floppy hat crowned his bizarre face. Every night, seated in the audience, I awaited my favorite moment, stretching my neck to see him better, while placing my hands under my buttocks to make myself a little taller. Phlegmatic, at one moment, leans over and, in slow motion, wraps his right hand around his ankle as if it were a snake slithering around the stem of a flowering plant. Then, slowly, he lifts his foot toward his face. Motionless, balancing on his other leg, he stares unblinkingly at the foot. I would try to see if I could remain still, hold my breath, and not blink, for as long as Todd stayed frozen. Others enter and dance around him; he doesn't quiver, breathless in his stillness for what seems like hours. Suddenly, without taking his eyes off the foot, he places it back on the floor and explodes into a high-stepping spinning dance. I would pant with delight. In seconds, this complicated movement evolves into a simple prance, performed with a nonchalant, saucy air.

* *The Spellbound Child* (*L'Enfant et les Sortilèges*), with music by Ravel, text by Colette, and decor by Aline Bernstein; and *The Four Temperaments*, with music by Paul Hindemith, scenery by Kurt Seligmann. The choreography was all Balanchine.

Todd Bolender in The Four Temperaments, *1946*

To this day, I consider Todd Bolender among the greatest dance artists I've ever seen on the stage, not just for *The Four Temperaments,* but in every role I saw him perform. His genius was in giving full value to every gesture of the dance, as if it were the only movement he would ever make, the beginning and end of the universe. Each movement, Todd imbued with drama and theater, as if the music and gestures contained dialogue, silent words holding secrets of Shakespeare and Chekhov.

I ended up dancing in *Four Temperaments* when I was seventeen, then eventually dancing the Sanguinic sections with Maria Tallchief. Lincoln loved *Four T's.* "Buster, go out front and watch Balanchine's invention in just bringing people on- and offstage." Generally, you don't dwell on entrances and exits; you look at the meat of the ballet. But the entrances and exits of *Four T's* are distinctive—varied, and, at times, goofy. Melancholic enters with a leap, lands on one leg, relevés and balances on the ball of his foot, twists, then collapses to the floor. In San-guinic, the man stalks on from stage left and assumes a heroic stance. The ballerina, from stage right, enters as if answering a question. She perches on pointe, puts one leg behind her, and slants way back, almost to the point of falling. They repeat, as if engaged in call and response, arriving at center, where they begin a thrilling conversation in dance. It never occurred to me in those Ballet Society days that someday I would be up there doing that entrance with those great dancers and sharing the stage with Todd. I never danced Todd's role, Phlegmatic. I would have refused, even if Balanchine had asked me. Todd was the zenith.

AHEARN TO D'AMBOISE

I have no idea how she did it, but in September 1946, just before rehearsals for the first season of Ballet Society commenced, my mother persuaded my father to change all our names from Ahearn to her maiden name, d'Amboise. "It's aristocratic, it's French, it has the 'd' apostrophe. It sounds better for the ballet, and it's a better name."

- Andrew Patrick Ahearn became André d'Amboise
- Georgiana d'Amboise Ahearn became Georgette d'Amboise
- John Ahearn became Jean Achilles d'Amboise
- Patrick Ahearn became Paul d'Amboise
- Madeleine Ahearn became Ninette d'Amboise

and

- Joseph Ahearn (me) became Jacques Joseph d'Amboise.

To this day, I am dumbfounded that Pop acquiesced. Maybe using d'Amboise as a professional stage name for the children might have made some sense. But to legally change the names of the entire family—including himself—is bizarre.

Lawyers were paid. Papers were signed, notarized, filed, and returned. A done deal. Afterward, I never heard Pop tell anyone he had once been "Ahearn." He introduced himself saying, "I'm Andy. Andy Damm-boyze," mispronouncing it with glee.

BALLET SOCIETY — SECOND SEASON

The creative forces at work during the two years of Ballet Society's existence were mind-boggling. Eight programs were presented, including premieres of sixteen new ballets. The finest artists in New York came together to realize the programs: Balanchine, Stravinsky, Lew Christensen, Isamu Noguchi, Merce Cunningham, John Cage— the list of collaborators goes on and on. The amount of choreography, productions—one program after another, one ballet after another— gives only a glimpse of the energy and passion in the proving ground that was Ballet Society.

The first time I danced for Balanchine, little was expected of me. I was not yet nine years old, a child doing a role in *A Midsummer Night's Dream.* The second time, at twelve, the assignment was to understudy the singing star in *L'Enfant* for the opening of Ballet Society. I was never expected to do anything but be on call. Several months later, in the second program of Ballet Society,* there was a world of difference. Lew Christensen had returned from the war and was reviving a ballet called *Pastorela* that he had created in 1941 for the American Ballet. *Pastorela* was a Mexican morality play. I starred as the angel, opposite Lew as the devil. In a vigorous pseudo-flamenco cockfight, with spurs on booted heel, the angel triumphs. Costarring with Lew Christensen, I was expected to perform and be professional.

I was a rambunctious brat backstage, bringing my street play to the corridors and dressing rooms of the theater. Misha Arshansky, who specialized in character roles with dramatic makeup, wigs, and assorted paraphernalia, was assigned to teach me how to put on makeup. His guttural voice was thick with a Russian accent, difficult to understand. Slamming me into a chair, he commanded, "Sit! No move. No talk. Eyes still, no blink." As he worked his magic on my face, he prepared

---

* The second program of Ballet Society's first season (January 1947) included three ballets: *Pastorela,* with choreography by Lew Christensen, music by Paul Bowles, based on the Mexican Christmas play *Los Pastores,* libretto by José Martinez, scenery and costumes by Alvin Colt; *Renard (The Fox),* with choreography by Balanchine, music by Stravinsky, scenery and costumes by Esteban Frances, and English text by Harvey Officer; and *Divertimento,* choreography by Balanchine to a score by Alexei Haieff, no scenery, and simple, stripped-down costumes. It was January 1947, and I was twelve and a half years old.

me with more than makeup. "You are no more American boy, running wild with bad manners. You must act grown up, and become a dancer, an artiste. Besides, you are starring in the role of an angel. Be one." It took a while to absorb his advice.

The Ballet Society programs made for a rich menu. There were modern dances (Iris Mayberry running around with her signature scarves) and Javanese performers (mysterious artists who kept to themselves, behaving like samurais onstage and off—they danced to the sound of their long-nailed fingers tap dancing on thin wooden boards held in the crook of an elbow, and seemed to move in another place and time). On the *Pastorela* program—*Renard* and *Divertimento.* I would sit out front after *Pastorela.* In *Renard,* I adored the undulating tail of the Fox's costume, and the way Todd played with that tail as if it were another limb, at times kissing it fondly on its tip. Todd's performance as the Fox was full of tongue-in-cheek humor and pepper-spiced. The dancing in *Divertimento* and jazzy rhythms of the music had me bouncing in my seat. Lew vigorously pounded out the rhythms of his variation, precise but stiffly. Another dancer, whose variation complemented Lew's, was John Taras. John's variation was soft, smooth, a marshmallow dancing.* But what brought me to rapture in *Divertimento* was the pas de deux with Maria Tallchief and Francisco Moncion, with its culmination of an inventive embrace. Frank's outstretched arms, reaching past Maria's shoulders, his hands clenching into fists, then repeatedly stretching his fingers yearningly, as he rocks in slow motion. Simultaneously, Maria, balancing on the tip of her left foot, tucks her head into the crook of Frank's neck, nuzzling. Then she gently strums the floor with her right foot, making a series of circles as if visualizing the musical phrase by stirring the air. I'd go home and practice every variation, and dream that someday, I would dance with Maria.

FAREL

Farel was a bully, and everyone was scared of him. No one ever called him anything except Farel. He wasn't big or strong. He seemed old,

---

* John would later have a lifelong and successful career as ballet master and choreographer in a variety of companies, eventually returning to join NYCB and hooking his life force to Balanchine.

his body hunched into pleats like a cold shrimp. Yellow fingers cupping a cigarette, he clamped furtively on the butt, swallowing his own lips and wrapping them around jaundiced teeth. He'd suck in, an arpeggio, then his arm would drop down and from the corner of his mouth, he'd vent a stream of smoke in a descending octave. As dependable as Old Faithful, the arm would pump up to repeat the cycle, the oil-rig piston of a tough guy. And I'm talking about a boy barely a teenager. He puffed, bobbed, and swayed constantly. We all felt his watery eyes staring at us. He may have been the author of "Don't cross Amsterdam Avenue; if you do, *they'll* get you," and "If *they* come around our block, we'll get *them*."

Silence with the occasional mumbled word was part of Farel's mystique. He used his grunts, mumbles, and half words as a shield. You never found out what was inside. What really shocked us was that HE CARRIED A *SWITCHBLADE!*

Growing up, we all had moments of juvenile delinquency, but by our teens, the consensus was that Farel was advanced. We imagined he had graduated into the camp of serious criminals.

Rumor on the block had Farel running with the Famwoods, a gang known for toughness, but recently, he had been ostracized. So he formed his own gang, a cluster of flunkies. You never saw them at Mass, Confession, or Communion. At our block games or school activities, they never participated, instead hovered, lurking at the edge of your eye, sort of a bevy of crows clustered on a ridge, sneering at the lesser animals cavorting in the meadow below.

On our block, when you were eight, nine, ten years old, you could join the Guerillas, who acted as lookouts for the Panthers (an older group into petty crimes). As a Guerilla, you blew the whistle and yelled, "Chickie! Chickie!" if you saw a cop or a cop car. Why "Chickie! Chickie!" was chosen as a signal I never knew; it was probably code for "Be scared!" "Danger!" or "Scatter! Make like a chicken!"

At eleven, twelve, and thirteen years old, you could become a Panther and perpetrate petty crimes—shoplifting, rifling through the glove compartments of parked cars, stealing into abandoned houses, warehouses, or boarded-up buildings. Or, down at the railroad tracks, breaking into railroad cars.

Then in early teens, you had a choice, the Vampires, Victory Boys, or Famwoods. Now you left misdemeanors behind and rose to felonies and battles with other gangs in street wars. Handguns were rare, so we made our own. We called them zip guns, and they were dangerous to the user.*

For several years, I managed to fit in some of these gang activities and still make my School of American Ballet classes after school. But by age fourteen, I was taking up to ten classes a week and gang activities faded away.

From the beginning of time, teen years have been difficult, frightening—breaking away from your family, making it on your own, finding your place in society. What will you do? be?

In elementary school at St. Rose's, the nuns programmed us to believe that when we reached our teens, we had two choices: aim for a secular life (a topic they rushed over quickly) or a religious life (dwelt on with rapture). "Maybe, God will choose you for a special vocation, to join His Church and be one of His." For girls, this higher calling was to become a nun (married to Jesus). Boys had a chance to become brothers or priests ("Little Jesuses here on earth"). The married life, if one was to choose it, existed solely for the procreation of children, to be brought up in the bosom of the Catholic Church. The nuns implied that being single and secular was fraught with danger and a lesser and unlikely path to heaven.

However, by high school, most of us weren't thinking about God anymore. Our parents worried about our future and old age. "Security—get a pension." Their words went in our ears and out again, leaving no mark.

Sex and money occupied all our thoughts.

Outside my schedule of dance classes, I always found time for sports. I would run from my house down to the handball courts in Riverside Park, and play with anyone who was there. I loved swatting viciously

---

* How to make a zip gun? First, carve out of hardwood a model of a pistol (a barrel with a handgrip, no trigger guard). Second, on the top of the barrel, scrape out a narrow groove that runs its length. Place a steel pipe in the groove and secure it by wrapping tape and multiple thick rubber bands around the barrel. The diameter of the pipe must be exactly the right size to fit a .22 shell, inserted with the rim resting on the edge of the pipe. Too small and the bullet falls out. Too big and you can't slip it in the pipe. Again using thick rubber bands, attach a big nail along the grip of the zip gun. The nail head functions as the hammer, pressing against the rim of the .22 shell that has been loaded into the pipe. Wedge a finger between the nail and the grip, pull the nail back as far as you can (cocking), and release it. The nail head slams into the bottom of the bullet, exploding the powder and propelling the bullet out of the pipe, occasionally blowing up your hand.

the hard rubber ball, and never used gloves, so my hands would bruise and swell. I imagined it made me tough, and it was a small price to pay for the strength of my swings. I was good at handball, right up there at the top, almost equal to our block's star athlete, Abie Grossfeld.

Late one summer afternoon, heading home from the handball courts, I arrived at a place where Riverside Park abutted the street's apartment houses—around 160th Street. Farel, surrounded by five of his henchmen, was lurking on the corner.

"Hi Farel, hi fellas," I said as I went by.

Farel ignored me. He didn't want to be interrupted; he was busy victimizing one of his crew, a pudgy and awkward red-faced boy with stubby arms. Farel had brought him to tears and was humiliating him. In an excess of stupid, impetuous, unthinking brashness, I yelled, "Cut it out, Farel. Leave him alone."

The gang was surprised, and Farel turned on me. "Fuck off, Ahearn—keep out of this, or you'll be sorry."

I shot back my own cliché. "Oh yeah, what the fuck are you going to do about it?" Comic-book dialogue.

Out came his switchblade. The pudgy victim scuttled backward against the building.

Without even thinking, I did a grand battement—a big kick—knocking his hand and sending the knife flying. The force of my kick spun me around on the ball of my foot 360 degrees. I arrived with both feet under me in plié, leaped in the air, and jumped so high my feet kicked down on top of his shoulders, smashing him to the ground. Farel lay stunned, when the virus of the bully infected me.

I ran over, picked up the knife, and came back. He was rolled in a fetal position. I pinned his shoulders, knelt down on his legs, and stabbed him in the buttocks, tearing through his jeans, piercing the skin, and drawing blood. "How do you like it, Farel, how do you like it?" I never looked at him; I was staring at the unbelieving faces of his gang, relishing my power and his humiliation.

Then it seemed like a bucket of water drenched me, a wash of shame. Curtains of emotion flooded from brain through belly to feet. I jumped up, flung the knife over the wall into the bushes, and fled, bewildered and frightened, appalled that violence and cruelty had boiled up with such speed and ease. What started as a cursory greeting had turned in seconds to a stabbing.

Late that night, the doorbell rang. The Boss answered, and soon she was at the door of my room. "Jacques, what have you done? The police are here. They want to speak to you." Two uniforms, big and Irish, were waiting in the hall near the door.

"Boss, I can handle it," I stammered. "I'll talk to them."

"Not on your life! I'm staying here to see what you've done."

One burly cop said, "You're Jock, right? Now, we know you had a fight with Farel, and it's an okay thing, you'll not be in trouble. We just want the knife."

When she heard "the knife," Boss gasped and stopped breathing. She did her Sarah Bernhardt act—clutched her heart and sagged against the wall. It worked, on me as well as the cops. I was more afraid of her than of them. "What do you mean? What knife?" she demanded.

"Sure now, Farel himself is at the station house at this very moment. And his gang now, they've told us your son took the knife. We'll be needing it. It's evidence."

The other cop spoke up. "That Farel, he's a bad one, been using that knife threatening and intimidating old people around the neighborhood. He makes them hand over their money."

I confessed, "I don't have it. I threw it away, into the bushes down at the park, around 160th Street."

"We'll be looking, and if it's there, we'll find it."

They turned and left. They *could* leave. I had to stay and face the Boss.

Within a week of the Farel fight, Boss announced, "Your brother wants you to come out to Chicago and spend the summer with him. It's a good chance to get you off the street, and it'll be good for you to be with your brother."

My brother Paul had joined the cast of the musical *Inside U.S.A.,* and was playing an extended run at the Shubert Theatre in Chicago.

"He will send you a ticket for the train. You'll stay with him and come back in September."

I thought my brother had asked for me. Only today, as I write this, do I realize that my mother was terrified about her delinquent son. She had called and set it up with Paul to get me off the street.

How excited I was! This was the real thing, on my own, boarding a super train at Penn Station, New York, and riding to South Street Station, Chicago. It was June of 1949. I was fourteen, five foot seven, weighed 130 pounds, and had just completed my first year of Bishop Dubois High School.

The ticket came, and my adventure started a little after eight a.m. I stuffed my bag with a few clothes, took the twenty dollars Boss gave me to eat with on the train, and headed down to Penn Station. After finding and boarding the correct train, I got myself ensconced in a window seat, and soon was staring at the New Jersey gasworks and refineries that so grossly greet you as you emerge from the Hudson tubes. A big black man in a white uniform with graying hair at his temples approached. "Are you planning to reserve yourself a berth?" he said as he checked my ticket.

"Huh?"

"You better, or you'll sleep all night in your seat. We don't get into Chicago till seven a.m. tomorrow."

This must be what you're supposed to do, the grown-up thing. "Okay. What's it cost?" It was nineteen dollars and something cents. He took my twenty, and I received a train car and berth number with the change. How sophisticated I was, handling that decision in just the right way. But the forty cents left in my hand made me uneasy. Something was wrong.

A short time later, a bell rang and back came the porter, full of good cheer, announcing, "Lunch. First serving." God, was I stupid. Not enough money to eat with, and about eighteen hours to go. "I'll just look out the window and won't think of food."

The railbed through New Jersey and Pennsylvania and across Ohio and Illinois passes vistas of woods and farmland, creeks and swamps, then more woods, farmland, creeks, and swamps, and so on and on. I stared out the window and watched myself as Daniel Boone, dressed in buckskin and a raccoon-tail hat, running across the countryside, leaping over creeks and dodging trees, keeping up with the train. I was a "courier du bois" who had to keep running without sustenance the whole way to Chicago.

Bells ringing, the porter announcing, "Lunch. Second serving . . ." Dizzy with hunger, I was inventing menus, and salivating.

Once in a while, we would flash through a town, and occasionally make a scheduled stop at the larger stations. Naturally, vendors were selling food. Where was Eve? Someone to offer me an apple!

"Dinner. Last call!" The sun was setting, and my empty stomach groaned. "Go to bed early; don't think about food." In an upper berth, I rolled and flipped and twitched all night, too hungry to sleep. "Jerk. You could have been eating. So what if you'd slept sitting up. You're not sleeping lying down."

At first light, I was back at the window, suffering through the call for breakfast. Then we pulled into Chicago's South Street Station. What if Paul wasn't there, or we missed each other? Where would I go? What would I do? I had no money and was *so* hungry. But there he was on the platform. He'd spotted my window-pressed face and was awaiting me as I stepped off the train.

"How was the trip?"

"Great," I grinned, too embarrassed to mention famine and sleeplessness.

"Come on. We're walking. It'll be good for you." He took my bag.

It was over three miles to East Huron Street, and I thought I would die as I struggled to keep up. Paul was short, and he had short legs, but his fast-twitch muscles moved in a blur. In later life, he took up running with a passion, knocking off marathons.

Undistinguished tract houses, three or four stories high, lined the streets all over the neighborhood that bordered Lake Michigan. At last, we stopped our dash. I followed my brother up a few steps, through a door, down a hall, and to a little room with the one bed we would share. Several members of the cast had also rented rooms in this little town house, which had a bathroom in the back for all. In show business, when you had a job and earned a salary, you skimped and saved any way you could, sort of storing up potatoes for the winter.

On a little hot plate, my brother warmed a can of Campbell's Chicken Noodle Soup. Oh, God! Was it delicious! A repast slurped down in seconds, and forever imprinted in the genetic makeup of my taste buds.

Paul and I snoozed, a quick nap, and then he had me up and race-walking several miles down Michigan Avenue and west to the Shubert Theatre. We arrived at the stage door just in time for the half-hour call for the matinee, and I was passed on to a stagehand, an older man with a potbelly. "Pete, this is my brother, Jacques. Call him Joebean, and keep him out of trouble."

So I found myself following Pete to the upper balcony and into the follow spot booth. It was hotter than the Sahara, crowded with several big metal cannon-shaped lighting instruments. Inside each were several rods similar to railroad spikes—carbons, I think. Electric current heated them red hot, and, when brought together in the barrel of the light cannon, they glowed brilliantly, and the glow, magnified by a fat lens, projected a light beam down to the stage. There was a wheel with colored cellophane gels at the end of the lens, and by turning the wheel you could tinge the light beam with varied colors, iris the beam to a pinspot, or open it up and spread it wide to cover the stage. The carbons would burn out, and at intermission, Pete would replace them with fresh ones, reloading the cannons.

Within a week, I had memorized the whole show, the dialogue, the songs, everyone's entrances and exits. Pete let me aim the beam during some of the ballads. Hooray. How I loved it. I was going to be a stagehand.

Over that summer of changes, I celebrated my fifteenth birthday and by September had grown to six foot one and weighed 145 pounds— a broomstick. It was time to return to New York. Paul delivered me to South Street Station with money in my pocket and my bag crammed with food. I signed up for every meal the porter announced and wolfed down snacks in between. Didn't take a berth, sat up, and noshed the night through. By the time I reached Penn Station, my pockets may have been lighter, but my stomach bulged.

A sophomore, and back at Bishop Dubois High School, I felt so worldly. I'd been to gangland Chicago on my own, and was going to be a stagehand.

September also found me back at the School of American Ballet, taking a full schedule of classes. Near the end of the month, Eddie Bigelow, a member of the New York City Ballet, who doubled as a kind of odd-jobs man and gofer—helping out in every aspect of production—came to me after class. "D'Amboise, come with me. Mr. Balanchine wants to talk to you." I followed him into a room, where Lincoln Kirstein, Jerry Robbins, and Balanchine had been auditioning.

Balanchine said, "Oh, well, we are making bigger the company. Maybe you would like to join?"

I was astonished, stunned, standing there grinning, speechless, thinking, "I can't do it. I have to finish school."

"How old are you now?"

I squeaked, "Fifteen."

Balanchine sniffed a bit and declared, "Maybe you should talk to parents and let us know."

In an alley in Chicago, outside the Shubert Theater, 1949

The Boss's response was an immediate HOORAY! Pop was less enthusiastic. "If you want to play around with all those highfalutin people for a few years, fine. But if you intend to be involved in theater, you better be a stagehand. It's the most amount of money for the least amount of work. And let me tell you, the greatest prima donna in the world can't function unless the little guy who pulls the rope opens the curtain." Pop always rooted for the underdog. He was a Yankees fan, but so perverse that in a competitive game, if the Dodgers were losing, he'd switch sides, dump the Yankees, and root for the Dodgers. Great, I thought. I could please both. Dance in the ballet, earn money, and eventually enroll in the stagehand union.

So I dropped out of high school and joined New York City Ballet. It was October and we were preparing for a three-week season at City Center. At my first rehearsal with Jerry Robbins, he called out, "Hey you! The lamppost with feet and teeth!"

THE BOSS, PART 2

From the time I was fifteen, I had been taking SAB's professional class, where Balanchine often taught. Small, unassuming, he radiated energy and total command. If ever he had any doubts (which he did), he never showed them. He wore small, open-necked polo shirts, short-sleeved, with black pants, and, like everyone else, smoked all the time. Visiting ballet celebrities flitted in and out of his classes, and occasionally Maria Tallchief, Vera Zorina, and Alexandra Danilova would be at the barre with Tanaquil LeClercq and me. Locker-room gossip, knowing that Tanny was Balanchine's favorite of the moment, delighted in comparing her with Balanchine's ex-wives.

Great male dancers from all over the world made the school their home. André Eglevsky, Igor Youskevitch, Lew Christensen, and William Dollar competed in class. I copied everything they did. If Eglevsky did ten pirouettes, I tried to do ten. When Youskevitch impressed with effortless double tours, I would slip into the "little studio" and spend hours trying to capture that ease and simplicity.

At SAB and as a member at NYCB, I was blessed with extraordinary teachers and models. Anatole Oboukhoff, a premier danseur of the Maryinsky Theater in St. Petersburg, always wore freshly pressed black pants, white socks, and black character shoes with no heel. He smelled of cologne, and his slender torso was caressed by a white, romantic, blousy long-sleeved shirt, open at the neck. In his breast pocket, he kept a handkerchief and a roll of peppermint Life Savers. Oboukhoff's face looked like a frowning prune with keen, dark brown eyes burning above the thin line of a determined mouth. Class began precisely on time. Outside the studio door, Oboukhoff would alert us to his entrance by clearing his throat in a series of grunts, as a lion coughs and growls in the jungle. He would then enter and, with a pistol-shot clap of his hands, launch us into the most exacting hour and a half. Like clockwork, we spent thirty minutes at the barres that lined the studio walls, practicing fundamentals by the hundreds, nonstop, without rest.

Anatole Oboukhoff teaching class at SAB Broadway studios, ca. 1951

No air conditioning in those days. On hot, muggy days, I would have to change my place halfway through the barre, because I was standing in a puddle of my own sweat. This portion of the class left our legs shaking, before we staggered to the center of the room for Oboukhoff's "Invention of the Day." Fifteen to twenty minutes long, its architecture formed a trilogy that challenged memory as well as body. Part One consisted of multiple repetitions of varied dance steps, basics, which segued into Part Two—slow, controlled adagio movement sequences and balances. Part Three, his coup de grâce, layered, endless combinations of vigorous leaps, moving forward and backward in space, then side to side, repeated over and over again. The trilogy abruptly terminated with a balance, holding still, posed. Dripping with sweat, pale and panting, we were afraid to look at Oboukhoff, fearing what was coming next: "LLLLLeffffft!" and we had to repeat the entire trilogy, only starting on the left side. In decades of classes I took with Oboukhoff, every single Invention of the Day was original; he never repeated himself.

During class, Oboukhoff made strange, rhythmical sounds, chugging with his voice, and finger snapping in accompaniment to the dancers. He never spoke without starting the sound of the first word somewhere in the distance, crescendoing into explosive *t*'s and vowels. First, he would cover his mouth with his handkerchief. Muffled by the handkerchief, he would start a throaty sound, and then, he would drop the handkerchief from his mouth like a curtain, and a word would erupt. "Mmmmm-ORE!" or "*Nnnnnynynyny-ET!*" or "Tttttttterrrrrri-bbbbbbbULL!" I recall once trembling in a balance on one leg, trying to hold steady in a slow promenade, my arms and legs stretched out and cramping. Oboukhoff strolled over, put his thumb and index finger right between my eyes, and snapped his fingers, trying to throw me off balance. I knew that if I fell, he would snort, "MmmmmmmeeeeesssssTA JACQUES! WwwwhaaaaTYou DO! (grrrrrr)!" If, however, I succeeded in holding my balance through the multiple finger snaps, Oboukhoff would reach out, take my hand, and place, in my palm, a single candy Life Saver. Sometimes the pianist would overlay, on whatever musical composition he or she was playing, a little tinkly rendition of "Who's Afraid of the Big Bad Wolf? . . ."

To end the class, Oboukhoff would give us his dessert. "Grrrrrrand hhhhhhhattement. BbbacK! Frrrrrrrront! Sssssssixxxxtttteen." Practically dead on our legs, we had to perform a series of high kicks to the side, sixteen moving back, and then sixteen moving forward. At that point, we would hold still, balanced on the balls of our feet, awaiting, unmoving, the one snap of his fingers that signaled the end of class. Or, on a whim, he might command us to repeat the entire sequence, this time staying raised on the balls of our feet. You never knew. It was a lottery that you didn't want to win.

The *lines* at the water fountain after! I don't know a dancer today who could make it through an Oboukhoff class. My sister adored him. She named her cat Anatole in his honor.

Years later, I asked Balanchine, "Tell me about Oboukhoff. What was he like in Russia?" "Oboukhoff was big star at Maryinsky Theatre, Petersburg," Balanchine informed. "He was *famous* for role of Prince in *Swan Lake.* Always dressed elegantly, you know, material, with velvet

Partnering Gloria Govrin in Oboukhoff's adagio class, ca. 1955

capes, embroidery that hung from shoulder to heels. Such a big star, people followed him, like prince with servants." Said Balanchine, "I was student, young, teenager, sitting in hallway of school, unhappy. We had these tests, academics, you know. I was not very good, mathematics, and knew I had failed. Oboukhoff came down hall, with entourage, stopped, stared at me, and said, 'Diga diga dyuhdyuh-you you papapass?' I shook head, 'No.' He answered, 'Geh geh geh G-IDIOT!' and stalked away. You see, Oboukhoff had 'diga diga diga' talk! He stuttered!"

Suddenly, Oboukhoff's eccentricities made sense to me. The mouth-covering handkerchief and all the histrionics and growling, frowning behavior were props to disguise a speech impediment and ward off his fear of communication. His Life Savers.

In adagio class, Oboukhoff taught me how to partner a ballerina, dance with and hold her. I learned all the classic pas de deux from him—*Swan Lake, Bluebird, Les Sylphides, Sleeping Beauty,* and *Nutcracker.* Many years later, shortly after our son George was born, his mother, Carrie, brought the baby to SAB. She was so proud of him. Seeing Oboukhoff, Carrie went up to him, handed him the baby, and said in her sweet voice, "Here's George, your next pupil." Clutching the baby, Oboukhoff started to tremble. Bewildered and with pleading eyes, he passed George back to Carrie. This gruff man had never held an infant.

Feeling bold, I once approached him, "Mr. Oboukhoff, what do you do when you're not teaching—weekends, or on vacation?" The startled man twisted his mouth into a grimace, puffed up his cheeks, and pushed out the sound. "FFFFFiiiish!" Fishing is a quiet, solitary sport. No need to talk.

And then there was Pierre Vladimiroff (Nijinsky's successor as premier danseur of the Maryinsky and rumored to be the last partner of Anna Pavlova, in the years before her death in 1931). "In classical roles, everyone considered Vladimiroff better than Nijinsky," Balanchine told me. Nijinsky was famous for his gigantic leaps, seemingly suspended in midair in slow motion. As was Vladimiroff. They were rivals. Balanchine continued, "When Vladimiroff leaped, he soared—he seemed to stop, pause, and suspend in midair. So light on feather feet. And his grand pirouettes"—rapid spins in place, balanced on one leg, with the other leg extended ninety degrees to the side. Balanchine described how, pirouetting, Vladimiroff would accelerate his spins to a blur, seemingly several revolutions a second. Then he would leap up, bending his supporting leg (the leaping leg) while continuing to revolve in the air (his other leg still extended at ninety degrees), then, after a full circle, land effortlessly, and continue spinning. This airborne spin he would repeat several times before closing his extended leg into fifteen or sixteen pirouettes that gradually slowed down, coming to a stop with a simple pose. He would lower and open his palms to the audience at the end of these pyrotechnics, calmly offering a simple and gracious *"Et voilà."*

In class, Vladimiroff stood more than erect; he seemed to lean backward. His cherubic face, Slavic features, and balding pate exuded sweetness. His hands, floppy and flowery, were soft fluttering petals. Vladimiroff's style was of the prince, not the peasant. "No!" he would say to us, "not with arms reaching up as if asking for something! *Peasants look up!* Prince is above. Everything else is beneath. Be light, on the balls of your feet. Let others be stuck on earth. You are a prince." After class, he elaborated and clarified: "A prince has everything worthy in himself and doesn't need to strive for things outside. Others bow and kneel to him from below. You must be self-contained, benevolent, and graciously lower your gaze. Only God is above." Later, when I danced in Florence in 1953, and first saw Michelangelo's sculpture of David, I recognized Vladimiroff's ideal. The nobility of the sculptured head and neck and serenity of the gaze—David looks downward modestly, not at his feet, but over the world. The simplicity and purity of dancing this way! Some think it feminine, and opt for heavy, heels-on-the-floor dancing, Soviet macho realism, and need to proclaim loudly through their dance, "I AM HERE!" That style of dancing carries with it heaviness.

Keeping the weight on the balls of your feet allows you to move quicker, lighter, and more effortlessly. Espoused by Balanchine, that technique didn't originate with him. Vladimiroff said he would walk into the theater heel-toe, heel-toe "like ordinary man"—go to the dressing room, put on makeup, then walk to the stage with his weight forward, on the balls of his feet. After he finished performing, he would walk out of the theater and the weight would go back into his heels—"ordinary man again."

When the Bolshoi Ballet was performing in New York City, the superb Russian dancer Vladimir Vasiliev,* invited me to join him in their company class. Messerer, the renowned teacher, officiated, and had only one correction for me: "Weight in the heels, Jacques. Stick them to the floor." I smiled and nodded, and tried to do as he asked (not very successfully). Messerer's suggestion would have made Vlady furious, for Vladimiroff advocated the pure, classical technique he'd learned in St. Petersburg, derived from the courtly behaviors of Europe. God, how I miss Vladimiroff and those classes!

Vladimiroff expressed the rivalry with Nijinsky with generosity and humility. He would stand in front of the young boys in class and describe, "I start here, leap in the air in sauté"—then he would walk

---

* If I had to reflect on the finest classical male ballet dancers of my time, Vladimir Vasiliev of the Bolshoi and the Danish dancer Eric Bruhn were, I feel, without peers.

In class with Pierre Vladimiroff

some eight or ten feet across the room—"and land here." Our heads nodded in amazement and admiration as Vladimiroff returned to stand in front of us again. "But when Nijinsky leaps in sauté, he starts here"—walking across the room until he came against the wall, and pointing and waving with his hand, through the wall, on and on, to the next room and beyond—"and lands there."

In the days when Vladimiroff and Nijinsky were dancing, the costumes for male dancers derived from the court wardrobe of the aristocracy: heeled, buckled shoes, hose, pantaloons to below the knee, belt, and sometimes a short sword. That's the reason you see so often in classical ballets the males standing in a pose with the right hand at the left waist, weight on the back (left) leg. It's the "draw your sword" position. As ballet developed, the costumes changed. Hose became tights all the way up, pantaloons shortened to allow freedom of movement, the tunic, a doublet similar to court attire, soft canvas shoes with little heels adorned the feet. In the Maryinsky under the tsar, these were the costumes male dancers wore. The dance belt we wear now (the ballet version of an athletic jock strap) didn't exist, and without the pantaloons the body hair and genitals could be seen through the tights.

Well. Nijinsky shocked the whole court by going onstage without pantaloons—just the sheer silk tights with nothing underneath—and was ostracized by the theater management. "So Vladimiroff replaced him as number one," Balanchine said.

Vladimiroff always said you must practice, practice, practice, repeat, repeat, thousands of times, rehearse, and rehearse, again and again. And then, when you go onstage, forget everything! Just listen to the music and dance. If you've done your practice, your body will do everything required, and your soul and spirit will be free and spontaneous. Your dancing will be lifted out of the rehearsal room, out of the ordinary, and you'll have freedom. If you try to make your performance a recreation of your rehearsal, you've lost it. But after performing, like a racehorse cooling down after the race, Vladimiroff would take off his costume, put on his practice clothes, and, keeping his fans waiting, go up to his favorite place in the theater's studio. There, he would do a short, ten-to-fifteen-minute barre, a few pliés, a few tendus, running through the alphabet of exercises to clean out any residue of performance excess and remind his body of the discipline and order that was the technique. The simplicity of the unadorned dancer.

His classes started with a short twenty minutes of routine barre exercises that quickly ran through the menu of basics. Then we moved into the center of the room, where he gave us a series of dance combinations that incorporated those basics, but with no barre to hold on to. Ten or fifteen minutes later, he launched us into a fifty- to fifty-five-minute smorgasbord of the most joyful combinations of dance steps. Some were variations borrowed from choreography he had performed himself, others were taken from memories of his own training back in St. Petersburg. I loved especially when he gave us some of the steps from his legendary roles—in *Les Sylphides, La Spectre de la Rose,* and *Sleeping Beauty.* His combinations took you all over the room, and required tremendous control of how you moved your body through space. We would perform each combination a few times before moving on to another. In fifty minutes of Vladimiroff's center, we would perform ten or twelve or fifteen varied combinations. Oboukhoff's classes emphasized gaining power through brute repetition, repetition, repetition. Vladimiroff's style was more filigreed, emphasizing variety and lightness. Nicholas Magallanes, a mentor to me, was always mumbling, "Someone should write these combinations down. They're going to be lost." Nicky was right. There were hundreds; today, I recall only a few.

Balanchine explained to me how Vladimiroff ended up teaching at SAB. "I told Lincoln, 'Vladimiroff must come with me, start a ballet school,' but he had engagements in Europe." Apparently, he later came to America with a small troupe from Europe—and wound up dancing on lousy stages in smoky cabarets. "Very unhappy," Balanchine said. "In Petersburg, after performance, fans would crowd stage door to wait for him. They would unhitch horses from his carriage, take reins themselves, pull carriage through snow—to honor him, to pay homage. Here after he danced, no applause, hardly anyone."

I envisioned Vladimiroff wearing white tights, in old-fashioned makeup and a powdered wig, dancing his variation from *Les Sylphides* as Balanchine described, "on tiny, slippery nightclub stage with audience of fat, cigar-smoking gangsters. They laughed at him. It hurt his soul," Balanchine said. "I invited him to come teach with me from beginning of the school."

What a fabulous place SAB was. Stamping and leaping in "character class,"* I learned folk dances, waltzes, polonaises, czardas, and mazurkas, all from a short, dark, and vigorous man with little command of English. Yurek Lazowski was his name, and he was an exceptional folk dancer. We dancers doffed our ballet shoes and put on shoes with little heels and/or boots. The girls donned skirts or wrapped scarves around their waists. The styles were difficult to achieve. Watching non-Slavs attempt mazurkas, czardas, polkas, you may view the steps, but you miss the spice. Much as I loved the classes, I never mastered the style. Or with any ethnic dances. From Balinese to flamenco—it is the rare dancer who can master a folk dance style outside his or her own culture. Somehow, the dance forms have their greatest veracity when the dancer's feet have been in touch with the earth of their homeland.

I was seventeen on tour in Spain. Five years earlier, for Ballet Society, I had been coached in flamenco footwork by Lew Christensen for our angel-versus-devil dance in *Pastorela,* and subsequently attended many flamenco performances in New York City. When I danced in the Liceu

---

* As opposed to classical ballet—the term "character class" meant ethnic or folk dance, primarily Central European and Slavic.

opera house in Barcelona in 1952, the curtain went up at ten p.m. and came down after midnight. Ravenous, I would head for Las Ramblas, the boulevard and heart of Barcelona, to find some lamplit restaurant, a *cave,* to drink *vino blanco,* gorge myself on tapas, *pollo,* and fresh sardines, while listening to flamenco guitarists and singers. The patrons were neighborhood. Seven years after World War II, there were few tourists in Franco's Spain. A fat lady diner, while being served by a waiter, would abruptly jump to her feet, push her chair aside, and burst into dance. The waiter, in turn, would gleefully set his tray on her chair and swirl in challenge as her partner. The flame caught, and soon other patrons joined, accompanying the couple with wild vocal outbursts, rhythmical clapping, and snapping fingers. Flamenco better than anything I had ever seen! The wine and music of a culture coursing like blood, and spilling out in dance. Great theater, and primeval. I was experiencing the real thing, and it wasn't painted fire. It seemed to be coming through the ground into the feet of the waiter and the patron, resonating through their bodies, their skin and bones, the gestures and expressions on their faces, and their speaking fingers and hands. Heat programmed on a cellular level, and transmuted through thousands of years of culture.

On the Iberian Peninsula and in parts of southern France—deep in caves where prehistoric art festoons the ceilings and walls—large, flat stones have been found covered with patterns of scuffmarks. The residue indicates that our prehistoric ancestors strapped the hooves of animals to their feet and stomped rhythms, patterns, and dances, vocalizing God-alone-knows-what kind of chants. In Barcelona's gypsy cave restaurants, in the wee hours of the morning, an umbilical cord stretched from the caves of 25,000 B.C. to the floor under my feet, reverberating millenniums of rhythms.

What culture does classical ballet come from? It really derives from dances the Italian/French aristocracy developed in the courts, with folk influences, but it is unique in the world because it jumps national barriers. Danilova once told me, "You are American boy—but when ballet dancer you are international, belong to the world, representing high art." It is bigger than any particular cultural or folk dance. It has been studied—what are the most economical movements, the most pleasing line—order, symmetry, and precision based on the principles of geometry. Classical ballet transcends the cultures—and Muriel Stu-

Muriel Stuart heading for me, 1959

art epitomized that transcendence, with her aristocratic carriage and demeanor.

At SAB, Muriel Stuart* was an anomaly—neither Russian nor American. She was British, and a superb teacher. A former soloist with Pavlova's ballet company, Muriel brought her elegant beauty, grandeur, and nobility of carriage to the dance studio, and transformed it into a *salle royale*. A vision of pastels, she smelled of lilacs, and wore flowing skirts and pink ballet shoes, with little flesh-colored callus pads on the backs of her heels so the shoes wouldn't rub them. Her long neck and slim, elegant torso were accentuated by the way she kept her shoulder

---

* Muriel Stuart collaborated with Lincoln Kirstein to write a technique manual, *The Classic Ballet* (1952), which has few peers.

blades drawn back and squeezed together, raising her chest and head. It made her appear glorious and heroic. I always thought of her as "heart-lifted." Wherever Muriel went, even in the streets of New York City, her feet glided.

Her class emphasized arms and placement, precise and demanding. "You will bring your arms here to the center of your chest and then directly overhead, exactly to here," she would announce and demonstrate, as if performing a Victorian melodrama. I dreaded only one thing in her class: THE CORRECTION. It started with Muriel at one end of the barre as she made her way down the line of struggling dancers. Whether coming from in front or in back, I knew I was the target. Arriving, she would pause for a moment, and then, with the delicate fingers of one hand, she would lift my wrist and guide me in a port des bras, at the same moment extending the little finger of the other hand to touch my behind, right at the base of the buttocks or just below the coccyx bone, and administer THE CORRECTION. *"Pull up here, dear."* I would blush with embarrassment and grin in adolescent self-consciousness.

Then there was Felia Doubrovska and her dramatic entrances. Students would be lined up at the barre, preparing for class, stretching and

"Et voilà! *Fifth position!" Felia Doubrovska, 1980*

gabbing, and the studio door would swing open slowly. Doubrovska would appear and press her body against the wall, making herself small, hiding, her head downcast and tucked into her shoulder (becoming wallpaper). She would then slide and creep along, making a series of freeze frames as in a Mata Hari spy film, until she reached a corner of the studio. Then, in a second, she would lose twenty years of age, gain six inches of height, turn to face us, transformed, and, smiling, float to the center of the room on tippy-toe, as if entering a spotlight onstage, and announce, "Fifth position!"

One morning, late in her life (I think she was in her eighties), she made her usual entrance. It was a gray winter morning, and we were all stiff and tired, preparing for morning class. After her slide along the wall, she did her move to center and called, "Fifth position!" Most of us responded lackadaisically, and half-heartedly got ready for the first plié. "Oh, no!" Doubrovska said in a gentle voice. "It is hard for me to come to class. I am eighty years old, and I am tired. But when *I* put my hand on the barre and take fifth position, no one would ever know this."

More time is spent by the dancer at the barre and in the studio—a lifetime more—than performing on the stage. It takes years, and generations of dancers, to transform a dance studio into hallowed ground. In the spring of 2003, I visited Cuba for the first time. Touring Alicia Alonso's ballet academy, I felt at home. Instantly, I recognized the atmosphere, the smells, the wooden floor so familiar to the *salles de ballet* of Europe, Russia, and the old SAB. The sweat-stained barre, polished from the touch of a century of dancers' grips, was lined with ghosts. At Alonso's ballet academy, I put my hand on the barre, touching the imprints of ten thousand dancers before me, took first position to prepare for a grand plié. Well, it was nice to dream. In 2003, I couldn't do a grand plié. The knees don't bend.

My training at SAB was not just ballet. Janet Collins taught modern dance. I had her once a week. She was café au lait, with light, chocolate-colored skin. Her solid, muscled body and powerful torso were shapely. She kept trying to teach me how to swirl and spiral down to the ground. I never got it, couldn't do it, and, frustrated, gave up. It went against my dreams of flying in the air.

Merce Cunningham also taught at the school. There was a bony kind of stringy strength to his physique, angular. No Botticelli look with curving lines of soft grace. More Marcel Duchamp's *Nude Descending a Staircase.* Cunningham's vision was not about going to the ground. You floated and improvised, inventing dance movements of randomness and accident. Merce choreographed a piece for Ballet Society called *The Seasons*. It was 1947, and that is when I first heard what a piano sounded like when it had been "prepared." John Cage, in doing the score for *The Seasons*, was experimenting in altering the sounds of the piano, and the results were bizarre. To me, they were outer space.

Though he played for ballet class and rehearsal, John Cage occasionally held lessons in theory and harmony for selected students. We gathered in the "little studio," the smallest of the three at Fifty-ninth and Madison. I sat in on several, and had no idea what John Cage was talking about or doing. Several years later, I heard a piece for "prepared" piano by the Japanese composer Toshiro Mayuzumi which was gorgeous. I asked Gordon Boelzner, NYCB's master pianist at that time, "How do you get that sound out of the piano?" and Gordon flipped off a tongue-in-cheek answer. "Oh, hardware. Nuts, bolts, bits and pieces of metal, they screw them into the soundboard and attach some of them to the piano strings." He wasn't kidding.

In 1966, Merce Cunningham revived his ballet *Summerspace* for NYCB, with music by Morton Feldman and scenery by Robert Rauschenberg. I watched rehearsals and, later, the premiere, and fervently wished that I had been asked to dance it. It was beautiful, all pointillist atmosphere. Sunlit, serene. A warm resonance filled the stage—a pale, caressing heat, versus a pressing, tropical one. Dancers, attired in dotted leotards, flitted, seemingly at random, entering and disappearing into the pointillist landscape, and melded into one unified work of art.

Everyone tried to educate me in my early years in NYCB. A fellow dancer in the corps, Dorothy Scott, insisted I see the Alwin Nikolais company. I went reluctantly, but after the curtain fell that evening, I walked out a fan. Who could resist a stage full of dancers as eggs—their bodies fetus-like inside spandex pouches? As they moved, the white ovoids shifted and changed shapes. Or dancers as strings erupting from the floor, and dropping down from the ceiling then stretching sideward into the wings? These eventually evolved using the arms, legs, and heads of dancers, to create an architectural network of cat's cradles and spiderwebs all over the stage. Quivering, the whole scene would change color and texture through brilliant lighting and evoked a magical, futuristic dreamscape. Nikolais even invented a dance for cans—before Andy Warhol's Campbell Soup became art.

Before I was through my teens, I had been introduced and exposed to artists who would, in later years, become legendary. Balanchine, Antony Tudor, Frederick Ashton, Jerome Robbins, Michael Kidd, Lew Christensen, Merce Cunningham, John Cranko, Martha Graham: they were my mentors, teachers, and choreographers. From morning to night, music was my floor, and dance did sport with song as I traversed the day. Through dance, I was called upon to make music visual, interpreting the art of Stravinsky, Mozart, Bach, Tchaikovsky, Morton Gould, Leonard Bernstein, Benjamin Britten, and Maurice Ravel, among others. Often, Stravinsky, Gould, and Bernstein would be in the orchestra pit conducting or at the piano playing. Several times, Balanchine conducted. My wife, Carrie, remembers:

> I was doing the semi-solo then, in the first movement of Bizet's *Symphony in C.* We were onstage in position when the curtain went up. We were supposed to move with the conductor's first downbeat, so all eyes were on the conductor's podium. We went into shock. There was Balanchine, dressed as Toscanini with a gray wig, high collar, and a jabot. When his baton flicked, we were off to the races. The tempo was so fast. I couldn't believe it. A five-minute movement sped by in less than three. We could barely keep up. I think the musicians had to skip notes to be able to play.

In the early fall of 1951, Balanchine was preparing for a fencing scene in his upcoming ballet, *Tyl Ulenspiegel,* starring Jerome Robbins. A handful of us were selected to learn fencing. I loved those lessons! At home, I would hang a shirt stuffed with assorted laundry inside my closet door, and, with the Swoboda epée, stab away at it for hours.

Meanwhile, on the block, my pals said to me, "We're picking a team to play the Famwoods Sunday. So, Dancing Guy, you got any time to play football?" I knew nothing about football, had never played it, but felt flattered that they asked. Besides, I could do anything. Impetuously, I replied, "Sure."

We didn't practice, just met at game time near the edge of the Hudson River, a grassy expanse, fence enclosed. I was to play right tackle. We had no offensive/defensive teams, just a bunch of buddies. But the Famwoods were organized. They had fans, uniforms, a slew of cheerleader girlfriends, and outnumbered us at least three to one. Among the onlookers in the Famwood cheering section lurked Farel. The game started, and we started losing. I didn't understand the game, didn't excel, never tackled anyone, and never had a chance to learn.

The Famwoods were way ahead, and on the line of scrimmage opposite me crouched the biggest guy on their team—a monster called Gaitlin. My job was to rush and block him off after the hike. When the play ended, full of anger and fury, he started shoving me. Immediately on cue, as if scripted, someone in the crowd started crowing, "Fight! Fight!" The Famwoods surrounded me, cutting me off. I crouched low, grabbed Gaitlin's ankles, and pulled him off his feet, yelling all the time, "I don't want to fight. I don't want to fight."

I was surprised at how easily he fell. I quickly crawled on top of him, embraced him around the neck, hugging and pressing him to the ground. He thrashed, struggled, and yelled, "You fuck, you fuck, you fuck!" to the Famwoods' chorus of "Fight, fight!" A nightmare opera, we must have looked like a violently copulating couple in the throes of climax, within a circle of decadent voyeurs.

Someone was shouting, "Let's get on with the game! Let's get on with the game! No fighting. Let's play football."

Some of my team managed to break through and part us. As I staggered to my feet, a Famwood, Johnny Ford, one of two look-alike brothers, with his tough Irish face and blond thatch of hair, started bellowing incoherently at Gaitlin.

My pitiful few teammates circled around me. We were all scared. Bobby Rosario, a pal from my team, had sidled over to the Famwoods, clustered around Gaitlin. As they broke their cluster and, led by Gaitlin, walked toward me. Bobby rushed ahead. He mumbled in my ear, "They're going to try and get you to fight. Don't fight. Whatever you do, don't fight." I was trembling.

Gaitlin loomed, his face twitching. "Come on, we haven't finished this."

"No," I said, "I'm not fighting. I'm not fighting!"

A bewildered look came over his face. He was dumb, ox-dumb. He literally turned around and said to the Ford brothers, "What do I do now? He doesn't want to fight."

Johnny Ford whispered into his ear, and Gaitlin came over and slapped me in the face. Everyone stood stunned. Immediately, I repeated what I had done before. Dropped to my knees, grabbed his ankles, and, pulling, knocked him flat on his ass. Then I scrambled on top of him, pinning him to the ground and hugging him, yelling my mantra, "I'm not fighting! I'm not fighting!"

The Famwoods circled again, keeping my pals away. Farel pushed my shirt up and started scraping a hair comb along my spine. "Cut it out! Play fair," I hollered, though I barely felt anything. And it seemed so easy holding Gaitlin pinned. I straddled him on my knees, riding astride his furiously bucking body. He was a paper giant. Then, as if from some distant place, slowly impinging on my consciousness, came awareness of kicks to my shins and legs. I started praying, and those old Hail Marys began to spew out of my soul.

Somebody lit a cigarette and pressed it against my arm. I jumped to my feet, still yelling, "I don't want to fight," and, shoving my way out of the circle, started running.

Running, running! Terrified! I could hear my heart oscillating in my brain, stewed with a cacophony of pounding feet and howls from the pack behind me. Blackout. Curtain.

The next thing I remember, I was half a mile away at a water fountain with Ryan, a friend from my block. He was washing my face with his handkerchief, and he was scared to death. It wasn't because the handkerchief was bloody, but because I'd been babbling incoherently for close to an hour. Then, suddenly, seemingly lucid, I was looking at him saying, "Where are we? What's happened?"

"You were in a fight, Jock. You were in a fight. I've been so scared— you've been talking funny for a long time. Are you okay now? I'm trying to take you home."

Over the next few hours, with many rest stops on the way, Ryan brought me home. Faded, dreamlike memories gradually came back; I began to recall flashes and images. Tackled, knocked down, and staggering back to my feet. Johnny Ford punched me in the face. Gaitlin and others of the Famwoods, as they ran up, punching away, too. I would be knocked down and stumble up, only to be punched down again. "My turn, my turn!" My friends began to intervene, and fights began breaking out all around. Bobby Rosario judo-throwing someone over his back, and the Famwoods leaving me to gang up on him. A police car rolling along the cyclone fence and then through a gap onto the turf of the field. (Abie Grossfeld, in later years, told me, "I called the cops.") Everyone scattering, dashing in every direction. Pictures of the Famwoods clambering up and over the fence, fleeing from the scene. And then nothing remembered until coming to at the water fountain with Ryan an hour later and a half mile away.

That was the end of my life on the block. Like an amputation. I never saw any of the Famwoods again. The ballet became my world. I stayed in touch with a handful of friends, mostly Abie and Jimmy. Several times, I'd invite them to come to the ballet. I would secret a half dozen of them, via the City Center fire escape, to the upper balcony. At my first performance (October 1949), they endured *Mother Goose Suite* (I was one of four silhouetted couples dancing in the darkened background, and could barely lift my ballerina, Jillana, not because she was heavy, but because my muscles had not fully developed); *Orpheus* (dressed in gray and carrying a papier-mâché rock, in even murkier lighting); and then in the last ballet, *Symphony in C,* I popped onto the brightly lit stage in the back row for a few minutes of the fourth movement. My clique in the balcony remained alert enough to spot me, and broke into raucous whistles and bellowing cheers. After the final bows, Maria Tallchief, the star of the company, announced to the cast, "Did you hear that wonderful audience, cheering and whistling from the balcony? Oh, they loved me tonight!"

My best friend, Jimmy, eschewed being a sneaker-inner. He bought his balcony ticket and strode in through the front door. Jim haunted City Center, whether I was dancing or not, clipped and saved every newspaper review, and kept diaries. His collection of NYCB memorabilia is impressive. "Jack-o," he wrote to me recently, "you ask me why I collected this stuff. Few people were doing it, as NYCB was not on the heap in those days. Also, Balanchine was amazing, though most people primarily looked at the dancers over what he was doing! And— during this time, it was just as exciting to see *who was in the audience* at the City Center as to who was on the stage:

- Alfred Kinsey (of the Kinsey Reports) at *Nutcracker,* taking addresses from gays who approached him at the premiere's intermission;
- Anna Freud at the ballet *Opus 34,* looking glum and dour;
- William Faulkner (with a discreet woman in black and pearls) in the City Center lobby during intermission, leaning against a radiator, smoking a pipe (and in a trench coat);
- Salvador Dalí in an aisle seat in Row R (being inconspicuous!)

with mustache and gold cane, always coming to New York in winter, staying at the St. Regis Hotel;

- W. H. Auden at the ballet in his bedroom slippers (even when it was snowing outside);
- Franchot Tone, the actor, a Balanchine admirer, trumpeting his praises in his sonorous voice at every opportunity, always seated with a beautiful blonde.

"The seats were by *no means full,* but the audience was as exciting as the dancers!"

Reading Jimmy's notes sparked memories of several NYCB matinees at City Center, where there were more dancers onstage than patrons in the audience. The house held some two thousand seats, and our company numbered less than fifty. Despite the possibility of bankruptcy, Lincoln was not about to give up, and Newbold Morris and Morton Baum, the pair of directors who had invited us to be City Center's resident dance company, kept their faith. Balanchine gave the impression he was unaware of the empty seats. Supremely confident, he never worried.

Maria Tallchief, Balanchine,
and Marc Chagall

In 1945, the Russian impresario Sol Hurok commissioned the visual artist Marc Chagall to design several drops and floor cloths, as well as costumes, for Ballet Theatre's production of Mikhail Fokine's *Firebird,* to be staged by Adolph Bolm. Chagall was reputed to have painted much of the scenery and costumes himself. In the fall of 1949, Balanchine planned to mount his own version of *Firebird,* starring his wife, Maria Tallchief. He persuaded Hurok to sell the Chagall decor to him, since the Bolm ballet had been dropped from Ballet Theatre's repertoire and the Chagall creations had been languishing in storage.

Stravinsky had rearranged and shortened the score—there were no long passages of music that allowed a choreographer to linger on character development. Balanchine's choreography was concise and direct. Bang! You're onstage, and within the first few gestures, the dance movements had to convey exactly who you are and what you're doing. From the Prince's first entrance to the Firebird's electric appearance—she zoomed out of the wings—Frank Moncion and Maria Tallchief were stunning. The spooky lighting, murky and evocative of the depths of the forest, reflected lighting designer Jean Rosenthal's genius. *Firebird* was the smash hit of the fall 1949 season.

I was in the monster scene, along with most of the corps de ballet. We popped out of the wings on a crashing chord, and burst into dance, to find ourselves slipping and tripping on Chagall's painted floor cloth. After a few performances, Balanchine eliminated the floor cloth.

It was also my first performance in a world premiere, and, to this day, *Firebird* resonates in my heart and memory. Toward the end of the ballet, just as the monsters are about to destroy the Prince and his love (the Maiden), the Firebird comes to the rescue. Holding a golden sword aloft in her hands, she dashes across the stage, and, after an enormous leap, gives the weapon to the Prince. Maria Tallchief's eyes flashed red and gold, and she whirled in a blur of piqué turns, riveting a circle around the Prince. He then slashes away with the sword at the monsters, knocking us left and right, till we collapse to the floor, vanquished.

Panting, we would lie on the floor, grateful for the respite. As if to an icon, the Prince bows to the Firebird in gratitude and obeisance, and, hand in hand, departs with his Maiden, both of them climbing and stepping over our monster bodies littering the stage, and leaving the Firebird alone. During what is called the berceuse in the music, she dances an exquisite solo in a golden follow spot.

This was my opportunity on the darkened stage floor. I would pillow my head in my arms, wrap myself in the haunting music, and, half dozing, prepare myself for a journey into the Firebird's realm. She floated above me, the glow from the follow spot reflected on the artwork of Chagall's extraordinary scenery—birds, bouquets of flowers, and trees in deep, rich colors. Depending on where Maria moved in her follow spot, Chagall's colors and images appeared and receded, ghostly, taking on a movement and life of their own, art pulsating.

Maria covered her tawny Native American skin with gold glitter, highlighting her cheekbones, arms, and upper torso. She even glued gold dust to her toe shoes. Her Firebird became a mysterious, metaphysical force. As she glided in her dance, I imagined regret in her eyes. This mythic bird—not for her, the love of a human Prince. Maria's performance evoked a feeling of ancientness, carrying the heavy weights and sorrows of thousands of years. You didn't think small-time watching her. It was eons, a fairy tale, archetypal.

At the end of her solo, the Firebird swoops toward the monsters, forcing them to roll, crawl, and slither into the wings, clearing us off her stage. Offstage, we clamber to our feet to hurry for a costume change, to transform ourselves from monsters into Russian courtiers for the final scene.

On her deserted stage, the Firebird moves backward in a bourrée, and, fluttering, turns and glides off into the forest. The gold light irises down to nothing, and the scenery starts to move. I would remain, mesmerized, staring at the spot where she'd just vanished. The scenery's movement brought me back to reality, and I frantically rolled into the wings rushing, late for costume change. Many others have danced *Firebird,* and beautifully, but for me, Maria was *the* Firebird.

Over two years later, mid-May 1952, *Firebird* highlighted our opening at the Théâtre des Champs-Élysées in Paris. Before the second performance, Balanchine burst into our dressing room in a rage, equipped with a big pair of scissors, followed by agitated members of the costume staff. He zigzagged among us in our crowded dressing room, cutting up the monster costumes. He ravaged the painted unitards that dressed our bodies and left intact only the varied feathered monster masks that encased our heads. Chunks and pieces of old Chagall costumes accumulated on the dressing-room floor. "Throw out! Throw out!" he stammered to the wardrobe crew, and stalked away. The scraps disappeared and were quickly replaced by tights and leotards—black, brown, and gray. Oh, what a delight! We hated wearing those unitards; they were old, moldy, thick, and stiff with cracked paint. Insects that had taken up residence in the interstices and crevices would sometimes crawl out on us. My dance mate in *Firebird,* Brooks Jackson, was allergic to something in the paint and would be covered with a rash after every performance. If *Firebird* was on the program, he protested like Job all day. That night, he danced a jig of joy. "Oh, Mary, thank God we're rid of those costumes! They were killing me." "What got into Balanchine?" I asked. Brooks knew all about it. He'd read it in the papers.

Marc Chagall had come to the Théâtre des Champs-Élysées, seen our *Firebird,* perhaps in dress rehearsal, and launched a public controversy, the kind the French love. He published an open letter to Balanchine in the French newspaper *Le Figaro.* "The . . . costumes are an outrageous caricature . . . the harmony [between sets and costumes] is now completely broken . . . the sets . . . betrayed by the unfavorable lighting . . ." He issued an ultimatum: "I demand that you remove my name (in so far as the costumes of the *Firebird* are concerned) from all posters, programs, and advertising."*

Infuriated, Balanchine had cut more than posters, programs, and advertisements. The Chagall costume scraps were never found. Like the floor cloth, they vanished.

Seventeen years after this incident, Balanchine restaged *Firebird.* It was 1970. In the revival, I was cast as the Prince to Gelsey Kirkland's Firebird. Balanchine had some of the original Chagall designs recreated for the much larger stage of the New York State Theater, with Karinska executing her version of the costumes—cartoonish cutouts of Chagall's birds, dinosaurs, trees, bushes, and forest beasts.

The buzz in the company was Gelsey was Balanchine's latest muse.

* *Le Figaro,* May 12, 1952. Quoted in Chujoy, *The New York City Ballet,* pp. 347–48.

She was a teenager and already an electric performer, a standout in the company. He chose Gelsey precisely because she was young and unformed. "The Firebird . . . is one of God's natural creatures."* Balanchine told me that Gelsey would dance it brilliantly as she had a spark of greatness. For the monster scene, he handed over the choreography to Jerome Robbins, and the dancers struggled to move in Karinska's enormous, foam-rubber costumes. Perhaps dictated by the costumes, Jerry's choreography was minimal and cutesy. Despite Gelsey's star-quality performance, Balanchine's new choreography lacked the visceral excitement, fire, and passion of the original. The ballet premiered May 28, and reviews were lukewarm at best. However, Gelsey had a triumph.

Regarding this new production of *Firebird,* I believe there was history at work. First, Gelsey was a budding muse, and he wanted to challenge and develop her. His experience with Maria Tallchief's monumental success in the first *Firebird* cautioned him. Balanchine's original *Firebird* molded and shaped Maria Tallchief, and her performance made the ballet a sensation, catapulting her to international stardom. He had had enough of celebrity stars in his life, to whom he had to kowtow and whom he had to please, and of cliques of fans who would attempt to dictate artistic policy: audiences chanting, "Tallchief! Tallchief!" as they had for the star Serge Lifar at the premiere of Balanchine's ballet *Apollon Musagète* in 1928. He didn't want this version to showcase and be a vehicle for a new star.

Secondly, he may have been making up to Chagall. Recreating Chagall's designs and featuring scenery over choreography might have salved the wounds of his own discomfort over that earlier controversy in Paris. Balanchine said, "I didn't want a woman. I didn't want a personality or a passionate performance . . . I didn't want people. I wanted Chagall."

Amazingly, he did a third version some two years later, with Karin von Aroldingen as the Firebird, and he eviscerated even more the Firebird's central place in the ballet. "In *Firebird,* everyone is a monster. It's a strange world. All of a sudden, you can't have a ballerina in a tutu come in and start turning."

Perhaps he was erasing the image of Tallchief's fabulous pirouettes. Karin was so encumbered by the new costume (yet again a new design),

* This and other Balanchine quotes in this episode are from Nancy Reynolds, *Repertory in Review: 40 Years of the New York City Ballet* (Dial Press, 1977), p. 100.

with wings and an elaborate headdress and trailing tail, that choreographic possibilities were almost nil. "I took the Firebird and made her a Chagall woman, like the figure on the front curtain, so now she looks like part of the mysterious world. Most important is the music accompanying Chagall—Chagall and Stravinsky. There is no Balanchine in there. You're not supposed to do anything. Just let the costumes flow. It's like a moving exhibit."*

This version of *Firebird* did not even rate a mention in my diary. I thought, "Going to a museum, gazing at a Chagall painting, and listening to the Stravinsky music on headphones would be more interesting." In any case, the entire evening of the *Firebird* premiere was eclipsed by the first performance of *Violin Concerto,* up there with *Apollo* and *Agon* as one of Balanchine's greatest masterworks.

Looking at the recreated scenery for this new *Firebird,* I wondered, "Where is the old Chagall scenery?" and started asking around. Generally, the replies were, "Uhh. Umm. I don't know. Maybe in a warehouse?" One night at a cocktail party, I blabbed out loud that in some warehouse Chagall's original *Firebird* drops lay sleeping. "Oh my God," piped up a voice. It was Campbell Wylie—a man knowledgable and passionate about visual arts—"you have Chagall's backdrops, and they're going to waste? Chagall painted those himself! You could cut them into picture-sized pieces, and sell them! You could probably raise hundreds of thousands of dollars. Maybe millions."

Making a stab as an art broker, I asked our company manager, Betty Cage, and Balanchine, "Where are the original Chagalls?" Neither knew, and both said, "Ask Ronnie Bates." Straight to our company stage manager, Ronnie, went I, and out of the side of his mouth, he mumbled, "Let me check it out." About a month later, he informed me, "I found them and it's a good thing. There was a lot of water damage from a leak in the warehouse. So we have them . . . and we don't. They're nothing but piles of moldy, wet, stuck-together, painted goo."

Balanchine, in his previous life, had risen from the ashes of dozens of missed opportunities, failed marriages, broken love affairs, disappointments, unrealized dreams, and short-lived companies. One of the biggest disappointments had been Lincoln! Believing Lincoln's grandiose promises—"Come to New York! We'll have the greatest

* Reynolds, *Repertory in Review.*

ballet company in the world!"—Balanchine and his manager/agent, Vladimir Dimitriev, had gotten off the boat in New York City on October 18, 1933, expecting to build a company for a theater with a school to feed it, only to be told by Lincoln, "We're going to Hartford [Connecticut]!" They didn't even know where Hartford was, somewhere in the provinces? They turned around, ready to go back to Europe. But time and circumstances sketched a different scenario, and now, some fifteen years and many adventures later, in 1948 at City Center, a company called New York City Ballet was formed. The dream becoming concrete.

Ultimately, by 1964, Balanchine would finally get from Lincoln precisely what Balanchine desired—his own company, made up of dancers trained from childhood at *his* School of American Ballet, performing in *his* theater, the New York State Theater in Lincoln Center.* Balanchine molded that school and sculpted that company. The partnership helped Lincoln realize his dream, as well—a world-class ballet academy and a world-class company—but on Balanchine's terms. The difference was (to Lincoln's bile) that Balanchine ran the show and realized the visions, not Lincoln. In the early days, Balanchine would address the dancers, "We—Lincoln and I—want this, you know. We are family." In the first decade, there was no guarantee that the company would survive. After Balanchine was safely ensconced in the New York State Theater, it became, "*I* want!"

The first international NYCB tour (by invitation from Covent Garden, England, in the summer of 1950), and subsequent tours arranged by the impresario Leon Leonidoff, kept NYCB alive for years. Leonidoff, a friend of Balanchine's from the Diaghilev days, took a chance, to everyone's benefit. Tours gave employment between short City Center seasons, allowing us to dance! dance! dance!—and eight performances a week, for months, during normally off-season periods, helped us evolve and solidify a style and reputation. Further, reports and reviews from the big European cities—Paris, London, Berlin, Hamburg, Milan, Amsterdam—drifted across the Atlantic and illuminated the New York audiences and critics to the jewel they had in their midst. We gained the Old World stamp of approval.

---

* Paid for primarily by tax dollars, the New York State Theater changed its name to the David H. Koch Theater when the billionaire donated a reputed $100 million for renovations.

My sister and I arriving in London, 1950

In 1950, ten months into my first year as a member of New York City Ballet, I was on my way to London. For a fledgling company that had started some two years before, and for this fifteen-year-old, it was incredible. I read a dozen books on the city of London and the history of England, and, dazed with delight, struggled to understand pence, shillings, pounds, and crowns.

Balanchine was ecstatic. He was forty-six years old, having left London for America close to seventeen years earlier, and was returning to perform at the Royal Opera House at Covent Garden with his new ballet company. Lincoln Kirstein was triumphant. For years, he had been shooting his mouth off to English friends about his great plans for ballet in America, and now he could flaunt his accomplishments. We had the theater to ourselves for five weeks (later extended by a week), then a short layoff, followed by engagements in three other cities.

Balanchine delighted in informing me of the proper manner of drinking tea, as there was a possibility the company would be hosted at a tea ceremony by the queen. "Diaghilev taught me. You know, with silver tongs, take only one lump of sugar, not greedy. And when you stir sugar, only half a swirl. Bzztt. Now, no sound—slurp, slurp—when you drink tea. And never finish tea to the end. Always leave a little in cup."

England in 1950 was still recovering from the devastation of war. Blackened shells of bombed-out buildings pockmarked the country. The company dancers were on their own to find accommodations, and I found a rooming house on Upper St. Martin's Lane; it had neither heat nor hot water. We were issued ration stamps for everything—soap, toilet paper, candy, food. Back home, I ate meat all the time, relishing my bacon in the morning, hamburgers at lunch, and sirloin or pork roast at night. In London, there was no meat. A stagehand, overhearing me complain, whispered that there was a place near the theater, called Nick's, run by a Greek, where you could get meat. It was horsemeat, a chewy chunk, bathed in Worcestershire sauce. Not so bad.

Balanchine and Cranko

Lincoln, while buzzing around London promoting NYCB, met John Cranko, a twenty-two-year-old up-and-coming choreographer. Born and raised in South Africa, Cranko had followed his muse to London and the Sadler's Wells Ballet.* He was the "hot boy" on the scene, and Frederick Ashton, the dean of British choreographers, had recommended him. Lincoln impetuously commissioned him to create a ballet for us, and announced his plans to Balanchine as a fait accompli.

We were a small company doing eight performances a week, the schedule was grueling, and now we had to fit in a new work by an unknown choreographer. We had early-morning ballet class, followed by nonstop rehearsals preparing for the night's repertoire and replacing injured dancers. When could we find the time? And who was this Cranko? We were intrigued. The company hummed with excitement. Balanchine was peeved.

The ballet would be called *The Witch,* and Cranko had chosen Melissa Hayden and Francisco Moncion to star. The music? Ravel's Piano Concerto no. 2 in G Major, and Dorothea Tanning, a dramatic and provocative designer, was commissioned to create costumes and decor. On the company's bulletin board, I was stunned to find my name listed, to be featured as one of a pair of ghoulish butlers, with Eddie Bigelow as my twin.

Cranko looked like one of us, a sandy-haired corps de ballet boy, undramatic, his demeanor quiet and unpretentious—but fascinating to watch in rehearsals, especially with Melissa and Frank. There were no definite steps or set movements, just vague suggestions of a dramatic effect he wished to achieve. As a director/playwright experiments with two great actors in developing a scene, Cranko collaborated with

* Sadler's Wells Ballet evolved into the Royal Ballet, and a second company was formed, the Sadler's Wells Theater Ballet.

Melissa and Frank, and all three developed the choreography together through trial and error.

At last, Cranko got around to Eddie and me. "Let's start," he said. "Try moving forward, heavy-footed and stuck together at the hip, like Siamese twins." I mumbled to Eddie, "I don't think he knows what he's doing!" Eddie replied with a grunt, "Do it. Just do it." "Do what?" I queried, and then gave up and copied Eddie.

Cranko was deeply influenced by Freddie Ashton, and developed choreography similarly. I realized this later, when Freddie was choreographing his first ballet for NYCB (*Illuminations*), and I was in it. In the following year, when Freddie was creating his second ballet, *Picnic at Tintagel*, I really got it, particularly when he was choreographing the love pas de deux between Isolde (Diana Adams) and Tristan (me). Freddie, who looked like the Penguin from *Batman* comic books, would curl up his fingers, clutch my shoulder, and, scrapping a little, say earnestly, "Jacques, my dear boy, I want you to listen to this passage in the music. Then I want you to spin to it, leap passionately, wildly, insanely, all around Diana"—one of the greatest beauties ever to go on toe. Freddie would pause for a moment, stare at me with rounded, watery eyes, then continue his direction. "Then, at the end of the musical phrase, throw yourself to the floor with both hands on her foot." Bewildered, I asked, "Freddie, what spins? What leaps? How many counts? What steps?" Exasperated, he answered, "Just do something, dear boy, invent anything, we'll worry about counts and steps later."

Balanchine, by contrast, would come to rehearsal understanding the structure of the music down to its DNA. He had taken the orchestral score and written his own piano breakdown—no waste of time, no doubts. He would go to the piano, look at the score, and then come over to us, invent and demonstrate a dance step, and we would execute it. We were trained by him, and so attuned, we could take his movements and transform what to others might seem a vague shuffle into a finished dance step. He was *never* vague about time or counts—and would make sound with his feet, beating out the rhythms precisely. Seldom would he change a step, and when he did, it was usually to adjust for some difficulty we were having. Rarely did he choreograph the position of our arms or how we were to enter or exit the stage—that was left to us. In later years, when Balanchine found it harder to demonstrate, he would comment, "If I can't move, I can't choreograph. I'll be finished."

On the other hand, Jerome Robbins told you what to think, before you made an entrance. He wanted to program his dancers to re-create the same performance every time, so he planned every single movement. Jerry would start by using a dancer's quirks, natural movements, and body shape, and then exploit and develop them into choreography. We soon learned that the first steps that Jerry worked out on you were the ones you would most likely end up with—but not until he had done a thousand variations and played endless journies of psychological games and manipulations on his cast. Rehearsals were miserable. He was constantly stressing his dancers, picking on them, embarrassing them, setting up conflicts among them, anything and everything his inventive mind could conjure to get more energy and passion out of them. Jerry could be charming and complimentary, and then, five minutes later, attack, insult, and crush your spirit—all to see how it would affect your mood and influence the dance movements. A few lucky dancers were spared.

One favored dancer, Carolyn George, moved quickly and lightly, and had enormous elevation. She was hard to keep earthbound. (Carolyn had been captain of the Highland Park High School basketball team when they won the Texas State Championship.) Jerry nicknamed her "Twitty Bird" and tended to choreograph fast, flitting movements for her. Out of Tanaquil LeClercq's long limbs and dramatic, mysterious elegance, Jerry shaped the nymph in *Afternoon of a Faun,* then built a ballet, *The Concert,* around her goofy sense of humor. Drawing on the power and dark intensity of Nora Kaye, Robbins created his great ballet *The Cage.*

Robbins took what you did naturally, enhanced, packaged, and presented it—he helped you become more of what you already were. Balanchine took the music, developed his own ideas of movement, and challenged you to become more than you thought you could be. With Robbins, you were amplified; with Balanchine, you were transformed.

While rehearsing *The Witch,* whenever Dorothea Tanning was around, I tried to not be caught staring at her arresting outfits. Once, she slashed the bodice of her dress, then gathered the gauzy fringes of torn material and pinned them together with a slew of safety pins, a nipple peeking out through metal lattice. The dancers would ooh and ah, gossiping, "Isn't she divine? She's married to Max Ernst!" I didn't want to seem stupid and ask, "Who's Max Ernst?" So I stayed stupid.

I remember Melissa as the witch, her thick, black hair, swirling. No marking the dance steps for her, she did everything full out, her

Lucky Jacques dancing with Tanny LeClercq in Jerome Robbins's Afternoon of a Faun, *1953*

gorgeous olive skin glowing with a sheen of sweat. Frank was mind-bogglingly handsome, with dark curly hair and rounded buns of power, supporting a muscular torso. Everyone loved being around Frank. Whenever he smiled, his face arranged itself into the essence of mirth; it was infectious. It was thrilling to watch them rehearse—Melissa, our company's great dramatic ballerina, and Frank, her equal in the power of his presence on the stage—cooking up what would become a fabulous performance.

The Witch premiered at the end of our final week in London, and then was scheduled to be repeated later, during our "tour of the provinces." Among my memories of the premiere: the dramatic lighting—spooky pools of light; the staccato Ravel score, charging the environment with energy; and, especially, Melissa and Frank's performance.

Eddie and I played a couple of servants to Melissa, who, in her witch guise, had blood-red streaks on the inner thighs of her dark tights, as if her "monthly" had gone insane. Dorothea costumed Eddie and me as bald-headed butlers, with skullcaps covering our hair and green makeup smeared over our faces.

The ballet was well received, but was not the smash hit expected. During the latter part of our London engagement, we faced half-empty houses, not because the public disliked us, but because most of the London cognoscenti and balletomanes had left for August vacations (that was why the Royal Opera House was available for all those weeks). However, many returned for our closing night. The house was packed with balletomanes and fans. It was a love fest. None of us had ever experienced such an ovation—flowers thrown all over the stage; doves released from the upper gallery; and, after twenty minutes of nonstop applause, a dilemma arose. The Cinderella deadline arrived, (hers was midnight; ours was eleven p.m.), for if the company remained onstage after that time, it meant the stage crew had to be paid overtime. The order was given to close the iron fire curtain and end the night. The massive iron wall came down, cutting off the fans still rhythmically clapping and stamping their feet. In the morning, a layoff-for-a-week began, and the company scattered. A paid vacation, albeit at half salary. I opted for a week in Paris.

On returning, before heading home to New York we would perform in Manchester, Liverpool, and Croydon—the Brits call them "the Provinces."

A GLASS OF MILK

Barely sixteen years old, loose in Paris, I ensconced myself in a garret at a pension near the Paris Opéra and haunted the booksellers along the Seine. The August weather was sumptuous. I can still feel the pale sun and conjure up the scent of the damp stones along the quay. Mornings, I took class at the Studio Wacker, the Paris mecca for ballet dancers. The dressing room was amazing; there wasn't any. You found a space in the hallway, stripped, put on dance clothes, and went in for the lesson. During class, I loved showing off and competing with dancers from all over the world, the American teenager who could jump so high and never put his heels on the floor.

Afternoons I spent tramping through every museum in the tourist brochures. Seedy men furtively offered, *"Le sex postcard?"* Of course, I was an easy mark, and bought them just as furtively, to discover nothing salacious—just photos of artwork, mostly nudes from paintings and sculptures in the Louvre. I already had a stack of them. One morning, I came across a sign, "Tour the Underground Rivers of Paris," so I skipped ballet class and took the tour. It was a sewer trip—a boat ride in rivers of *merde*—claimed to be the same route Jean Valjean had taken fleeing Inspector Javert. The river wasn't so bad, just brown water, but Jean Valjean didn't have a boat. Oh, the scent! Staggering at first, but during the hour or so our bateau wended its way through the underground maze, I got used to it. As cigarette smoke sticks to your hair and clothes, so did the sewer stench stick to me for the rest of the day. To air myself off, I purchased a fishing line and hook, baited it with bread, and spent the afternoon on the banks of the Seine, fishing.

The next day, I bought a medieval-looking dagger, a bottle of cheap *vin rouge,* a chunk of cheese, and a loaf of bread and, ferreting a blanket from my room, boarded the train to Saint-Germain-en-Laye. From the station, I walked through cobblestone village streets to a forest on the outskirts. Deep in the woods, I made a campsite, ate my cheese, drank the whole bottle, and passed out, to dream through the night of tournaments, knights, Lancelot, and Guinevere.

Back in Paris, a meal at a two-star restaurant at Le Gare Saint-Lazare resonates as a formative experience. The restaurant's elegant wood paneling and some twelve tables were waiting and expectant, dressed with white tablecloths, crystal, and silver settings. I was the only customer. Three bony waiters in black suits and white shirts, their collars frayed, buzzed around me, their aged bow ties tinged with a patina of iridescent brownish highlights. Five years since the Bosh had left, the French were still struggling. My pocketful of dollars made me rich. The rate of exchange was 350 francs to the dollar—on the black market, three times as much.

After perusal of the menu, with a beaming waiter hovering and his two buddies in the background watching my every move, I ordered an Alsatian dish, the house specialty, *choucroute garnie*—sauerkraut cooked in champagne with black peppercorns and caraway seeds. It arrived, a steaming mountain on a giant silver platter, encircled with boiled potatoes and covered with varied sausages, slabs of ham and pork, rashers of bacon, and, on the side, a plate containing half a dozen assorted mustards. *"Et pour boire, Monsieur?"* the pleased waiter inquired.

A moment's hesitation from me. Ah! To drink. *"Un verre de lait, s'il vous plaît."*

Don't forget, I was sixteen and used to guzzling down two quarts of milk a day. With a disbelieving look, the waiter's face fell. His two buddies, lurking in the background, froze.

"Ce n'est pas possible, Monsieur," the waiter's little eyeballs were twitching.

"Pourquoi ce n'est pas possible? Je veux un verre de lait and a big one, if you don't mind." I switched to English. The waiter retreated to confer with his cronies and, bolstered by their support, checked out his English, then returned and announced, "Milk, you cannot have."

Stridently, I yelled, "I don't see any other customers here! It's not as if this restaurant is loaded with patrons. Do I have to go somewhere else to get a glass of milk?" The Ugly American had flared out of this pimply faced teenager.

Adrenaline surged on all sides. The waiter scurried back and the trio disappeared to the back of the restaurant, while I sat there fuming. They returned moments later with the maître d', a slight man, his straight black hair plastered flat against his skull. He stood ahead of the triangle of waiters, pursed his lips, and announced in elegant tones, "Monsieur, it is not possible to give you milk with your *choucroute*. This cannot be done."

"Why not?" I barked, half rising from my seat, both hands planted on the table.

To which he parried, "Monsieur, milk is a food. *Choucroute* is a food. And one does not drink the kind of food that is milk while one eats the kind of food that is *choucroute.*"

Triggered by whatever gods of gastronomy enlightened me, I sat down, took a big breath, and, somewhat calmed, asked, "Then tell me what would be the right drink to have."

They danced with delight. Oh, the smiles, the nods of relief and sighs of amiability from the quartet. "May I recommend," said the maitre d', *"une bière d'Alsace,* or a wine *peut-être*—a white, a Gewürztraminer—it has a perfume spicy, slightly sweet—with the *choucroute,* a good balance."

Thus, I discovered *choucroute garnie* and Gewürztraminer!

The platter held enough for four people. I ate it all, including most of the mustards, and drank every drop of the scrumptious wine. With each mouthful and sip, the audience of delighted gastronomical mentors watched on, a bevy of mothers cooing as their baby stuffed himself. Sated, I sat back in my chair and searched out the last morsel of juicy pork, still stuck at the back of my teeth, my tongue caressing it. Oh, so happy! And slightly drunk.

The maître d' approached, victorious. *"Monsieur, voulez vous une dessert?* We have *les pâtisseries, le sorbet,* and a wonderful baked Alaska."

Before he could go on, I said, in my disordered French, *"Non, non, non, merci. Je suis fini. Le choucroute, c'est superb, mais ça suffit.* Enough, I can't eat another bite. *L'addition, s'il vous plaît.* The bill."

The maître d' disappeared. A few moments later, one of the waiters came with the check on a small, rectangular silver plate and retired. I reached in my pocket, pulled out a wad of dollars, and started counting them out. Looking up, I saw the quartet slowly approaching, a procession led by the maître d'. In his hand, he carried a grand silver platter. On it were a bowl of sugar, a silver spoon, and a little vase with a single flower, standing in attendance to a glass of milk. *"Mes compliments, Monsieur."*

Early October, I was back on the block. My buddies were hanging out on the corner, a cigarette in every mouth. All of them were heavier and taller. Despite my enthusiastic accounts of London and Paris, their sole preoccupation was who could best fake that they were old enough to get the beer, and whose parents weren't in, so we could party in their apartment. After twenty minutes of discussion, it was decided that the biggest and oldest looking, Peter Heevy, could pull off the beer, and we could use Joe Keene's pad; both his parents were at work. "Come on, Jock," they urged. Six or seven of us squeezed into Joe's tiny room—some on the floor, some on the bed. Behind the closed door, we munched potato chips and drank beer, and every other word was a street expletive. The room soon filled with cigarette smoke and my eyes and nose dripped. Someone started passing around a deck of dirty playing cards with photos of naked women copulating with unappetizing men, animals, and objects. I sat there numb, thinking, "I have grown into another world, stratospheres away from the life of gangs, the streets, and its dead-end culture." Saved by dance, the arts, and, of course, *choucroute* and Gewürztraminer! I mumbled excuses and left.

After my adventures in Paris, our tour recommenced in Manchester, a factory town still devastated five years after the Battle of Britain and never considered a mecca for the arts. Manchester's damp, clammy air was thick with oily soot, generated by chunks of bituminous coal, the only available fuel to burn in the fireplace grates of most homes throughout the British Isles.* A half hour in that environment and your skin was speckled. Imagine your lungs! Many buildings were facades, bodiless and eviscerated . . . compliments of the Luftwaffe. Our visit was to be a morale-building Band-Aid for the citizens, sponsored by the government. *The Witch* was a bonus.

Two hours before our first performance, I walked down the narrow cobblestone streets, heading for the theater. There was minimal electric power. Buildings pressed around me, and after the second or third floor, their architecture vanished, rising up into formless gloom. Near the theater, the streets were empty—no cars, no people, nothing. My footsteps were the only sound. Were there *any* citizens in this town? A single light bulb occasionally dangled at intersections. How perfect. I loved it! The light's alchemy transformed the black soot dust into green soup, served by a malevolent host, in honor of the opening night of *The Witch.*

Going through the stage door, there wasn't a doorman. Would we have an audience?

* In the "Black Fog" of London, England, in the winter of 1952, at least four thousand deaths were due to stagnant air masses of coal smog.

They came! The curtain opened to a full house, and a triumph for *The Witch.* Applause roared from a standing, cheering audience. Melissa and Frank's performances were hair-raising, riveting; company members packed the wings to watch them. This was a wonderful ballet . . . at least, I thought so.

Less than a month later, back in New York, and preparing for our fall season, I noticed *The Witch* was not in our repertoire. Rumor had it that Ravel's score had copyright problems in the United States. However, in

My sister Ninette, the teenage ballerina, 1948

the ensuing years, NYCB did many tours outside America. The ballet was never done again. It disappeared like a faded specter.

A couple of years later, my sister Ninette married Dr. Mel Kiddon, our lanky, good-looking company medic. He lost his equilibrium and tumbled into her eyes. At first I thought he was English, and he did nothing to dispel that impression, but he was from New Jersey, a bright medical student who had received a scholarship to study in London. An Anglophile, he adopted the camouflage of a Brit. On the mantel over the fireplace in their home, they had Dorothea Tanning's painting of the set from *The Witch*. It glowed there for years in their apartment. On visits to them, I never failed to walk up to the painting and say, "Oh, *The Witch!* What ever happened to you?"

As his career developed, Cranko found the soil of the British Isles unproductive, so he accepted a position as director of the ballet in Stuttgart, Germany. Choreographing full-length, dramatic ballets based on literature, he found a signature style for himself, and lifted a regional company to international stature. *Romeo and Juliet, The Taming of the Shrew,* and *Eugene Onegin* were major successes. He built his company around two stars: a Brazilian ballerina, Marcia Haydée, noted for her dramatic interpretations, and a superb American male dancer, Richard Cragun (I admired Cragun—one of the few male dancers who could easily knock off a triple tour en l'air).

In 1973, Stravinsky had been dead several years, Balanchine was close to seventy, and Cranko, at forty-five, was close to the age Balanchine had been when they first met in London. New York City Ballet was in its spring season at Lincoln Center, and Cranko's renowned Stuttgart Ballet was performing across the plaza at the Metropolitan Opera House. Hype and marketing about the Stuttgart Ballet was intense, and the critics were in a laudatory chorus about Cranko's works, in particular *Eugene Onegin.*

Savoring poetry, I had read and reread Pushkin's *Eugene Onegin* in a variety of translations. Once, I had gone to Balanchine to show him a particular passage (chapter six, stanza 31) in Russian and ask his opinion on which was the best of several English translations I had found. He perused them, reflected a moment, and declared, "None. You cannot translate this. Only in Russian can you understand Pushkin. So much more than 'lump of snow'!"

Onegin has shot his friend, Lensky. Filled with remorse, Onegin cradles Lensky in his arms and witnesses in Lensky's eyes the curtain of death slowly descend. At that very second, deep in the forest, a sheet of snow (*gliba snegovàya*), glittering in sunlight, slid silently down a slope.*

Balanchine explained that the phrase "*gliba snegovàya*" has more meanings than can be translated. The way it is used, the words imply the voyage of a life—past, present, and future—everything one has already done, what one is now, and the myriad possibilities of what one could do and be in the future. *Gliba snegovàya* evokes a sense that the totality and potential of Lensky has silently slipped away. A mountain of a life, yet vulnerable to melting.

A few days later, Balanchine gave me his four-volume translation by Vladimir Nabokov of *Eugene Onegin*: "Here is gift for you. In it is everything you need to know about everything."

Every morning, Balanchine taught a company class. His routine: enter the studio precisely on time; head to the piano; greet the pianist; then, after a few words of conversation, he would snap his fingers, and class would begin. If a practice bag had been left on the piano, or there was a coffee cup or debris left there, he would personally clear it before starting—the practice bag to the corner, the coffee cup or debris in the wastebasket. On rare occasions, he would single out a dancer to greet with a few personal comments, before the snap of his fingers established the tempo for our pliés.

One morning, in 1973, an agitated Balanchine entered, skipped the pianist, and made a beeline for me. "You know, Jacques, last night, I see this ballet, by Cranko, where he took *Onegin* to make choreography. And the music, you know, different pieces of Tchaikovsky, put together, no attention to harmonies. Bad. And the worst, the letter, the beautiful letter to Tatiana—Pushkin's poetry. Cranko has man put hand on ballerina behind, between legs, and lift in air, then run around

* Three translations of this stanza from *Eugene Onegin*:

Nabokov translation (revised ed. 1975):	*Walter Arndt translation (1963):*	*Douglas Hofstadter translation (1999):*
Gently he lays his hand upon his breast	In silence to his bosom raising	And on his breast he gently places
and falls. His misty gaze	A hand, he took no other breath,	His hand, then crumples to the dirt.
expresses death, not anguish.	And sank, and fell. Opaquely glazing,	The foggy look upon his face is
Thus, slowly, down the slope of hills,	His eyes expressed not pain, but death.	Of death expressive, not of hurt.
in the sun with sparks shining,	So, gently down the slope subsiding,	Once, slowly down some sloping mountain,
a *lump of snow* descends.	A sparkling *sheet of snow* comes sliding.	Aglow as though sun's frozen fountain,
		A lonely *snowball* fell and rolled.

stage like weightlifter in circus." I put an agreeable expression on my face and nodded. Balanchine continued, "Oh! What he has done to Pushkin and Tchaikovsky."

"Is it worth seeing, Mr. B?" A moment of silence, a twitch of his nose, and he mumbled, "If you want . . . you can."

A little later in June, I was in class, and once again Balanchine entered the room and headed right to me, all excited. "Jacques, did you read paper this morning?" "No, I didn't." What did I miss?

"Well, you see what happened to Cranko? He was in airplane, over forty thousand feet, up there near heaven, and died." He paused, expectant. My mouth fell open. "Oh, no! How? What happened?"

Balanchine leaned back and pronounced, "You see? Tchaikovsky got together with Pushkin and Stravinsky." Balanchine clapped his hands together and yelled, "BANG!" All the dancers in the room froze, and then he announced, "THEY STOPPED HIM!"

Approaching the upper atmosphere, Cranko had choked on a piece of food while strapped into his seat. The Heimlich maneuver could have saved him.

Lincoln and Lew

What are the *gliba snegovàya*s of George Balanchine and Lincoln Kirstein? Nobody can sum up these giants—or perhaps any human being—but there are a handful of defining moments in my relationship with each, and I recount them in hopes to illuminate, in some small degree, the marvels and complexities of both. In many ways, they were the teachers and mentors who wrote the scripts for the roles I would play in my life.

They came from different worlds—one Russian, one American; one poor, one rich; one short, one tall. One, the professional, a supreme master, and, arguably, the greatest artist in the field of dance in the twentieth century. The other, a flawed genius who aspired to be the supreme arbiter of all the arts in the twentieth century. Although of small stature, and having only one lung—its twin lost to tuberculosis—Balanchine had great confidence, was unflappable; Lincoln, with his tall and powerful frame, was riddled with doubts gnawing at his convictions.

United in their love of arts, and ballet in particular, their paths crossed. Balanchine often remarked, "Ballet is woman . . . Man is partner, you know. In service to woman. You see?" To Lincoln, the ballerina was peripheral. He saw only the male, and the male was always the focus of Lincoln's vision of ballet.

"You're a dancer today, Buster, because I wanted to fuck Lew Christensen."

Lincoln Kirstein's growling voice reverberated, as he rubbed my hair affectionately. He relished shocking statements, pointed, rude, and jarring. No honeyed packaging for him. His blunt opinions, riveted with truth (the way he saw it), were aimed to knock you off-balance, shake your tightrope, and manipulate you. Grand and menacing, Lincoln was. Primal. At this moment, he had coalesced into a black hole looming over me.

I had just turned fifteen, and was in my first week of rehearsal in the corps of New York City Ballet. This was the first of many times Lincoln would bestow this confession/blessing on me, usually with his hand on my head, as if he were the pope imparting great dogma to the anointed—other times pontificating with a stabbing finger, accusing and threatening the chosen one.

"There wouldn't be any of this if it wasn't for Lew. I did everything for Lew."

"What did he mean by everything?" I thought. The ballet company, the school, the teachers, the students, the pianists, Balanchine, the costumes, the building, me? He did mean all of that.

"Don't you forget it, buster. It's all because of Lew."

"I first saw him in a vaudeville act with his brother, Willam," Lincoln recounted. Their act was billed "The Christensen Brothers and Company." The brothers were Mormons from Ogden, Utah, but a rare type of Mormon. They smoked and drank, danced, played musical instruments, knew and loved theater and the visual arts, and somehow managed to meld it all together in a raucous act with the "company." The "company" consisted of two lovely girls, their dancing partners. (There was a third brother, Harold, but he opted not to be a performer; instead, he went to West Point, graduated, and became a ballet teacher.) As young boys in Utah, William and Lew had their hearts and minds captured by the arts. They dreamed of careers in those fields, and were destined to spend a lifetime in exploration and service to those arts. They were constantly seeking out any person who could teach, guide, and further them in their careers, and every opportunity to travel to wherever the arts were flourishing had them on their way.

Willam was a dramatic performer: short, dynamic, and bursting with ideas on theater. Lew, graced with an over-six-foot frame, had a superbly proportioned body and gorgeous, golden-haired movie-star looks. He was an exceptional ballet dancer with amazing virtuosity, speed, and precision. Both were inspired choreographers. Willam was charming and outgoing. Lew, shy and reticent. Both were stubborn.

With their dancing partners, the brothers invented and choreographed an acrobatic-cum-ballet tour de force spiced with virtuoso "tricks." They would fling the girls dramatically in the air and snatch them back safely to earth. They got themselves onto the vaudeville circuit, and their schedule was grueling—two shows a day, more on the weekend—and Lincoln went to see them.

"I fell in love with Lew Christensen," he bellowed again and again. "One look was all it took!" Lincoln always sounded angry, even when he wasn't.

THE CHRISTENSEN BROTHERS

On tour with their partners, from right, Willam Christensen and Lew Chris-
tensen, late 1920s. The third brother, Harold, opted for West Point and later
became a respected teacher of ballet.

He was schizophrenic and multi-frantic, and tortured by ideas and
ambitions, pebbles in his brain case, rattling. In every field and in every
way, his ballooning and bizarre imagination birthed idiotic concepts
and projects, as well as brilliant ideas, spewing out from the boiling
soup that was his psyche. He was obsessed with a romanticized dream
of the American Blue-Collar Worker. The laborer, muscles gleaming as
he toils in steel mills, cornfields, or garages—courageous, with a rough
humor, unsophisticated, but with dignity; unspoiled, yet with discipline. The doughboy, the sailor in bell-bottoms, the gymnast, the base-

Who wouldn't do everything for him? Lew Christensen in 1937. Such a beauty!

ball player, the boxer, the teenager mowing the lawn on a hot summer day with sweat glistening on his arms, sensual and innocent, all were in Lincoln's mind's eye.

Lew ignited this vision. A god from Brigham City, Utah: but simple, modest, and American, he was the Apollo of the Desert, and a classical ballet dancer to boot. Lew became the muse to Lincoln's dreams, the lodestar that drove him to succeed in realizing his greatest achievement—founding the School of American Ballet, and its affiliate, New York City Ballet. Lincoln brought Balanchine to the U.S. because of Lew. That's what Lincoln meant when he said, "I did everything for Lew."

Did Lincoln go backstage after Lew's performance and say, "I'm going to start a ballet company for you"? If he did, how did Lew respond? I have no idea. On this, Lincoln never enlightened me.

In his time, Napoleon the conqueror had been appalled with the way graveyards littered the city of Venice—neither orderly nor sanitary—so he cleared out the nearby island of San Michele and made it into the Isle of the Dead. Barges served as hearses on the watery byways of Venice, conveying the deceased to the cemetery. In 1929, Lincoln was touristing his way through Venice, and in his wanderings stumbled onto a funeral ceremony. A corpse was being loaded onto a black and gold barge.

After inquiring, Lincoln discovered that the principal attraction, the corpse, had been the impresario Sergei Diaghilev. Thunderstruck, Lincoln felt he had a message from God. He would be the next to wear Sergei's shoes.

Lincoln would be the Gardener in Chief of a ballet company for all time. Outdoing Diaghilev, he would choose and commission choreographers, dancers, painters, scenic designers, costumers, librettists, poets, photographers, composers, musicians—he would guide architects in designing plans for rehearsal studios and theaters for dance, and artists in writing books on ballet technique. He even took classes in ballet. Hard to imagine he could find ballet shoes of a size to fit his feet, or tights to cover his legs; he was some six foot four, over two hundred pounds, doing pliés at the barre, an elephant at a tea party. No earthbound ambitions for Lincoln—he planned to be the artistic tsar in the creation of a New World.

Lincoln needed a ballet master to come to America to plant the seeds and nurture his garden. Léonide Massine, a vibrant performer/choreographer and onetime lover of Diaghilev, was not interested. Another on Diaghilev's dance card, Serge Lifar, had clawed himself up to run the Paris Opéra Ballet.

Given the cold shoulder by Massine and Lifar, in October 1933 Lincoln approached Balanchine, who was ripe for something new, even as big a change as leaving Europe. Despondent over the disbanding of his little start-up company, his loss of the Paris Opéra, and periodically ill from recurrent bouts of tuberculosis, Balanchine, at the urging of this giant, mad capitalist, agreed to journey to America. Always the pragmatist, he interrupted Lincoln's avalanche of words: "But first a school."

Lincoln, while recounting this history to me, his mouth full of hors d'oeuvres at our lunch, growled, "Lifar was getting the Paris Opera, and Massine just wanted to make money and buy his island in Italy. Only George saw the vision."

Expanding his dream, Lincoln envisioned a conservatory to rival the Imperial School of St. Petersburg. He dreamed of hundreds of young male dancers with exquisite manners, learning the arts. Lincoln designed uniforms for them, badged with a lyre emblem. There were ballerinas in his vision, but they were vague shapes in the background.

When Lincoln got Balanchine, he got Balanchine's enterprising manager, Vladimir Dimitriev, who negotiated the terms, details, and contracts. Balanchine felt deeply indebted to Dimitriev, and insisted that he come to New York as part of the new partnership.

DIMITRIEV

In 1923, barely two years after Balanchine graduated from the Ballet School in Petrograd,* Vladimir Dimitriev (a singer of the Theater of Musical Drama and later of the Maryinsky Opera) helped Balanchine launch "Evenings of Young Ballet" with a company of some fifteen young dancers from the Maryinsky. An important alliance/collaboration/partnership had been formed.

I remember Dimitriev at SAB in 1942. Even though he had been replaced as director of the school (first by Lincoln, then Eugenie Ouroussow), he occasionally came around because his wife, Kyra Blank, taught the beginner's classes. I came out of her class once, and a greasy-looking man was talking to Miss Ouroussow. One of the mothers whispered to the Boss, "That's Dimitriev, he's Kyra Blank's husband. He came from Russia, like they all did."

Lenin died in 1924, and life in Russia plunged into deeper darkness as Stalin took charge. George Kennan, America's ambassador to Russia, and a great diplomat and Russian scholar, told me, "Stalin had yellow eyes. He lived at night, and if at any moment he decided to call someone, they had better be available. All over the eleven time zones of the Soviet Union, Communist Party members, bureaucrats, sat at their desks, awaiting word from the Kremlin, 'He's gone to sleep.' Then it would be safe to close down, collapse, maybe go home, before they would have to be back at their offices."

Nearly everyone wanted desperately to get out of the country. For-

* This city built by Tsar Peter the Great juggled the names Petrograd, St. Petersburg, and Leningrad.

eign visas were seemingly impossible to secure, especially for artists, but wily Dimitriev managed a miracle, manipulating the Soviet bureaucrats into providing passports and visas for a small group of artists, headed by himself and Balanchine. Calling themselves the Soviet State Dancers, the troupe included three singers, a conductor, and five dancers, among them Tamara Gevergeyeva, Balanchine's first wife, later known in the U.S. as the actress Tamara Geva; Alexandra Danilova, who would become Balanchine's second wife* and, by the time she put away her toe shoes, a prima ballerina of international renown; Nicholas Efimov, who later became a premier danseur at the Paris Opéra; and Lydia Ivanova, who never made it.[†]

Setting out (supposedly) to propagandize the prowess of Soviet ballet in the West, late in 1924 they boarded a boat for Germany and embarked on a nail-biting, white-knuckled journey. As punishment for defection involved either imprisonment in a Siberian gulag or execution, they expected cannons to fire on the ship and stop them in their tracks.

Dimitriev was the wheeler-dealer confidence man they depended on. They landed in Berlin with tattered clothes, a few sleazy costumes, and little money. However, in another feat of legerdemain, Dimitriev managed to arrange a paid tour of summer camps along the Rhine.

"We took any job we could, anywhere," Balanchine recalled, but they were no longer starving. "In Germany, it was so wonderful, the food. I remember the cheapest meal—boiled potato with herring and chopped onion. And you put olive oil on top, and ate with white bread and German beer. So good. We hadn't seen white bread since the tsar died." Years later, in New York, we would often hang out at the Empire Coffee Shop on the corner of Sixty-third and Broadway, and Balanchine would order boiled potato, herring or anchovies, chopped onion, and Beck's beer. *"Best meal!"*

Somewhere along the way, the troupe received a message from the Soviet Union demanding, "Return immediately!" The conductor and

---

* Danilova and Balanchine never actually married, but they lived together in what may be considered a common-law marriage.

† Lydia Ivanova, a promising ballerina, was included among the original members of the group. Before the group received permission to depart, she drowned in a mysterious accident. Ivanova was rumored to be mistress to a high party official, Danilova told me: "He did not want her to leave, so he had her, as you say in your country, rubbed out."

three singers returned; Balanchine, Dimitriev, and the others elected to defect.

After the tour of the Rhineland, Dimitriev set out scheming and networking, and before long, the company received an invitation from Diaghilev to audition for his Ballets Russes. Danilova, having been a soloist at the Maryinsky, was insulted to be expected to audition. Bernard Taper describes Sergei Diaghilev as "that extraordinary figure who had made a unique impact on the cultural life of Europe and who, as a personality, has been an endless source of speculation and fascination."

Luckily, Diaghilev was impressed, and all four dancers were invited to join. Soon afterward, Balanchine became ballet master of Diaghilev's famed and historic company. He was twenty years old. Perhaps out of loyalty and gratitude, perhaps because of a prearranged agreement, during these years Balanchine and the others contributed one fifth of their salaries to Dimitriev. Years later, Balanchine told me, "When I go to Hollywood, or do Broadway show, I send money to Dimitriev." I asked, "Dimitriev's been out of your life for decades, why do you keep giving him money?" to which he replied, "I would not be alive if it were not for Dimitriev!"

In 1929, Diaghilev died, and the company, full of intrigues, struggled. Right around the time Lincoln received, at Diaghilev's funeral, his "message from God," Balanchine accepted a position as ballet master at the Royal Opera House in Copenhagen. Soon after, the director of a theater in Monte Carlo, René Blum, gathered what was left of the scattered Diaghilev company, and formed a new company, the Ballets Russes de Monte Carlo. Balanchine was the first choreographer he invited to join. Before long, though, Balanchine butted heads with Colonel de Basil, a wealthy entrepreneur who had elbowed his way into Blum's company and named himself codirector. Balanchine left after one season.

A wealthy patron and fan, Edward James, helped Balanchine form his own company, Les Ballets 1933, to perform in Paris. If de Basil could do it, why couldn't they? Lincoln Kirstein attended performances of Les Ballets 1933 in Paris and then, later, London, and it confirmed his belief in, and enthusiasm for, the work of this young choreographer. Lincoln felt Balanchine was continuing to create ballets in the spirit of Diaghilev. With few prospects for the future, after the London season

Les Ballets 1933 disbanded. Lo and behold, Lincoln Kirstein appeared and made his offer.

Balanchine had a passion for American movies—westerns and musicals—so he shelved his dream of running the Paris Opéra and, with Dimitriev in tow, headed for the wide-open spaces of the New World.

There's a photograph I saw in a newspaper of Lincoln and his friend and cosponsor Eddie Warburg meeting Balanchine and Dimitriev on their arrival in New York. It's written on their faces, their body language, right there in that photograph—the smiling Americans, full of promise; the Russians, suspicious, afraid of being taken advantage of, and thinking, "What's in it for me, and how can I manipulate these rich guys?" When informed that their home would be Hartford, Connecticut, I can imagine, "WHAT! HARTFORD? WHAT YOU MEAN, CONNECTICUT?! WHAT ABOUT NEW YORK CITY?" That was the day they thought they would quit and head back to Europe.

Fortunately for Lincoln (and perhaps ballet in America), Balanchine suffered a relapse of tuberculosis and had to be hospitalized before he and Dimitriev could return. By the time he was released from the hospital, Lincoln and Eddie Warburg had found an alternate space for the school in New York City—three grungy, dimly lit studios at Fifty-ninth Street and Madison Avenue. Balanchine and Dimitriev agreed to stay. My sister, Ninette, in later years remembered, "The elevator was slow, but the wallpaper in the lobby was impressive."

Lincoln garnered seed money. There was never enough. Begging from friends and relatives was to be Lincoln's lot in life. The majority of funds in the operating pot came from Eddie Warburg, supplemented by some of Lincoln's own, mostly his parents'. And they managed to prepare, furnish, and open the School of American Ballet at Fifty-ninth Street. Balanchine wanted his company. The school was the crucible for his dancers. As soon as he could, he was at work preparing ballets, using the best of the school's students, augmented by a handful of the few professional dancers available. Meanwhile, Lincoln labored frantically, seeking venues for performances. Eventually, a company evolved, the American Ballet, directed by Balanchine. It didn't last long, their monies quickly spent. When the empty pot resonated, "No more, no more!" Eddie Warburg echoed, "Enough, Lincoln. No more." By the middle of 1938, the American Ballet had fallen apart.

Balanchine packed up and left to further explore the worlds of Broadway and Hollywood. Lincoln formed another company, Ballet Caravan, and installed Lew Christensen as ballet master and dancing star and himself as director. They mustered a group of young dancers, many of whom later became stars in their own right: Todd Bolender, Eugene Loring, and Michael Kidd were foremost among them. During my years with the New York City Ballet, Betty Cage was the company manager, and told me that her mentor and predecessor, Frances Hawkins, had saved Ballet Caravan, this child of Lincoln, through bookings, wise diplomacy, and calling on myriad personal contacts so the fledgling company could perform. They found work anywhere possible, and survived, performing in school halls, college athletic department gyms, community centers, movies and vaudeville theaters. Eventually, Lincoln's childhood pal Nelson Rockefeller arranged a Latin American tour funded by the U.S. State Department. In the summer of 1941, Ballet Caravan went off to dance under a panoply starring the Southern Cross.

TOURING SOUTH AMERICA WITH BALLET CARAVAN

Lew told me, "You have no idea how tough a tour can be." They'd be riding a bus along precipitous roads, wending their way through the Andes, with three-thousand-foot drops on one side and sheer cliffs on the other. Then, without warning or, seemingly, logic, the bus driver would stop in the middle of the road, climb down, and stretch out on the warm hood of the bus to sleep. The dancers would look at each other, shake their heads, and, abandoned to fend for themselves, sit or go pee on the side of the road, until the driver woke up and took the wheel again.*

---

* At the Royal Opera House, empty between matinee and evening, a fellow corps de ballet dancer, Kaye Sargent, and I would slip into the Royal Box to neck passionately, panting in regal style. She subsequently married the head electrician at the opera, Bill McGee, and moved to London for good. In later years, we would get together with several dancers from the Royal Ballet and laugh, gossiping over the conditions we overcame on ballet tours. The worst I remember was the Liceu in Barcelona—the one toilet in all of Europe, it seemed, that *did* have a bowl sporting a wooden rim, only the rim was encrusted with dried feces (other toilets were just

During a confessional four-hour lunch in the early 1960s, Lincoln told me that in dealing with Nelson's machinations in South America, he came to understand the use of power. "You can move people around like chess pieces!" Lincoln said. "Nelson and I were like brothers. His mother was another mother to me." Lincoln shifted in his seat. "After the Ballet Caravan tour, I went back to South America, this time as a spy for Nelson, to report on the quality of the U.S. State Department offices, and to scope out artists and buy works for him." Arousing the enmity of the State Department bureaucrats, Lincoln was arrested in São Paolo. "I was stupid enough to send information to Nelson via mail," he explained. At our lunch, Lincoln would abruptly stand, walk away, pivot, return, plop down, and resume—continuing from where he left off or, tacking, beginning a new anecdote. Episodes tumbled out of him, seemingly at random.

"I was put in a stone room, small, with a hole in the middle of the floor. In the corner was a metal bed stand, no mattress. I kept telling them, 'Call the American embassy, it's a mistake!' After several hours, an American consulate aide came. I was so relieved, and told him to call Nelson, that I was working for him, and he had given me authorization to send back reports. It was early in the day, and the aide said he would be back shortly to get me out. He never came. I spent the night crouching on top of the bed frame—the floor was covered with vermin— assorted bugs and rats. I didn't dare use the hole, because I would have had to walk cross the floor, and God knows what would have come out of it."

---

holes in the ground). Shaun O'Brien, a fellow dancer, solved our Liceu problem by saving local newspapers and cutting out covers for the rim. ("The problem, Daisy," Shaun called me endearingly, "is the newsprint rubs off and tattoos your buns.") Dancers from the Royal Ballet described their tours in the deserts of the Middle East, where they danced on raised wooden platforms built for the occasion—with the orchestra abutting the stage, ensconced in fold-up chairs, at ground level. "If you needed to go to the loo, you had to go under the stage, squat and do your duty, staring at the orchestra members playing while over your head, the sounds of the dancers' feet reverberated." And ubiquitous flies. Kaye's friend Anne, an ex-member of the corps, recounted, "I do think the worst horror was putting on your makeup. The flies were so thick, they covered the mirror. You would whisk them away with your hand, or blow with your breath to open up a clear space on the mirror, and by the time you'd put on your lipstick, the mirror was full of flies again." I imagine that Ballet Caravan's tour had tales to equal or outdo these.

Recounting the story, Lincoln implied he spent a terrified night sobbing. An over-six-foot giant, manic-depressive, in a claustrophobic South American prison, imagining he would be buried forever. "The next day, late in the morning, that embassy prick came by to get me out, all smiles and friendship. When I was free of that prison, I screamed at him, 'Why did you let me spend the night there? Why didn't you come sooner?' 'Oh, Lincoln, that was on Nelson's orders,' the aide smirked. 'He said an overnight stay would teach you a lesson. Humility, you know.' " As Lincoln was filling my ear with this story, I kept thinking—did Nelson truly give those orders? Were the diplomats at the American embassy pissed off and playing with Lincoln? Or was it Lincoln's own paranoia, embellished? Why was he arrested? For sending covert information to Nelson, or because the authorities were aware he had been soliciting and picking up young men? Lincoln had a habit of frequenting the gay baths in New York (especially in Harlem). Some of my fellow dancers at the ballet told me they had been there with him.

"He was showing me that he held the cards." Lincoln continued, "Buster, a favor given could be taken away, and don't you forget it." Lincoln needed Nelson; Nelson didn't need Lincoln. The same dynamic would define (and condemn) Lincoln's relationship with Balanchine.

Ballet Caravan, Lincoln's child, faded away and disbanded.

WORLD WAR II

Everything changed on December 7, 1941. Pearl Harbor.

Lew was drafted, and Lincoln ran to the nearest recruiting station. He could have had a commission as an officer, but he enlisted as a private—a man in his mid-thirties lined up, volunteering with teenagers. He liked the idea of being with the grunt workers and doughboys and in the forefront of the fighting, sweating with the men in the trenches.

After completing basic training, a dismayed Lincoln found himself sweating, not in the trenches, but behind a desk at an Army base, screaming in frustration while others fought battles raging all over the world. "I enlisted in the Army. I wanted to get right out to the front lines. Instead, they punished me. Kept me in an Army base down south—guarding a stove. I couldn't stand it!" (Who did he mean by "they"? Nelson? Lincoln's enemies in the State Department? The Pentagon?)

Lew ended up in the European theater, assigned to head a detail whose miserable task was to search the battlefields for the maimed and the dead. Whenever there was a lull in fighting or an engagement terminated, Lew and his squad would collect bodies, search for identifying dog tags, try to match them with body parts, assemble them, bag them, and get them off the field for burial.

Meanwhile, manic that the war might pass him, Lincoln was pulling every string he could. Eventually, Nelson and old Joe Kennedy's lobbyist in Washington made calls and wrote letters, and Lincoln found himself in Europe. He was to become part of a team designated to track down and rescue artwork confiscated by the Nazis. "It wasn't all honey, Buster. It was hairy," Lincoln recounted. "I was assigned to drive a jeep for a colonel in General Patton's army, and it was back and forth across the front lines. Patton was one of America's greatest warriors. I met him once. I went to take a piss in the portable latrine set up at the hospital's triage center. I found the general in the latrine, leaning over a urinal, his head pressed against the wall, with tears streaming down his face, while his cock was pissing."

One day, returning with an officer from battlefield reconnaissance somewhere in Europe, Lincoln—the driver—was forced to slam his jeep to a stop. A soldier had leaped onto the muddy road in front of them, and was waving and beseeching. The officer bellowed, "What the hell's going on? Why are you stopping us?"

The soldier stuttered, "There's something wrong. Our sergeant, our sergeant, he's gone crazy. He's crazy. Over here, over here. Help us."

The officer whispered to Lincoln, "Stick close to me, soldier," and got out to follow the agitated trooper into a field. The shapes of half a dozen soldiers, hunched with concern, were clustered around a figure sitting on a log. The center of their attention was a bare-chested, bronzed and muscled, golden-haired soldier, who was heaving, sobbing, and howling. The officer, an Old Establishment, "keep order no matter what" type, strolled over and yelled out a command: "STAND UP, SOLDIER! STAND UP!"

Lew Christensen jumped to his feet, blank-faced and pop-eyed, his hinged arm continually saluting as he mouthed, "Aye aye, sir. Aye aye, sir. Aye aye, sir." The officer, his own nerves frayed, broke down: "I'm sorry, I'm sorry."

Lincoln took charge. "I know the man, sir. I'll take care of him, he's the star of my ballet company." The officer probably thought he was hearing things, or that his driver, too, had gone off the deep end. "The officer was completely useless, like a child," Lincoln boasted. "I got Lew and the officer over to the jeep, and drove them back to command headquarters." He delivered Lew to the medics, and would not see him again until after Germany was defeated.

Lew's Army experiences are recounted by Debra Hickenlooper Sowell in her book *The Christensen Brothers: An American Dance Epic.* In it she describes Lew as a lieutenant administering a captured German city and running into Lincoln. Lew told him he doubted he would dance again.

Berlin fell. Lincoln was helping to track down, catalog, and return artwork stolen by the Nazis. When finally mustered out, Lincoln returned to New York, bursting with energy.

He unshelved his dreams, reconnected with Balanchine, and birthed Ballet Society, an elitist organization—after all, ballet was the art of the aristocracy, and in the New World, the aristocrats were the wealthy. Several hundred patrons became members, among them many of Lincoln's well-heeled friends. Lincoln handled everything: he chose the orchestra, commissioned the artists, watched all the rehearsals, and buzzed around, a giant raven constantly on the move. Besides Balanchine, Lincoln assembled several other choreographers, hired dancers, booked theaters, and gave the choice seats to members of ballet society. The ordinary public could buy tickets to fill any remaining places. Lincoln persuaded Lew to join the company as choreographer, ballet master, and principal dancer.

Every performance, I sat out front, mesmerized. Already an opinionated critic at twelve years old, I remember watching Lew Christensen dance and thinking, "Oh, he's not that great. Not as great as what I've been hearing." Years later, in April 1953, when I was eighteen years old and Lew was teaching me his role in the 1938 ballet *Filling Station,* he confided, "After the war, I was finished as a dancer. On the vaudeville circuit, I used to do sixteen double tours on a dime, night after night. But after the army boots, I could never get it back. My time has gone,

Jacques."* This marvelous, sensitive man, mumbling excuses to a gauche teenager.

I am writing this account from excerpts in my diary, scrawled after many conversations through the years, with Lincoln, Lew, Bill, and Balanchine. "I wrote a poem about meeting Lew during the war," Lincoln told me, and gave me a copy of his book, *Rhymes of a PFC.*† "Auden likes it," he claimed. "Said it was my best work." A hundred copies were privately printed before the first public edition. Lincoln dedicated number 52 to me. I treasure it. The poem about Lew is called "Vaudeville."

---

* Over the years, I got to know and care a great deal for Lew and Willam. Carrie, my wife, danced with and for Willam when he was director of San Francisco Ballet. Willam then formed the ballet company at the University of Utah, which evolved into Ballet West. I was a regular guest with both groups, and headed Ballet West's first European tour. Bill always importuned me to come codirect Ballet West with him, and then take it over. He was such a creative force, constantly planning new ballets, never playing it safe, teaching every class. When in his nineties, I heard he had been moved to a nursing home, so I called him. "My time has gone!" he yelled into the phone. "It's too late for me! I can't move! I can't demonstrate a dance step! I can't teach a class! Time has passed me by." Then, in a subdued voice, "I always loved you, Jacques, from the first time I saw you dance." It touches such an emotional chord in me. Ironic, too, that the two brothers, unbeknownst to each other, spoke almost identical words—"My time has gone." Lew, speaking of the end of his career as a dancer in the early fifties; Bill, speaking of the end of his career as a ballet master.

† *Rhymes of a PFC,* 1964; *Rhymes and More Rhymes of a PFC,* 1966, first printed edition for the public. Both have the "Vaudeville" poem and one called "Patton," in which the general takes a leak.

> Inspecting cots of amputees, unshaken obviously,
> Approves the stitch above the wrist,
> the slice below the knee;
> Hides in th'enlisted men's latrine so he can quietly
> Have one good hearty cry.
>
> This soldier has to take a leak, finds someone sobbing there.
> To my horror it's an officer; his stars make this quite clear.
> I gasp: "Oh, sir, are you all right?" Patton grumbles: "Fair.
> Something's in my eye."

VAUDEVILLE

Pete Petersen, before this bit, a professional entertainer;
He and a partner tossed two girls on the Two-a-Day,
Swung them by their heels and snatched them in mid-air,
Billed as "Pete's Meteors: Acrobatic Adagio & Classical Ballet."
His vulnerable grin, efficiency, or bland physique
Lands him in Graves' Registration, a slot few strive to seek.
He follows death around picking up pieces,
Recovering men and portions of men so that by dawn
Only the landscape bares its wounds, the dead are gone.
Near Echternach, after the last stand they had the heart to make
With much personal slaughter by small arms at close range,
I drive for an officer sent down to look things over.
There is Pete slouched on a stump, catching his wind.
On your feet: salute. "Yes, sir?"
"Bad here, what?" "Yes, sir."
Good manners or knowing no word can ever condone
What happened, what he had to do, has done,
Spares further grief. Pete sits down.
A shimmering pulsation of exhaustion fixes him
In its throbbing aura like footlights when the curtain rises.
His act is over. Nothing now till the next show.
He takes his break while stagehands move the scenery,
And the performing dogs are led up from below.

Boss Leaves Pop

As members of the NYCB, Ninette and I were earning salaries. Having switched from ballet to Broadway, brother Paul was earning his living in musical theater, while John, now engaged to the lovely Mary Cruthers, was working as an assistant manager at Woolworth's.

Boss dreamed of becoming a nurse, but without a high school diploma there was no chance, so she attended night school and became a nurse's aide. "It's the same as a nurse! I give shots and medications, and do the ministering just like they do, only they don't have to empty bedpans."

After the war, Pop had returned to his old job at Columbia Presbyterian Hospital, and, before the decade was out, found himself replaced by a machine, since hospital management had automated the elevators. Boss became the full-time wage earner. "Andy, become a nurse's aide like me," she urged, and enrolled him in the same nursing school she had attended.

My father's version: "As soon as I finished the course, she threw me out of the house."

Coming home from rehearsal, I opened the apartment door, and there was Pop, waiting. He immediately launched into a diatribe about my mother, menopause, and madness. "They go crazy!" he cried, as though it was fact that when women go through menopause they lose their minds, ipso facto. "She threw me out! She's mad, your mother, insane! I went all my life with holes in my pants so that you could have your dancing lessons and your fancy, artsy world. And now your mother is throwing me out! It's the menopause doing it to her. She's not in her right mind!"

Frantic and crazy, my father made a pain in the ass of himself, a broken record of unending complaints about his victimization and the madness of the mother. "Do *you* think it's rational for a woman whose husband has supported her . . . ?" The minute my father visited John and his family to unload his grievances, John said, "Don't talk to me about my mother," and closed the door. John had his own life; he and his bride, Mary, were living on Long Island, starting a family, and John was working brutal hours at Woolworth's. Paul had been drafted into the Army and was enduring the rigors of basic training in Fort Hood, Texas, so he was spared Pop's rants.

Ninette and I bore the brunt. But, because I was the youngest and Boss's pet, Pop zeroed in on me: "Talk to your mother, she can't do this to me. It's your fault." Imagine as a teenager—my father told me, "We haven't had sex in years, Jacques!" Hard enough to imagine your parents copulating. The mind balks, images forming blank out. "We've been sleeping in the same bed, but for the last ten years, she hasn't let me touch her!"

When I accused Boss of throwing Pop out, she replied, "It's between your father and me. I don't talk about it."

My father wrote letters to all Boss's relatives in Lewiston, Maine, and demanded a hearing. Then he went up to Maine and filled the ear of anyone who would listen with his message, "Georgette's gone crazy. She's insane." He was persuasive, and convinced my aunts—Boss's sisters—to hold a tribunal. With letters and phone calls, the aunts summoned my mother and me to Maine. (Ninette extricated herself from the tornado. She was hot and heavy with Dr. Mel Kiddon.)

In Maine, I was interviewed by each of the aunts about my father and mother's relationship, and to my shame, I parroted my father's statements, "She must be crazy. Menopause, you know. It makes women crazy!" (Diagnosis from a seventeen-year-old.) Boss stuck out her chin and told her sisters, "Mind your own business. It's my marriage." Balanced against my father's ranting and raving, her confidence was unshakable and her reasoning true. "*Vas y!*" the tribunal told my father, and the whole chimera collapsed.

My mother never said a word in defense of herself for leaving my father. She'd clench her jaw, put her nose in the air (the "Napoleon" stance), and say, "I'm not divorcing him. We just can't live together." She did divorce him, eventually, but it took *a while.*

Pop, in New York, rented a room in a boardinghouse near our block. He went back to Columbia Presbyterian. Now he spent his eight-hour shift (never a minute more) going up and down the newly automated elevator, this time as a nurse's aide. When he wasn't working, he walked all over the city, from Washington Heights to the Battery, sometimes circumnavigating the whole of Manhattan Island. He bought newspapers, smoked his cigars, ate and read alone at various workmen's cafeterias.

Boss sought out "private-duty" clients, with sleepover duty. I was rarely home, leaving at eight o'clock in the morning for class and rehearsals, returning at midnight after performances, raiding the ice-box for whatever Boss may have left. I was breaking out on my own, earning a salary, and falling in love with a ballerina, Carolyn George.

Carolyn George

In spring 1952, a lovely, effervescent dancer showed up for company class, and I spotted her the minute she walked into the room. She had hazel eyes, a slim body. Quirky, she leaped and flitted all over the dance studio. She flew, and I was hard put to match the height of her leaps! Although her torso was considered skinny, she had a ballerina's muscled legs, and probably part of the reason for her extraordinary elevation was her combination of quick-twitch muscles and thin bones.

She came full of dreams to New York City and filled her days with dance. As she wrote in her diary:

> I shall never forget my first drive down the great white way. I was so excited, I planned to be a Broadway star, a dancing star. I moved into a room on 125th St. at Claremont Avenue. It was a small, dingy, green room, smeared with dirt. I tried to wash the walls clean with Spic and Span. One window looking out on a dirty air well and a shared bath, which I would timidly sneek into. Was I miserable? NO! My heart sang from dawn to dusk. I was alive and living in New York City. It was the

Carrie in Times Square, 1946

Carrie, happiest in the air—you can't keep a good girl down—Seattle, 1962

center of the universe and when anything happened here it was headlines around the world.

The School of American Ballet was said to be the best, so that's where
I spent my time and my few dollars. Two to three classes a day. Mostly I
ate caramel popcorn, sandwiches and coffee at Chock full o' Nuts. What
an adventure for a nice girl from Dallas, Texas, Highland Park, sheltered
from the realities of the outside world. But I seemed to be efficient. I
found out about auditions.

She got into the cast of *Bloomer Girl* and toured the country, switched
to the show *Oklahoma!* and eventually ended up as a ballerina at the San

Francisco Ballet. After three years, she decided she felt ready to dance for Balanchine, so in the spring of 1952, she had come to New York to audition. Lincoln Kirstein told her, "We like you, but there's no opening, and no money to pay an extra dancer. After our European tour this summer, there may be a place for you. Come back then." So Carolyn took another job. She auditioned for and accepted a role in Jerome Robbins's new musical, *Call Me Madam.* But within a few days, everything changed. In Carolyn's words,

I had barely assimilated into the show when a call came. "One of our dancers has had an appendectomy. Would you like to join the company for the European tour?" Would I! My first day off from *Call Me Madam,* I rushed to the City Center Theater to watch a performance of the ballet company, my future home. The ballet mistress, Vida Brown, took one look at me, saw I was healthy, and said, "We need you in our ballet company now!" Stunned, I was still trying to comprehend what she meant as I was whisked upstairs to the dressing room and pulled into pink tights. The opening ballet for the evening was *Swan Lake.* Someone pulled my hair back into a bun and stuck white feathers over my ears. Another dancer kept trying to fit toe shoes on my feet, and decided that Tanaquil LeClercq's shoes were the best fit. By the time I reached the wings (without makeup but in full costume), the Prince and the Swan Queen were just finishing their first encounter. The swans' entrance music started, and I was pushed onstage as one of the swans whispered, "Follow me." I was given whispered instructions throughout the ballet, what steps to dance and where to dance them, by the nearest swan. In what seemed like seconds, the Prince was kneeling in despair, the Swan Queen exiting dramatically, and the curtain closed. I was trembling like a leaf. Lots of hugs, smiles, and "Welcome to New York City Ballet" marked my hectic and unusual entrance to the company. In the course of the following week, I continued to perform each night in *Call Me Madam* while training my replacement for that show, found my birth certificate, got a passport, packed for the six-month tour, squeezed in company classes, and flew off to Spain with the New York City Ballet.

I fell in love right away! When she chatted with her pals in the hallways after class (they all called her Carrie), her giggle was infectious, and she had a charming, light, Texas drawl. I started asking around about her—the FBI couldn't have done better. Carrie came from High-

Carrie in a café. Is that a white horse kissing her head?

A train station break in Montreux, Switzerland; dreaming of Carrie as I watch her have a coffee

land Park, a suburb of Dallas—3641 Mockingbird Lane—had gone to Highland Park High School, had been a marksman on the rifle team, and was captain of the basketball team. She had trained in dance with the legendary Kingsbury Sisters, and had performed in summer stock at the Texas State Fair in Dallas. She had a younger sister, Marilyn; her ancestors were the first settlers of what was to become Waco, Texas, and they once owned most of the land along the adjacent Brazos River. One descendant on her mother's side, John Carroll, signed the Declaration of Independence.

After our six-month tour in 1952, it took me another three months to gather the courage to ask her for a date. Giggling, she said, "Okay." We sat together in the top row of the upper balcony for the City Opera's production of Rossini's *La Cenerentola*. I think Carrie was sitting next to me, and the stage seemed a half mile away. Opera and ballet were siblings at City Center. Though a ticket in the upper balcony cost a buck, I got ours for free. I was not yet eighteen; Carrie was twenty-four. She must have gone out with me from pity.

It took months of dating before I found enough boldness to kiss her; even then, it was only a brush of the lips. Later, when I tried to touch her breast with my hand, she gently pushed me away and let me know, in the sweetest way possible, that this was too much. "I don't want to be serious."

A curtain dropped. I was filled with teenage hurt. A switch went off, and I refused to talk to her, ignored her in class, avoided her in the hallways, and wouldn't look at her. As we were the highest jumpers in the company, Balanchine cast us together in the airborne third movement of *Symphony in C.* We would dance together, rehearse, and perform. Carrie smelled of the outdoors, healthy, fresh, clean, wet straw, and touching her onstage was thrilling. I would partner her beautifully there, and present her during the bows as a precious flower, but as soon as the curtain closed on the last bow, I would strut off without a word—as if the intimacy of partnering meant nothing. Jekyll and Hyde!

However, I stalked her secretly. In ballet class, I'd spot where she was at the barre and take a place on the opposite side of the room, yet watch her the whole time. I learned her rehearsal schedule and would peek into the room to ogle her. Outside the stage door, I would lurk across the street and follow her home or to a restaurant if she went out, to see who she was with. At night I shadowed her, gazing up at her apartment in the brownstone where she and her roommate (Arlouine Case) lived, trying to figure out which window was hers. I learned who her best buddies were, and then I wouldn't talk to them, either. Poor Carrie. I snubbed her and her friends . . . for a year!

That spring, Lew Christensen revived his ballet *Filling Station* for me. It was a superb role, and I had a delicious success. At the premiere, I was doing a series of leaps in a circle and heard the audience starting to cheer and applaud. I was amazed. I had never heard that before—for me. At the end of the ballet, waves of applause came from the audience, and I was called on for bow after bow. Dozens. Finally, I came offstage and had only minutes to change my costume for the next ballet. People crowded around—Virgil Thomson (the composer of *Filling Station*),* Paul Cad-

---

* Virgil, famous for his collaboration with Gertrude Stein on the opera *Four Saints in Three Acts,* was to become a good friend. He introduced me to the artist Maurice Grosser. Partners in the past, they had split but remained loving friends. "Jacques, it's Virgil Thomson here. Could you come over for lunch? I have someone I want you to meet. Maurice Grosser. He wants to paint a portrait of you. I'm at the Chelsea Hotel on Twenty-third Street." I answered, "Sure, I know the place. George Kleinsinger lives there. He composed the music for a Broadway show I was in, *Shinbone Alley.*" Virgil continued in his fey and pouty St. Louis, Missouri, voice, "Oh, George. He's got so many tropical plants in his apartment, it's a rain forest . . . he keeps a python for a pet! I don't know how he can play his piano with a snake wrapped around the piano legs and its head on the pedals," then coyly, "or further up."

Virgil was ovoid and infirm, stuck in his chair like a decadent cardinal glued onto a throne. Hairless, with fat little jowls and round eyes that seemed to have no eyelashes, he stared without blinking, and his rosebud cupid's mouth would open and close like a little fish. An ancient baby, who summoned maternal instincts—you wanted to stroke and cuddle him. Pricilla Rey, a dear friend of Virgil's and of mine, laughingly remarked, "All those women around him, their milk flowed in his presence."

Virgil was clever with a biting wit that somehow avoided nastiness; it was barbed, but without pain.

I arrived to find him surrounded by lady friends, and a nurse. "Jacques, dear, you've caught me with my court. These are my ladies. They worship me. Don't you, ladies? Oh, and this is Maurice Grosser. I know him well," glancing coyly at Maurice as if they had just been caught necking, "and you, Jacques, don't know him at all. But you will. . . . " A statement, pregnant with mysterious import, implying that the secrets of the Addams Family awaited me.

Maurice was nondescript, of medium height, medium everything, with a sallow complexion, but he had a gentle charm. And a few days later, I found myself sitting for a portrait by Maurice.

Awed by Lincoln Kirstein, Virgil often asked me, "What does Lincoln think of my music? . . . Does he mention me? You think Lincoln would want me to do another work for the ballet company?"

Paul Cadmus's drawing for Filling Station

Costume as rendered on Jacques, 1953

mus (costumes and decor),* and the celebrated modern choreographer José Limón (whom I had never met, but whose work I admired).† They had rushed backstage to meet and congratulate me as I exited the stage. I made excuses: "Thank you, thank you, I gotta change costumes. I'm in

---

* Paul Cadmus, a contemporary visual artist, was Lincoln's brother-in-law, and was hired by Lincoln to create scenery for many ballets. His sister, Fidelma Cadmus, was married to Lincoln, and they loved cats. Whatever love Fidelma and Lincoln shared was symbolized by their love for cats. Fidelma was fragile—around her, you felt she could crack and disintegrate. Paul had done a series of lifesize paintings of the Seven Deadly Sins, which were filled with brilliant colors, twisted shapes, vibrant, energetic, Gothic. They made you uncomfortable. Paintings you don't want to sleep with. Lincoln adored them. They lined the hallway of his house.

† Choreographer José Limón's *There Is a Time,* based on verses from Ecclesiastes, was groundbreaking, still a classic in the world of modern dance, as is his *Moor's Pavane.* He was very handsome and dramatic. I just remember him standing there trying to talk to me—I was trying to change costumes, he kept talking— and he had beautiful hands, and knew they were beautiful, so whenever he addressed you, he made sure his hands were between your faces—gesturing, posing, demonstrating, revolving so you could get a look at them from every angle. I liked him very much.

the next ballet." In subsequent days, fan letters arrived, among them, several from Charles Goren, the bridge master. As a result, I took up bridge. For years, I kept and treasured the superb actress Eileen Heckart's note, and still have the city planner Lewis Mumford's letter. The script and substance form the shape of a diamond, with my name at the apex and his at the base. One newspaper headlined its review, "Rookie Hits Home Run!"

Every morning Balanchine taught class. Occasionally, he would give private lessons to a chosen few. Nicholas Magallanes, Tanaquil LeClercq, Maria Tallchief, and I were a regular quartet. As scientists will test out their theories and hypotheses in experiments, Balanchine used these private lessons to test new ideas on technique. The exercises he developed on us were integrated into daily company class. Skills in speed and strength developed as a result, with emphasis on precision and extreme extensions, and maximum turnout.

Russian ballerinas are trained so that arms, head, hands, and torso fully participate in every movement. The entire body is integrated to communicate the full expression of the drama of dance. Balanchine was reminded of this when the Bolshoi Ballet first performed in New York in the 1950s. For several months after, our classes doubled in length, with a full hour devoted to simple, repetitive exercises using the arms, head, and upper torso.

Balanchine was always analyzing movement, and his style and technique changed as he experimented. There is still controversy over many of Balanchine's techniques. Here's an example. You know how you keep your heels on the floor in plié? Well, somewhere along the way, people started saying that Balanchine said, "Don't put your heels on the floor." He didn't say that. When dancing classical ballet, Balanchine had discovered that keeping the weight of your body lightly on the smallest possible place—directly underneath you, and on the balls of your feet—affords greater agility and quickness. He never said, "Don't put your heels down" but, rather, "Focus weight on the balls of your feet, not on your heels." That was Vladimiroff, too.

After the success of *Filling Station* and back in rehearsals, I was still my boisterous and effusive self. Then . . . Carrie would walk into the room. Her friends would wave and shout, "Hi, Carrie!" I would repair to the rosin box and pretend to fix my shoe. Carrie and her friends thought, "What an arrogant brat! Success has gone to *his* head! He's creepy."

WOOED BY HOLLYWOOD, OCTOBER 1953

Dancing *Filling Station* that summer in San Francisco, I came offstage on a high. During the performance, I had knocked off thirteen pirouettes in slow motion, my record to that date. In the wings, two suntanned guys accosted me—Hollywood types, good-looking, laid-back, and dressed in polo shirts, brown loafers, and sport coats splashed with pastel-colored handkerchiefs. "I'm a producer and filmmaker, Jack Cummings," one barked at me. He pointed. "And this is Stanley Donen, he's the director. We're doing a movie, *Seven Brides for Seven Brothers,* and we want you to be one of the brothers." They stared at me expectantly, waiting for the significance of their statement to buckle my knees.

Over dinner they later filled me in with details. *Seven Brides for Seven Brothers* was to be the title of their movie, a sunny, Hollywood adaptation of Plutarch's dark tale *Rape of the Sabine Women.* Michael Kidd was to choreograph. I was ignorant of Stanley Donen's or Jack Cummings's accomplishments (and there were many), but I'd read Plutarch, and I knew of Michael Kidd. Michael had had a career with American Ballet Theatre, and was well known as a superb dancer, performer, and choreographer. He had even danced with Ballet Caravan, the early company Lincoln Kirstein had conjured.

When I told Balanchine Michael Kidd was choreographing the movie, he raised a finger like a pontiff, sniffed, and pronounced judgment, "Good!" Then he warned, "You know, Jacques, if you're not careful, they will own you. You will have sold your soul for seven years." He arranged for his lawyer, Mr. Krohn, to negotiate my contract with MGM. On Balanchine's advice, Krohn contracted me to return from Hollywood by February 1954, in time to star in Balanchine's new production of *The Nutcracker.* Within the week, Balanchine gave me a three-month leave of absence from the company, though it meant missing the last few weeks of our upcoming European tour and part of our winter season in New York.

ITALY 1953

So I said yes to Cummings and Donen and went off with the NYCB to Europe. The tour was grueling and glorious, with most of it in Italy, and I danced dozens of new roles—some of them with Carrie. Every time I took her hand to go onstage, I felt a surge in my heart. Offstage, I wouldn't speak to her, even in Italian.

Dancing Hugh Laing's role in *Lilac Garden* was my big challenge of that tour. My dressing-room mates thought it hilarious that this teenager (me) was dancing as the object of Nora Kaye's affections in Antony Tudor's great romantic ballet. Nora, the ballet diva, was some fifteen years my senior, already in her thirties and thinking of retirement.* My role had been created for Hugh, who was much older than I. He was graced with matinee-idol looks and had passionate, dramatic energy. There I was in his role, boyishly welcoming the amorous advances of an older woman. "You change the whole dynamic," the elegant Brooks Jackson drawled in his nasal voice. "She's robbing the cradle . . ." Brooks played Nora's elderly husband in the ballet. "Seducing a baby in his playpen." The sophisticated Italian audiences loved the ballet, and we were a big success. As youths, many may have been devirgined by their babysitters, cooks, housekeepers, gardeners, or close relatives.

Since 1952, Balanchine's buddy Leon Leonidoff had arranged our European tours. For Italy, he had hired three Florentine stagehands to work as crew, and I ended up hanging around with them. Alfredo, dapper, always dressed in a suit jacket, struck me as a confidence man; tiny Osvaldo, charming, laughing, and active as a buzzing insect, always

---

* After that 1953 tour of Europe, Nora (who inspired Jerry Robbins's fantastic ballet *The Cage*) and her lover, the to-be-world-famous movie director Herbert Ross (*Pennies from Heaven, Turning Point*), decided to quit dance. They bought a Mercedes, and were passing through the Black Forest at breakneck speed on the autobahn, when, on a whim, Nora opened a window and flung her toe shoes out. "Enough, I'm going to live! I'm not going to dance anymore, I'm going to *eat!* Herbert, head for Italy," she demanded. Within a few weeks, she was the size of a horse. When she died in 1987, Herbert arranged for a spot at Westwood Memorial Park in Los Angeles (also the site of the graves of Marilyn Monroe, Jack Lemmon, Walter Matthau, and many other entertainment luminaries), and, when he died, Herbert had himself buried there—*on top of her!* Isaac Stern, who had previously been married to Nora, refused to speak to her for years after she and Herbert toured Europe. He was furious because they'd bought a German car. Slights real or imagined are hard to let go of—Isabel Brown told me that on her deathbed, Nora refused to let Jerry Robbins in to say goodbye—because he had named several artists during the McCarthy hearings in the 1950s. Jerry was left sobbing outside her closed hospital door.

had something to say. Osvaldo was a kind of Sancho Panza to the hero of the trio, tall Gulio, who could have been lifted out of a Caravaggio painting. A beautiful hunk of Northern Italian male, Gulio's classical profile, heroic Roman nose, and smooth, ivory skin graced a body on par with Michelangelo's *David*. He had the entire company, male and female, undulating with desire. None of the trio was ever without a cigarette in his mouth.

When we had an engagement in a city, the company would book, in advance, a room in a hotel near the theater. If you didn't like the hotel, you were responsible for paying the first night, and then could go find your own digs. We had no per diem, only our salaries. Mine was thirty-five dollars a week. Most dancers let the company book them for the first night, then wandered the streets to find a cheap pension for the rest of the stay. On the advice of my three Italian buddies, I developed a penny-pinching system that worked: don't book a room in advance, follow Osvaldo's lead.

"Not to worry, we no have a room, we find *albergo* when we get there," Osvaldo assured me. Therefore, fresh off the bus or train, the four of us would lug our bags to the stage door of the opera house. Immediately, Osvaldo would burst into a torrent of Italian, to various members of the stage crew, seeking advice on a place to stay. We usually ended up in the homes of the theater's cleaning women. These Italian families had so little—often, they gave me their children's room and crowded their young ones onto mats on the floor of their bedroom. I paid the equivalent of one U.S. dollar a night—620 lire. The arrangement included a light supper, left on the kitchen table for my after-performance repast—usually several cheeses, bread, olives, and, occasionally, a tomato. A carafe of water as well, and, every once in a while, one of wine. Simple, delicious, heart-and-stomach warming.

This system worked—until Naples. Decades earlier, Mussolini had promised to make the Italian trains run on time, but since he had been hung off a balcony, the Italians (and their train system) reverted to a more lax sense of time. The bullet train the Italians were so proud of, the Rapido, ran four hours behind schedule, and we arrived in Naples at two o'clock in the morning. The whole company boarded the bus that had been patiently waiting, and drove off to the arranged hotel, leaving the four of us with our bags on the station platform. "Osvaldo," I cried, "the Teatro San Carlo's been closed for hours! How are we going to find a family to stay with?" He seemed a little embarrassed, but assured me, "*Sì, sì . . . sì!* No worry, no worry, Jacques! We find a bed." "*Dove?* Osvaldo, where?" I bellowed. With a sheepish grin, he answered, "Oh, hee, hee, hee. Now we go out to find women of the street, and we pay to sleep in their beds." With that, the three of them picked up their bags and scattered. I found a bench in the train station.

On the previous year's tour, crossing borders from one country to another, I had discovered that at an Italian bank, you could take a U.S. dollar and say, "I want French francs," and you'd get 350. Take a dollar's worth of lire (620) and say, "I want to exchange these Italian lire for French francs," and you'd get 380, thirty francs more! In the Italians' eyes, their lire had greater value than the rest of the world acknowledged, especially the French. "Holy smokes, Jacques," I thought. "Take your dollars, exchange them for lire, then buy French francs in Italy, and store those francs for the company's next engagement in France. You're going to make a profit!"

On my day off, I'd head for the bank, change five dollars to lire, and then scoot over to the Cambio (a special bank for exchanging foreign currency), where my dollar's worth of lire bought me the thirty extra French francs. It was big finance, and it took several hours of my day. By the end of the afternoon, I'd have gained a profit of about forty cents (?!)—less the fees for changing money. Only now, as I'm writing this, does it strike me that, with those fees, I must have been losing money with each transaction.*

In Milan, we performed at the famous La Scala opera house for several weeks. I made friends with several of the Italian dancers, especially the young ones—fourteen-year-old Carla Fracci,[†] already lighting up the room with her beauty and talent; and Mario Pistoni, not much older than I, a superb technician. They laughed at my atrocious Italian and stew of assorted languages, French, English, Spanish, and Italian, melded and spiced with mime. "*Insalata di lingua mista*" they dubbed it. They arranged for me to join their morning classes, eight fifteen to nine fifteen a.m. Why so early? NYCB was in residence at the theater, so had command of the dance studio, and needed it all day. That left early morning as the only alternative for the Italians. I'd be up by six

---

* Years later I asked a friend, the financial genius George Soros, how to invest in currency exchange. His answer: "DON'T!"

[†] Years later, I had the privilege of partnering Carla Fracci in the pas de deux from *Swan Lake* in a tiny space on a floor of cement. It was a television special and Carla's first performance in the U.S.

a.m. and on my way by seven, arriving at the theater in time to join my Italian friends in their class. Madame Bulnes, the legendary dance teacher from Argentina, presided. She had revitalized the training and quality of the La Scala company, and taught a brutal, vigorous class. As soon as it ended, I'd head to the theater buffet, gobble several brioches, which settled in my stomach, well drenched with eight to ten double espressos. By nine thirty a.m., hyped and jagged, I'd be in Balanchine's class, twitching and relishing every leap and spin.

During the short break between company class and rehearsal, Balanchine would test me playfully, "Do ten pirouettes, and I give you a hundred lire." Then would follow a slew of virtuoso dance steps to test me, dredged up from his past experience and incredible imagination. The commencement of rehearsals stopped our games. We danced from eleven a.m. to six p.m., with an hour break for lunch. At six p.m., I'd race out, grab a bite, and return to the theater in time to put on makeup, do a warm-up, and, as there were always last-minute injuries, fit in eleventh-hour emergency rehearsals for replacements. Then, into costume, and, by eight o'clock, be onstage ready for the call. "Places, dancers. Curtain going up."

Milan's buildings bore the scars of World War II, pockmarked with bulletholes and shrapnel indentations. The local Italian people, having endured the Mussolini and Hitler regimes some eight years before, had their own scars. Ballet fans saved their lire for months to buy a ticket to see the *Americani* in the New York City Ballet. No one can imagine the success in those days. How we were loved and admired.

The last performance in each city was always triumphant. As in London in 1950 and our European tour in 1952, the applause at the end of the performance lasted close to a half an hour. We'd take bow after bow. The curtain would close, but the audience kept applauding and stamping, so up it would go, then down and up and down and up, dozens and dozens of times. Thrilling as it was, the exhausted dancers eventually importuned the stage manager, "Bring in the fire curtain!" It was the only way to silence the enthusiasm and determination of the fans.

With matinees Saturday and Sunday, we did eight performances a week. Monday was our day off, and my Italian dancer friends often took me to the local *piscina* (swimming pool), and I treated them to lunch at the local trattorias. Biffi Scala, the restaurant next to La Scala, was Balanchine's favorite hangout. I could never afford it, but he relished describing to me the meals he enjoyed there—lunch, dinner, and after-performance feasting. I'd be waiting in the wings ready to make an entrance in *Lilac Garden,* and he'd be whispering to me, "You know, Biffi Scala—the *tortellini alla panna.* It has a little hint of nutmeg."

In Venice, one night after the curtain came down at the Teatro La Fenice, famished, I headed out with Osvaldo and company to eat. Yuri Bardyguine,* our stage manager for the tour and Osvaldo's boss, latched on to us. A kind of sophisticated, glib Russian survivalist who spoke half a dozen languages, Yuri addressed Giulio, Osvaldo, and Alfredo in machine-gun Italian. I had no idea what they were discussing. Suddenly, Osvaldo beckoning scooted off, leading us through several twisting passageways, over and around various canals, to a narrow cul de sac enclosed by a few three-story buildings. We stopped on the doorstep of the house with the red light. Blabbing nervously, "Hey! Where are we going to eat?" They'd answer, *"Oh, senti! Un momento!"* Abruptly, Yuri turned around and said to me, "Let's just go in for a minute and take a look."

We were greeted by the madam, a tough, flat-faced woman in her fifties, flouncing in a print frock, with a cigarette in her mouth and her hair dyed jet-black. She led us to a small sitting room decorated with faux Middle Eastern touches—its rug and curtains patterned in dark browns, deep reds, and blues. There was a table with a tasseled lamp, a long sofa, and several foldout chairs arranged in a semicircle facing a bare wall. "Pass-a-port." Yuri produced his and told me, "Show her your passport." Then the entire group fell into machine-gun Italian, with Yuri nodding in my direction. The madam, her anthracite eyes dancing, gestured for us to sit, and left the room.

Yuri announced, "For your education, it's time, you're eighteen."

They didn't come out all at once. First, one lady entered, probably the same age as the madam. For a moment, I thought they were sisters. As she paraded around, wearing shiny black high heels, black fishnet stockings and panties, and a pointy black bra, I couldn't take my eyes off her stomach. A half a dozen jagged scars descended from her ribcage to disappear somewhere beneath those black panties. I imagined a consort of cesareans. She lingered just long enough to sit on Yuri's lap and cadge a cigarette.

Next came a redhead about the same age as number one, her dyed hair a clump of dried straw. She wore red shoes, and I never saw anyone

* Yuri went on to marry the ballerina Patricia Wilde, one of NYCB's stars.

more bowlegged. My eyes didn't venture any higher. The third was the youngest, in her teens or early twenties, with pale, white skin, but really fat, pregnant-fat. The mandatory blonde, she wore white shoes with thick, tall heels and white cotton knee socks adorned with a blue garter just below the right knee. This time my eyes worked their way up. A scant piece of see-through gauze, tied at the waist with a bow, in no way obstructing the view of her frilly, pink panties. Her belly rose like the moon in full from those panties. At the top of the moon rested a white half-bra, and you could see her maraschino-cherry nipples popping out. She was pretty, with pale blue eyes, a Kewpie-doll mouth, and a blue ribbon in her hair.

I was so ashamed . . . of us. My heart went out to the women. When each came out, I would act the gentleman, standing, nodding, and saying, "You are very lovely, *mille grazie, signorina, mille grazie.*"

During their varied entrances and exits, a gleeful Yuri would question, "Well, what about this one, Jacques? Hey, do you like this one?" Alternately blanching with fear, then blushing with shame, I squeaked out, "No, no, no, I don't want to. I don't want to." Osvaldo, Giulio, and Alfredo tried to shrink into the sofa.

Moments after number three had been displayed, the madam reentered, accompanied by one and two. The room was crowded for *the choice,* with the women standing around the bare wall. "Come on, Jacques!" Yuri urged. "It won't take long, we'll wait for you!" I stood, bowed to the ladies, turned and faced Yuri, and announced, "I'll find a trattoria myself." My Italian buddies leaped to their feet, saying, "Oh no, no, we'll all go," and so we fled.

Later, I thought to myself, "Maybe when Yuri was a boy, his father, or brother, or some buddy took him to a whorehouse." He must have felt this was a rite of passage, something necessary for teenagers to go through. Yuri thought he was doing me a favor. The incident tainted my relationship with him and the three Italians. I never had the same sense of trust, and hung around them less and less.

On the first day in a new city, heading for the opera house, we dancers often stopped, agog, to watch the Italian stage crews unload from the lorry four-hundred-pound costume and scenery trunks. The crewmen—most of them scrawny, some of them aged, and all of them smoking—would strap one of these trunks to the back of one of their fellows, who, in turn, doubled over, would wend his way up the stairs, transporting the load to a stage-level storage area. We were their audi-

Janie Mason in LA, during NYCB's tour in California

ence, and they loved our applause as, one by one, they would stagger up the stairs, their cigarettes cramped in their mouths, puffing like a loco motive. It was their moment in the spotlight.

Our company class also had its dramatic performers, and the star was Janie Mason. A superb dancer with excellent technique, Janie was extremely beautiful, and so nearsighted that without her glasses, her world was a blur. Think: full breasts, high on her torso, and, balancing those breasts, lower down, a pair of perfect, rounded buttocks— a petite, teenage Brigitte Bardot. Janie arrived for morning class early, even before the stage crew had turned on the work lights. When the rest of us showed up, Janie would have dramatically posed herself on center stage, splayed in a split under the ghost light (a bare light bulb on a stand in center stage), and reading an enormous book. Every once in a while, she would shift her split, sometimes with the right leg front, then the left, then back again, without ever interrupting her reading. Engrossed, Janie would read right up until Balanchine started the pliés.

"What are you reading that's so interesting?" he sometimes asked. Janie's act never changed, though the books did! For several weeks, she pored over the dictionary; next, her nose was buried in a volume of Encyclopædia Britannica, or some philosophical tome, Nietzsche or Kierkegaard. A week later, it was Buddhist texts, then she switched to *The Prophet,* by Kahlil Gibran. It seemed she carried her own library.

When I read Terry Southern's book *Candy,** I thought he must have known Janie. An easy mark, Janie handed out money to anyone on the street she thought looked needy. Often, the stage doorman would have to bar crowds of street urchins and beggars who had followed her to the theater. Big-hearted Betty Cage,† our company manager, paid Janie's hotel bill several times, as she had given away her paycheck.

Janie had other idiosyncrasies. One day, she went to the dressing room early, collected all the ballerinas' tights (more than forty pairs), and, as a favor, laundered them. The problem was the tights were different colors, so, when laundered together, they came out splotched and tie-dyed. "Oh, I didn't know that would happen," her heart-shaped lips pouted.

Carrie told me that more than anything, Janie's eating habits irritated those who shared her dressing room. She would purchase food and bring it to the theater, leaving most of it uneaten overnight on her makeup table. You would think the rats would get it, but no! It was the cats! Brought in as pets to rid the theater of vermin, they had long ago staged a coup and taken over. Treated royally by the stage crew, they were talismans, fearless and arrogant. They would head for Janie's makeup table, gobble up her food, declare squatting rights in the practice bags and costumes, and mark their new territory with urine. No one dared touch them. They especially liked to lick the glue that hardened the tips of the dancers' toe shoes.

The feline capital of Italy's opera houses was the Teatro San Carlo in Naples, where cats easily outnumbered ballerinas. On opening night, in the middle of Balanchine's ballet *Symphony in C,* we discovered their power. In the finale of that sunlit celebration of Bizet's music, a large, gray tiger slowly and saucily padded across the back of the stage, up

---

* *Candy,* by Terry Southern and Mason Hoffenberg (G. P. Putnam, 1964).
† Betty introduced Carrie, and many others, to the art of tai chi. She coauthored a book on tai chi with Edward Maisel. In the years after Balanchine's death she led a class in tai chi until she lost her appetite for living, stopped eating, was hospitalized, and died.

from stage left to upstage right. The orchestra kept playing, and the dancers never stopped, but the gray tiger did. Pausing for a moment, up in center, she cast a blasé gaze at the audience, stretched, preened, yawned, and then ambled off. The audience erupted into cheers.

Everyone traveled with a wardrobe trunk. Tours averaged from three and a half to six months, and in many places you couldn't buy soap, makeup, or toilet paper, so the trunks served as storage for haberdashery, groceries, hardware, and apothecary needs. In addition, we all had a large, black, metal case to carry makeup, dancing shoes, and assorted practice clothes. These, the company transported for us. Our personal suitcases, we lugged around ourselves. Between cities, the company usually booked a couple of railroad cars, generally added to the back of the train, and those trips sometimes lasted as long as eighteen or nineteen hours. We brought our own food on board and shared lavish, winesodden feasts during these trips, while playing continual games of poker, canasta, bridge, or assorted word games.

Upon arrival, being at the back of the train, the dancers found themselves miles from the entrance to a terminal, where the taxis and buses were. No porters around, no pushcarts, and, back then, no wheels on your luggage, so all of us, exhausted, dragged our own suitcases—except Janie. She would manage, somehow, to get her enormous suitcase, bigger than herself, off the train and onto the platform. Then, she would pose, and wait. With a helpless, bewildered look on her face, and her lascivious curves, she didn't wait long. A honey trap! The siren soon drew Romeos vying for the privilege of carrying her suitcase. As the commedia dell'arte scene unfolded, the rest of us would stand around to enjoy. A handsome and vigorous Italian swain would approach. "*Oh! Signorina! Per favore* . . ." Another would shove him aside. "No, no, *permette,* I would be honored, *cara signorina!*" Beaming to Janie, and sometimes adding a gallant bow, the most aggressive would finally seize the suitcase, then blanch. In her suitcase, besides her library, Janie kept several iron exercise weights and a pair of iron shoes that she wore around her hotel room, explaining to her roommate, "Oh, they strengthen the quadriceps and slim the gluteus maximus." Romeo, macho and determined, would crouch down, grit his teeth, and manhandle the burden to his shoulder, then stagger all the way down the platform, following Janie's swaying buttocks to the taxi stand. The other suitors scattered, breathing sighs of relief.

If we were crossing a border and had to go through customs, an even better scene ensued, for Janie was a sure thing to have her bags searched. When the iron shoes were revealed, the customs agent would usually call out, "Hey, Giuseppe, *vedere*! Look!" Then, as her other treasures were revealed, more and more Marios, Carlos, and Giovannis would rush over. What, besides the barbells and iron shoes, emerged from Janie's bag? Well, besides the assortment of reading material, there were wheels of brie and other assorted cheeses wrapped in panties; zucchini, broccoli, and artichokes tucked into bras, shoes, and sweaters; and many a stocking leg stuffed with fruits and nuts. Ah, Janie, with your goofy and passionate nature how bizarre you were, and how much fun. She was our company mascot.

Janie left the company after a few years. We heard she had gotten married, and, rumor had it, in the Dominican Republic, wearing a topless wedding gown. Years later, a story circulated that Janie was living in Mexico and had adopted the unwanted babies of various prostitutes. There was even the suggestion that the babies had come from Janie's own establishment. I met her again in Sun Valley, Idaho, about twenty years ago. She was married and proud to tell me that she had put several of her adopted children through college. (The following year, I heard—read—she had been arrested. It seemed she lost her temper in a fight with her husband, and went at him with a pair of scissors, or a kitchen knife, whatever.)

Since I wasn't speaking to Carrie and had dumped my Italian trio, I began to hang out with Barbara Bocher, a teenage ballerina. Another corps de ballet girl, Allegra Kent, perhaps the youngest dancer on the tour, would tag along wherever Barbara and I went. Allegra drove me nuts.

It was my habit to gobble two or three full meals at a sitting—insalata, pasta, a main course (sometimes a second), followed by another round of insalata and pasta, then several desserts—always with a bottle of vino, though neither Barbara nor Allegra drank. Occasionally, as an epilogue, I'd order a third pasta. Barbara would order one sensible dish, then politely converse and wait for me to finish stuffing myself, planning to get a spoonful of one of my desserts. Allegra never said a word, except early on, when we first ordered, as the waiter would stand, expectantly. I would say, "So, Allegra, what are you going to have?" She would stare at me, and reply dramatically. "What do you mean?" I'd repeat, "I mean, what do you want to order? What are you going to eat?" She'd answer, "Oh, we're eating?" Irritated, I'd run through the

On tour with Allegra Kent

. . . and with a pigeon, 1953

menu, describing the entrees I knew so well, and launch myself into a sales pitch. When I finally ran down, she would warble, "Nothing." I'd bellow, "Come on! You have to eat something!" Allegra would then squeak out "Oh, alright, then, *fagiolini senza burro*"—green beans without butter. Convinced she meant to insult their menu, the Italian waiter was livid. She never relented. For three and a half months, all through Italy, she ate only plain, unseasoned vegetables. We got to calling her "Allegra Senza Burro."

Shaun O'Brien would ask, "Hey, Daisy, who are you dancing with tonight?" "Senza Burro," I'd reply, and the whole dressing room knew it was Allegra.

Trieste, a seaport on the Adriatic, was claimed for Yugoslavia by their Communist dictator, Marshal Tito. Behind the scenes, Austria was lobbying to make Trieste part of their country. The Italian newspapers countered, "Trieste belongs to Italy!" Since the Cold War was in full bloom, the U.S. government actively supported Italy. Most of the dockworkers of Trieste were communists and favored Yugoslavia, so strikes and protests agitated the city constantly, and the ensuing chaos generated riots on a regular schedule.

Posted on the bulletin board backstage at the theater, we'd find a notice, "Riots planned for tomorrow. Get to the theater early before matinee." I remember walking down a bustling street on a Saturday around ten thirty a.m., and hearing the iron shutters and gates on storefronts being closed down behind me, "Bang! Bang!" The sound spread along the side streets, like cages slamming shut in prison cells, one after the other, throughout the city, and not a cop in sight. As I made my way to the stage door, I glanced back. People had vanished from the streets.

Inside the theater, everything was normal. Outside, thousands of protesters had materialized to sweep down the avenues, chanting and singing songs, waving placards and banners. Riots erupted when rival mobs crossed at intersections. The theater crew told us that, parked in lorries on side streets, the carabinieri—police—waited in case they were needed. Despite the emotional thunderstorms, it was all over within an hour. Stores reopened, our orchestra tuned up, and an enthusiastic citizenry discarded their picket signs and filled the theater for the matinee.

I left for Hollywood after the matinee. My last image: an exhausted Todd Bolender, hacking with bronchitis, stretched out on a wardrobe trunk, trying to catch his breath before his next entrance. Dancers were dropping like flies with injuries, illness, and exhaustion, and the tour had several weeks left to go. I felt like a deserter.

Carrie told me about the end of that tour, in Amsterdam, with a ballet company so depleted that when the choreography called for the entire cast to appear in the finale, "there were more injured dancers watching from the wings than there were healthy dancers performing on the stage." The finale of the ballet, *Bourrée Fantasque,* features several lines of dancers in rows across the stage, eight dancers to a line, "But in my line," Carrie laughed, "there were only two of us left—Janie Mason all the way stage right, and me, stage left, looking at each other across the six empty spaces."

HOLLYWOOD

From Trieste, I took the Rapido to Milan, and boarded a red-eye flight to Hollywood. No jets in those days, so propeller planes required several stops for refueling and changing crews. The trip lasted two days. Despite exhaustion, descending into Hollywood was magical: the city lights glowed reddish orange, a million campfires burning through smog. Jack Donaldson met me at the airport. A caricature of a struggling Hollywood agent, all bluster and hyperbole. Jack was a ballet groupie, young looking for his late forties, though he already showed a hint of double chin. He had latched on to me, but his biggest love was the movie business—the wheeling and dealing, the gossip, and the stars. "Do you realize what an opportunity this is?" he harped. "Jack Cummings is one of the great producers at MGM, and Stanley Donen's a legend! Have you ever heard of *On the Town* or *Singin' in the Rain?* You can't get any better. Gene Kelly is getting older, and the silver screen will be looking for a new, athletic, male dancing star! You could be it!" Dear Jack tried his best. He had ambitions for me; I had none. Doing a film was exciting, but as a career move? No. For me, it was just a game to play for a while, another challenge, a new cast.

Another of Jack's clients, Morgan Jones, owned a small house on upper Laurel Canyon Road, and he rented me a room. Morgan, an actor in his mid-twenties, had a solid, muscular body, blue eyes, and the freckles of a redhead. Charming and matter-of-fact, he offered a litany of rooming-together details. "There's the door. The key's in the flowerpot. This is my shelf in the fridge. If you're up early, tiptoe." Then he revealed his great secret. "It'll make me millions!" he boasted. "Except for my house, everybody in LA has a swimming pool, and those pools need to be kept clean. Mostly leaves and smog dust. It's hard to reach the stuff in the middle. But . . ." He held up a small bottle of clear liquid. "With these mystery drops, cleaning's a piece of cake! Here, I'll show you." Morgan filled his biggest kitchen pot with water, scattered crumpled leaves and broken matchsticks over the surface, and, with a tiny eyedropper and a dramatic wave of his hand, hocus-pocused a single drop into the center of the pot. Immediately, the floating debris moved outward, in concentric circles, to the sides of the pot. " 'Morgan's Magic Drops,' " he exclaimed. "Now, all that debris is easy to scoop up from the sides!" "Wow! How did you do that?" I asked. He nodded with self-satisfaction. "It's a secret." Was he nuts, or was he on to something big? "But Morgan," I persisted, "swimming pools are big. How are you going to get those drops into the center of the pool?" Preening, he whispered, "Squirt gun."

Jack Donaldson laughed. "He's pulling your leg. It's nothing but household detergent [a new product in the early 1950s]. It has that effect on water."

I discovered the difference between Hollywood and NYCB within the first few days. Michael Kidd would say, "Call for the brothers— tomorrow nine o'clock." I would get there at eight a.m., don my tights and ballet shoes, do a barre, and by nine be warmed up, dripping with sweat, and ready to dance. That's how it was at the ballet. Not so on the movie set. At nine, a couple of the crew, the assistant director, and a few of the brothers would wander in with cups of coffee and doughnuts, schmoozing or reading a newspaper, and would make themselves comfortable. "What's happening?" I'd pipe up. "Is rehearsal canceled?" "Nah, we don't start on time." I don't know if that's true today with the big salaries and budgets, but in those days, it struck me as unprofessional.

Eventually, Michael and Stanley would show up, probably coming in from an earlier production meeting, so we usually started rehearsing around ten o'clock. At eleven o'clock, you'd hear, "Coffee break!" and everyone would stop for more coffee and doughnuts. Some half hour later, we would be back rehearsing. Between eleven thirty and one, work would get done, till "Break for lunch. Back at two." After lunch, we rarely started on time, usually a half hour to forty-five minutes late. Exact time became elastic, but we always broke at five.

I resisted for a while, doing another ballet class during lunch so that at two o'clock I'd be ready to go again. Finally, I caved in and joined the culture, wolfing down the coffee and doughnuts, beginning to salivate just before lunch, and dashing to the commissary to gobble. I gained twenty pounds before the film was done. After lunch, cross-country running through the sets with Russ Tamblyn, and, often, playing handball with Tommy Rall against the sides of the sound studios, until the movie machine got moving again.

Russ taught me how to jump from an eighteen-foot height, and, on hitting the ground, take up the force with a body roll. "It's how they train parachutists to land," he confided. He was a tumbler who had studied dance and used both skills to great effect. He was a superb actor, insightful, thoughtful, and the scenes he did during the shoot always seemed the truest.

The female star of the movie, playing the role of Milly, was Jane Powell—lovely, petite, and vivacious. I immediately developed a crush on her, but I was shy. Years later, I heard that Jane told an audience, "Oh, Jacques d'Amboise? He was one of the brothers, but he never said much. I thought it was because he was French and didn't speak English."

On the romantic scene, Morgan tried to set me up with a girl. One weekend, with dreams of seduction, I cooked her a dinner, but after ten minutes or so of necking (pathetic on my part), she got up and left. After the first few kisses, she realized the teenager on the other end of her lips was a neophyte. Although I had just turned nineteen, emotionally I was eleven. I cleaned the dishes, relieved.

I had no car, but it didn't matter; I couldn't drive. To get to Culver City and the MGM studios, I'd leave Morgan's house and walk down from upper Laurel Canyon Road to the taxi stand on Franklin Avenue and Hollywood, about two miles. When film shooting started, the call would be, "Brothers in makeup at six a.m.!" which meant I had to be on my way by four. A rare car would pass me on Laurel Canyon Road, and I'd thrust out my thumb, but never had any luck. Until one morning.

A black sedan barreling down Laurel Canyon Road stopped. "Hi! Gee, thanks. Wow. I never thought anybody would be out this early," I jabbered, clambering into the elegant car's passenger seat. The profile of a stunning, strong-featured man greeted my gaze. He didn't say a word; his hands clutched the steering wheel. In an attempt to fill the palpable void emanating from my mysterious driver, I never stopped talking. "I'm just going down as far as you can take me. I gotta get to

Culver City." Big silence. "Usually, I catch a cab at Franklin and Holly-wood. You see, I'm shooting a movie, *Seven Brides for Seven Brothers . . .*" Babble, babble, babble. We stopped at Franklin and Hollywood, and he leaned across my body and pushed open the passenger door at my side. "Gee, thanks, thanks a lot. That was a big help, getting me down here. Well, so long, now!" I closed the door, and the car zoomed off.

Every morning, around four fifteen a.m., Monday through Friday, the sedan would drive down, my thumb would go out, and he'd pick me up. Over the next three weeks, I blurted out my life story—yammering about New York, the ballet, my family, adventures on the *Seven Brides* set, and gossip about the cast. This taciturn man, I suspected, was ago-nizingly shy. He exuded masculinity, and had gorgeous skin, with a healthy blush of red stroked across his cheek. I never remember seeing the left side of his face. And always, at Franklin and Hollywood, he'd lean across my lap to push open my door. Once, after he'd given me this cue to exit, I held the door open. "You've been coming down at the crack of dawn every morning to give me a ride. I'm thinking you must be an angel from heaven. Where do you live? And what do you do?" He mumbled, "Last house on the top of the hill," waited for me to close the door, then bent his head as I shut it gently and he took off.

One morning, the car didn't show, and I never saw him again.

Morgan was intrigued. "Let's go up and find the house." We drove up the hill, winding and winding, until we came upon a plateau at the top, with the most incredible view overlooking Hollywood, and crowned with a solitary house. There was no sedan in the driveway, but I insisted, "This must be it—it's supposed to be the last house on the top of the hill." "Holy shit!" Morgan said. "I know this house! You've been picked up by Rock Hudson and never knew it!"

In the plot, the seven brothers, all redheads, had been christened by their father at birth with biblical names—in alphabetical order. The firstborn, Adam, was played by Howard Keel, already a star, and mag-nificent. Howard was giant in stature, bighearted, big-voiced, a big man with big talent. He met his match in energy, talent, and charm, if not in height, with his costar, the adorable Jane Powell. The number two brother, Benjamin, was acted by Jeff Richards, a handsome, laconic actor. Gossip reported he had been a star baseball player before Thespis touched him. Then came number three—Caleb—Matt Mattox, the best dancer of us all. He was a disciple of Jack Cole, the genius who revolutionized Broadway dance. Jerome Robbins, Michael Bennett, and especially Bob Fosse were deeply influenced by Jack's innovations in dance vocabulary and choreography. Matt Mattox was among the greatest male dancers I have ever seen. We became friends for life. Daniel and Ephraim—brothers four and five, Marc Platt and I—were always paired together, and worked as a team. And next to last, the F in the alphabet, Frankincense, was Tommy Rall. A major talent, he was destined to win a Tony on Broadway for *Milk and Honey,* and star (as an opera singer) in the title role of *Le Jongleur de Notre-Dame* in Sarah Caldwell's Opera Company of Boston. Last of the seven was Gideon, boyish Russ Tamblyn. Within a few years, his star would light up the movie *West Side Story.* Curiously, the title, *Seven Brides for Seven Brothers,* gives equal billing to the brides, but the movie was truly about the brothers. We kidnapped the women and, after sundry adventures, won them over as our brides. Michael paired me with Virginia Gibson (her original name had been Gorsky). She was fresh like a spring flower, a freckle-faced American beauty, with class. I lucked out.

Work generally finished around five o'clock, and Marc would drop me off in Hollywood. There, I would wander around, maybe catch a flick, and haunt the sex shops on Hollywood Boulevard. Compared to today, they were antiseptic, even prim. Usually, I'd pig out at Musso & Frank, where marvelously blasé, worldly, old-time waiters reigned as kings over their sections of tables. Filmmaking was old hat to Marc; in the past, he had starred with Rita Hayworth and Janet Blair in several movies, and he constantly griped to me that playing one of seven brothers was a comedown. Marc had changed his name several times. In his Ballet Russe days, he was known as Platoff, because that surname sounded more Russian. Name changing was a virus. I knew Jerome Robbins had been born Rabinowitz; Nora Kaye, Koreff; and even our choreographer, Michael Kidd, had originally been named Michael Greenwald. But who was I to talk? The Boss had morphed me from Joseph Jacques Ahearn to Jacques Joseph d'Amboise.

For a while, one of the brides, Julie Newmar,* replaced the vanished Rock Hudson as my a.m. chauffeur. We'd make a date at the taxi stand, she'd pick me up at five a.m. and zoom off, driving erratically and fast. She'd say, "Don't talk to me, I'm not awake yet," open up a book on the steering wheel, and start reading. As a driver, she was at her bizarre

---

* Later to be Catwoman in the 1960s television show *Batman.*

zenith. Over six feet tall, and large-breasted, she dripped sensuality with each husky pant that started and ended every sentence. Her mind worked constantly. Julie was smart, but camouflaged her intelligence by playing the innocent, sweet thing who didn't quite understand what was happening to or around her. She caught up and passed every car on the highway. We'd talk a few platitudes and exchange a bit of gossip, but often, there was no conversation at all, as Julie was engrossed in her book while driving. I'd sit, rigid, and she would bury her nose down between the pages, propping the book on the steering wheel, occasionally glancing up at the road. A few trips with Julie cured me of trying to bum rides; I opted to pay the hefty taxi fare.

Weekends had me en route to Mexico and Tijuana, a border town some two hours' drive south of LA. Already legendary for its danger, reputedly filled with thieves, bandits, drug addicts, pickpockets, and prostitutes, Tijuana thrilled me. Jack Donaldson and his buddy Scotty Groves would pick me up on Saturday morning. Wreathed in cigarette smoke, Scotty could not talk without coughing, and the cough sounded like the squish your boots make when traversing a marsh. He boasted, "I smoke when I'm taking a shower," as if it were a badge of honor. I thought, "This guy's on his last legs." A gambling man, Scotty loved Las Vegas, but Tijuana had the racetrack, and horses were his primary passion. He claimed, "I've sat in every seat at that racetrack, and my winnings pay my rent!" Though Jack never placed bets, Scotty bet on everything, even Tijuana's bullfights. In Barcelona the year before, I had been to the bullfights, and witnessed the archaic theater of the bullring: the pageantry, colors, beauty, skill, and art balanced against danger, cruelty, and death. In a spontaneous pas de deux, the matador and bull dance together—the possibility of maiming or death for the matador and certain destruction for the bull drive their choreography.

As a prologue, to give the matador an edge and prepare the bull for his confrontation, two acrobatic, deft, and nimble men (banderilleros) enter the ring. Carrying a pair of barbed darts decorated with colored ribbons (banderillas), they take turns rushing at the bull, attempting to stab their darts into the muscles in the back of the bull's neck, while avoiding the horns by leaping and twisting their bodies out of the way at the last second. Watching the banderilleros avoid the bull's horns, I envisioned the bull dances of ancient Crete. Accounts describe how naked, nubile dancers (teens and subteens, boys and girls) would run straight at the bull and seize its horns, or leap and land with their feet on its head. Using the toss of the bull's head as a springboard, these Cretan dancers were catapulted into spinning, twisting aerial feats or left squirming impaled on a horn.

To me, the least sympathetic of the cast is the picador. He prances in on a padded horse, brandishing a lance, for the picador's role is to lacerate and weaken the powerful muscles at the back of the bull's head. The shaft has a crosspiece to prevent the blade from sliding too deep into the bull. The immense strength of the bull is phenomenal; I have seen it hook its horns under the padding of the horse and toss both horse and picador over the barricade and out of the ring. Sometimes, the horse gets gored. Though I love the pageantry and music, every time the bull dies and they drag off the now lifeless piece of meat, I feel sickened and wish I weren't there.

Not so in Portugal, where the bull is not slain. A horse and rider enter the ring to shift and dodge, adroitly avoiding the charges of the bull. The high point comes when a daisy chain of garishly dressed heroes line up to face the bull. The most courageous (or the loser of the coin toss) stands at the head of the line, wearing generous padding and backed up by a long line of cronies. They attempt to bring the bull's full charge to a stop. Lucky for them, the bull's horns are padded too. His charge smashes into number one and sends him reeling into the second, and so on, until, like dominoes, their combined mass hopefully slows and stops the bull. Just as likely, they could be scattered like rag dolls, flung all over the arena on their behinds. It all depends on luck, skill, and the angle of the bull's charge. Courageous, foolhardy, comic, and highly entertaining!

God, how we feasted in Tijuana, where the cuisine was varied, scrumptious, and fascinating. Tamales filled with esoteric fruits, corn puddings with spices alien to me. Chicken mole? With chocolate sauce? "Scotty," I said, "I can't imagine it. It's like putting ketchup on ice cream, they just don't go!" But oh, yes they do. And was it delicious. Mexican chocolate is different; it's *real*. Between puffs of cigarette, Scotty claimed that chocolate came from Mexico. "Before Cortés, the world didn't know about it."

Tijuana's dangers? I never saw any. Or if I did, I didn't know it.

Our soundstage vibrated with energy. There was buzz about *Seven Brides for Seven Brothers*. When the cast and stars from other stages had a break, they would rush over to our set to watch.

The adaptation of Plutarch's tale was inventive and goofy, the music, top-notch, the lyrics by Johnny Mercer couldn't have been better, but it was the alchemy of Stanley and Michael that transformed the material into something surprising and extraordinary. Co-captains for every artistic decision, they had handpicked the cast, and molded and guided us. The entire cast, including extras, consisted of a conglomerate—jazz dancers and acrobats from Las Vegas; hoofers from Broadway; dozens of assorted Hollywood stuntmen; even a buddy of mine, Kelly Brown, from American Ballet Theatre, who happened to be a hell of a horseman. Our athleticism gave the entire film an energy and precision that make the barn scene and the fight with the townspeople standouts. Michael was a brilliant choreographer, and nobody knew how to film dance better than Stanley. Yet no one expected *Seven Brides* to become one of the greatest musicals in the history of Hollywood. Stanley and Michael deserve the credit.

In the midst of shooting, we'd hear "Reloading!" or "Replacing lights!" followed by "Take a break, kids!" then we'd all slouch around. Suddenly, Tommy Rall would bound out of his chair, look at me, and say, "You want to see a brandy?" Then he'd back up to give himself room, and flip over, his head upside down, in a kind of cartwheel without hands—first, to one side, then the other, then back again. Abruptly, he'd stop, walk back to his chair, and plop down. It was kind of crazy. Michael used it during the movie's "Competition Dance," where Tommy triumphs over all his rivals, with a series of brandies performed on top of two parallel sawhorses. If he had missed by an inch, he would have broken legs and head, and have died.

I once bragged to Tommy that I could knock off several consecutive entrechats huit—where you leap vertically and open and close your feet, alternating positions four times before landing*—but "I've never managed to make entrechat dix," I lamented. Tom mumbled laconically, "Yeah, I can do entrechat dix. I've done it a lot. I'd do them now for you, but not with these boots on. How about I do a bunch of double and triple tours in a row?" He didn't wait for an answer, just got up, stood in front of me in fifth position, and propelled himself into the air,

---

* They call it "huit" (eight, in French) because the four changes are multiplied by two since there are two feet.

spinning twice to the right. Bouncing off the cement floor, he repeated the double tour, then knocked off a triple. Just like a ball rebounding off a hard surface, Tommy continued the sequence—double tour, double tour, triple tour, double, double, triple—over and over again. We got vertigo watching. As with the brandy, he abruptly stopped and, without a word, strode directly to his chair and sat down. His nonchalant "It's a piece of cake" attitude was endearing.

In my memory, only one display of consecutive tours overshadows Tommy's—Phillip Mosco's. Phil was a dancing friend I had known from my early days at SAB. Everyone was in love with Phil, men and women, but he was straight, as far as I knew. Endowed with a beautiful, triangular face, and gorgeous blue eyes, topped with black eyelashes half the length of my thumb, he had the most perfectly proportioned body, amazing elevation, and the energy of a herd of antelope. It was nothing for Phil to get up at dawn and run a six-mile loop in Manhattan's Central Park. Occasionally, he'd sprint toward a tree, and, using that momentum, run up the trunk, leap, and seize a limb sixteen or eighteen feet off the ground. He'd swarm the tree to the top, then descend like a gibbon, swinging and dropping off branches to land on his feet, and bound off to continue his run—all before his early-morning ballet class. By early evening, he would have completed at least two more dance classes, and be abroad for a night of partying or servicing his slew of girlfriends.

Phil tried to fix me up with a blond teenager at the Ballet Arts studio in Carnegie Hall. I was sixteen, and protested, "She wouldn't be interested in me. I'm sure she's in love with you, Phil. Why don't *you* make out with her?" "No, too young!" he said. "Older women are better. It's her mother I want!"

One day, after ballet class at a studio in Los Angeles, Phil claimed he could do a sequence of double tours, alternating with flamenco spins and multiple pirouettes, and keep repeating them. Immediately, he launched off, calling out, on each double tour, "There's one!" "There's two!" "And three!" Unfortunately, around number eight, he landed crookedly and started ricocheting to his side. A panicky look came to his eyes, but he was determined, continuing to count. As he yelled out, "Fourteen!" he fell through the glass door at the entrance to the studio. Phil injured his leg, and the shattering glass badly cut the tendons in one of his wrists. After recovering in the hospital, he did get back to dancing—to find himself a legend. "You heard about Phil Mosco? The guy who double-toured through a glass door!"*

Dancing in movies was an experience worlds from the ballet. From morning to night in a ballet company, it is dance, dance, perform, perform. In movies, eight bars of music into a sequence, the director yells, "Cut!" and you wait twenty minutes or a half hour before hearing, "Let's shoot that again . . ." It may use most of the day to do eight takes for one little dance sequence. I found it difficult to sustain enthusiasm when you stop and start, stop and start, and, by the end of the day, you've only done a few dance steps. Performing with a ballet company, you're in conversation with the audience, not a camera; it's immediate, and there's no going back to redo, repair, or camouflage. If you leaped high, you leaped high; no camera angle enhances your elevation. In a movie, the cameras could dance for us, come into our faces, focus on the feet, and even spin around and capture our dancing from behind or above. Later, the editor can restructure everything. Audience and applause can be added. I felt somehow truth was missing. I had to learn a different mindset.

We were scheduled to wrap the film shortly after the new year, but were so far behind that shooting had to be extended. Balanchine was mounting the first production of *Nutcracker* back in New York, and I was supposed to be there. So, to the shock of the producer, director, and entire cast and crew, I said no to extending my contract, but I eventually agreed to an extra few weeks. And then, "After that, no matter what, I'm going back to the ballet." Stanley and Michael reorganized the shooting schedule, cramming in as many of the brothers' scenes as possible before I left. The assistant director has the worst job in the film

* Phil showed up to visit New York in June 2004. He came to watch National Dance Institute's Saturday children's class, and I introduced him to the dancing star Donlin Foreman, saying, "This is my buddy Phil. We've known each other from ancient times. He's eighty years old and in a hell of a lot better shape than me. Feel those pecs." "How do you do it?" asked Donlin. "Three times a night!" Phil proclaimed. Phil's falling through the glass door feat was topped only by an incident I didn't witness, but heard about. I was living on 163rd and St. Nicholas Avenue, and must have been ten or eleven years old. An old couple lived in my building. The old man, Albert, got out of bed one morning. Stiff and tired, he was having trouble getting his leg into his pants. He got one in, and then, as he was trying to get the other in, he lost his balance and started hopping to catch up, all the while conversing with his wife, who was sitting in bed. He hopped himself right out the window, fell four floors, and died.

business—the front man, spokesperson, overseer, major domo, gofer, mule driver, and scapegoat describe that rotten job; my leaving the movie to return to the ballet company pissed him off. He got his revenge with his "mispronunciation ploy." Broadcasting over the speaker system, he'd say, "All right, cast, your break is over. Hurry up! *Drambuie* is in a rush." Or another one: "All the brothers on the set. *Dembones* has to go back to the ballet." I'd just grin and count the days until I'd return to Balanchine, and what I felt was my real world.

I left the picture with one scene unfinished, where the brothers pace the floor waiting for the birth of Milly's baby. Michael put the assistant choreographer, Alex Romero, in a duplicate of my costume, slapped a red wig on his head, and stuck him in the back to fill in for me. Today, they could take my photo and digitally morph me into the scene with close-ups.

I complained, then, about doing movies, but am so thankful now, and I treasure every bit part and scene I was lucky enough to be in. Today, when I choreograph a dance, I simultaneously plan how it could be directed, filmed, and edited.

COURTING CARRIE

I flew into New York City and immediately dashed to the City Center Theater, arriving just in time to catch the evening's premiere of *The Nutcracker*. Lincoln Kirstein gave me his seat in the first row of the mezzanine. Balanchine's exquisite choreography raised my heart to my throat: Maria Tallchief glittered as the Sugar Plum Fairy, Nicholas Magallanes made an elegant Cavalier, and Tanny stole the show as the Dew Drop in the "Waltz of the Flowers," but I hardly noticed. My eyes sought out Carrie whenever she was onstage. I remember how she always said, to my surprise, that she didn't enjoy all the battements tendus and exercises at the barre. I loved them, and did them by the thousands, so I thought everyone else did. To her, ballet class was a bit of a chore, and although rehearsals were more interesting, for Carrie the *best* was to be onstage and dance. That's where she felt happiest.

The next morning after class, I approached her and squeaked out, "Hi! Want to go to a movie with me?" Her mouth fell open. "You haven't spoken to me in a year!" Then she giggled, and answered, "Okay." It was February 26, 1954.

One of her favorite places was Carnegie Tavern, a big, German-style alehouse that occupied the southwest corner of Carnegie Hall. On Fifty-sixth Street and Seventh Avenue, it was half a block up from the stage door of City Center. After the curtain closed, Carrie and I would dash there as quickly as we could, for their enormous, frosty tankards of beer and "the Carnegie Special," an indulgence of a sandwich—rye bread, an inch-thick pile of thinly sliced ham, topped with a slice of raw onion, wearing a hat of Swiss cheese and slathered with Russian dressing before being bracketed with the other bread slice. I would guzzle, nosh, and gab incessantly while Carrie sipped, ate daintily, and giggled. Garrulousness with your mouth full is not romantic; I would often notice Carrie fighting to stay awake.

Today, I wonder why she suffered me. Perhaps our love of dance, energy, and optimism knit us together.

In our ballet company, everyone knows who's going together—you're branded as an item if you carry someone's practice bag. "Oh, look, Roland's carrying Janice's bag . . . Oh, there's Billy carrying Juan's bag." Before long, there was a chorus of, "Oh, look who's carrying Carrie's bag!" I hefted her bag until we were married in 1956. Two years of penance for my year of dumb pride!

In 1955, NYCB was once again touring the cities of Europe. On arriving, Carrie and I secretly developed a system to be able to stay together, but needed help to pull it off. Fellow company members Roland Vasquez and his girlfriend, Janice Mitoff, agreed to be coconspirators. Roland and I would book a double room in a hotel. We'd dump our bags, slip outside the hotel, and inform our female counterparts our room number. "Try and get the same floor," we urged. Carrie and Janice would then go to the desk and book their double, requesting the designated floor. After performances, our quartet would sup together, and, in the hotel lobby, stage a dramatic scene of separation, loudly proclaiming, "Goodnight, you all!" and "Yeah, see you in the morning!" Roland and I would then repair to our room. Precisely a half hour later, I would scope the hall, and if it was deserted, slip out and head for Carrie's room, toothbrush in hand, passing Janice on her way to Roland. In the morning, the reverse: peek through a crack in the door and, if the coast was clear, scoot back to Roland, passing a sleepy Janice.

I doubt anyone in the hotel was fooled. I can't speak for Roland and Janice, but Carrie and I were innocents. We just wanted a chance to

Balanchine wreathed with NYCB dancers in Monaco. I'm standing far left, Carrie up the stairs third from left, and Roland Vasquez standing top center, 1955. The quintet of ballerinas sitting left to right are Jillana, Tanaquil LeClercq, Patricia Wilde, Diana Adams, saucy Melissa Hayden.

sleep in each other's arms. When we married a year later we were both virgins.

Bordeaux was NYCB's last engagement in France, and I needed to do something special for Carrie. Since dancers are consumed with a passion for eating, I inquired of our company pianist, the sophisticated Nicholas Kopeikine, "Kolya, what's the best restaurant in Bordeaux?" "The restaurant in the Hotel Au Chapon Fin." It hadn't taken him a second to reply. "Ooooh, oooh, it's divine," he cooed, rolling his eyes, "it has Michelin stars." Kolya had been there with Diaghilev, and insisted, "You *must* take her to Chapon Fin." Aware of Kolya's advice, Balanchine applauded the choice. "Order Mouton Rothschild! It is the best of the wines," he advised.

On our day off, I took Carrie to the restaurant. An elegant maître d' greeted us. "We're dancers, we're here with NYCB, we're hungry and heard about your restaurant. What's your specialty? What would you recommend?" Delighted, he announced, "For Americans with an appetite, I recommend *notre Chateaubriand avec sauce béarnaise.*" Now, he may have recommended the most expensive thing on the menu. But so what! Into the pond, now for the swim. "What should we have with it?" I asked. "Monsieur, let me surprise you with the legumes."

Ensconced in plush red velvet armchairs, Carrie and I noticed every table in the restaurant was equipped with several miniature stools. "What are they?" she wondered. Padded and puffy, a down comforter crowning four stubby legs, they were gout stools, meant to rest the swollen feet of patrons whose indulgence in culinary excess had been thought to generate this painful affliction. Their presence proclaimed the clientele's willingness to suffer for the privilege of savoring the restaurant's rich cuisine.

When the sommelier came, I stuck my nose in the air, extended a finger as if preaching, and intoned, "A bottle of Mouton, *s'il vous plaît.* Your very best year!" *That* would impress Carrie.

As lovers have their song, Mouton Rothschild became our wine.*

Now, to the meal. The Chateaubriand—it is beef steak, enormous, the size of a loaf of bread, rubbed with a little oil and placed in an extremely hot oven, charred quickly, then removed from the excessive heat and finished off at a lower temperature, but just a little bit. This

---

* In later years, whenever I choreographed a ballet, Balanchine would send me a case of Mouton Rothschild along with a note: "For your ballet."

preparation creates an outside that is crusty, thick, and almost chewy—
rare in the spine of its center, the surrounding flesh oozing the juicy
essence of *meat*. The flavor—fantastic. Nearby proudly standing was the
king of sauces, about to enter the stage. A silver tureen of sauce béarnaise—thick, cadmium yellow, and fragrant of tarragon and lemon—
expectantly staring at us and the steak. Ah! The coupling, when it
came, exquisite. Up until then, I had always enjoyed ketchup or mustard with my steak. What a revelation! The perfume generated by the
marriage of these flavors explored the nasal passages, palate, and
tongue, leaving ghosts dancing behind to titillate. Sauce béarnaise
joined Mouton Rothschild as *our* sauce. With the Chateaubriand came
the maître d's surprises.

Tomates à la Provençale, basically a half-moon of a tomato freckled
with garlic, parsley, olive oil, Dijon mustard, and a dusting of grated
Parmesan cheese. Broiled and presented, they were quickly consumed.
Heaven! However, it was something as ordinary as creamed spinach
that dazzled. Take a mouthful, and you would discover a tiny crouton
hiding amid the creamy greenness. Biting one, an explosion of garlic
juices poured out, the aroma bursting in your mouth. It was a royal
hunt seeking these little golden nuggets, finding one, anticipating
the biting—and *bang*—the molar crush and sumptuousness follow
through! It makes one realize the importance of proportions. You
wanted to find these delightful tidbits, but there weren't many, so perfect was the balance that their garlic expression did not overwhelm the
exquisite simplicity of spinach and buttery cream. Allow me to
describe the *pommes soufflés*. It's a French fry that looks like a finger—
except when you bite into it, it doesn't have potato in the middle, it's a
puff, a potato crust that magically encloses the hot vapor of "potato-
ness."

Carrie and I have attempted to recreate this experience—in many
restaurants and our own kitchen—for over half a century. All attempts
were mere foothills to the heights of that Chapon Fin feast.

A week later, Carrie got the flu, a day or two before we were to leave
Bordeaux and fly to Lisbon. Usually, nothing could stop Carrie from
dancing, but this time, there was no way. She sat shivering in the dressing room. "I know exactly what she needs," Balanchine said, and, grab-
bing my elbow, ushered me to the buffet of the theater and demanded a
bottle of cognac. The portly bartender announced, "We do not sell bottles." Balanchine sniffed, "Well, maybe a bottle of Coca-Cola." Then,

he took that bottle of Coca-Cola into the bathroom, poured its contents into the sink, and returned with the empty bottle in his pocket. "Now, give my friend and me hookers of cognac. Nine, please." The unfazed bartender poured the cognac. For every shot of cognac Balanchine poured into himself, he poured one into the Coca-Cola bottle, saying, "One for me, one for the bottle, and one for you, Jacques!" insisting I "bottoms-up" to Carrie's quick recovery.

Meanwhile, I was twitching with anxiety and thinking, "HURRY UP, GEORGE!" The knowing bartender handed Balanchine a cork with the bill, and we headed back to the dressing room, Coke bottle in hand, loaded with cognac. I tried to get Carrie to swallow a sip, but she was shaking too much. Eddie Bigelow and I carried her, shivering, out of the theater. It was intermission. Eleanor Barzin, lady friend of our conductor, Leon, and an heiress to Mrs. Merriweather Post's fortune, spied us. Elegant Eleanor removed her ankle-length fur coat and wrapped it around Carrie. All Carrie could think of, she told me later, was that her makeup and sweat were ruining the fur. "That coat . . . I'll never be rich enough to have a coat like that, and Eleanor is wrapping it around me to keep me warm."

When I finally got Carrie tucked into bed, I drank all the cognac and proposed. Trembling and feverish, she made me kneel by the bed and repeat it formally, before chattering out a "yes."

The next day the company flew on to Lisbon. I wouldn't leave without Carrie, so they left without us. A day or two later, she was better, and we boarded the cargo plane (carrying the scenery and wardrobe trunks) and flew to Lisbon, strapped into some kind of jump seat on either side of the cockpit. Carrie keeping warm in Eleanor's fur.

She soon recovered in warm and balmy Lisbon.

In the 1950s, Portugal was ruled by the dictator Salazar, and his Ministry of Culture assigned a guy to keep tabs on us. José de Jesus Santos was short and pale-faced, with black hair, a long, thin nose, and gleaming eyes that continually flicked back and forth like windshield wipers. On inquiring, "Are you a dancer, performer, or something?" he would reply, "I am sent by God to assist you," or "Fate has sent me to be of service." His English was impeccable, and he was charming as he buzzed around. When I complained to him that the stage of Lisbon opera house had the most extreme rake of any stage I had danced on—the footlights were at least seventeen feet lower than the back wall of the stage—"It's like dancing on the side of a hill!"—he replied, "Oh, but we built it that way to enhance your enormous leaps." Word was out that he was reporting to Salazar and the Secret Service— ensuring that there were no agitators or communists among us. There weren't, just dancers, and soon José de Jesus ceased his buzzing around and began enjoying his entrée to this exotic ballet company.

The Portuguese are natural romantics. Where America's national story tells of George Washington cutting down a cherry tree, their story recounts the love of Inês de Castro and Pedro I of Portugal, and of lost love, tragedy, murder, and revenge. Love continues into the tomb. José de Jesus Santos decided to advance my romance with Carrie, suggesting that on our day off, we travel to Estoril. "All the deposed royalty of the world have made it their home in exile. It is a place of flowers, palaces, and sunlight."

José de Jesus took charge of us, planning and organizing the whole adventure: pickup, bus tickets, hotel, and delivery. "You must stay overnight. If you will permit me, I will come as your guide. Give me your passports." In Portugal, you couldn't check into a hotel without surrendering your passport, and certainly, no man and woman could stay together unless married. In Estoril, we had no Roland and Janet, just José de Jesus. But he was superb. On entering the hotel lobby, he assured us, "I'll take care of everything." He marched up to the desk, spoke a few words, and flashed something in his wallet to the now white-faced and fawning clerk. Within minutes, we were escorted into an elegant suite, "The best in the hotel!" the bellhop announced. That's when we knew for sure José was a Secret Services big shot. Beaming, José de Jesus bowed, announced, "You have the wedding suite," and disappeared. We didn't spot him again until two days later, when he boarded the return bus with us. "I had a few odds and ends to take care of," he grinned.

Every couple needs an Estoril. Spotlessly clean. Flower bedecked, and next to a stunning beach. Gorgeous waves. On the last night, Carrie and I lingered barefoot at the edge of the surf. The full moon, reflected on the water, made a beam path to us, and no matter where we trod it followed, illuminating us and the surf, which bubbled with lights like diamonds and miniature supernovas.

After Balanchine's stormy parting from Maria Tallchief (an annulment, on the grounds that she wanted a baby—he didn't), he soon married Tanny. The stick-skinny, gawky teenager, Nymph to my childhood Puck, had blossomed into an exquisite, witty, sophisticated princess.

Balanchine had watched and nurtured her for years, intrigued by her talent. Through her teens, he choreographed for her, and waited. She had captured the eyes and heart of the king. They married December 31, 1952.

The Balanchines included us in their family life. Routinely, Tanny would say, "Come over for dinner. We'll play cards after." As it was the fifties, steak every night was the norm. Porterhouse, rare, served with Dijon mustard, a salad of romaine lettuce with a dressing of olive-oil, lemon, and garlic, and new potatoes roasted in their skin with butter, parsley, and rosemary. This was the usual menu Tanny chose and chef Balanchine served. Her wit, barbed and directed at everything and anyone (including herself), was unpredictable, yet veined with affection. Having decided on the dinner menu, she would announce, "Oh! This again?" Delivered with mock surprise and a hint of indignation. Dessert was never anything but ice cream. "I thought we'd have something new," Tanny would declare. Mouton Rothschild was the wine—two bottles in the course of an evening. I was responsible for the downing of one. "Have another glass," Tanny would quip. "Here, let me pour it for you." Then, turning to Balanchine, she'd add, "If he does, George, we're sure to win, even with you as my card partner." After dinner, Balanchine would sit, patiently playing endless rounds of canasta. Sometimes, either from boredom or just to pique an outburst from Tanny, he would throw down a wrong card, dissolving her strategy.

During the next day's rehearsal, Tanny would pick up from the night before. She'd draw away from me, dramatically, as I partnered her. "Do I detect a little purple staining the whites of your ballet shoes? Jacques, I can't believe it! You're sweating wine!"*

ORDER OF THE GARTER

When Carrie and I announced our engagement, Balanchine pointed his finger at us: "You know, you *have* to marry, same day, Tanny and I. December 31."

There was no doubt we would have a Catholic wedding, else the Boss

* We loved to eat, Tanny and I; dancing kept us slim, so the sky's the limit on the cuisine. Tanny even did a cookbook where different ballet friends gave their favorite recipes. I gave her a stack and most of them ended up in her book. The number of mine she included is second only to Balanchine's.

would have choked. Carrie had to promise to baptize and raise our future children as Roman Catholics, and often had to rush from NYCB rehearsals to endure an hour of lessons in dogma from the priest. She recalls the composer Samuel Barber watching a run-through of Todd Bolender's ballet *Souvenirs*. "He couldn't believe that in the middle of the pas de deux, Todd was letting me leave!" "She's going for a catechism lesson," he whispered in Barber's car.

The ballet garter is waiting

The church, St. Thomas More, was already booked for December 31, so we chose the next day, January 1. "Goody," Tanny said, "it's close enough." Over the next decade, Tanny, Balanchine, Carrie, and I celebrated every New Year's Eve together, with Balanchine raising his glass. "Special time," he would sniff. "At midnight tonight, our day ends, your day begins."

I bought a new suit, and wore a silver tie. Carrie's wedding dress was a light rose color, and beneath her wedding dress she put on the ballet's Order of the Garter.* It adorned her left leg above the knee.

At various nuptials over the year, this pink symbol had been passed from dancer to dancer. Carrie thinks it began its odyssey June 13, 1951, at the wedding of San Francisco Ballet's ballerina Patricia Johnston.

---

* With a few exceptions, all who have used the Order of the Garter have been ballet stars or well-known performers: Pat Johnston and F. N. Bibbins (June 13, 1951); Joan Vickers and Stanley Davis (December 18, 1952); Sally Streets and Alex Nichols, parents of NYCB ballerina Kyra Nichols (October 1955); Carolyn George and Jacques d'Amboise (January 1, 1956); Edith Brozek and Frank McMann (May 26, 1957); Sally Bailey and John Flynn (June 22, 1957); Marilyn George and Dan Sheffield (July 22, 1957); Jillana and Ben Janney (May 27, 1960); Vida Brown and Stanley Olinick (June 26, 1964); Wintress Perkins and Warren Wetzel (February 17, 1968); Kyra Nichols and Daniel Duell (September 3, 1978); Kay Mazzo and Albert Bellas (December 21, 1978); Marcia Rubine and John Masten (July 22, 1979); Marjorie Spohn and Alexander Hyatt (September 13, 1981); Diane Lyons and Eli Boatwright Jr. (April 14, 1990); Catherine d'Amboise and Peter Brill (April 20, 1991); Charlotte d'Amboise and Terrence Mann (January 20, 1996); Kathleen Donlin and John Badalament (July 29, 2000). After Kelly Crandall and Christopher d'Amboise married in August 2008, the pink garter went to Kay Gayner for her marriage to Frank Wood, September 26, 2009, and the garter is presently awaiting its next limb.

Wedding Day, St. Thomas More, 1956

About a year and a half later, the garter took up residence on the limb of a fellow dancer, Joan Vickers, till Joan passed it on to Sally Streets. Sally had danced with us in NYCB for several years, and after her wedding in October of 1955, she launched the rosy circlet cross-country to the East Coast, to nestle on Carrie's lovely gam.

Our wedding took place between the matinee and evening performances of *The Nutcracker,* with the entire company in attendance. When the priest finally said, "I now pronounce you man and wife," I grabbed Carrie's hand and ran down the aisle. My brother John leaped to block us at the front door. "You forgot to kiss the bride, stupid!"

That evening, we boarded a plane for Port-au-Prince, Haiti. Balanchine's joke: he listed our names on the bulletin board to perform *Nutcracker* that night.

A Honeymoon in Haiti

Leaving in midwinter and arriving a few hours later on a tropical island was like being smacked in the face. With the first breath of that hot, muggy, flower-scented atmosphere, our sinuses were swamped. Ears overflowed with sounds of clamoring birds, insects, and unknown creatures, all jabbering like a rambunctious family with a slew of children. When night fell, the atmosphere's perfume doubled, and the cacophony intensified, with distant drums and chanting voices joining in.

On our first step out of the airport terminal in Port-au-Prince, a taxi driver with dark chocolate skin hooked us. "Monsieur, Madame, I am George, destined to be your driver!" A round-faced, pudgy man in his early thirties, sweet-speaking Haitian George was prescient, and he became our guide and driver for the next two weeks. George kept a photograph of his wife and son clipped to his taxi's visor, and commented melodiously on every tree, building, and thoroughfare we passed on the way to our hotel.

The hotel room was high-ceilinged, with one tiny window, and cement walls sweating with condensation. A jail cell. On opening our suitcases, rice spilt onto the floor. Carrie's sister, Marilyn, had sprinkled rice in the layers between our clothes; we even found grains in the toothpaste. Carrie couldn't get over it. "When did she do it? When did she have time?" We laughed and collapsed, exhausted.

In the morning, Haitian George moved us out of our jail cell accommodations and over to the Hotel Oloffson. Thick greenery and tropical flowers entwined and competed with Victorian filigree in the entryway. Tchaikovsky's Second Piano Concerto was playing on a speaker system throughout the hotel, as if welcoming a pair of newlywed ballet dancers. A slow-moving man greeted us. I imagined that years in the tropics and a fondness for Haitian rum had directed his metabolism and sensibilities to legato tempos and decadence. Dressed in an open-necked white shirt, a once-trim frame had rounded excessively. "I will take care of you during your stay here." ("Maybe it's Mr. Oloffson himself!" I whispered to Carrie.) He turned out to be charming, and led us to our room along a wedding cake of tiered balconies, decorated with green and white carved wood and cast iron. Outside our room stood a tree, festooned with exotic, bulbous fruits. "Coffee," Haitian George announced. "Sure, after we get settled in our room," we answered. "It grows on trees, my young friends, the coffee." Pointing to the tree, he continued, "Not quite ready for your cup."

Over the next few days, George guided us through an incredible open-air market, its tin roof radiating heat in all directions. The astonishing beauty of the women in multicolored outfits—not one fat person—most milled about barefoot or sandaled. Drums and singing all the time. One *Vogue*-model-gorgeous young woman with a withered old woman, maybe grandmother or mother, sat on a blanket, with a cluster of five bananas to sell. How far had they walked to get to this marketplace? Later in my life, when I traveled to other Third World countries, I learned this was common—and that five bananas was probably considered goodly merchandise.

Within a week, Carrie and I ventured up the hill toward Pétionville, Haiti's version of the old San Francisco's Nob Hill, hoping to pop in on Katherine Dunham's school.* We found a caretaker, who told us, "Madame is away. The school is closed."

I knew of Katherine Dunham from seeing her dancers in New York—and most amusingly, from Balanchine's description of how she saved his life.

In the mid-1940s, SAB was abuzz with the breakup of Balanchine and his then wife, Vera Zorina, the movie-star beauty. Gossip was rife as to who would be the ballerina to next catch his eye (it turned out to be Maria Tallchief).

Twenty years later, still sucking the thumb of rejection, Balanchine filled my ear. Vera's real name was Brigitta, and Balanchine always referred to her that way. "Brigitta did not want me anymore, so she threw me out. I remember, you know, standing outside on sidewalk,

---

* Katherine Dunham, a titan in the world of modern dance, was renowned for bringing traditional Haitian dance forms to America and incorporating these forms into contemporary dance idiom. She and Balanchine met in 1940, while she and her troupe appeared in the musical *Cabin in the Sky*, directed by Balanchine. She died in 2006, at the age of ninety-six, destitute. Friends were paying her apartment costs.

looking up at window, and thinking, 'I am homeless. What to do?' I went to bench in Central Park."

Later that night, he found his way to the Barbizon-Plaza for Women, a hotel right off Central Park South that had an annex for tourists. I believe he stayed there years before when he first arrived in New York City. "No toothbrush, no shaving kit. Nothing." He spent days in his room, "not expecting Brigitta to take me back," he said, crushed and stinging from rejection. "I was destroyed."

Katherine Dunham was performing in New York City with her dance troupe. "I don't know how she heard," Balanchine said, "but someone told her that 'Balanchine is in hotel with broken heart.' Late at night, I hear—knock, knock, knock—at door. And there was Dunham, with six of the most *beautiful* dancers from her company. Octoroons." (He loved the word "octoroons.") "Loaded with baskets of food and champagne. They came in and we danced and partied," he raised a finger in the air, "all night! I will never forget Dunham for this. She cured me."

Willam Christensen, years later, corroborated Balanchine. Bill was walking across Central Park at two o'clock in the morning on his way home from a party. It was freezing cold, and he spotted a figure huddled on a park bench. "George?!?" he said. Balanchine looked up, nodded, and sniffed. "Brigitta threw me out." Bill stood for a moment, nodded sagely, replied, "Oh!" and walked on.

Why Haiti for our honeymoon? Carrie had been intrigued by Haiti ever since she first read Kenneth Roberts's *Lydia Bailey.* I had recently delved into a riveting biography of Henri Christophe, titled *Black Majesty: The Life of Christophe, King of Haiti,* and we were both drawn to the island's exotic landscape, culture, and history.

Determined not to miss Henri Christophe's fantastic palace and citadel, we grabbed a few days to visit Cap-Haitien. The town was studded with exquisite little houses, painted in different colors, and bursting with flowers—right out of the best of Haitian paintings.

Since it was the richest of the French colonies, Napoleon exploited Haiti's wealth for his wars. When the slaves revolted, he sent a fleet with an army of elite troops to crush the insurgency. Led by General Leclerc and fueled by arrogance, the French underestimated the passionately driven guerilla fighters, and their allies, malaria and tropical heat. The French armies were defeated, and fled.

For the plantation owners who had made Haiti their home, the world turned from white to black, and those colonials not dead fled with many of their servants, leaving behind a bevy of European chefs, musicians, acrobats, and performers who had found employment entertaining them. A number of these artists emigrated to the southern coast of the United States and brought their sensibilities with them— baroque music and French folk songs, spiced with Haitian and African influences—a bouillabaisse melding to jambalaya. Many of these artist-refugees found employment in service to southern planters.

Alan Jones, a choreographer, aficionado, and scholar of baroque dance, described how the indigenous music and dance of Georgia and the Carolinas were galvanized and transformed by this infusion. Among records from a Carolina plantation, he discovered a description of a baroque pas de deux danced on a tightrope by two acrobat-dancers from French Haiti. To my delight, Kay Gayner already knew about these influences: "Pockets of the Georgia Sea Islands, where I grew up, are renowned for preserving the language, storytelling, and arts of Gullah slave culture, and the Haitian presence there was powerful. Gullah is a unique mixture of the rhythms, rituals, dance movements, and language of West Africa, Brazil, and Haiti." While writing this book, on a whim I took a break with Kay and, bound and limited by a single line, an imaginary tightrope sketched on the floor, invented and danced a minuet.

After the French defeat in Haiti, one of the leaders of the slave rebellion, Henri Christophe, built himself a kingdom, with the town Cap-Haitien as its capital. On a hill outside the town, he built a model of a famous palace in Potsdam, Germany, Sans-Souci. He envisioned himself as a new Louis XIV, only black, and as king, he needed a court of nobles, so he dubbed many of his cronies with made-up aristocratic titles and names—the Duke of Marmalade, Count Frangipani, Lady Marzipan. Clad in fantastic uniforms and ball gowns, the king and his court held ballets and cotillions. His Royal Highness insisted that pink be the prevailing color for the gowns, as he felt the blushing shade best complemented the black skin of his noble ladies.

Haunted by fears the French might return, Henri built himself an escape aerie overlooking his Sans-Souci, a fortress on a mountaintop so enormous it transformed the shape of the mountain, with walls so thick that a horse and carriage could drive along the wall's edges with space to spare. He forced his subjects to drag hundreds of giant cannons up the mountain and install them with tens of thousands of cannonballs stacked in pyramids nearby, ready to be fired. Unknown numbers of "liberated" slaves died building Henri's folly—all in preparation for the return of the French. Not one cannon ever discharged a shot.

Within ten years, his subjects revolted. As the revolutionaries infested Sans-Souci, Henri retreated to his bedroom, wrapped himself in a white satin robe, put a pistol to his head, and killed himself with a golden bullet he had years before prepared for the occasion. Improvising a stretcher using two poles and a bedsheet, an elderly servant, with Christophe's queen and their two young daughters, labored most of the night to cart his body up the steep trail to the citadel. They buried him in a pit and covered it with lime. Today, in the middle of the castle's parade ground sits an enormous mass of hardened lime, like a giant loaf of white bread.

Back in Port-au-Prince, Haitian George announced, "We're going to go to a vodun ceremony. Real—not for tourists." In teeming darkness (no streetlamps), George drove us over twisting roads, seemingly drawn by distant drums, until we pulled into a dirt driveway before a one-story, tin-roofed house. Drumming rumbled from the open door of the house. George cautioned, "Wait. Stay," and got out of the car. We heard him speaking to someone, but we couldn't see whom—an occasional flash of teeth and white eyeballs glistened—and every once in a while, I'd recognize a word of something that sounded familiar, a sort of French, that sang. What would be, *"Parlez-vous français?"* came out, *"Oom pah pahlee français?"*—an "Oom pa pah," and a "pahlee" in musical counterpoint to the drums.

"All okay," George announced.

At the hut's entrance, we tiptoed over symbols laid out on the ground—giant snowflakes sketched in powdered seashells, making delicate star-shaped designs. The markings' significance and power would refuse entry to unwanted spirits, as well as offer a sort of welcome mat to good gods. Haitian George popped his eyes and whispered, "Or ghosts . . ."

Lit only by a few oil lamps and candles, the house was packed with some hundred bodies sitting in a circle, and several standing amid the shadows along the wall. Red dots twinkled on and off as everyone smoked. One side of the circle had a bit of space, where the *houngan,* the priest, stood near a table. The table held a clear bottle and a glass, both filled with rum.

Haitian George squeezed us in against the back wall. No one seemed to pay attention to us, two lone white people in the hut. A bottle was passed around, and everybody would take a slug and pass it on. We faked it. Two or three drummers sat near the *houngan,* who gradually began to chant and dance to their rhythms. As he was dancing and spinning, he launched into dialogue with the congregation, shouting out phrases (incantations? running commentary? gossip?), and they'd pick up his phrases and shout their own back. All the while, the drummers played, and the *houngan* gulped from the bottle. Maybe he was doing stand-up comedy, or advising on family health, "Your child is sick, he overate. You're not feeding him the right food!" And so on. We were mesmerized. Soon, rather than swallowing the rum, he began to spit it out over the crowd, like a baptism, blessing us with sprayed rum.

In his dance, his body shifted and moved—all improvised. Wonderful! A few people got up to join, and then more and more, and the chanting grew raucous. Not everybody, but roughly eighty out of a hundred, were up and dancing. We three sat stuck to the wall.

Someone held up a live chicken, and cut its throat. The drums went wild. The *houngan* grabbed the bleeding chicken by its feet and whirled it over the crowd, as in the Roman Catholic ceremony when the priest flings holy water out of the aspergillum, the congregation is sprinkled—with this ceremony we were blooded.

The chanting crescendoed and, out of the dancers, a girl became the center, a teenager with caffe-latte skin. Though she wasn't specifically dressed in anything special—no veil or fancy dress—everyone danced around her, the chosen one.

The *houngan* circled and spit rum in her face, and then the space around her began to open up, as the people backed away from her. I believe they improvised their dances, but all seemed to move in a counterclockwise direction. The chosen one's eyes were wide, popping out, staring. She started to shake and tremble, and the music changed, throbbing louder and faster.

Suddenly, she started to flail her arms and legs, and propelled herself, flying as if she had been blasted backward. She would fall against people, and then hurl herself forward, twist, fall, and fly. She bounced from one wall of people to another, and the minute she'd hit them, she would push at them and dance away, wilder and wilder until you thought she was going to shatter her arms and legs. The drums hurt our ears.

I never saw her blink or close her eyes. Maybe her pupils were tiny and had rolled up. I don't know, but her eyes were white saucers in her face. Finally, she froze, held, then collapsed to the ground and started to convulse, flopping as if she were a live fish frying in a pan of oil. Everyone ignored her and resumed dancing. Just as I began to think she might die, some attendants came, seized and carried her out.

George said, "That's it, they'll keep dancing now." He explained that the spirit (or whatever it is) enters the chosen one and throws him or her around, until, finally, the person goes into a trance. "Soon others will be possessed and fall into a trance. The spirit might leapfrog to many, or maybe none—till dawn."

We hung around another twenty minutes or so, watching the dancing and the *houngan* spitting his rum, and then we took off.

Seductive Haiti. The people are charming, the art, the colors, the energy, the music, the sounds, the history. We vowed to go back: "Keep in touch, George. We'll see you next year!" We never did. Papa Doc took over.*

Before visiting, while there, and to this day, I hold Haitian people high in my admiration, and feel ashamed of the misguided policies the United States has had, and still has, toward Haitians and their island nation. Just fifteen years after Sam Adams and the Sons of Liberty sparked the American Revolution and ousted the British, the black slaves in Haiti—on their Caribbean island off the southern coast of the young United States—kicked out their white plantation owners and the French (1791–1804). It wasn't until 1862, when the Confederate states seceded from the union, that the U.S. gave diplomatic recognition to Haiti. We even occupied Haiti for decades with U.S. Marines.

Contraception is anathema to the Catholic Church, but the Curia reluctantly suggests an alternative, the rhythm method. "Catholic roulette," Carrie called it. Sure enough, two months after we returned from Haiti, Carrie became pregnant.

The baby was due November 2 or 3, 1956, so when NYCB announced another European tour for the fall, Carrie realized she would have to stay behind.

I planned to leave the tour at the end of October, to be in New York

---

* François Duvalier, known as Papa Doc, was elected President of Haiti in 1956. By 1964, he had installed himself as President for Life. That life left him in 1971 and left his power to Baby Doc, his son, Jean-Claude.

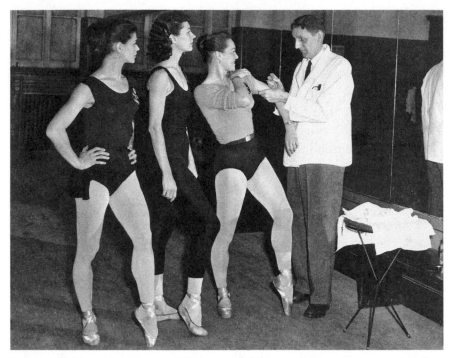

Dr. Mel Kiddon giving Patricia Wilde her polio shot, with Diana Adams and Melissa Hayden waiting for theirs, 1956. Tanny LeClercq protested, "I hate shots! They make me sick. I'll get mine when I come back."

in time for the birth. The tour was brutal and exhausting. Tanny, Diana Adams, and Melissa Hayden were my partners in practically every ballet in the repertoire. At the end of October, on closing night in Cologne, Germany, Tanny and I danced two ballets together (*Concerto Barocco* and *Western Symphony*). Thin, tired, and both suffering from bronchitis, we coughed in the dressing rooms, the wings, and onstage in each other's faces, trying our best to muffle the hacking sounds— until the bows. While our heads were lowered, we could take the opportunity to let loose bellowing coughs. The American consulate gave an after-performance party, but my flight to New York City was early in the morning, so I gave Tanny a hug onstage, and said goodbye. I was never to embrace her again while she was standing.

In the morning, the company flew to their next engagement, Copenhagen, and within a few days Tanny collapsed and was rushed to the hospital, where she went into a coma and woke up in an iron lung. Polio. After Copenhagen, the company went on to Stockholm to finish the tour. Balanchine, his aplomb shredded, abandoned all responsibilities, and spent every moment tending Tanny. They would remain in Denmark for months.

When I saw Balanchine later in New York, he confessed to me, "She was in this place, iron lung, to make her breathe. She told me, 'Stop smoking, it's hurting me!' " Balanchine made a gesture with his hand like the blade of a guillotine, demonstrating an irrevocable change, "I stopped!" He never smoked again, and displayed disfavor to anyone who did. Then Balanchine presented me with a package, saying, "Tanny asked me to get you this gift. Very direct orders. 'A Danish sweater with silver buttons,' she said." It hangs today in my closet.

Our baby was late. We expected him November 2, but he popped out November 11. Carolyn's maiden name was George, my mother's name was Georgette, so naming our first son George was preordained. Balanchine enjoyed the thought that George had been named for him. "Very nice name," he declared.

I was twenty-two years old and had managed to escape being drafted for the war in Korea, because they were not yet inducting married men. When China joined the war on the side of the North Koreans, and American and coalition forces were in full retreat, the draft was expanded to include married men, but not yet those with children. George saved me.

When Balanchine returned with Tanny to New York, he sought out a friend, Dr. Henry Jordan, a renowned orthopedic and hemophilia specialist at Lenox Hill Hospital. "As soon as possible, take Tanny to the treatment center in Warm Springs, Georgia. Do as much physical therapy as possible," Jordan advised. "Little by little, she'll recover, no one knows how much, and then her improvement will stop." He predicted, "She has a window of about two and a half years from the onset." Balanchine was angry: "No, she'll get better. I'll *make* her better. She'll dance again!" He denounced Dr. Jordan and anyone who spoke otherwise. After settling Tanny at the spa in Warm Springs, Balanchine shuttled back and forth, alternately working with the doctors on Tanny's recovery and doing his best to run his ballet company. When he later brought her back to New York, he tended her day and night, cooking for her, cleaning, bathing and massaging her, bending and stretching her legs, lifting her and inventing his own forms of physical therapy. "I would bend legs and stretch, then take her out of bed, hold up from behind with her feet on my feet, and practice walking."

Tanny didn't get better.* Almost eight years passed before Balanchine would admit to himself that Dr. Jordan was right.†

---

* The polio vaccine had just come out before we left for tour, and many of us had been immunized. Some, including Tanny, opted not to have the vaccination then. Shortly after Copenhagen, Ann Crowell, one of the dancers in the corps de ballet, complained of a pulled muscle in her shoulder blade, which didn't seem to get better. Years later, a doctor told her she had had polio, and the muscle in her shoulder had died. Rumor had it that the consul general's wife in Cologne contracted polio after the party they had given the company. Who knows how many others could have gotten it, had we not been immunized or lucky.

† Maria Tallchief first brought Dr. Jordan to Balanchine. I think Maria had been injured and went to Lenox Hill Hospital for treatment, and that's how she met him.

When I knew Jordan, he said, "Maria Tallchief brought me to the world of ballet. After dealing with broken bones and withered bodies all my life, what a wonderful thing it is to see the ballet, to see what these joints can do, how they can be transformed into the most beautiful of art, gravity-less. It fills my dreams and inspires me never to give up on my patients. The human body is extraordinary."

Jordan continued in his soft voice, "In the early fifties, I went to a cocktail party and, standing around in conversation, met a Frenchman. We were both reminiscing about World War I, "Oh yes, I was in the squadron, so and so . . ." "Oh, yes!" the Frenchman said. "A fighter pilot." "I was one too, but against the Luftwaffe." Jordan modestly told him, "I'm afraid I wasn't a very good pilot. For I got shot down over France early on, crashed in a farmer's field." It seemed his French opponent landed, arranged for an ambulance to take care of him, and then took off again. Jordan spent the rest of the war mending his multitude of broken bones. The experience inspired him to seek a profession in orthopedics. He later inquired and learned the name of the Frenchman who had shot him down but never saw him. Now, speaking to *this* Frenchman, Jordan asked, "Did you ever know a pilot named so-and-so?" The man replied, "You're looking at him!"

Dr. Gould, I met through Dr. Jordan. Wilbur James Gould was an ear, nose, and throat specialist and would become a close friend to my family, as did the surgeon Dr. Liebler, who handled my first knee operation.

Dr. Gould told me, "Jordan is a saint. In New York City when you start to cross the Triboro Bridge to Queens from Manhattan right around the tolls there is an enormous beige stone building to your right. It's the hospital for the criminally insane. Every time I pass that building I think of him. Each week Jordan maybe had a day or sometimes half a day off. He donated that time making the rounds, treating the inmates incarcerated there."

Apollo
(The Apollo of
Madison Square Garden)

A ny idea or dream I had of a life outside the world of dance, whether as a stagehand, doctor, or archaeologist, went out the window the season I danced the ballet *Apollo.*

Anyone who knew anything about ballet, or music, anxiously anticipated NYCB's fall 1957 season. Stravinsky and Balanchine would premiere the third work in a trilogy that had started with their first collaboration some thirty years before. The first installment, *Apollon Musagète,* premiered with Diaghilev's Ballets Russes in 1928. The second, *Orpheus,* following the idea of Grecian themes, premiered at Ballet Society in 1948. And now, the summation of the trilogy, *Agon,* was scheduled to premiere. This season, the trilogy would be complete, and the three ballets would be performed together for the first time.

Balanchine said *Apollo* was the turning point in his life as a choreographer. It was the first time he and Stravinsky collaborated on an original score. Balanchine was twenty-three when he began choreographing *Apollo* for the reigning star of Diaghilev's company, Serge Lifar. "I worked with him for a *year* before the premiere!" Balanchine told me.

Apollo had become legendary; every male dancer wanted to star in it. When I was twenty-three, Balanchine revived it for me. It would be the turning point in my life as a dancer. Years before, Balanchine had summed up his *Apollo* with one sentence: "A wild, untamed youth learns nobility through art." Now as we rehearsed, he described a story to each step.

"You are born, already grown up. But you are baby, know nothing, and have tantrums. To calm you down, handmaidens bring you music, a lute, and teach you how to play. But you play like peasant, rake hands over strings, and use lute like child uses toy. You don't know what to do with it—measure body with it, measure floor, and, like child, you put aside and forget. You leave your toy on the floor. Now, you try to walk to better things, but can't control how you move. You stagger, leap in circles. Finally, on your knees, you beg help from Papa, and he fills you with energy and power, and you become like teenager throwing around energy. You waste it! So Papa says, 'STOP! Go back to your music, and call for muses to come and inspire you.' "

Returning to the lute, Apollo plays, more refined now, and summons the muses of poetry, mime, and dance. He gives each the symbol or instrument of her art—the scroll of poetry, the mask of silence, and the lyre of music and dance. In sequence, each muse makes a presentation: "The First (Calliope) shows you what she's written, but you don't acknowledge—she has nothing new to tell you. You are a god, already know everything."

The second (Polyhymnia) speaks when she should not, and Apollo admonishes her. The third (Terpsichore) finds favor: "Terpsichore pleases you, and you bless her and dance together. Sometimes you play with her, like dodge game. Then, you take her on your back for nice flying. Coda begins, and you dance like thunderstorm, and muses try to hold you back. They want you to practice, ride chariot of sun across sky, and bring sunlight, prophecy, music, and dance to the world. Now, life as boy is over. Papa says, 'You are grown up. Come up to Olympus to be with family.' The muses try to hold you back, but you make them bow to you, and leave them to ascend to your home."

Lifar had Balanchine working out the choreography with him, one on one, for a year; I had Balanchine for a couple of weeks. He showed me all the steps, danced them himself, coached me a few times, played the ballerina and made me partner him, and then left me alone to rehearse in a ballet studio that was dirty, grimy, with one mirrored wall. His interest was in inventing the choreography for *Agon.*

Nicholas Kopeikine, the company pianist, helped me. A rotund man with a distinguished leonine head and fat, chubby fingers that flitted lightly over the keys like butterflies, he had known Balanchine from the early days with Diaghilev. In Russia, Kopeikine's father's company manufactured the brass buttons on the uniforms of the tsar's soldiers. In rehearsal, Koyla, we called him, kept nodding at me, saying, "Good, good, you will be good." Kolya was cultured and sophisticated, a soft tabby cat, gray-haired with wobbly jowls, his suit littered with cigarette ashes from the never-absent butt pointing from his lips. He took it upon himself to mentor and mother me, and I listened to everything

Apollo blesses Terpsichore (Allegra Kent), the muse of music and dance, 1957

he said. "All you have to do is copy how Balanchine dances it." He would delight me with bits of his history: "I should have been girl. I had nine sisters. Mama, Papa didn't know they really had ten girls. It's just one had a peepee by mistake." Then: "To cross the border out of Russia, I went with pigs in railroad car, on hands and knees wearing skin."

I kept waiting for Balanchine to come around and see how I was

Stravinsky showing Balanchine his completed score to Agon, *1957. Kolya seated at the piano, delighted. I had been rehearsing* Apollo *next door, and had rushed in to watch.*

doing, coach me more—but he was obsessed with *Agon* and rarely showed up and, when he did, had nothing to say. I couldn't believe it. I'd finish the variation and knew it wasn't good, but he wouldn't say anything. At orchestra and, later, the dress rehearsal, Balanchine offered me no feedback.

Preview night came, a benefit for NYCB. After, people said I danced well, but I knew better, and was crushed, embarrassed, shamed. My performance had: *No Stamina*—I don't believe that in the previous weeks I had danced through the demanding choreography without making a pause, a breather; *No Style*—poor musical phrasing, with my hands so full trying to do the steps, I had no idea most of the time if I was ahead of or behind the music; *No Control*—at the end of *Apollo's* major variation, I ended on the floor facing the backdrop instead of the audience.

That night, in my dingy dressing room at City Center, I waited for Balanchine to come upstairs and fantasized him saying, "Awful! How can you go on so unprepared! Tomorrow, all day, *I* will rehearse you . . . and the next day and the next . . . over and over each phrase, gesture, expression, *we* will work!"

In the dressing room below, I overheard the muffled voice of Balanchine talking to the three ballerinas who had danced with me. My heart pounded as he left them, and then I heard his footsteps fade away, going downstairs, instead of up to me.

Miserable, I sat there sweating in my jockstrap, thinking, "That's it. I'm quitting dance. I'll finish the season and after that, no more." Louie the doorman came to turn out the lights and found me sitting numb and dejected. "I'm closing up . . . you got to get out . . . I'm locking the

Balanchine demonstrating, 1962

door." I dressed, went down to the bulletin board where the rehearsal schedules are posted, and scrawled, "FOR JACQUES—tomorrow, Wednesday and Thursday—Apollo rehearsal 3 hours a.m., 3 hours p.m. *ALONE* . . ." and underlined it.

I got what I asked. Alone in a studio, I took each step, analyzed it, and practiced, repeating it over and over again at different tempi— slow motion, then fast, faster—even danced with my eyes shut, to explore the possibilities in the movement. I would repeat this regimen with the next movement. Then, I'd do the first and second steps together to find the flow between them. Next, progress to the third step, and repeat. Now, put first, second, and third together, finding the bridges. And so on, until I'd rehearsed every step in the ballet, including how my arms, head, torso, and legs were positioned even while in the middle of lifting the ballerina, practicing my partnering without a partner. It took two hours to get through a two-and-a-half-to-three- minute variation. I even practiced breathing, where and how I would breathe. By the time I performed the role again, I'd made a quantum leap and stumbled upon an interesting paradox: through detailed prac- tice and countless repetitions, there is freedom. Vladimiroff had told me that, but you only learn by doing . . . maybe.

Previous to my experience in *Apollo,* I would perform my roles the best I could, rehearsing only the hours required by the choreographer or the demands of the ballerina who was my partner. I enjoyed perform- ing in a thoughtless sort of way, improving a bit and, generally, having success.

Apollo launched me on a new trajectory. For each role, I began to set goals, analyze how to reach them, and, laboring alone, strive to reach the imagined criteria, until those original goals were no longer a chal- lenge. Skills were acquired, and increased skills demand increased goals. I'd set the bar higher, and launch myself anew. In the artist's pur- suit, there is no ultimate end—whether musician, painter, actor, writer, choreographer, architect, director, poet, or dancer. I believe that pursu- ing and perfecting, as well as performing, foster a kind of morality. There is no place in the strict discipline and mathematics of the art forms that are music and dance for anything false.

If someone of quality mentors you, you are lucky. If that someone is Balanchine, you are blessed. His was more than teaching, it was a phi- losophy of manners. The best mentor sets up an environment for discovery, suggests and demonstrates, and leaves the artist alone to explore. Years later, when I was directing the musical *Lady in the Dark,* a dear friend and superb actor, Michael Tolan, advised, "Go into your rehearsals loaded with bullets. Know everything about the play, the characters, the history, the style—but don't tell your actors anything about their characters. Leave them alone. They will find out more about their characters than you ever dreamed. They will surprise, delight, and amaze you. By trying to do it for them, you deprive them, and, ultimately, you waste a tremendous resource."

I heard from Balanchine the same thing. "Class is to analyze how to do the gesture. After you leave class, you must practice alone—practice your tendus by the thousands—while eating your eggs and brushing your teeth." Then he would say, "Something will happen with your body. You will develop speed and strength. Virtuosity. The rest is up to—" and he would make one of his characteristic gestures heavenward, indicating it had something to do with divine forces.

Some of those "divine" forces must have been helping me: by the second performance of *Apollo, stamina, style,* and *control* were mine.

Dancing became so much more interesting, an odyssey toward excellence. In this singular striving toward an ideal, with only yourself as competition—no coach, no audience, just you, motivating and pushing—I found a joy. In my son Christopher's book, *Leap Year,** he writes about how, when doing a challenging role, he'd be tossing and turning in bed at night, dancing in his mind, unable to sleep. He would go to the theater at two o'clock in the morning, turn on the lights in the rehearsal studio, and practice alone until five a.m. All our company dancers remember when the passionate Melissa Hayden had a role to dance, rehearsal rooms would be unavailable. She actually seemed to be in *all* three of them—at the same time.

Just to get ready for class in the morning, the dancer warms up, sometimes for an hour or so. Then after class comes a day full of hours of rehearsals, one after the other. Any additional time is devoted to working out little details of the choreography—honing, perfecting. Through it all, there is a sense of building toward performance.

Then arrives "Curtain going up!"—the peak. Now you're free to forget everything, listen to the music, and dance.

* Christopher d'Amboise, *Leap Year* (Doubleday, 1982).

Elation builds, you feel in complete command of the stage—your world—and the space it encompasses. It even seems you can master time. Occasionally, you become a doppelgänger, seemingly outside yourself, watching yourself dance, and partaking in reciprocal joy. Even time seems to slow.

After the performance, I'd be on such a high I felt I could envelop everything—audience, orchestra, stagehands, lights, curtains—and later, in the streets, the passersby. I could swallow them all with relish. While onstage, I often thought, "If all I have left to live is these next few minutes of dancing, it's worth it." At night I'd dream "dance."

Distance runners speak of an endorphin high, how after running a long race, there is a sense of exhilaration. It comes, in some ways, from the release of tension after the race. The body tingles, there is an enormous sense of accomplishment. George Hirsch, a friend and world-class marathon runner, cajoled me to run the marathon in New York. "Why don't you try it? It's the first time they're going to run through all five boroughs." In 1976, I did, and after, celebrating at Tavern on the Green, I reflected, "Oh, if this is the runner's rush, it's what's been happening to me after every performance all these years."

*Jacques d'Amboise's drawings illustrating the evolution
of the decor of* Apollo *over decades*

The three muses: from left, Patricia McBride, Allegra Kent, and Patricia Neary, 1957

Of course, not every performance succeeds, even if the dancer is the only one who realizes its shortcomings. The usual peaks of elation may be matched by equivalent depths of depression.

In that 1957 premiere of *Agon,* Apollo had a new look. Previous productions had used colorful and elaborate scenery. As Apollo, Lifar wore a Grecian-style tunic cut to a miniskirt, decorated with gold clasps, and danced in ballet shoes emulating sandals. Laces crisscrossing up his calves. In subsequent revivals in America, Lew, then Nicky Magallanes, and Eglevsky, appeared in similar costume and wore elaborate wigs or curled their hair and sprayed it gold. In Balanchine's revival for me, he wanted a new look, pared down to essentials, black and white. Mount Olympus became a thin black staircase, silhouetted against a blue sky. Onstage, the enormous rock where Apollo sat became a diminutive black stool. No ornament at all, minimalist. I danced bare-chested, with only a thin white drapery of cloth over one shoulder, held by a solitary gold button, black tights, and white ballet shoes. Michael Arshansky couldn't wait to play with my hair. "No!" Balanchine objected. "Hair is fine. Simple, teenage American boy hair." The serenity of the strings in the music and purity of the choreography brings Apollo, in his apotheosis, into the sunlit sky. It was a perfect prelude to *Agon,* itself stark, etched in black and white. The new *Apollo* seemed thoroughly modern, as if the thirty years since its creation had vanished with the snap of a finger. Music and dance. Stravinsky and Balanchine, seamlessly pairing the sunlight of *Apollo* and the crackling radiation of *Agon,* lifting all up past the Van Allen belt.

And *Agon,* what a glory. Can you imagine the sight of two bodies—one, Arthur Mitchell, a black male, the other, Diana Adams, a milk-white ballerina—together on the stage in 1957? Clad in the simplest of form-fitting dance clothes, their pas de deux began with an entrance upstage left and moved diagonally like an express train to cross to the footlights on stage right. During their subsequent dance, there are times when Diana is held aloft with her legs spread, making an upside-down T over Arthur's head. At the end of their pas de deux, brimming with sensuality, yet tasteful and with simplicity, Arthur is at her feet, his head close to her thigh. The hush from the audience, as if in concert they had stopped breathing, was prelude to an ear-throbbing roar, reverberating in the street outside the theater. Again, Balanchine decades before anyone else.

Whenever *Apollo* was staged, Balanchine would coach, refine, and demonstrate. He loved dancing every part himself—the birth pangs of Apollo's mother, Leto, on top of the platform; the muses' variations; Apollo playing his lute. Balanchine was beautiful to watch. In the course of the next twenty years dancing the role, I received more time and guidance from him than Lifar or anyone else. We discussed *Apollo* in cafés over countless meals. After every performance, he would come

Half hour before curtain, clearing the stage, 1962

to the stage with some comment, suggestion, or piece of advice.* I knew he wanted to dance it himself, and was out front performing the role along with me in his imagination.

When NYCB first performed in Monte Carlo, Balanchine seemed obsessed. "This is where Lifar and I rehearsed *Apollo,* in this theater, on this stage." For the whole week, in every rehearsal, he insisted on going to the stage and standing in the wings; he would watch me practicing.

* According to Bernard Taper, in his *Balanchine* (p. 10), a pianist friend of Balanchine's had seen a performance of *Apollo* at City Center and had been so impressed that he went backstage to congratulate the dancers, and found Balanchine rehearsing first Patricia Wilde, then me. "Balanchine turned to d'Amboise, and the visitor could see them going over various sequences together—facing each other, like one man looking in a mirror, while both of them danced. Occasionally, they would stop for a few words of comment. D'Amboise would nod vigorously. Balanchine would smile agreement at something d'Amboise said, and then they would spring into action again, face to face, about three feet apart. Time passed as they continued to work, and the backstage visitor watched them wonderingly. Dancers began to gather onstage for the next ballet, which was to be *Agon.* Bells could be heard ringing, announcing the imminent curtain. Stagehands hurried to their places. Totally preoccupied, Balanchine and d'Amboise ignored it all. When the pianist finally left, without having a chance to congratulate anyone, they were still at it. They were gone from the stage, though, when the curtain went up on *Agon.* At the very last second, perhaps, the stage manager had taken each of them by an arm and led them off. The visitor, back in his seat, could not help wondering if they might not still be working away in the wings."

He was a shadow or mirror. He wouldn't leave, even when the cleaning crew came and tried to sweep me off. He told me he hated that Lifar had had such a big success with *Apollo* while Balanchine got poor reviews. He sniffed, "One critic said, 'When does a god crawl on knees?' " Then Balanchine gleefully pronounced, "So I say to critic, 'When have you seen a god?' "

From 1957 to the late 1970s, I did this ballet, staged it, and performed it all over the world. Better dancers than me have performed the role, but I had Balanchine, and I followed Kopeikine's advice: "Copy Balanchine." I never was good enough for what is inherent in the ballet, never equaled the monumental challenges and possibilities it offered, but the attempt transformed me from dancer to artist. If I skipped one performance, I felt I'd lost that opportunity to improve. The span of a dancer's performing time is limited.

A few years ago, Arthur Mitchell asked me to work with Dance Theatre of Harlem on *Apollo,* and shortly after, Helgi Tomasson invited me to San Francisco to coach his dancers. Rasta Thomas at DTH and Gonzalo Garcia of SFB, were the Apollos, both beautiful male dancers of charisma and superb technique. The ballerinas from both companies excelled. But I was too old to be able to dance it for them. As I tried to demonstrate, I would say, "I'm sorry. This is not what it should look like, you have to see Balanchine." In many dances, particularly *Prodigal Son,* any time he demonstrated his choreography, my mouth would open at the beauty of his movement. Coaching a slew of marvelous male dancers who danced the role over the years—Jerome Robbins, Francisco Moncion, Hugh Laing, Eddie Villella, Misha Baryshnikov—Balanchine would demonstrate and all paled in comparison. He wrung tears from your heart. Maria Tallchief, at a recent symposium, when asked about developing her extraordinary interpretations of Balanchine's choreography, responded, "Oh, I only had to look at George. He was so beautiful, the way he demonstrated the movements." Can you imagine what he was like at twenty-three, inventing and teaching *Apollo* and *Prodigal Son* to Lifar?

After dancing in Germany in the 1960s, a critic titled me "the Apollo of Madison Square Garden." Though I'm not sure he meant it as a compliment, the phrase resonates. Balanchine's *Apollo* is my story. A wild, untamed youth gains nobility through the arts. A New York City street boy from Washington Heights transformed by the art of the aerial.

· · ·

In late March of 1958, when my son George was a year and a half old, NYCB embarked on a tour of Japan, Australia, and the Philippines. Paul Szilard, a successful impresario who, as a dancer, had shared the barre with me in many a ballet class, booked our company for the six-month tour. Balanchine stayed home with Tanny; I took Carrie and little George with me on the Japan Airlines flight. Our ballet company had the run of the whole plane. Over two days, we hopped and refueled from San Francisco to Hawaii, Wake Island, and at last Tokyo. Carrie, George, and I sat right behind the cockpit, and despite George's continual squalling, the senior pilot, Captain Hench, took to us. "This is the last propeller flight that I'll fly for Japan Airlines," he confided. "Jets are the future, and I've been back in school learning how to fly them." He had young children of his own in San Francisco, but after our arrival in Tokyo he stayed an extra week, to help us settle in. "Best to stay in a traditional Japanese hotel. I'll arrange it—the Matsudaira—you'll have your own private cottage, surrounded by gardens."

What a dear Captain Hench was. "I'll get you the babysitter," he insisted. "TB is rampant in Japan, so she'll have to be tested. And I'll be sure to have pasteurized milk delivered to you—it's scarce here." Captain Hench made sure the milk wasn't delivered in bottles, but in sealed cartons, because, he warned, "People with TB sometimes spit into bottles." Our cottage sat solo in the midst of a garden of glorious flowers. Made of wood with paper walls that slid open to the outdoors, it had two rooms, one for us, and one for George and a babysitter. After he got us settled, Captain Hench returned to his own family in San Francisco. I never saw him again.*

Walking down the streets of Tokyo, George attracted crowds. They followed us, staring at his yellow hair, longing to touch and stroke it. We took him everywhere—dressing rooms, backstage, out front, and to after-performance dinners. At the restaurant table, I'd take the belt off my pants and attach George to a chair, seatbelt-style. A real show-biz trouper, he'd eat a few bites, squirm, wiggle, complain a bit, then pass out.

The two superstars of the company, Maria Tallchief and André

---

* Decades later, I received a letter from Captain Hench's daughters. Apparently, he was recently deceased, and had saved, among his effects, stacks of newspaper clippings about our family.

Wearing Tanny LeClercq's sweater and jumping over George, Australia, 1958

Eglevsky, skipped out of the tour. Maria informed Paul she was leaving after Tokyo, and nothing could dissuade her. André attempted to follow, but Paul, angry and distraught, insisted that he stay, "at least for the opening in Australia." As our plane was landing in Sydney, Paul sat, scheming with our manager, Betty Cage. "How can I face the press in Australia? I will have to confess that Maria walked out on us. Maybe if

I make up some grand excuse . . . How about I tell a big lie! She is pregnant, and her doctor said she will lose the baby if she dances?" "Well, if you want to lie," Betty mumbled, "I guess I can't stop you."

Recently, laughing over our many years of adventures together, Paul told me, "Can you imagine? I found out later Maria *was* pregnant, and, it's fantastic! The doctor *had* told her not to dance. You see? I'm a fortune-teller!"

After the opening in Sydney, André left, and the papers trumpeted, "Isn't Australia good enough for the superstars?" It was thrown upon Melissa Hayden and me to carry the company. The critics in Sydney were skeptical, but we eventually won them over. The audiences thrilled to Balanchine's choreography, and our reviews were glowing. Milly and I danced, and danced, and danced for two months, in Sydney, followed by two months in Melbourne, till it was time to say goodbye to the many Aussie friends and fans we had made. We headed for our final engagement, in the Philippines.

Paul Szilard is Hungarian. In ballet class in the late 1940s and '50s, he always wore a white short-sleeve T-shirt, black tights, white socks, and white ballet shoes, everything sparklingly clean. He was as neat and clean as a dancer and seemed to know everything and everyone. To this day, Paul, now in his nineties, books tours for the Alvin Ailey and Martha Graham dance companies, and quietly sends money to dancers he hears are in need.

Paul had spent World War II in Manila during the Japanese occupation, until he was liberated by the American G.I.s under General Douglas MacArthur. He cashed in those early connections to bring the company to Manila for the final week of our tour.

It was the end of September, and hot. The Philippine people were thrilled that we were there. It was a little over a decade since the Japanese had been forced out. Recovery was slow. Our theater was about an hour's drive, on the outskirts of Manila. We drove in a bus through dark roads, no lights, just twilight from the sun. The houses on the side of the road were teeming with people, waving at us and calling out greetings in Tagalog, their language. The houses were wood and carved with figures and designs, built off the ground on stilts, hoping to catch a breeze and be above the bugs, insects, and jungle stuff.

On arriving, we discovered our theater was a giant metal Quonset hut, aluminum or tin. Shaped as if a half of a watermelon was hollowed out, but over a city block long—three thousand folding chairs filled 90 percent of it. I doubt if more than the first few rows of people could really see. We were dancing on four-foot-high wooden risers covered with splintered plywood. The orchestra sat on the dirt floor at the base of the risers. Hopefully, to make a breeze, they had cut holes on the side of the hut and peeled back the metal like opening a can of sardines. All day long, the hot sun had been cooking this oven, and, open as it was, millions of mosquitoes were buzzing in residence. We had no need to do a warm-up to prepare for performance—I did one plié and found myself in a puddle of sweat. As we performed, we slipped on our own droplets on the floor. By the end of four ballets, the floor was sopping wet. All the dancers' muscles were cramping from loss of fluids, potassium, and salt. Looking out front into the audience, we saw three thousand flapping fans . . . not just people but their white programs trying to make a breeze.

The actor and singer George Irving and I once shared a bottle of wine (actually, several). I posed the question, "George, how old were you when you first did it? How did you lose your virginity?" His answer involved the outskirts of Manila.

George was drafted during World War II. After basic training, recruits lined up, and were told, "You're going to Japan; you're going to Europe; you're going to Italy; you're going to France; you're going to . . ." When George reached the front of the line, the guy deciding looked up and recognized him. They had done summer stock together. "Hey George, how did you get in the infantry?" "Drafted!" George replied. "Well, you should be in the USO, in the entertainment arm, performing! How about the Pacific?"

So that's how George got to the Philippines. He said they performed day and night, averaging twenty performances a week, sometimes at four o'clock in the morning, in a clearing in the jungle, under makeshift klieg lights, surrounded by exhausted troops. After a long stint, he went to Manila on an R & R break. The soldiers, excited about the whorehouses, chanted, "Let's go, let's go!" So George decided to try it.

"I took a shower, shaved, put on my best dress uniform, cut my fingernails, and perfumed and covered myself in talcum powder, because I wanted the experience to be perfect," he told me.

He got out of the jeep with the other soldiers. Dozens and dozens of troops were around, most of them drunk, some coming out of the brothels holding naked women upside down with their legs spread, yelling, "This is what you're going to get! This is what you're going to get!"

"I was so traumatized," George said, "but I was determined to do it." Inside, there were cubbyholes with sheets dividing rows of mattresses lying on the floor. "I don't doubt the Japanese had just left, because we could still hear shooting off in the jungle. I was not going to let this be a bad experience, so I stood at attention next to the poor girl in the bed, and sang Cole Porter."

> *Night and day, you are the one.*
> *Only you beneath the moon or under the sun . . .*

What did the girl think? The Japanese were bad enough, and now the drunken Americans. Here was a singing madman, moaning at her. All George heard in reply to his serenade was, "Hurry up and pom pom."

MILLY

Melissa Hayden was a perfect example of doing everything possible to be your best onstage. We would be on a concert tour. Milly would want to get up and go to the theater first thing in the morning and do barre. Or she'd get out of bed and do barre in her room. She even traveled with a full-length mirror. At breakfast, she would sit down, eat like a stevedore, then consume forty different colored vitamin pills—she'd lay them out on the table like a mosaic. She'd find a place to get a massage after class, check the floor of the theater, go out front and look at the stage to see the sight lines, take a nap after rehearsal. We'd come to the theater, always an hour earlier than everyone else, and she'd want to rehearse constantly, "Can we do it again?" She had a ritual in the dressing room, and carried a syringe to give herself vitamin B_{12} shots for extra energy, just before curtain. Everything was timed and worked out so that when the overture played she was ready to make her entrance onstage, she was at her peak.

If she didn't feel at her peak, to get her adrenaline up, she'd pick a fight. Once, just before our entrance in *Swan Lake,* we could hear the music in a countdown, Thirty, twenty-nine, twenty-eight . . . I was busy trying to get myself together, jumping and stretching, when I spotted that dissatisfied look on her face. "Milly, save it. Leave me alone." Twenty-one . . . twenty . . . nineteen . . .

"Well, I don't feel ready," she complained. "I don't have enough energy. I have to get my adrenaline going. Let me go pick a fight with a stagehand."

As the countdown continued, fifteen, fourteen, thirteen . . . , she'd approach some unsuspecting member of the crew. "Hey! I have to make an entrance here. Move your ass. Move up to the front where you can see me better!" At that point, it's like ten, nine, eight . . . and she's arguing with this guy, who's furious at her, and he's opening his mouth to call out "BITCH!" . . . then three, two, one and she's onstage, transforming that conflict into a performance of riveting drama.

At the end of the bows, when the curtain came down, she'd yell, "Where the hell is he? Where's that wonderful man? I owe it all to him!" She would seek out that stagehand to hug him and kiss him, saying, "Thank you, thank you, I needed you! Wasn't I great?!" Tremendous generosity of spirit, drive, and ego.

Milly depended more than anybody I know on the music. If the music didn't give her joy, pleasure, and excitement, she would be angry. Partnering her onstage was exciting, but hair-raising. She would feel the impulse to throw herself in a different direction or add an extra pirouette, change a step, or go to a different place! You never knew what was going to happen, everything was spontaneous, there would be something different at every performance. She had favorite pairs of toe shoes, and she would set them up in the wings—in one pair, she thought she did better pirouettes, another pair were for adagio, and another, softer pair for jumps (not so noisy when you land). During performance, she would exit into a wing, and, in ten seconds, switch to the shoes that best suited her next variation, her fingers a blur of untying and tying ribbons. So versatile and one of the greatest dramatic ballerinas on the stage, she had over sixty ballets in her repertoire from NYCB alone. The opera world had Maria Callas; the ballet, Melissa Hayden.

Compassion and generosity—she could hide nothing, in personal or public life. She never held back, never played it safe. She mothered two beautiful children, Stuart and Jennifer. Loyalty and Integrity were her other children. "If anything doesn't work in my life, it's not going to be because I didn't do everything possible to make it work."

Melissa Hayden joined NYCB the same year I did. I was fifteen; she was twenty-six. We danced together and became lifelong friends. Ballets were choreographed for us, and we explored, as artistic siblings, the art of dance. On that Australian tour, both of us danced into a bond of admiration and caring—connected forever.

Carrie, George, and I had our own little house in Sydney, right on Bondi Beach, and oh! how the Aussies took care of us. Carrie, paddling with George at the edge of the surf, was warned, "Lady, if you hear a klaxon blast, it just means the sharks are coming in, so you and the little tyke should consider getting out of the water." It seemed to ring several times a day. I first saw an emu (the Australian version of an ostrich, its head atop a neck taller than my six foot two); the adorable koala bears, feasting on the leaves of eucalyptus trees; and kangaroos, cute until you see a re-creation of what they were like in prehistoric times (eight feet tall). At morning rush hour in Sydney, there would be queues of workers lined up, not for coffee and doughnuts, but for the juice and pulp of Queensland pineapples. The vendors would place a whole pineapple into a machine that, in one movement, would flay and core the pineapple, while a separate arm descended to crush the prepared fruit into a waiting container. In about six seconds, the customer would be guzzling chilled, pulped pineapple. So refreshing, just the thought of it got me out of bed in the morning. As the poet Hafiz wrote:

> 'Tis life's pure river
> 'tis sugar's giver

With our extensive repertoire, we presented a variety of ballets each week, but the Australian fans complained. Through word of mouth or by reading a review, they'd hear about a program, and want to see that exact program. We began to oblige, doing the same dance program several days in a row. Since Eglevsky had left, I stepped into all his virtuoso roles and had my own repertoire to dance, plus partner to most of the ballerinas. In one evening's program, I'd be supporting the lovely Diana Adams in *Concerto Barocco,* dancing the faun to Allegra Kent's nymph in *Afternoon of a Faun,* followed by *Pas de Dix* with the dynamic Patricia Wilde, then with Milly, leading the finale of *Stars and Stripes.* During a week, sometimes the ballerinas would change, but there was no respite for me. Doing the same program over and over was hard on the body, because you're taxing the same muscles in the same way, night after night, and on weekend matinees. For those four months, I had the stage to myself for rehearsals during the day, and the chance to refine and explore my roles each night. I took the lessons I had learned doing *Apollo* the year before, put them into practice, and when we returned to New York I was dancing with a different attitude about myself. Before, it was always "Tallchief and Eglevsky" headlining. Now, it was "Hayden and d'Amboise" as well. Melissa had always been a star, but now I realized I could stand with her.

For a quarter of a century, Milly and I danced together, guesting with other companies, doing concerts and television—every opportunity to get onstage together. We became like an old couple, an institution, a caricature—in the ballet *Stars and Stripes,* the company nicknamed us "Ike and Mamie" after President Eisenhower and his wife. I danced my first full-length *Coppélia, Giselle,* and *Swan Lake* with her, and choreographed a production of *Firebird* for her.

In the fall of 1958, I returned to New York to discover the exquisite Violette Verdy had joined our company, and we were to dance together in Birgit Cullberg's ballet *Medea.* I was to be Jason; Violette, King Creon's daughter, Creusa; and Melissa, Medea. The ballet triumphed. Balanchine hated it. He complained to me that the choreography was unrelated to Bartók's music, but I think he was peeved at the ballet's success and audience acclaim.

Balanchine rarely did a ballet with the idea of building up the male dancer as star. If he needed a crowd-pleasing work, he would find music of quality and dancers who interested him, and he would create a wonderful ballet. But those were not the works closest to his heart; some of his own ballets he came to hate or actively resent, when he thought the principal performers and their performances superseded the choreography. When a dance artist had a tremendous success, with screaming fans, and the choreography faded into the shadows under the celebrity star, he fumed. Several times, he had been given assignments by Diaghilev to create star vehicles for Lifar, Diaghilev's lover. Balanchine created *Apollo* and *Prodigal Son* for Lifar, and to this day they are stellar roles for the male dancer, but Balanchine did not want to be at the mercy of anyone telling him what to do—ballet critics, fans, patrons, or ballerinas. He ranted to me that audiences and critics had talked only about Lifar and not about "Balanchine," and this was more than thirty years after the fact.

It was a dilemma he lived with all his life. He tried his best to avoid it, but audiences, patrons, management, and the stars themselves defeated him. He knew he needed stars, and with his ballets he created many of them, but he resented their success and hated their demands.

Lincoln insisted that Balanchine create a star vehicle for Jerry Robbins; *Tyl Ulenspiegel* resulted. It did not last long in the repertory. In each subsequent production of *Firebird* he diminished the star's role. The audience would be screaming and cheering the firebird during the ballet, and Balanchine would say to me, "Why are they clapping? Who wants to hear clapping? It's the music we want to hear." When they applauded the star on the entrance, he'd say, "Music hasn't even started, and dance not begun, and already they clap? It doesn't matter what will happen. They've already lost their ears and their eyes."

Tired of hearing audiences declare they only bought tickets to see Tallchief and Eglevsky in *Sylvia: Pas de Deux*, he ripped it out of the repertory. "I gave this to Eglevsky, you know, for his concerts." Over the years, the Delibes music for *Sylvia* found fading life in Balanchine's watered-down versions, first *Pas de Deux and Divertissement* and ultimately, diminished more, into the ballet *La Source.*

In the mid-1970s, Mr. B and I are in the wings. *Apollo* is onstage tonight, danced by Peter Martins. We're watching a truncated version, missing the prologue (the birth of Apollo), and with a cut-and-pasted ending. No more Apollo ascending a staircase into the sky, an unstoppable force caressed by sunlight as the music fades into the ionosphere. Rather, Apollo now ends onstage, embraced by the muses, in an echo of an earlier pose. "Why did you do that, Mr. B? Cut Stravinsky's music, cut out the prologue, and change the choreography for the ending?" Without looking at me, musing to himself, he whispers, "You know, audience only want to see stars, and stars only want to make poses, not do my steps. So I give them what they want. Poses. Like for magazine." Then, turning to look at me, he pauses a second, and adds, "Like van Gogh—cut off his own ear!"

EPISODES: BALANCHINE AND INVENTION

Spring 1959 brought an extraordinary dance event. Balanchine and Martha Graham, titans of the dance world, were to celebrate the music of Anton von Webern. A ballet titled *Episodes,* it would be a collaboration between NYCB dancers and some of Martha's dancers, with Paul Taylor as a solo guest. Lincoln had seen Taylor dance and admired him.

Balanchine, too, was impressed, and invited him to dance with us. Paul had an extremely muscular body and strange, pale eyes that stared at the audience as he danced. An amazing, facile dancer, he managed to look simian as well as feline. Balanchine created a bizarre solo for him, and I watched from the wings during every performance. Paul's movements, the shape of his body, and the way he moved were the opposite of traditional ideas of gracefulness and symmetry. With tremendous muscular power, his movements were grotesque. They seemed to the eye, at first, awkward, odd shapes and patterns, that Paul transformed into riveting beauty. Fascinating, intriguing. He was (and remains) a great artist.

For *Episodes,* Balanchine called me to rehearse with Diana. "You know, we will do version of first man and first woman." The music was Webern's *Six Pieces for Orchestra,* a thrilling composition, and, as was his wont with me, Balanchine described to me how he envisioned the ballet:

> You know, you are naked. Two—Adam and Eve, naked, you see? And you're next to each other, in pose, knees turn in, and you're looking up, frozen and afraid. And, because you have eaten apple already, you are a little bit ashamed. You want to cover yourself, but you can't find, you know, leaf. But there's some hair on the floor, so you grab each piece of hair, and start to cover yourself. Girl on one side, boy on other, you wrap around, between legs, around body, and you're turning as you wrap— you, Jacques, to the left, against the clock, and Diana, to the right. Hair is long, looong, long hair, and after maybe thirty, forty feet, it comes together, and it's attached to the head of a bat-like witch. She has hair attached to her head, and she's lying on back, facing sky. Underneath her is dancer, on hands and knees, dressed as toad. As you pull hair, hair pulls her, and toad moves. So, you two, on body winding hair, are pulling toad with bat woman riding on its back. And just when you're completely wrapped like a cocoon, hair has come to end, and there is face of bat between you, upside down, staring at you, and you are looking back at this bat. Four men in black, two on each side, come and grab bat, spread-eagle bat, lift up in air, and start to run with her like kite that swoops down and up, all around the stage. Well, when they do that, you see, run with bat, it pulls hair and spins you out of hair cocoon, and into each other's arms, naked again. Toad hops off frightened, and the bat, with all the hair flying around, swoops offstage. All of this is done

with just spotlight on center, and another to follow bat. Audience does not see the floor of the stage. Now, when bat has left, stage lights up, and we see, all over the floor, clothes—blue jeans, blouses, right? Jackets. And we start pas de deux.

Balanchine started choreographing this pas de deux. I'm holding Diana, she leans over, picks up the edge of a skirt. As she makes a développé, she gets one leg into the skirt, and while supporting her, I am following choreography that eventually gets my legs into blue jeans, and continuing this most inventive dance of turning, twisting with contorted lifts, and rollings on the floor, up, down and around again. In less than a minute, we're both standing, holding hands, attired in blue jeans, skirt, blouse, bandana—a pair of contemporary hippies, ready to dance for today. It was terrific, it was thrilling!

We'd had about four days of rehearsal, and had arrived at where the dressing pas de deux was complete, when . . . knock, knock, knock on the studio door. Balanchine opens it, it's Martha Graham. She had been in a nearby rehearsal studio, choreographing a piece to another of Webern's scores. Her choreography involved the relationship between Mary Queen of Scots and Queen Elizabeth, and Martha had run out of music. She'd come to Balanchine to ask, "Do you know of any more music of Webern that I could use?"

Balanchine nodded, walked over to the piano, and took the score, *Six Pieces for Orchestra,* that he had just spent four days using for his choreography, and handed it to her. He then turned and announced to us, "You know, maybe we won't do. Another time, maybe. Martha needs it." Diana and I looked at each other, our mouths fell open, "Whhaat?"

The next day, Balanchine and I met for breakfast. "You have to choreograph, Jacques, you must choreograph all the time." And I said, "What do you mean, all the time?" He said, "Not necessary to put onstage. You must just choreograph. Make up dances all the time. Give yourself impediments." He explained, "You know, make pas de deux and have no pirouettes—no pirouettes. Or, ballerina must never, ever, be in second position. Or, like we did, pas de deux while you get dressed. And then if you do this, don't expect to put it on the stage. It's exercise. A person wants to write—don't write a novel right away; first you write a thousand short stories and poems, letters, but you learn how to write. Maybe someday you have great novel. Same with music, choreography, painting—you exercise!" he urged. Then he invented a scenario for pas de deux on the spot. "For example, imagine pas de deux where you don't see each other. You reach for each other and you always miss. And then, all of a sudden, you touch! And now, you can't unstick. You are stuck forever." Well, I started to laugh, and I said, "What a great idea! Why don't you do it?" "No, it's an exercise for you to do," he replied.

The next day, on the bulletin board, it said, "Diana and Jacques— 5 Pieces for Orchestra." Balanchine had another Webern piece, and in less than two hours, he choreographed to it a dance similar to the one he'd described at breakfast the day before. He must have gone to bed and thought about it; then, in the morning, he found some music and posted a message for us on the bulletin board, "Come to rehearsal."

This time, the choreography did get performed. On a dimly lit stage, a man enters upstage right, the woman, downstage left. As if balancing on a tightrope stretched diagonally between them, they move toward each other, reaching and yearning to embrace—but they miss, pass by without touching. Then abruptly they turn, face each other, and again try, in frantic lunges, but always missing by inches. Suddenly, as the woman reaches away, the man captures her hand, and within a few moments, puts his head between her legs and stands up, as all stage lights go out, except for a small spot around his face. You see her two white legs emerging from behind his head. Her legs wrap around his arms, and with his fingers extended, the effect is of a giant pair of deer's antlers. He runs around, seeking her, and then poses, a frightened deer in headlights. The lights fade to black, then come up, to reveal their arms around each other, nonchalantly standing, serene, in a pool of light. At the antlers scene, the audience reacted in different ways. It was so inventive and unusual that there were chortles of delight and bursts of applause. Some ballet fans told me they thought Balanchine's choreography was inspired by a shamanistic ritual.

Balanchine visualized inventions in his brain ahead of time. Using the music as a blueprint, his imagination built an entire structure before he invented a single step on his dancers. On many occasions, he described the scenery, the lighting, the order and narrative of his ballets before any sets were built, or even scenic artists hired. *Vienna Waltzes, Robert Schumann's "Davidsbündlertänze," Union Jack,* the pas de deux *Meditation, A Midsummer Night's Dream,* and *The Figure in the Carpet* are just some of the ballets he described to me in detail, at times almost a year before a dancer did a step in rehearsal. But every piece of choreography—ensemble, pas

Episodes, *1962*

de deux, solos, finales—the dance steps themselves were invented right on the dancers, in the present. No preconceived steps in his mind. All inspired and invented on a certain dancer and the way they moved. There were many times that he would trust me, "Make some turn here, Jacques, you know, in place. Four counts of eight, while I fix the dancers behind you." I would invent something, show him, and he would either keep it, edit it, or suggest something else.

Opus 34 (1954) was a ballet set to Schoenberg music that has become legend, at least as long as those who danced it, or saw it, still live. The score was so dense that two conductors in the pit were needed to handle its complexity, with Balanchine—the third conductor—onstage, hidden, tucked in the wings, gesturing and counting out loud for the dancers. Quite often in his ballets, Balanchine would fill musical phrases with the dancers holding hands, getting tangled and tied up in knots, and then unraveling through his choreographic legerdemain. In the ballet *Concerto Barocco,* it happens in the second movement. Every time I see it, I smile with delight at its invention and beauty.

In *Opus 34,* he had maneuvered twenty-four dancers, ensnaring them in a seething mass. As the movements continued, it disentangled—as if some mathematical formula, defying solution for centuries, had been solved in front of your eyes. The choreography so described the architecture of the music as to make you exclaim, "Oh, it's the Truth we're hearing." In another part of *Opus,* there was a macabre dance for Tanny LeClercq and Herbert Bliss that took place in an operating room, where they represented two flayed bodies in a flopping pas de deux—a pair of medical models of veins, blood vessels, muscles, sinew, viscera, and nerve endings that had slipped off the surgery table.

In the 1954 ballet *Ivesiana,* Balanchine invented haunting choreography to Charles Ives's composition *The Unanswered Question.* It starred the teenage ballerina Allegra Kent and caused a sensation. The nubile Allegra is borne by four males, as if they are transporting a sacred icon. She falls and swoops, twisted, contorted, bent into a ball, then spread, her legs akimbo. Her airborne peregrinations, at one time, have her being passed around the waists of her bearers as if they were threading a belt through loops. And always that beautiful, serene face, staring innocently and unaffectedly at the audience, as if she were in another world. Never does she touch the earth. Throughout this procession and meandering around the stage, a bare-chested man follows her, with out-stretched arms, yearningly seeking her, never leaving his knees. Waiting in the wings with my partner, Tanny, for our entrance in the dance Balanchine invented for us, *George Washington's Barn Dance,* I remember reflecting that there will never be a choreographer to equal him. Inventing some four hundred ballets. Analytic, spiritual, the musicality of him, the quality of taste, the surprises, inventing worlds outside of the ordinary as if he had conjured planets and satellites, other moons, right outside of our globe, that we had never imagined existed. And his generosity was unmatched. When you read the letters of Stravinsky, you get a sense of his tightfistedness, his concern about royalties—you never got that with Balanchine. The god of dance touched him. He was blessed, so he gave. "You diminish yourself by putting a price tag on your work. One does not own dance."

When I see his ballets danced today, I realize they miss his presence. Anyone who tries to teach Balanchine ballets somehow fails. We are the dancers who danced the roles, and are trying to express and re-create what was taught us, but it's not the same. Besides, Balanchine would re-create movement—he'd change the steps to challenge a different type of dancer! He was the pinnacle. If Balanchine did it or said it, it became dogma. Carrie, in 1946, on her first visit to New York, wrote in her diary:

> Balanchine was our God. It's not so easy to explain. We didn't pray to him. We asked for help for our dancing because he was all knowing, all seeing, you believed with all your heart that what he saw in your dancing was absolutely true, and right. No one else I have ever known had such a clear vision of what we were each struggling to do.
>
> The enormity of this only became apparent to me much later.
>
> What a luxury—a God, a leader, you believe without doubt, and can follow in blind faith. You can accomplish 100% more because you don't have to question every move you make . . . just follow . . . As soon as you comprehended & executed one more step in the progression he had set up for you—Mr. B was quick to give assurances.
>
> Each individual was different and he never tried to make the techniques the same for each, and his goals for each dancer were different— using their differences in physical and mental make-up to bring out their individuality rather than make a dance mold for all.
>
> Everyone goes on and on about "the Balanchine technique"—analyzing it to death . . . it was so simple.—Each dancer must learn to move as fast as possible . . . jump as high as possible . . . use your feet so that they

were like a hand . . . arabesque as high as possible. This was America &
his dream of America was BIG—BOLD—FREE . . . and in some cases
RAUNCHY.

That's why I was so shocked to see him petty about Cranko, or jealous because Ashton was working with Diana Adams, or pissed off
because he didn't think Birgit Cullberg's ballet *Medea* was as good as
the applause it received, or peeved that William Dollar's ballet *The Duel*
was always a smashing success. His own ballet *Minkus Pas de Trois,* a
star vehicle for André Eglevsky, he later claimed he hated because the
Minkus music was so bad. The truth was, though, the audience
screamed for Eglevsky. And Balanchine's reaction to the brilliance of
Jerome Robbins's *The Cage,* choreographed to Stravinsky music, the
turf Balanchine claimed as his own, was sad. If the ballet was being performed, he would avoid the stage, and if I mentioned "Jerry's *Cage,*"
he would look away and change the subject. On the other hand,
HOORAY! If Balanchine didn't have those flaws, he'd be hard to take,
too perfect. I mean, thank God there were those streaks of pettiness.

Of the two, the more sympathetic, to me, was Lincoln—a flawed
savant, stumbling through a minefield. Being subjected to the wild
oscillating stylus of his emotional electrocardiogram did not put me
off. I'd want to calm him and stroke him, "It's all right, Lincoln." But
when Balanchine revealed a jealousy, I'd want to deny it, walk away,
tuck any criticism of him in the bottom of the drawer and forget it.

"Miracle" George

The birth of our son George had interrupted Carrie's career, but she got back to dancing with NYCB in Australia, and when *Nutcracker* performances ended our fall season in January 1959, she took two-year-old George to visit her family in Highland Park, Texas. While there, she noticed a tiny, pebble-like growth on the inside of his right nostril. Off they went to the hospital to have it checked. The doctors removed the pebble and did a biopsy of the tissue. The results were devastating: "It's rhabdomyosarcoma, a deadly cancer." Carrie grabbed George and flew back to New York, to find me in bed with the measles.

At Lenox Hill Hospital, Dr. Jordan brought in Jim Gould. A second biopsy confirmed rhabdomyosarcoma and further revealed that some of the cells at the edge of the growth had been cut in half, indicating that the cancer had not been "encapsulated," and had probably spread.

Within a week, a handful of doctors—all experts in their varied fields—held a closed-door meeting to confer on George's diagnosis and treatment. We had been waiting outside for more than an hour when a long-faced Jim Gould came out. "This kind of cancer is rare and very deadly. There's nothing we can recommend—not radiation or surgery. Radiation will burn and scar him terribly. As for surgery, even the chief surgeon said, 'No way. You would have to excise half the baby's face.' " Their unanimous consensus was that no treatment could help. "Even with intense radiation or surgery, no one with rhabdomyosarcoma has survived more than a year or two."

Carrie and I stood, numb and hopeless. Jim disappeared for a few moments, made arrangements, then returned and said, "I'm driving you home." Carrie and I squeezed into the front seat of Jim's car, holding hands, and a voice in my mind repeated, "Don't let yourself think about George, he's gone. Worry about your wife." When Jim stopped the car in front of our apartment building, we sat, silent. It was pouring rain. Then from Carrie, "How much time?" Jim sighed, "Within the year." "What do we do?" whispered Carrie. "Well, I want to see him every week." Jim looked away. "But if I were you, I would plan to take him soon to some beautiful beach, go to the Caribbean, swim and play with him, while you can." We stepped out of the car into the rain, to find ourselves sloshing in ankle-deep water. The drain on the street corner was blocked and the gutter had flooded.

The next day, we went to the children's ward to pick up George. The room was dimly lit, but we found him in one corner. He stood, holding on to the edge of his crib, shaking it and howling, with his little halo of blond hair and a nose full of packing, dripping blood. There were other children in the ward, but I saw only his little face and tiny hands, shaking the bars of the crib.

Carrie rushed over, and in her soft voice started soothing him. I couldn't stand to stay in the room. I fled into the next ward. Eight or ten cribs lined the walls, occupied by other children with serious illnesses. "Want to see me jump over a chair?" I announced enthusiastically. "But I better land lightly and right on this spot, because I'm a cat!" I leaped, landed, and my tiny audience was intrigued. "Want to see how a cat moves?" I performed a cat dance. "Here comes a chicken!" I squawked and scuttled in and out among the cribs—anything to entertain them and distract myself; I couldn't face my own son. I didn't have the courage. That's why, every time I look at Carrie, I think how *strong* she is, how strong mothers have to be. I think it may have been the first time I used dance to engage children. The beginning of what would later become National Dance Institute.

The news about George spread. Everyone knew and loved him. I got a call to go to SAB to talk to Eugenie Ouroussow, the school's director, and her number one assistant, Natalie Molostwoff (we called her "Black Natasha" because of her swarthy skin, coal-black hair, throaty voice, and serious demeanor). They eagerly advised me that there was hope for George. "There's a doctor in Chicago who has developed a cancer cure—it's a serum derived from animals who had survived cancers." Both swore they knew of friends who, due to the shots, had their cancers go into remission. Natasha dramatically recounted, "They opened Sasha up and he was *riddled* with cancer"—those are the words she used, "*riddled* with cancer." But he'd gone to Chicago, taken the shots, and, "in six months, was completely cured."

I jotted down the doctor's name, collected information about him, and presented it to Jim Gould. "What do you think?" Jim was glum. "I've heard of this doctor and his serum. I have my doubts. But let me investigate, and I'll get back to you." Within a few days, Jim called. "This doctor has been claiming these cures for years, and the American Medical Association has asked him for documented proof and his files, but he has refused to show anything to the Oversight Board." Jim went on, "I don't know what to tell you, because our doctors offer you nothing. But I believe you would be investing your energies, money, and hope in a pipe dream." We were ready to sell everything we owned, move to Chicago, and take a chance on this doctor's serum injections. They were expensive—once a day for six months at around a hundred dollars a shot (1959 dollars). "I can't tell a parent who is going to lose a child not to grab at every straw, but, if it was my child, I wouldn't trust this doctor," said Jim.

We agonized, concluded we had to trust in Jim, give up the chimera of the miracle serum, and accept that George was doomed. Rigid with grief, Carrie worried, "Where do you bury a baby in New York?" and tearfully demanded, "I want another baby."

A few days later, Balanchine pulled me out of class at SAB. "What about Eugenie's doctor? The one in Chicago?" I informed him of Jim's assessment. He stared at me a long time, then said, "It's your wife's fault for smoking! She poisoned him with her cigarettes! You have to *make* her stop smoking!"

Before Balanchine quit smoking, he used to give cartons of cigarettes to people as gifts, even if they didn't smoke. But now that he had quit, everyone had to stop. "Mr. B," I said, "Carrie's tried to quit before, but it's so hard." He commanded, "Divorce her if she doesn't!"

A month passed, then two, then five, and George showed no sign of cancer. Jim was amazed; Carrie was pregnant; I was in limbo. Our second son, elfin Christopher, arrived February 4, 1960, to be greeted by George, now a bouncing, healthy three-year-old. Jim ordered a reexamination of the original tissue, and with the results unchanged, concluded, "There was no mistake in our diagnosis. George should be dead." We celebrated, and dubbed George "the Miracle." "No need to come regularly anymore," Jim advised. "Just watch him." Any time George had a stomachache, sniffle in his nose, we headed straight for Dr. Gould.

Life was now doves and roses, so we planned a trip on the *Queen Mary* for our quartet. Then, horror! Carrie noticed on George a return of that little growth, in the same place the cancer had formed before. Jim ordered a biopsy and discovered the rhabdomyosarcoma was back. He performed the surgery himself, and, still in his greens, announced to us, "I got it all out, in a little capsule." He offered some hope, "In the time that has passed, a new radiation treatment has been developed, where it is possible to eradicate cells in a one-millimeter area, without affecting any of the surrounding tissue."

Queen Mary was dumped, and George started treatments. Once a week, we'd take him to Lenox Hill Hospital, and in a small room, he'd lie, strap-wrapped on a slab, with beanbags attached around the sides of his head to prevent movement. The radiation machine was shaped like a giant metal breast hanging on tracks from the ceiling. With a gyroscopic mechanism, it was possible to maneuver and twist its nipple-like nozzle to any angle. The actual treatment took only a few seconds, then we'd open the door and dash back in, release George, and cover him with hugs and kisses. Once a week, for something like six weeks, and then Jim Gould said, "Now, we watch and pray."

As George grew, the tiny portion of tissue destroyed in the treatments didn't. The result is a slightly crooked smile that women find irresistible. Charmed and charming, "the Miracle" grew to become a strapping, handsome man. Forty years later, we hiked the entire Appalachian Trail together. I was sixty-five; he was forty-four. Over the trail's 2,180 miles, George took care of me, worrying, "How're you holding up, Dad?" Most memorable were our rest breaks, two animals slouched in repose on the side of the trail, gabbing about every subject, from philosophy to feet. Each time I look at him, I think, "He's alive! He's a miracle!"

When Chris was three, we thought, "Should we try for another?" It seemed we could call out "BABY" and Carrie was pregnant. And so we did. By the end of her term she was enormous. It was impossible for her to sleep in a bed. The weight of her stomach would push down so much that she couldn't breathe. Poor wife! She slept in a rocking chair.

On Monday, May 11, at four thirty a.m. Carrie called out, "I think the baby is coming!" Having sprained my back at the matinee the day before, I was crawling

Photo snapped by Heidi Preuss, an Olympic skier and fellow hiker, 1999, as George hovers over his dad

Diane Smarr, 1964

around on my hands and knees, worthless, so I called my buddy Dick Boehm, "Come quick!"

Later, when I was waiting with Dick at Lenox Hill Hospital with a hot pad on my back, Dr. Buele popped out of the operating room and announced two words, "Twins . . . girls!" We were all stunned; so was Carrie.

A week later Carrie was home with the girls—we named them Charlotte and Catherine. Thank God Carrie's mother, Ona, and the Boss were there to help, as I was off to dance in Munich, leaving Miracle George ecstatic with his new bitty playmates and Chris, suspicious.

But soon Diane Smarr would enter our life. Sent by the gods to enrich and transform our lives. She was a teenager hired as a babysitter to help us; she became and continues to be part of our family. A bundle of caring goodness, Diane is spiritual, and at her center she carries wisdom, morality, modesty, and a sense of humor. There are none that I admire more. Over the next half century Diane married twice and had two children, Heidi and Shaw. I eventually enticed young Shaw to dance, but Heidi slipped through my fingers.

The world of dance and theater rubbed off on Diane. She once produced, directed, and choreographed a production for her church called *The Devil on Trial.* Sort of a street theater in a church. She cast her fellow worshippers brilliantly. If it had been taped for television an Emmy could have been garnered.

Carrie did return to the NYCB, but as the company photographer, not a dancer. She had always dabbled as an amateur, but now a pro, having for several years studied at the photographic institute in Rockport, Maine. Her mentors and teachers were the tops in their field, in particular Ernst Haas, who took her under his wing. Our homes, and many of our friends' homes, are enhanced by her art.

My father rarely came to see me perform. If I asked, "Pa, do you want to come to the ballet?" he would gaze past me and answer, "What's on the program? I don't know if there's anything I want to see." Every once in a while, he would show up and inform an usherette, "I'm Andy Dam-

boize, my son's dancing," and get a
free seat. When I would see him
later, he would wait for me to ask,
"Did you like the ballet, Pop?" In
reply, I would get, "Oh, that partner you were dancing with . . .
what's her name, Melissa Hayden?
She's a hell of a dancer." Or, "That
little guy, Eddie Villella, boy can he
jump!" or, "Francisco Moncion, he's
a handsome-looking guy. He was
the star of the evening. What is he?
Spanish, black?" Never a word
about me or my performance. And
yet I imagined he told his friends
and acquaintances that his son was

Diane Smarr with the twins, 1965

a star in the ballet. "That's Pop," I thought. I would like to believe he
was proud of me, but letting me know that would have meant admit-
ting that the Boss was right, all those dancing lessons had paid off. As
for Carrie, Pop never said a word to me about her. I vaguely remember
him standing on the outskirts at our wedding—hiding from the Boss,
who sat in the front row, sobbing loudly throughout the ceremony.

Boss devoted herself to nursing her private clients and saving money.
With her baby (me) out of the house, all her children married off, and
Pop dumped, full-time work became all-time. She made herself nurse's
outfits, complete with stylish nurse's hats—costuming herself as a chic,
French Canadian Florence Nightingale. Dressed for the role, she minis-
tered, gave her patients orders and their shots, sewed clothes, shopped,
cooked (they ate fantastically), cleaned, redecorated their houses, did
secretarial work, gave advice, ran errands, and emptied bedpans—
twenty-four-hour duty, seven days a week. When the show closed (a
patient recovered or died), her performance ended, and she would be
laid off, but never for long. She'd find a new patient, don her little
white uniform, and resume the life of nurturing and bossing.

She insisted on being paid in cash and invested every nickel in blue-
chip stocks, for close to eight years. "I don't need anything. I make
everything myself and save every penny. I don't need to pay taxes."

During those years, she gave my brother John money to help buy a
house on Long Island after he and Mary got married, and my brother

Carrie's self-portrait

Paul, too, when he married his love, Kathleen, and moved to Maine. When Carrie and I, in the early 1960s, tried to buy a town house on Seventy-first Street, no bank would give us a mortgage. Ballet dancers were not considered good investments. Boss gave us some money for the down payment, and Carrie's parents made up the difference. Gerry Goldsmith, the husband of a dear friend, Barbara, guaranteed the bank he would make good if we defaulted, so we got a mortgage and bought a home.

By that time, Boss had saved a couple of hundred thousand dollars. Her apartment on 163rd Street was empty, and as she aged, she was determined not to burden anyone, so she moved to the west coast of Florida, bought herself a little house, and started a garden. "I always loved it when your father and I lived in Florida. It's warmer here, and Clearwater is cheaper than New York!"

My father must have been spying on her, because he trailed her to Florida and lived in a cheap rooming house near her. At church on Sundays, he would sit in the pew behind her, grinding his teeth and muttering to the back of her head, "Why are you in church? You're living in sin, Georgette. God won't forgive you until you come back to your husband." She never acknowledged him, looked at him, or acted like she heard him—for seventeen years.

While in Florida, Pop sought private-duty clients, and ended up nursing a celebrity. Bill Stern was a famous radio and television announcer, sports commentator, and emcee of *The Colgate Sports Newsreel*. He was old, rich, and dying. Pop relished discussing his wealthy client: "He's a hell of a storyteller, but what did it get him?" and "He's got a big mansion, a swimming pool, half a dozen cars in his garage, a cook, gardener, chauffeur, a housekeeper, and me. No one swims in his pool; the staff show up, do their work, and leave. The only person he has to talk to is me—when I come by to give him his shots, bathe him, and empty his bedpan!" True to Pop's mantra—"The underdog is the one to root for . . . they're going to end up being the winners!"—his anecdotes ended with his familiar moral: "The biggest celebrity, the richest person in the world, ultimately has to have someone empty the bedpan. It's the little people in the world, doing things like that, that make it run!"

He spent his falls and winters stalking and tormenting my mother in Florida. In late spring, he would take a bus up to Maine to spend summers with my brother Paul. On the way, he would occasionally stop by our house in New York, unannounced, knock on the door, and say to a harassed Carrie as she opened it, "I'm just passing through and need a place to put my head."

An excerpt from my diary, May 27, 1973 (I was recovering in the hospital after my first knee surgery): "Carrie said Pop arrived last night. The bell rang, she opened the front door, and he popped out his dentures. 'I almost fell over,' she said. Mumbling without his teeth, he announced, 'All I want is a cup of coffee and the living room couch.' "

Pa never stayed more than a day or two—a break in the bus ride— but while in New York he would walk and walk from dawn till night, all over the city, buying and reading newspapers, especially Florida newspapers and the *Wall Street Journal*. Sometimes at breakfast, I would give him his tea and make him an Egg Trudy sandwich, and I'd watch him sit at the table, industriously making marks and notations on a piece of paper. "What are you doing, Pop?" He would get this look in his eye and reply, "Scheming. I'm scheming." Turns out he had tracked down which stocks my mother had purchased, and was following their ups and downs.

The Boss found out. I think he wrote her a letter, saying she had to give him half of her income, since they were still married. Boss went to see the local Catholic priest: "What do I do, Father?" The enlightened priest answered, "What? You've been separated seventeen years, and you're not divorced yet? What are you waiting for?"

Pa contested the divorce, the judge threw him out of court, and a curtain came down on the major chapter of his life. He was free. So he started dating a variety of women, taking them out dancing, writing them love letters. Sleeping with them? I don't know—but I hope so. But he kept my mother's name. "Hi! What's your name?" "Andy Damboize," he'd reply. It's the name on his grave.

Eventually, he retired and went to Maine to live with Paul and Kathleen, and started fishing full-time, though he never caught a fish. Paul and Kathleen had six children, and he regaled every one of them with his wonderful Irish stories, the same tales he had recounted to my siblings and to me. We loved them and would importune, "Pop! Tell another, tell another!" but when we heard, "All right, I'll tell you the story of Jimmy McGorry, and now my tale is done!" we'd groan with disappointment, because it was a signoff, his way of saying "Enough." The tales were done for the night.

I was teaching a group of children in an auditorium at St. Patrick's School in Jersey City when the principal, Sister Maeve,* called me out of rehearsal, and led me into an office to answer an urgent phone call. "Hello, this is Dr. Mulet. Do you know a Georgette d'Amboise?" Boss had died of cardiac arrest, the police were at her condo, and I was to call them to get the details. It seemed she went in her sleep. I hung up, numbed and brain-scrambled, and called Carrie. "I'm going with you," Carrie said. "I've been through this, with the death of my mom. You won't be able to function or make a decision. You're going to need someone."

Diary entry, January 23, 1984:

> I am amazed at how I have not broken down. How great she was, and what a lesson to me. To be what she wished and imagined me to be—

---

* Sister Maeve is the finest principal, teacher, and most loving human being I know. A Druid . . . wearing the insignia of the Sister of Charity, she represents the best in Christianity and the true message of the "Prince of Peace": "Love your neighbor." Best of all is her Irish sense of humor, which leavens and pops up accompanied by a raucous laugh.

I think I can aim at that. My wife is great as well. The women who have been part of me have been extraordinary. Last time I spoke with Boss, less than a month ago, she had me laughing about a dear friend, James V. Bowler, a newspaper columnist, being her gigolo—his word. Boss: "My gigolo is coming over to call on me, bringing me my groceries." She talked about him, how smart he is, how sophisticated. "He knows about everything! Everything there is, he knows about dance and music and art." She had me laughing, and we had a good laugh together. I promised to come down to visit her by the end of February or early March. "Oh I wish I could hold and hug you, my Jacques."

Carrie and I jumped on a plane to Tampa. We were met by James V. Bowler and taken to her apartment. A neighbor, Steve, had given the Boss's extra key to the police, but we managed to get in via Ruth Smith, a lady in the condo office. Inside, Boss's tiny slippers were next to the bed, where she had died. The house was not a mess, although she had not been able to keep it spick-and-span, as was her wont. While Carrie started cleaning the kitchen and bathroom, I got into Boss's bed, and tried to fit my body into the indentations where hers had last lain. I talked to her, whispering so Carrie wouldn't hear. After a while, I got out of the bed, stripped off the sheets, threw them out, and put the mattress outside to air. Carrie picked out clothes she thought the Boss would like to be buried in. That night, I slept on the floor and Carrie slept in the narrow hide-a-bed couch.

My siblings arrived, and I discovered that Boss had left pages and pages of notes for each of us, with detailed orders about funeral arrangements and exact instructions for how her belongings would be distributed. From Boss's last letters and orders:

> I have at Fortune Federal an account holder's T.R.I.T.F. . . . You can draw all the amount, it is to pay for my funeral expenses. You will buy a modest coffin—you will find a white silk dress in among my other dresses; you can also choose another off-white evening dress that could be suitable. I have made arrangements with Moss Funeral Home Inc., they will give you all the help you need. You'll find their card among these papers. My church, St. Catherine of Siena on Belcher Road, talk to the priest for the Funeral Mass. I want singing at my Mass, the organist at the church, her name Jo Malina, ask that she will sing Charles Gounod—Ave Maria . . .

She left three thousand dollars to cover funeral expenses, and though she suggested no flowers for the service, we got them. She left whatever monies remained (between eighty and ninety thousand dollars) to be divided among us. She left me her car, my sister the furniture, with phone numbers of the nearest Goodwill in case Ninette chose to donate it. All of her artwork, every lamp, crucifix, and other artifact she had made (and the house was full of them), was listed and bequeathed to one of her children or their spouses. A box labeled "for Jacques" contained my 1942 *Midsummer Night's Dream* Puck costume, with the pair of little golden horns still attached to its elastic holding band, and the handheld pipes she had conjured and constructed nestled on top. Everyone got a little something. Her portrait, which had hung in the living room all our lives, she also left to me—to the chagrin of my siblings. Predictably, she had arranged for her own cemetery plot, prepaid its cost and maintenance, and left monies to the Catholic church for a memorial Mass once a year, in perpetuity. A note addressed to all of us was found next to her bed:

> To my dear Family,
> Please do not buy any flowers, but in your kindness of heart, I will need prayers, Masses, for my poor soul. I know that you love me, and will think of me, I will need your help to go to heaven. May the Good Lord have mercy on my helpless sinful soul.
> Thank you all my dear loved ones for the pleasure you have given me. Especially Jacques, all the attentions, devotions, love he has given me through the goodness of his heart. Thank you Jacques you have made my life beautiful with your generosity—and interesting deeds. My dear children, I am sorry if I have offended you in any way during my life on earth, if so I ask your pardon.
> We will be reunited in heaven one day with the grace of God, where we will all be very happy, loving God through the Mercy of Our Lord Jesus Christ forever and ever. Amen. Thank you again my dear ones. May God bless you. Farewell until I will see you all again in Eternity.
> Your mother,
> Georgette

Boss died in 1984. The January before, when I visited her, my mother spoke to me for the first time in a negative way about my father. "Around the time we were evicted, you were five years old, Jacques, and

I was so sick. I had appendicitis but didn't know it, and my appendix burst. I asked your father to get a taxi to take me to the hospital. 'We don't have any money for that,' he said, 'why can't you walk?' And then in the hospital, sitting by my bed, he whispered in my ear, 'Die, Georgette, why don't you die?' " Poor Pop. I can imagine how he must have dreaded coming home, without any work, to face her harping. I don't think my sister and brothers know this.

In March of 1989, I visited Pop in Maine. He was living in a nursing home Paul and Kathleen had arranged for him, a comfortable, spacious place. When I arrived, he showed me some of his correspondence—love letters to and from his collection of women. He was frail and failing, but he took my elbow and walked me into a kind of recreation room, the common area. A couple of old guys were playing checkers, several women were watching a soap opera, and some reluctant children wandered, visiting aged grandparents. Pop moved a few chairs around to give himself some space and me a place to sit, and then he started performing a dance, a kind of soft-shoe shuffle, a lazy man's slow-motion

Pop doing his dance for anyone who would watch, 1989

wind-about. No one else in the room seemed startled—the men didn't look up from their checkers game, the soap opera kept the ladies mesmerized—and I realized his dancing was nothing new to them, he did it all the time. "Andy's at it again!" I watched him for quite a while, and he was pretty good. The soap opera finished and another had started, but he continued his wind-about. Then I interrupted him, "Gotta go, Pop. But I'll be back to visit you again. Bye, Pop!" I gave him a hug and slipped away. He didn't seem to notice. I left him dancing. A little over a week later, he died.

Quentin Keynes

At the dress rehearsal of Freddie Ashton's *Picnic at Tintagel* (February 1952), a tall Englishman came backstage. "Hello, Jacques d'Amboise? I'm Quentin Keynes." In clipped manner and commanding speech, he explained, "I'm a friend of Freddie's, just passing through. Do you mind if I film your rehearsal?" He pointed to a handheld 16 mm camera. "It works with cartridges—they're good for several minutes, then I unload and toss in another. Not ideal, as it causes gaps in the footage." I shrugged. "Sure! Why not?" After all, he was a friend of Freddie's and had an English accent.

I had to wear a wig, a red beard stuck on with gobs of spirit gum, and heavy makeup. Seeing what a neophyte I was, fumbling with the makeup and paraphernalia, the designer, Cecil Beaton, came to the rescue. "Like this, my dear," he advised as he painted my face. "Don't complain. You're a character in a myth, so nothing is ordinary; everything is exaggerated. Your costume, the scenery, the wig, demand it." The costume was cumbersome, but what truly made me uncomfortable was knowing I was not equal to the intricacies and physical demands of the role. Waiting to make an entrance, I watched my heart pound and pulsate through my costume, and thought, "This is my last season. I'll be dead of a heart attack within a year." At seventeen, the role was beyond my experience, skills as an actor, or physical strength. I'd go onstage filled with fear. Thankfully, onstage, the nervousness disappeared.

The ballet premiered the next day, and Quentin came backstage, declaring he loved it. At first, I thought, "What a creepy guy, but interesting . . . and persistent." He started hanging around the theater, and informed me that his great-grandfather was Charles Darwin. His father, Sir Geoffrey Keynes, a renowned surgeon at the Royal College of Surgeons, was one of the great bibliographers and collectors of William Blake's poems and paintings. Quentin continued recounting celestial genealogy: "You've heard of Lord Maynard Keynes? My uncle." The famous economist John Maynard Keynes was among the group of British patrons that had supported young George Balanchine's com-

Quentin Keynes in search of the dodo, Mauritius, 1952

pany Les Ballets 1933, and Keynes's wife, Lydia Lopokova, was an ex-ballerina from Diaghilev's company. Quentin grew up surrounded by artists, scholars, and celebrities, and name-dropped shamelessly. Lord *This* and Lady *That* (and the queen) spackled his stories.

"Jock-o, I'm staying at a brownstone down the street"—he was sponging off someone—"you've got to come over on your day off. I've some fantastic dance films you've got to see—outtakes from *Dark Rapture,* a marvelous film shot in Africa! Prudery, you know—the distributors feared viewers would not accept the jiggling breasts of women, and the men's privies bouncing around. But I got them! And I'll show you some of *my* latest films."

Africa had caught Quentin's imagination early on, and he spent a lifetime traveling through the Dark Continent—up, down, and sideways—never without a camera.

The clips from *Dark Rapture* were mind-boggling. Thousands of tribespeople danced on a dusty, African plain. As their multitude of voices chanted, *"Ahhee bo-bo, impahh-sighyee, ahhee bo-bo,"* over a thousand men—some dressed in loincloths, others naked—would vault into the air, and thunder down in unison. Simultaneously, another thousand or so would sing and stamp out a different rhythm in counterpoint. Several angles showed columns of women wearing nothing but little loincloths, five abreast, singing and dancing in endless lines, snaking paths through the men. The camera panned to reveal dozens of hollowed tree trunks (many over two hundred feet long), lined, on both sides, with hundreds of muscular men beating out complex rhythms with bludgeons held in both hands. The drummers would switch rhythms, following some mysterious signal, and, as far as the camera's lens reached, an ocean of dancers responded, their feet and voices in a dialogue with the drumming.

Quentin explained, "The *Dark Rapture* crew filmed over several days, and the dancing never stopped, day or night."

The quality of the film was poor, the sound, tinny, but in the parlor of a New York City brownstone in the East Fifties, in 1952, I thrilled to the music and dance in this flickering old film. The clips captured a life force as awesome as Niagara Falls, as natural as a thousand whales cavorting, flopping and smashing their tails on the ocean's surface, or the thundering migration of a million buffalo across the plains for days on end. In the nineteenth century in America, passenger pigeons once flew so thickly in the sky, they blocked out the sun, and day plants closed their petals, thinking it was night. Roosting at night, the pigeons so covered the branches of the forests that their weight would crack and break tree limbs. The gathering of tribespeople in *Dark Rapture* was no less monumental—human culture expressed through rituals of music and dance. And, of course, bouncing breasts and genitals were titillating to a teenager. "Well, Jock-o, I'm going to Africa this summer. Do you want to come along?"

Quentin's passions included book collecting—Charles Darwin and James Joyce, foremost, as well as any account of adventuring in Africa. His idol was the adventurer-explorer Sir Richard Burton, and he snapped up anything written by or about Burton. To finance his indulgences, Quentin gave lectures and showed his movies in prep schools all over England and the United States. He never took a hotel room and avoided paying for any meal. Driving a fancy sports car and sponging off people wherever he went, he'd spend most of the school year enticing teenagers to pay a fee to join him on his next safari. By late spring, perhaps nineteen or twenty youths would have signed up. Their monies covered his and the expedition's expenses, and any leftover funds helped expand his book collection. Quentin got a free trip and a slew of gofers. "We'll set up camp here. Who's going to volunteer to go for water?" Quentin would ask. The boys would also become his film crew, camera and gear carriers. "Jock-o, everybody pitches in."

"I should go," I imagined, and saw myself winning the admiration of the natives, cavorting, dancing, and leaping, the white boy soaring over bonfires—naked, naturally. But at the ballet, principal roles were tumbling to me. And there was talk of a European tour after the spring season. "If I go to Africa, I'll miss ballet class, just when I feel I'm beginning to learn how to dance." So I put it off. "Maybe someday, Quent."

Quentin and I became good friends. Quentin drove the Boss crazy, and, later, Carrie, because without notice, he'd appear on the doorstep and say, "I can park my car in the street when I stay with you!" He loved to be catered to. "Oh, at breakfast, I drink a lot of tea, could you keep the kettle on? I take at least twelve or fifteen cups. And it's got to be hot. Thanks, dear, you make such wonderful tea. Could you get me another pot?"

I introduced him to Jimmy Comiskey, and another lover of books, Dick Boehm. Dick was a buddy, about my age, who attended every performance of ballet and opera in New York City. Dick and Jimmy were automatically added to Quentin's "Do you mind if I stay with you?" list.

In Milan, during the company's 1953 Italian tour, Quentin drove up to the theater in a brand-new Austin Healey convertible. "Where can I find Jacques d'Amboise?" he demanded. For the next ten days, he attended every performance, and my fellow dancers ached with envy at my being picked up at the stage door by this mysterious man in his roaring sports car. But he never treated for a thing. I treated him. Tickets to the ballet and our meals.

He wandered in and out of my life for years (and Jimmy's, too; less so with Dick, as he was more adept at fending Quentin off). One visit, he persuaded me to buy a limited edition of Sir Richard Burton's translation of *The Arabian Nights.* "Don't miss it!" he urged. I spent a hundred and fifty dollars for the fifteen-volume set, a lot of money for me. Returning from tour the next year, I discovered that the Boss, assuming *Arabian Nights* shared the same category with the *Kama Sutra* (in her mind anti-Catholic and pornographic), had glued culinary recipes over many of the pages in volume 4, obscuring the prose Sir Richard had labored so hard to translate.

Some time in the early 1960s, Quentin contacted me. "I'm planning to buy a new camera, and my old one would be great for you, Jock-o. Do you want it?" Aware Quentin didn't plan a gift, I asked, "How much?"

For something like forty bucks, I bought his Bell and Howell 16 mm cartridge-load camera. After all, it had traveled all over Africa, seen and filmed a lot. I tested it out with a few home movies of Miracle George misbehaving in Riverside Park with his five-year-old girlfriend, Katherine Hamer. I planned to use the camera intensively on NYCB's first tour of the Soviet Union, scheduled for the fall of 1962.*

RUSSIA

Almost forty years before, Balanchine had left Russia. Now he was going back. I packed an entire suitcase with film cartridges and, with my roommate for the tour, Shaun O'Brien, planned how to record our adventures in Europe and the Soviet Union.

At my first company class, in September of 1949, Shaun stood in front of me at the barre, wearing lime-green ballet shoes. Dramatic and flamboyant, he had enormous turnout—I remember him doing ronds de jambe en l'air, staring intently over his shoulder at his lime-green foot tracing circles in the air. Glamorous, muscular, and handsome, he became a mentor to me. I hung around him, like a groupie, and he became my closest friend in the company.

Shaun's dancing was neat, clean, and fluid, but his genius was doing character roles—he was *brilliant* as Drosselmeyer in *The Nutcracker,* and in the ballet *Harlequinade* he was without equal. His special talent was commedia dell'arte characters—the fat buffoon, the comic grandfather. Lincoln never missed a performance of *Harlequinade* when Shaun was dancing. "High art," Lincoln called it. In life, he was affected and fey, but never onstage—unless the role demanded it. His performance as Dr. Coppélius in *Coppélia* is legendary.

With Shaun's wicked Irish sense of humor and ability to tell a story, he could elevate the mundane to the hilarious, and would regale you for hours with a story about a cab ride. His anger could be devastating (when I was complaining in the dressing room and being a brat, he once cowed me, bellowing, "Oh, blow it out your ass!"). There wasn't a topic Shaun couldn't dredge up information on; as you conversed, the more he seemed to know. Passing a statue in a plaza or museum any-

---

* In 2003, at the age of eighty-one, Quentin died of spinal cancer. For over fifty years, he brought high school students, on their summer breaks, to Africa, believing the experience would change them from adolescents to men. Many of them did follow that change during those summers. His library of books and manuscripts brought in well over six million dollars at auction.

Partying with Cris Alexander and Shaun O'Brien, London, early 1980s

where in Europe, Shaun would spend the next twenty minutes describing relevant details and the entire history of the artwork. With his partner, Cris Alexander, a Broadway gypsy, superb artist and photographer, slim and elegant, crackling with intelligence, they made a partnership in life for every couple to envy. Our second son, Christopher, is named for Cris Alexander.

THE PAPER BAG

Shaun O'Brien's treatment for a filmed travelogue of NYCB's tour of Europe and the Soviet Union, 1962: Suggested Scenes

I. About twelve inches high, and six wide, your ordinary brown paper bag sits, opened, on a table at the Vier Jahreszeiten Hotel in Hamburg. The silverware and crystal gleam, embroidered napkins await unfolding. A pair of pale, delicate hands close the bag, carefully pleating its top, folding exactly twice. Could something be in it? It is lifted out of frame, then the camera pans to record the décor of the restaurant and hotel.

II. Off stage at the Staatsoper in Hamburg, ballerinas crush rosin with their toe shoes. Next to the rosin box sits the paper bag, observing.

III. Berlin Opera House. The paper bag watches rehearsal from a seat in the otherwise empty house.

IV. Vienna, inside St. Stephen's Cathedral. We see a shadowy figure place the paper bag on a pew, next to local patrons, enjoying an organ concert.

At the School of American Ballet, Vladimiroff had a request. He had heard NYCB would leave in the spring of 1962 for a tour of Europe that would culminate with some two months behind the Iron Curtain. Vladimiroff regaled me with his memories of the beautiful Maryinsky Theater in St. Petersburg, where I would be dancing, and, in particular, he dwelt on the dance studio above the stage. How glorious it was, with its decoration and enormous high ceiling. How he had spent a lifetime exercising there, honing his art. He sketched me a map of the studio, located his exact spot at the barre—his place—and handed me the map. "When you do barre at Maryinsky, do it in my place."

For close to four months, the paper bag traveled with NYCB from theater to hotel, opera house, museum, and stage, starting in New York and ending in Baku, Azerbaijan, on the Caspian Sea. Shaun's inventive imagination garnered many of the company's dancers to star in his paper bag travelogue.

Our tour started in Germany at the Hamburg opera house. Hamburg was a sister city to New York, and Balanchine's ballets were an important part of the Hamburg Ballet's repertoire. The intendant, Rolf Liebermann, was a Balanchine groupie.

While there, Shaun recruited me to star in his travelogue, but a smashing event took me out of the picture.

HAMBURG

Thursday, August 30, 1962. A fantastic rehearsal with Balanchine. I floated through the new choreography in the first movement of *Symphony in C*. He had decided to replace musical repeats previously deleted and had invented stunning variations for the ballerina and me.

The company had a free night, so Vicky Simon, a ballerina friend, agreed to be my date for dinner. A charming brunette, she met me at the streetcar stop in front of the Staatsoper. I was delighting in the life and light of Vicky's darting brown eyes, above a pair of lovely breasts, oblivious to my surroundings.

A streetcar hit me.

A day later, I came out of a coma at the Hafenkrankenhaus, a hospital in Hamburg's St. Pauli district. With multiple ribs broken on my left side and one on my right, each breath hurt, and so did the hole in the back of my head, which matched another in the front. The right side of my face was steak tartare, scraped from forehead to chin. I thought to myself, "Maybe better to die."

Another day later, less foggy, I became aware that Betty Cage and Mel Kiddon were holding my hands. A comforting pair—Mel, of course, was a doctor, and Betty, a witch, but a good one. Swarthy, with intense brown eyes and hair, she was rumored to be spiced with Native American and African blood. She read the Tarot, and always had a prophecy. At her dinner parties, the exotic foods she prepared were followed by séances and Ouija board magic. Her most successful spells, though, kept Lincoln's madness and Balanchine's creative genius in balance, so that somehow, NYCB did not fragment. I needed her magic and Mel's medicine.

According to the police report, a streetcar had rounded a corner and slammed into my back. Witnesses described how the impact sent me flying into Vicky and then crash-landing onto the pavement, where I slid along, for a while, on my forehead and face. Poor Vicky went airborne, too, and eventually thudded down and smashed her face into the curb, splitting her lip and knocking out her front teeth. Midflight, Vicky took down two overweight German Hausfrauen like dominoes, and they joined the aerials, windmilling, somersaulting, and, on landing, breaking legs. Mel's description made me laugh, but not for long; it hurt.

"Your clothes were shredded and we can't find your shoes!" He seemed delighted. "We think the streetcar knocked you out of them, then ran over them!" Betty finally spoke up in her dry, matter-of-fact monotone: "The report says the streetcar conductor complained, 'I rang my bells! Why didn't he hear me?'"

"I'm so sorry, I failed Mr. B, I failed the company." I mumbled this mantra to the two of them before passing out for another day.

The Hafenkrankenhaus doctor spoke four languages, and in each ordered, "No moving! Stay on your back for at least a week." Eschewing the bedpan one night, I stumbled determinedly to the nearby bathroom. A pair of porcine-looking German nurses the size of Volkswagens caught me, and reprimanded me so terrifyingly I regressed to kindergarten.

Carrie sent a message from New York. "Should I come over?" She was at home, caring for Miracle George, close to six years old, and his two-year-old brother, Christopher, and must have been scared to death she would end up a widow. I urged her not to worry and not to come. If I couldn't get back to dancing, I'd be on my way home.

The company opened. Jonathan Watts replaced me in *Raymonda,* and Arthur Mitchell in *Western Symphony.* "Did Balanchine ask about me?" I inquired of Mel, plaintively. He hedged, "Mr. B's so distraught about the debacle of *Liebeslieder,* he speaks of nothing else."

Balanchine had expected *Liebeslieder Waltzer* would bring all of Germany to its feet, cheering. Instead, the Hamburg premiere caused a scandal. It seemed the singers had angered the audience. *"Raus!* Get them off!" Hordes of voices bellowed from the audience, "Without singers!" Mel told me Balanchine blamed our conductor, Robert Irving. "You hired them! Bad singers, and no one knows *Liebeslieder* better than the Germans. They grow up with *Liebeslieder* like Americans grow up with 'Jingle Bells'!" Peeved, Balanchine canceled the ballet for the rest of the tour.

Certain cities held special meaning for Balanchine—London, Paris, Monte Carlo, Hamburg, and Berlin. Berlin was the city Balanchine recalled with admiration after leaving chaos-stricken Leningrad. Twenty years old, he had survived the Bolshevik Revolution, civil war, the advent of Leninism, and escaped Russia before the reign of the monstrous yellow-eyed killer, "Uncle Joe" Stalin. Germany's own monster, Adolf Hitler, had not yet risen to power when Balanchine was in Europe, but was waiting in the wings.

Despite the disappointing reception of *Liebeslieder,* Germany continued to hold a special place in Balanchine's heart, as did, in later years, the German ballerina Karin von Aroldingen, whom he nurtured, guided, and adored. *Vienna Waltzes* and *Liebeslieder Waltzer* were among the many ballets Balanchine left Karin when he died. Of *Vienna Waltzes,* Karin recalls, "He used to stand in the wings and mumble to anyone within earshot, 'Oh, it's so romantic. The man in the woods with the lady.' " I was originally that man in the woods with Karin—in spring 1977, Balanchine started shaping his choreography for us in Washington, D.C., but my knee went *kaputt,* so I returned to New York. The beautiful dancer Sean Lavery replaced me and eventually premiered the work.

A bevy of ballerinas from NYCB and the Hamburg Ballet streamed in and out of my hospital room over the next days. Two teenage stunners from the Hamburg Ballet, Gaby Holtz and Dörte Rüter (think Miss Teen Universe, *only better*), informed me, with giggles, "On our way to class every morning, we walk by the spot where it happened. The blood's still there!"

On leaving my bedside on September 5, Mel, the instigator, said he wanted Vicky and me to file a lawsuit against the city of Hamburg and the streetcar company, for assault.

Ten days after impact (September 9), the doctors let me out for a short walk. Instead I cabbed to the spot and back. Gaby and Dörte were right: almost a yard in diameter, a thick, Rorschach-like stain flourished, blackening the sidewalk. I fled back to my hospital bed.

About two weeks after Vicky had her teeth knocked out, September 14, she got new ones, and had healed enough to rejoin the company, then performing in Zurich.

On October 6, the company was scheduled to leave from Vienna for Moscow. Would I be healed enough to make the plane to Russia?? It was either be on that plane or go home. An old German friend, Max Niehaus, visited my bedside every day, and arranged for me to come to his apartment in Munich to convalesce. "It's not so far from Vienna," he assured me.

I was released on September 15 from the hospital, and after feasting at an auf Wiedersehen party with Gaby and Dörte, I grabbed a plane to Munich and ate everything offered on the flight. Meeting me on arrival, Max was dancing like a little boy with a new toy. Back at his apartment, I slurped down a repast he'd prepared that was big enough for six.

Max worshipped Balanchine. I met Max in Munich in 1953. A fan and a friend, he seemed ancient to me. Stooped, with a few wisps of white hair, rheumy eyes behind thick glasses, he had no chin. His little, pursed mouth perpetually seemed to have just sucked a lemon. When speaking, he commenced with a whining hum, "Hmmmmmm *wie geht's,* Jacques?" His English accent was classic German Jew from the Borscht belt (though he wasn't Jewish). He spoke several languages—French, Italian, Spanish, and a smattering of Greek. As were many Germans, he was also conversant in Dutch and Danish. In all his languages, he always hummed.

Max was a sophisticate whose knowledge and interests seemed to include everything there is—economics, political science, literature, and art. His interests were global. "Hmmmmmm, Jacques. You must go to Crete, hmmmmmm. When there, I learned all about art and life." A liberal and virulently antireligious, he complained, "The nuns may have saved me from Hitler. They hid me in a convent, but made me go to Vespers, kneel, and say the Rosary at four o'clock in the morning." He adored Voltaire and Nietzsche, but his crowning passion was dance—from ancient to avant-garde—and ballet in particular. Max used his connections to publish a dance calendar, an eclectic collection of photographs of dancers from all over the world, which included birth dates and a little biography of each.

Throughout his life, Max showered me with friendship and gifts— Tanagra statues, sculptures, and several prints, including Renoir and Degas drawings, and, most treasured, a silver coin from the time of Alexander the Great, in pristine condition. Max attempted to write a book about me as the ultimate Balanchine dancer, and in the summer of 1963 submitted it to Lincoln, who hated it. Lincoln wrote me a letter that began:

> Dear Jacques:
> Mr. Niehaus' manuscript can do you no harm; if it has pictures in it, it will probably sell enough copies not to do the publishers any harm, either.

The letter ended:

> The manuscript is perfectly (and I mean flawlessly) awful. There is nothing more embarrassing than the obituary of a living person . . .
> I will write a short, hopeful and snappy foreword.
> With love to you and Carrie,
> Lincoln

Max had a wife, Gertrude. She would flit by like a shadow some-where in their apartment. There was a son, too, Rolf, a solidly built, beefy teenager. Hefting beer barrels off a truck at his job was a piece of cake for him. He'd speak to me in avalanches of German, punctuated, every once in a while, with "*Verstehen? Verstehen?* [Do you understand?]" I'd nod vigorously and say, "Yah, yah!!" even though I had no idea what "*Verstehen*" meant. After a while, Rolf caught on that I didn't understand a word he said, so he gave up. Max joked that he found it hard to believe Rolf was his son, as "he has no interest in anything to do with art. Maybe when I was in the convent, Gertrude . . . ?"

Max would be sitting outside my room at dawn, and, on hearing me stir, would rush to the kitchen to prepare breakfast. When I emerged, he'd be there to announce, "Hmmmmmm *Frühstück* [breakfast] waits!" The array of food was staggering—multitudes of sausages, pâtés, and varied cold cuts and cheeses. "Wurst is from Bavaria, *Käse* [cheese] from Alsace-Lorraine, and *Senf* [mustard]—three kinds." Max loved strong cheeses—there was always a hint of Gorgonzola on his breath. A trio of hard-boiled eggs, each in a porcelain cup, accompanied four different kinds of bread, a slab of butter, and assorted condiments and jams. Teas, café au lait, espresso, and a pot of hot chocolate kept warm on trivets. A bowl of raspberries accompanied the colors of flowers in a vase he squeezed between the plates of cheeses. When he found out I loved pudding, he made tureens of vanilla pudding drizzled with raspberry sauce for me, morning and night. I used to lick the bowl.

I ate, slept, and recuperated.

One morning, Max told me a little about his youth. He was born in the town of Wesel, and between World War I and World War II, under the Weimar Republic, became mayor (a sort of Bürgermeister) of another small town on the Rhine—and, as a member of the Republic, a target for the Nazis when they took over. "After the convent, I hid out in this apartment, Jacques. Hmmmm, it was terrible. Word would go out, 'Curfew tonight!' That meant they would be moving the *Jüdin* through the streets to the train station. We would hear over the loudspeakers, 'NO ONE OUT! NO PHOTOGRAPHS! NO WINDOWS OPEN! EVERYTHING SHUTTERED!' We could hear them crying and wailing for help," Max confessed. "We would cover our ears, hide under the bed as *Kinder* do. In the morning, we would smile and nod to our neighbors, as if nothing had happened. We knew, but were afraid. No one trusted anyone. One word, one report, and you would join the *Jüdin*."

I was counting on making that plane to Russia. Max took me to the Munich airport on September 29, and with gingerly hugs, sent me on my way to Vienna. Shaun was waiting for me at our hotel, the Sacher, where he had just been shooting a scene with our fellow dancer Deni Lamont, the paper bag, and a Sacher torte. We immediately went off to the theater. Mr. B was there, and ill at ease. Through my whole convalescence, I had never heard a word from him. I'd like to believe he felt a little guilty. Anyway, I hugged him. Lincoln walked over and was much more honest, glowering, "Well, Buster, we didn't think we'd see you alive again!"

Shaun kept me busy, insisting I join him to film the paper bag scene at St. Stephen's Cathedral. He had tickets for *Rosenkavalier* at the opera, and tons of gossip. "Daisy!"* he'd coo, "Taras and his boyfriend had a row at the restaurant the other night. The boyfriend stood up dramatically, and slowly poured a glass of wine over Taras's head! Taras let the wine drip down his face. He sat unblinking and unmoving, until a little twitch at the edge of his upper lip marked time."

Within a day—October 1—I tried my first barre, and lasted three minutes. So I sat and watched, jealous of everyone able to move. In the next day's class, I lasted maybe ten minutes, up to the rond de jambe. It was impossible to do center work. Any attempt to jump was too painful.

On October 5, the last day before Russia, Shaun corralled me to go to Vienna's legendary gay bar, announcing, "We're all heading to the Piccadilly for one last fling! Daisy, it's like before crossing the Sahara—you load up with water!" It had been rumored that there was only one gay bar in all of Russia.

The airplane landed at Sheremetyevo Airport in Moscow, and we looked out at an enormous crowd at the gate. The dancers deplaned first and waited at the foot of the stairs for Balanchine, who timed a grand entrance with Diana Adams at his side. I caught the whole thing on film with Quentin Keynes's camera. Balanchine made a big deal of introducing Diana as his prima ballerina, bobbing and beaming with delight as he presented her to his brother, Andrei, whom he had not seen in four decades. We hung around for hours, while the press photographed and interviewed Balanchine, flashes and microphones shoved in his face. We were exhausted, looking around in trepidation at the

---

* Early on, Brooks and Shaun had given me the nickname Daisy. Another backstage ritual—everybody called you by your mother's name. They'd say, "Who's dancing *Tchaikovsky Pas de Deux* tonight? Georgette!" Deni Lamont was Alice, and Shaun was Elsie.

dark, dismal airport. Why was it so dim? I looked up. Take a light bulb the size of a baby's fist, about eighteen watts, bury it in the bottom of a large brown coffee can, and glue it to the ceiling. The miserable, descending light was like spit in the shadows. And there were a lot of them. A claustrophobic caging of illumination that became, for me, a metaphor of the strictures Leninism imposed on Russia.

I'm dumping on the Soviet system, not the Russian people, and definitely not their dancers. Among the greatest performances of *Swan Lake* was Ludmila Semenyaka's and once Allegra Kent and I in Munich sat in the audience watching Marina Kondratieva dance Giselle. We looked at each other: "I think that's the best Giselle I have ever seen!" we both declared simultaneously. Some of those superb artists became friends—especially Vladimir Vasiliev and Shamil Yagudin. Peers to admire and emulate. Vasiliev, at his height, I believed, was the best male ballet dancer in the world. Yagudin, his compatriot at the Bolshoi Ballet, in his leaps flew over the heads of his fellow dancers. Today, Allegra and I often attend the American Ballet Theatre performances. There we luxuriate in joy and wonder at the artistry of the ballerinas Diana Vishneva and Natalia Osipova. They represent the art of ballet at its apex, where dance has been lifted from the earth to another realm and its artists seemingly transformed into another species.

In Russia, Balanchine conducted himself with his usual aplomb. "Welcome to the home of classical ballet," one Soviet dignitary said. Later, on the bus, Balanchine, swelling with pride, recounted his reply. He'd parried, "No. Russia is home of romantic ballet. America is home of classical ballet!"—meaning himself!

The bus took us to the hideous Hotel Ukraine. Stalin built seven of these monstrosities, known to the Russians as "Stalin's wedding cakes," and they did seem to me a marriage, a union, joining futuristic rockets imagined by H. G. Wells and the castle Gormenghast of Mervyn Peake's book *Titus Groan*—hulking conglomerations of dirty yellow blocks with towers and turrets, many topped by red flags enhanced by hidden wind machines and spotlights. Their gargantuan mass made one feel like a dot. Of the "wedding cakes," only one, the Ukraine, is a hotel. A hotel with not enough elevators. There may have been a bank of six or eight that would carry twenty victims each, but forty or fifty elevators would barely have sufficed. We dancers would wait and wait and wait, amid mobs of locals bundled in their winter clothes, surly and stuffed bears. Each elevator was operated by a disgruntled, rounded woman in a blue skirt, white blouse, and red kerchief. I never saw jewelry or makeup on any of them.

There was no getting your room key in the lobby; you had to go to your floor and check in with another miserable lump, sitting behind a desk in the hallway. All keys passed through her hands, and we had to check them with her every time we left or returned to our rooms. She lived there twenty-four hours a day, catching naps in the wee hours of the morning on a cot near her desk. Of course she was grumpy.

Dinner that night was surprisingly good—delicious piroshki, stacks of dark bread, sliced cucumbers, radishes, and pickles led to borscht, watery but tasty. The dessert, *morozhenoye* (ice cream), wonderful, but the entrée, Chicken à la Kiev, yikes! The meat was gray leather, and when hacked into, the so-called butter filling squished out like pale congealed worms. For drinks, every table had a half-dozen numbered bottles— sweet sodas, the numbers designating a variety of nonexistent flavors. You could buy cheap but surprisingly good champagne, slightly sweet but a bargain at three rubles, and at the same price, bottles of rough, red wine from Georgia, more purple than red in color. Balanchine was determined to introduce me to the mineral water from his childhood, Borzhomi.* "For health, you must drink every day," he told me. It tasted like rotten eggs and sulfur, and the mineral content, while ruining your gallbladder, probably generates kidney stones all while coating your esophagus with copper. Surprisingly, over time, I got addicted.

Throughout the trip, we followed a routine. Early breakfast at the hotel, bus to the theater, class, rehearsal, lunch at the theater buffet, and, after more rehearsal, performance, and bus back for late supper at the hotel. With Quentin's camera, I tried to film the company in the dining room, but our Russian interpreters and handlers commanded, *"Nyet! Nyet photographe!"*

These guides—their jobs (and their necks) depended on shepherding us from place to place, keeping the group together and watching for strays. If dancers or staff opted to find their own way to the theater, the guides became agitated. We'd pile into the bus, and they would inquire, "Are we missing anybody?" We'd answer, "Don't worry, if they're not on the bus, they're going on their own." Shocked that we

---

* A Russian friend, Grisha, tells me that Russia's boss, Vladimir Putin, recently banned Borzhomi and Georgian wine, in an effort to punish Georgians for their rebellious separation from Russia.

would allow individuals to leave the pack, they'd ask, "They're not with the group, don't you *care* about them?" "Fuck 'em!" we'd laugh.

I laugh now. Back then, the environment was miserable. Imagine the widest street you've ever seen—the Champs-Élysées, Pennsylvania Avenue—all over Moscow, there were streets like that, only wider. Seldom did a car drive by, just sidewalks with droves of people bundled up against the cold in thick layers of blue, gray, and brown, walking with their heads down. Some corners were packed with queues, waiting for a bus. Rarely did one come by, and they were stuffed, like sausages, with people. In the gutters, women in babushkas swept with bundles of twigs tied with rags, stick brooms of witches. Occasionally, a black limousine with a red flag on its hood would pass, transporting dignitaries. Even rarer, a truck would pass, loaded with cabbages, then stop at a designated site and dump a heap of cabbages on the sidewalk. People stood in lines that stretched for blocks to buy them.

When we dancers would walk Moscow's streets, passing the multitudes, I never saw one person look up to watch us. It's not that they didn't scope us, they were just afraid to be seen watching. "Do you think they would be reported?" we discussed at dinner. If anyone in the crowd was caught staring, perhaps a KGB agent might call them out or report them—"Why are you looking at their clothes? Don't you think our Russian clothes are good enough?" or "Do you know these people? Then why look at them? What's your name?" The police-state mentality, frightening, infected our moods. In relief, our company became more cohesive and insular, solidarity against the atmosphere. For the first time in my life, I began to feel lonely and despondent.

After several days of rehearsal, NYCB opened at the Bolshoi Theater in Moscow. Still infirm, I sat in the box with Balanchine and Lincoln. An excerpt from my diary:

> October 9, Tuesday. Moscow opening night. Company was great. First the boys: Arthur [Mitchell] in *Western* the best he has ever done; Eddie [Villella] in *Agon,* the same; Conrad [Ludlow] and Nicky [Magallanes] both partnered beautifully. *Serenade* with Patty Wilde, Allegra, Jillana, and Patricia McBride—outstanding. The corps, fabulous. In *Interplay,* Patty McBride, Conrad, Tony [Blum], good. Its Pas de deux a success. In *Agon,* Melissa great and Allegra too. Again, corps fabulous. *Western Symphony* closed, it was wonderful. Reception lukewarm, all the way through,

although Arthur had a big, personal success, as he did in Europe.* Mr. B depressed, I think. I was proud as hell of the best ballet in the world, and unhappy over its reception.

Opening night, when the dignitaries and moneyed class were in the audience, the response was tepid. The critics played it safe—in their reviews, they didn't like us, they didn't hate us—until Official Word circulated that it was okay to like us. Several nights after the opening, the audience began to fill with diehard balletomanes. From then on, reception was unpredictable. Sometimes, a ballet we thought would be a smash hit would lay an egg; other times, a sleeper ballet would receive roaring accolades. A few nights after the opening, I was in the company box. The audience adored Violette Verdy and Eddie Villella in *Donizetti Variations*. To everyone's astonishment (and Balanchine's chagrin), Eddie repeated his variation in an encore. Balanchine was peeved that Eddie and Violette had been such a success, especially Eddie. I cheered, even though I was envious and frustrated that I wasn't up there dancing too. I was determined to get back onstage and, in my daydreams, imagined that if I ever did an encore, I would not repeat my variation, but invent a new one.[†]

After opening at the Bolshoi, the company moved to the Kremlin and its Great Palace of Congress, a six-thousand-seat theater, I was told, built a year before. We were scheduled to perform there for a couple of weeks, before returning to the Bolshoi for a final few performances. After company class, I'd spend the day, and most evenings as well, totally immersed in a variety of exercises, driving to get back on that stage. Skill and strength were compounding, so occasionally I'd take an evening off to seek out performances of opera, theater, and ballet around Moscow.

---

* Arthur Mitchell joined the company in 1954, and became a principal dancer within a year or two. Every time we toured Europe, he was a sensation—this beautiful black American ballet dancer of such accomplishment and grace. There would literally be hundreds of fans at the stage door waiting for him after performances. At that time, as far as I know, there wasn't a black dancer in any other major ballet company in America.

[†] Several years later, I put that dream to a test, dancing *Nutcracker* in Salt Lake City. I invented and danced a different variation every night to the same music, for ten performances in a row.

Our bus was not allowed close to the Kremlin wall. Each day, leaving the warmth of our bus, we'd scurry up to the fortress walls and crowd through a narrow aperture to arrive in a low-ceilinged vestibule, where an awful doorman waited with a pair of flunkies. Each dancer had to show proof of his or her identity, and this surly clerk would scrutinize it, compare it to some ledger, peruse and mull over it, stare at you, stare back at the identity card, and, at last, wave you through. Endless! Every day for two weeks, the company allowed twenty minutes extra in our schedule just to get past this prick.

Pavel Gerdt was an early teacher of Balanchine, and his favorite. His daughter had come to watch our company class, and offered to teach the ballerinas the next day. She served up a difficult technique class, and Suki Schorer, Milly, Gloria Govrin, and Violette Verdy were outstanding. Violette, with her wild French passion, worked so intensely in class that it threw her into a nervous and excited state. Afterward, she couldn't stop talking, and couldn't rehearse for the rest of the day. Balanchine, observing the class with me, kept mumbling in my ear, "You know . . . I wish Diana was in class. Gerdt should see Diana!"

Ever the optimist, I told Balanchine I would be ready to dance by late October. Assuming that Diana would be ready, he scheduled us to dance *Episodes* at the matinee on the 27th.

Poor Balanchine was constantly plagued. Dancers were complaining and making demands; others were getting injured. The corps was exhausted, and creating ballet programs with enough variety, yet not overworking the cast, became impossible. Dignitaries and fans were pulling at him. The minister of culture wanted to take him around and show him off, and demanded he participate in various political and diplomatic activities. Journalists clamored for interviews, and Soviet musicians, writers, choreographers, and dancers all wanted a part of him. The Soviet pundits sought for him to declare publicly how great the Soviet Union was. "Better now, everything better now, wouldn't you say?" Balanchine answered, "*Nyet.*" At the behest of the Soviet authorities, and probably for himself, Balanchine's brother, Andrei, continually asked favors. A well-known composer, he boasted to Balanchine, "I make four hundred rubles a month. The average composer, maybe eighty-nine." Andrei gave Balanchine one of his scores, urging him to create a ballet. He painted the picture, "Two brothers! One makes the music, the other makes choreography." Balanchine told me, "I don't know how to tell him his music is awful."

Meanwhile, the Bolshoi Ballet gave a performance of their "modern" works, and our dancers were invited to attend. In the minds of the Soviets, the four ballets on the program represented the pinnacle of avant-garde choreography, but they turned out to be bad copies of modern dances seen in the West in the 1930s and '40s. The closing ballet was a Marxist critique, a "message" ballet—the oppressed rising up against the landlords—full of excessive, earth-stomping energy, punching, and heroic sentiment. The finale included the entire cast onstage, waving red flags. Balanchine called it "Soviet garbage." How easily art and artist can be tainted by imposed ideology.

The night of October 13, I was hanging around my dressing room backstage when Balanchine stopped by. "We need something easy to fill out program. What about pas de deux from *A Midsummer Night's Dream?* It's easy, not difficult. You think you can do? We will do to piano only." This pas de deux was not in the repertoire we'd brought with us, so he almost fell over when I told him, "Oh! I have the orchestra scores with me. They're in my theater bag. And of course I'll do it." He felt it was a sign from God, and scheduled me to dance it within the week.

A couple of days later, Shaun, Deni Lamont, and a crowd of us went to a production of the full-length *Le Corsaire* at the Stanislavsky Theater. At that time, no full-length production of *Le Corsaire* (that I know of) had been seen in the West. The ballet was a campy melodrama, like watching Douglas Fairbanks swashbuckling. Sitting in the "Royal Box" were Khrushchev, his wife, and the president of Finland. Standing off Khrushchev's left shoulder was a bull of a man, a bodyguard dressed in black leather, with his two hands folded over his groin. During the performance, I'd occasionally crane my neck back to look up at the box, and I'd swear that bodyguard's gaze fixed directly on me.

The next day, when I finally got past Comrade Prick at the Kremlin gate, I dashed to class, and standing outside the ballet studio was Khrushchev's bodyguard, sizing up each dancer. Later, at rehearsal, he was in the theater watching from the audience. Perhaps it was paranoid on my part, but I was convinced he had singled me out the previous night, and had come by this morning to verify I really was a dancer.

Two months earlier, I'd been lying in a hospital cot in Hamburg, not knowing if I'd ever dance again. On October 19, I stepped onto a stage in Moscow to perform the pas de deux in *A Midsummer Night's Dream* with Melissa Hayden. Oh God, to dance again, what a joy!

The next day, Jonathan Watts, a principal dancer and elegant cavalier who covered many of my roles, got injured dancing *Raymonda* at the matinee, so that ballet was replaced with *Scotch Symphony* for the evening program. I had a half hour's notice, and was off like a bird. My ballerina, Allegra Kent, danced beautifully, but was worried for me. My torso was weak, I couldn't lift well, and I got winded quickly, but I got through—decently.

Soon after, I danced the ballet *Episodes* with Diana, who had recovered from another of her injuries. *Episodes* was set to Anton von Webern's music—serial, twelve-tone, and perhaps never played before in Russia, certainly never for a ballet. Diana confessed to me her fears, "They're gonna hate this ballet, and its music. We're gonna lay an egg." It turned out the reverse—not only were the musicians thrilled with the score, but along with Bizet's *Symphony in C,* it may have been the NYCB company's biggest success.

Twenty days from my first barre back in Vienna, I was relieved and thrilled to be performing again, but I wouldn't consider myself truly "back" till I was able to conquer *Tchaikovsky Pas de Deux, Raymonda,* and, especially, *Apollo.*

There was a group of interpreters assigned to us by the Soviet agency Intourist (the government's official tourist bureau)—Julia, Valentine, Felix, and Leda, an attractive girl who never said a word and seemed to be a gofer for everyone else. "Anything you want or need, tell us. Anywhere you want to go, tell us. We are here for you," was announced to all of us. Mousey little Julia rarely spoke up, and Felix hid in a corner, so Shaun immediately decided Valentine would be the one to cultivate. The U.S. State Department watched over us as well, and assigned their agent to look after us. As he was diminutive in size, we dubbed him Tommy Tuck. Our mail came, via diplomatic pouch, to the American Embassy, and Tuck relished the mail call. He would hand out letters and report the contents publicly. "Oh, Jacques, you have a letter. Christopher's over his cold!" The little rat was making sure we got the message: our State Department was opening and reading our correspondence. We wanted to slap him.

Our outgoing mail was also sent via the embassy's diplomatic pouches, and forget about sending packages. If you wanted to send home a gift, you had to persuade someone on their way back to the U.S. to carry it, à la courier. The balletomane Bert Martinson (of Martinson

Coffee)* had joined us for the early part of our tour, and was on his way home. So I saddled him with a parcel—a wooden tinkertoy, whose painted sections fitted together vertically to make a colorful tower of the Kremlin, including the red star at its apex. It was a gift for George's sixth birthday.

Phone calls were possible occasionally, if you made your request days ahead, informing your Intourist handler. A time would be arranged, and perhaps a connection. You would sit in your hotel room and wait for the message, "Come down, your call is going through." Then you would sit by the international phone booth in the lobby, possibly for hours, while a connection was made. Sometimes I would hear Carrie talking to me, but she couldn't hear my answer. We speculated that they wanted to be informed of what people outside the country said, but didn't want information about Russia going out.

Shaun hoped to visit the seat of the Russian Orthodox Church, the monastery of Zagorsk, their Vatican. It would be a paper bag opportunity, too. Zagorsk was some ninety kilometers outside of Moscow, and Shaun needed help to get there. For a week, he tried to persuade Valentine to take us. "There is no such place," we were told at first. Then, "Oh yes, Zagorsk. It's closed now." Then, "Only open on certain days, but nobody goes there, only old women." Then, "There may be a bus, but we don't know." Finally, somewhere around the third week of our stay in Moscow, Shaun purred, "Valentine, dear, we'll pay for a taxi to take us there, wait while we tour the place, and then drive us all back," and Valentine relented. "You must have your passports." Soon, we were driving through the countryside. Valentine in front, next to the driver, and Shaun and I in the back, munching dried fruit. On either side of the road lay flat fields of mud, no walls, fences, or foliage. Against the gray sky, thick, muscular telephone wires curved from pole to pole, and every once in a while, you'd pass a hovel—a one-story shed. At a crossroad about forty kilometers out of town, we came to a concrete building with a radio tower, laden with antennae. A barrier lowered across the road, and a militiaman waved us down. Our taxi driver stopped the car and froze. Valentine turned pale and twitched. "Uh-oh," came out of Shaun. The militiaman demanded something and there was an inter-

* Bert Martinson died from an insect bite. In 1989, I would lose my right index finger to the bite of a brown recluse spider.

lude of rapid Russian. The driver handed over some papers; Valentine fished out ID, then he turned around to us, and said, "Give him your passports!" The officer, taking everything, stalked away. Shaun leaned out of the car and shouted, "*Nyet politico! Artistes! Artistes!*" Valentine and the driver sat like stones, deaf to our questions. For twenty minutes. Then the militiaman returned, handed back our passports and ID papers, grunted a few words, and left. Valentine turned back to face us, his voice high-pitched. "It's all right, it's all right, he called Julia at the hotel, and she said let us go." Shaun and I stared at each other. "Julia? The mouse who attended all the Intourist meetings without saying a word? Who sat in the corner of the dining room? She was the boss!"

Zagorsk is a walled complex of cupola-crowned churches. Fabulous. Outside among the churches stood a scattering of old women, black-garbed. And in the doorway of the biggest church sat one man without any teeth. A guardian. Inside were clusters of little old women paying court to various icons. In the dark, dingy gloom, lit with a few preciously hoarded candles and the occasional electric light bulb strung on a makeshift wire, the church's every inch was layered with icons and murals. We left all our rubles as a donation, and Shaun did several paper bag cutaways. My favorite: he photographed me next to the guardian, sitting as if we were a couple at a flick, sharing a paper bag of popcorn.

Back at the hotel a few days later, Shaun stumbled in on Julia, holding a conference. "Daisy, I went down early for breakfast, and the doors to the dining room were locked. I rattled the door because I heard people in there, and when someone opened it, I saw the interpreters sitting around a table, looking terrified, with Julia haranguing them."

One of our dancers got through to the U.S. on a phone call: "Oh my God, do you realize there's a big crisis going on, and we may be going to war with Russia!"

The Cuban missile crisis had been brewing, but none of the dancers knew it. The U.S. Embassy played dumb. Then, one morning at breakfast, we were officially told to avoid the embassy that day between the hours of two and five p.m. "The Russians are staging a demonstration. Not a good idea to be around." For an hour or so, shouting protestors threw bottles of ink at the walls of the embassy while cameras rolled. When the photo op was over, that was it. They dispersed. Years later, Betty Cage confessed, "I didn't sleep much. We had escape plan A, B, and C." Plan A: look into chartering a plane so, if word came from the U.S. Embassy saying, "It's about to happen, get out, get out!" we could hopefully bus to the waiting plane and flee. Plan B: if we were too late for a plane, surreptitiously keep the bus on call twenty-four hours, so that if we got the word "War has been declared," the whole company could pack into the bus, and maybe have a chance to get inside the American Embassy. Plan C: no luck, interred in a gulag, doing barre in barracks. In her laconic, deadpan monotone, Betty elaborated on Plan C: "Well, the Bolshoi Ballet company is touring America. They care about their dancers. Maybe our state department will too, then we'll get traded. Or maybe not."

The Russian Literary Guild planned, for their union's annual celebration, a show—a potpourri of Slavic arts, featuring folk dancers, a violinist, ballet, a vaudeville act, and an opera singer. And the guild was pressuring Balanchine to have his dancers perform. Balanchine dissembled; the minister of culture insisted.

There was no way he could squeeze out of it, so I suggested, "Why don't Allegra and I do the pas de deux from *A Midsummer Night's Dream*? It's not taxing, and can be done in a small space." That night, we went to the Literary Guild and, in the wee hours, on a stage the size of an index card—maybe fifteen feet by ten—performed before a hall packed with vodka-swilling trolls. Hating every second, Balanchine introduced us and disappeared, hiding backstage. Allegra and I adjusted the choreography to fit the index card; a series of lifts ordinarily done on a long diagonal became oscillating cabrioles, one to the right, pivot, one to the left, pivot, to the right, to the left. The audience talked and drank the whole time, and I don't remember any applause when we finished. We were followed by an accordion player who received an ovation.

Balanchine was a wreck, miserable with bursitis of the rotator cuff, and it seemed everywhere he went, people hugged him or patted him on the shoulder. Lincoln and Betty Cage made arrangements for him to return to New York after Leningrad. "He's got to get away," Betty explained, "if only for a week. He's cracking up." Betty told me Tanny called and told Lincoln that she didn't want Balanchine to come back, but Lincoln insisted, "He *needs* to get out for a while." I had the feeling it was his obsession with Diana Adams that was cracking their marriage.

We'd had enough of Moscow. We were ready for Leningrad. But our closing night at the Bolshoi left no doubt we were a triumph. I felt terrific dancing *Scotch Symphony* with Milly. *Episodes* and *Symphony in C*

An enormous potted plant, Hotel Astoria, Leningrad

closed the program. The applause went on so long, Balanchine made a speech to the audience, "We have to leave now . . . ," and, deliberately using the tzarist name for Leningrad, " . . . you know, leave for PETROGRAD!"

A bevy of Balanchine's old classmates met him at the station in Leningrad. With a drawn face, he later told me, "I had to be nice."

Our hotel in Leningrad, the Astoria, built in 1912, was once an Art Nouveau honey. Now seedy, a frayed lady with runny makeup, it was an apt setting for the paper bag travelogue. We had no sooner settled in our room than Shaun collected Allegra and headed for the lobby. There we met Balanchine, flanked by Lincoln, who was tap dancing with excitement. "We go now to Maryinsky [the Kirov]," Balanchine sniffed. "You want to come?" They waited while I ran to my room, grabbed Quentin's camera and a pocketful of blank cassettes, and trotted off after them, leaving director Shaun in the lobby with his set—a potted plant—and his two stars, Allegra and the paper bag.

> *The lobby of the once-posh Astoria. The leaves of an enormous potted plant slowly part as if a curtain is split, to reveal pixie-faced Allegra. She looks around nervously, then slowly allows the fronds to close, hurries around, and crosses in front of the plant and moves out of the picture, leaving the camera to zoom in on a close-up of a paper bag nestled at the base of the planter.*

Balanchine, Lincoln, and I set off on a nostalgia tour. Four decades before, Balanchine had danced, choreographed, and loved here. He refused to use the word "Leningrad." His hatred of Lenin was intense. "That awful man with beard." Leningrad was known as St. Petersburg before Soviet rule, and the Kirov Theater was known as the Maryinsky. "It's Petrograd! And Maryinsky!" he would assert. He seemed in a daze as I filmed him, traipsing through the streets and along the canals of the city, with Lincoln looming off his shoulder. Balanchine would stop, point to a second-floor window, and say, "I stayed here," and later at another building, "Ah. Here in her room, Tamara served me tea." Each time he paused to expound on memories ignited, I filmed, but *also* I wanted to hear his stories. So I'd listen a bit, scoot back to capture the two of them on my 16 mm, then rush back to demand, "What did you just say? I missed it! Say it again."

A policewoman, Leningrad

"This must be the year of the cabbage," I thought. As in Moscow, piles of cabbages were dumped on the corners of alleys and streets. In store windows, you'd see cabbages arranged carefully in geometric configurations—squares, rectangles, circles, and pyramids displayed window dressing à la Bergdorf or Saks. I filmed it all.

Soon, we turned a corner, and there was the Maryinsky Theater. Nearby was a column plastered with posters and notices, and Balanchine translated delightedly, "NYCB," and the listing of our program. I backed away to catch both of them in the frame, but a policewoman materialized. "*Nyet! Nyet! Nyet!*" she commanded, advancing. Tendrils of shoulder-length hair straggled from her austere military hat, emblazoned with a red star.

Certain we were headed for the gulag, Lincoln started squeaking, "Oh my God, George. George!" It never crossed my mind to worry; Balanchine was there. And sure enough, leaning back to make himself taller and looking down his nose, he described to the policewoman who he was, who we were, and, pointing to the poster, concluded, "*Amerikanski balyet!*" I moved in to get a shot of her scowling face, and, like a frightened little girl fending off Dracula, she raised her open palms to me, gasped out an apprehensive "*Nyet, nyet,*" and fled.

Unfortunately, we couldn't get in the theater that morning, only circled it, but I captured it all on film. Later, when inside, I thought it the most beautiful theater I had ever seen. The Bolshoi is red and yellow gold; the Maryinsky is blue and pale gold, almost silver, and gentler, somehow. Too bad we only had two performances there.

Vladimiroff had charged me with his request, so at the first company class, I went very early to find his spot at the barre in the theater's dance studio. The room was smaller, narrower than I expected, dank, musty, with grime-streaked walls. The ceiling was not the shimmering yellow gold Vladimiroff had described, but some twenty feet high and a dishwater gray, speckled with dust and neglect. I stood at the place designated on his map and imagined my hand on the wooden bar holding his from a half century before.

We took a sightseeing tour of the city the next day. The guide was full of propaganda nonsense. Discounting St. Isaac's Cathedral, "Why do you want to go there? You will only see the oppression religion has made on the people. Better things to see." She then expounded on Soviet architecture and nonferrous metalworks factories.

We opened at the Maryinsky on Halloween. I danced the closing ballet, *Western Symphony.* During the bows, Balanchine made a short but charming speech, but backstage he confessed to me, "These awful people, in such a beautiful theater." A gray dullness had settled over the country, and the elegance and manners of the aristocratic audiences he remembered from his boyhood were gone. When people dressed to the nines and laughter and confidence filled the theater, Balanchine had performed at the Maryinsky, as a mouse in *Nutcracker.* "Everything changes. With revolution and Lenin, people were eating rats in street," he ranted.

At this point, Balanchine's resilience and aplomb began to break down. He'd survived the pressures and demands of three weeks in Moscow, and now found his beloved Petrograd degraded to a shell of its former self, as well as suffering the continual disappointment of Diana Adams dancing so rarely. He might watch Jillana, Melissa, Pat Neary, Violette, or other dancers performing his choreography beautifully, but it didn't satisfy him. It was *Diana* he wanted to see doing his steps.

All the ballets generally received more praise in Leningrad than in Moscow. One night at dinner, I spoke at length to a man from the United States Information Services. An old-time State Department diplomat, he had stopped on his way to Estonia. Knowledgeable about ballet, a fan of Russia and especially the young ballerina Maya Plisetskaya, he spoke of communism, capitalism, and degrees of freedom. He believed Julia, the guide, was a member of the Secret Police. "I spotted her in New York City with the Soviet delegation . . ." He warned me, "At the dinner table, you have to be careful what you say, because the waiters report to their superiors." They would be queried, "What was the conversation at your dinner table? Who said what?"

We were becoming more independent and subversive, many of us dodging our handlers to venture off on our own. Leningrad was less depressing than Moscow, but only by a degree. We visited beautiful cathedrals and palaces where the gorgeous icons had been replaced by hundreds of posters, leaflets, and mind-numbing propaganda proclaiming the virtues of the hammer and sickle, and always images of Lenin. Every day off was crammed with adventures. Touring the Hermitage Museum, with its stunning architecture and artwork. Watching class at the Kirov School, everyone agreed the early training is superb, world class, but as the dancers hit their teens, fourteen or fifteen years old, they lose individuality and begin working to make themselves carbon copies of the current luminary of the day. But I guess all young dancers emulate their stars. I had Eglevsky as my model.

On November 1, we moved to another theater, and the following day, Friday, I danced *Raymonda Variations,* Balanchine's homage to the composer Glazounov. "He used to play rehearsal for us at Maryinsky." The ballet had been choreographed as a showcase for Patricia Wilde and me, with two virtuoso male variations. I was slender and ready, but Robert Irving pushed the tempo, and I spent the last variation expending all my energy trying not to be late.

The next night, Violette and Eddie brought down the house in *Donizetti.* Balanchine tried to avoid watching during their dancing, and kept chatting to me in the wings about his plans to revive *Ballet Imperial* for the New York spring season. To my amazement, he mumbled, "Maybe for Allegra." Had he finally realized Diana didn't want to dance?

At last, I danced *Apollo.* It went well, and I found myself euphoric and ravenous to dance it again. Balanchine was swamped with fans and spent hours talking with admirers, but that night, at the theater buffet, he lamented, "I am choking and have to get away."

He'd been to the dingy apartment of a friend, "two rooms, tiny, dirty," Balanchine said. His friend very proudly said, "We have it alone, George. We don't even have to share the toilet. Do you want to make pee-pee?" Balanchine sighed, "Next week, I escape, you know. Go back for little while to New York. But back in time for Tbilisi."

A few nights later, Melissa and I danced *Tchaikovsky Pas de Deux,* and I looked forward to proving that my recovery was complete. When the curtain came down on *Concerto Barocco,* there was a smattering of applause. As Melissa and I waited in the wings for our entrance, I remember thinking, "Oh my God, they don't like us; we're going to flop." It turned out to be the reverse. We danced the ballet. After my variation, I took a series of six bows. Milly and I spent more time taking bows than the eight or nine minutes the ballet took to dance.

Balanchine stormed backstage, apoplectic, and accosted me in the wings. Milly had escaped to her dressing room to prepare for the next ballet. He was almost incoherent. "*Tchaikovsky Pas de Deux* is not for us! It is circus!" and "It's Melissa's fault!" He'd wanted to see Diana Adams doing those steps he had choreographed for her, and not anyone else.* "Jacques, you can have this ballet for concerts and television! I'm taking it out of the company's repertoire. I don't want to see it. I give it to you."

Despite his tirade, I was exhilarated. A little over nine weeks before, I had been a bloody, broken pile in front of the Hamburg Staatsoper. Tonight, I was back to the skills of the pre–streetcar smash.

The next day, I said au revoir to a shifty-eyed, nervous Balanchine, who was implementing his escape plan. "Mr. B, last night, you were so distraught. I know you didn't mean what you said about Milly and *Tchaikovsky Pas de Deux,* about taking it out of the repertoire and letting me have it for concerts and TV. Give my love to Tanny and please go see Carrie in New York. We'll see you when you get back in Tbilisi." He dropped his head and mumbled, looking like a wet dog being reprimanded, then left. He skipped our closing night in Leningrad.

Kiev is the city that claims, "Russia was born here." Assorted Viking princes—Vladimir, Oleg, and others—extended their powers over the

---

* Earlier, Mr. B had described to me his plans for the premiere of his full-length *Midsummer Night's Dream.* The tall and regal Diana would be his Titania, and a canopy of fat leaves created by the set designer David Hays would be lowered to make her appear even taller. "She will look like giantess, big, beautiful." Her choreography would be slow, with long, sweeping movements, and her handmaidens, the tallest girls in the corps. Whereas when Oberon was onstage, a new canopy of leaves above would be smaller and suspended as high as possible, so the compact Eddie Villella would seem diminutive by contrast. His choreography would be quick, electric, virtuoso, and buzzing all over the stage. To further enhance the effect, Oberon would command a court of tiny creatures of the forest, butterflies and elves—danced by bevies of children from SAB, to contrast with Titania's tall entourage. But as it happened, when it all came to pass, Diana didn't make the premiere. Melissa replaced her as Titania. Before Balanchine died, he left *Midsummer Night's Dream* as his gift to Diana, whom I never saw dance the role.
    Every time Diana opted out, Milly came to the rescue. To his ire, Balanchine had to depend on her. Eventually, Milly won him over, but it took most of her career.

Floating around in Tchaikovsky Pas de Deux, *so happy, 1962*

Slavic cities, and established the river port city of Kiev as their capital. For a few centuries, it was the most important cultural and intellectual city in Eastern Europe. Built on a bluff that slopes down to the river Dnieper, it was home to the Cathedral of St. Sophia. Kiev is the seat of the Ukrainian church, and honeycombed beneath the church, as well as the city, are tomb-niches connected by miles of passages. Shaun, determined to film a paper bag scene in one of those tombs, requested a visit. And also a visit to Babi Yar, a ravine on the outskirts of the city, notorious for the over 100,000 people slaughtered there by the Nazi SS. A year before, the Russian poet Yevgeny Yevtushenko had written about Babi Yar, and many among us had read his poem. Our Russian guides were reluctant to admit that the slaughter had been primarily Jews. "Mostly Russian comrades," they'd insist, "our people, not just Jews, it was anyone who spoke out against the Nazis."

"Babi Yar, you can visit on your own. But we will arrange for you a tour of the catacombs," said our Intourist guide. Outside the bluff, we lined up single file to enter a doorway and snake our way through the underground maze. Off to the sides of our tunnel were niches containing mummies—at times, a pile of something wrapped in rags, other times a carved wooden figure covered with jewels and gilded crowns. "These jewels are paste. The real ones were stolen from the people by monks," our lady guide informed us. As we inched along, she would point to some niche on the right and announce, "This is not real mummy; it is fabrication." Then, pointing to the left, "This is real mummy. Pass this down to your comrades, please." So, through the tunnels of the catacombs, the guide's words were whispered from one dancer to the next, "This mummy is real . . . this is *fake*," until it came to Frank Moncion, in line before Shaun and me. When the message reached Frank, he made a ridiculous face, pointed right, and said, "*Da* mummy," then pointing left, "*Nyet* mummy. Pass it." From that point on, the dancers joined in, chanting musical variations of "*Da* mummy, *nyet* mummy," down the line, accompanied by roaring cascades of laughter. When we finally collected in an open chamber outside the tunnel, the company continued chanting the lyrics, and the tour guide's face twitched with anger. Some thirty years later, my son Christopher, then artistic director of the Pennsylvania Ballet, choreographed a piece called *Da Mummy, Nyet Mummy*. Curious critics asked, "What does it mean?" Chris solemnly answered, "Long story, family history."

In Kiev, I danced almost everything with Allegra. And she was the company's sensation—all the talk and spotlight was on her. Early on, there was a dewy-eyed teenager who stood waiting at the stage door. He approached me and stammered, "I saw you dance with Allegra. She is so beautiful!" I remarked, "Your English is excellent!" "Thank you, I study." He gathered his courage and continued, "Do you think I could approach Miss Kent?" "Sure, just go up and talk to her!" But he was too modest to do so, and left.

The next night, he was back. Thinking that with him as our guide, we could ditch the rest of the company and sup adventurously with the Kievians, I went up to him. "Why don't you come out after the performance? I'll ask Allegra. We'll have dinner together." Stunned, he was making some incomprehensible sounds. "Pick your favorite restaurant," I suggested. He may have picked the most expensive "in" place he could think of—not the student dive I'd hoped for. During the dinner, he filled us with his dreams. "I am going to be scientist, but to do it, I must go to Novosibirsk. It is where the elite go." He described how only the top of the class would be allowed to go; otherwise, you would be assigned to a factory school, or to study an occupation the government determined. Our dinner didn't last long. The service was awful, and Allegra, acting her kooky self, squirming dramatically to get back to the hotel.

All memories of Kiev are eclipsed by Shaun's arrest. I was to dance *Swan Lake* that night with Diana, but, of course, she canceled and was replaced by Allegra. The half-hour call came and Shaun, who played the sorcerer, von Rothbart, was not in the theater. Fifteen-minute call, no Shaun, and, calling the hotel, no answer in his room. Eddie Bigelow came to the rescue, put on Shaun's costume, and did the role he'd originated some ten years before.

Halfway through the performance, we got the news. "Shaun's in jail." Much later we heard the details from him. In the early morning, he had gone to film the tracks of birds in the snow, planning to use the footage in his travelogue. In a transition, a picture of the tracks would dissolve to people's feet slushing their way to St. Sophia Cathedral, where you'd see the paper bag at the foot of a sculpture of a Russian saint.

Some police up the road saw this *Amerikanski* with his head lowered, and his camera pointing at the snow. "Photographing snow? In Russia?" They nabbed him, thrust him in the back of their jeep, drove to headquarters, and shoved him in a cell. Details were recounted by him at dinner that night, when the released Shaun made a grand entrance to the dining room. "Oh my dears, wait till I tell you what happened to me!" Lincoln, who wanted to be there, had earlier ordered, "When he shows up, don't let him say anything until I'm there!" But no one could stop Shaun when he had an audience. He immediately told us the whole story, and didn't mind at all when Lincoln showed up later and he had to give a repeat.

"All I was doing was filming bird tracks in the snow, when these militiamen grabbed me and threw me in their jeep, then drove me somewhere. I was afraid I would pee." While under interrogation the whole day, Shaun protested, "*Artiste!* I'm an *artiste! Nyet politico!* I don't know anything." "One after another, they kept barking at me in Russian. It was hours before they brought an interpreter." Every time they asked a question, Shaun would reply, "*Nyet politico. Balyet. Artiste!* New York City *Balyet. Teatr, Teatr.* Balanchine, Balanchine!!! *Artiste! Nyet politico!*"

The police had gone to our hotel and taken all the film footage found in our room—including my cassettes. "They stuck me in a cell," Shaun continued, "while they developed the film! I kept thinking I'd be released. But by six o'clock, I was terrified. They took me to a room with three generals, glittering in medals!" Shaun recounted how they had plied him with questions about Kennedy, the U.S. government, and how he felt about communism. "I have no opinion, I'm an *artiste.* I know nothing. *Balyet, balyet,* Balanchine!" Finally, one of the generals spoke up, in perfect English. "We have watched the film you have taken, and what is the paper bag in front of church? And if you are artist, what is so artistic about a toilet bowl flushing?" "I'm sunk now," Shaun thought, but answered, "Well, it's what you call a cutaway. You zoom in on the waters of a flushing toilet bowl, and come up with the image of a windshield wiper in the rain, and find you're in a new city . . ." Eventually, late in the evening, they returned all the confiscated film and my cassettes to Shaun and dumped him at our hotel's dining-room door.

In 2010, when I recounted this incident to my Russian friend Grisha, he angrily commented, "It's no different now. The police!" he yelled. "They need to discover spies—if there are no real ones, they invent one! That's how they get promoted; uncover a spy, move up a notch in power! Today it's a terrorist!"

Mr. B showed up at the end of our engagement in Kiev. I'd exited the stage between variations, breathing heavily in the wings, dripping with sweat, and there he was. I wet him with my hug, and just before I went back onstage for the finale, he called out, "In New York, I see Carrie." Balanchine returned with more than just good news. He had a stack of mail for everyone, and from Carrie came a photograph Cris Alexander had taken of our Chris. Not yet three years old, he sits at Hermione Gingold's makeup table, adorned with her costume jewelry, a diamond tiara on his head. Taken with his own beauty, he beams the essence of delight. I made myself a pest showing it to everyone.

Two days later, we were in Tbilisi, Georgia, home of Balanchine's ancestors. Also where Vakhtang Chabukiani reigned supreme.

TBILISI, GEORGIA

Chabukiani was a great star of the Soviet ballet, and a supernova in his native Georgia. I had been inspired by old black-and-white footage of him in the film *Stars of the Russian Ballet*. I watched it over and over again at the bygone Cameo movie theater,

Chris d'Amboise, 1962

below Forty-second Street, on Seventh Avenue. Nicholas Kopeikine had played piano accompaniment for Chabukiani on his tour of the States in the 1930s, and was a fan as well. He often shook his jowls as he declared to me, "Oooh, ooooh . . . you are the American Chabukiani. Oooooh."*

The first night in Tbilisi, I went to see Chabukiani dance in a three-act ballet, *Laurencia*. He had a fabulous, charismatic personality onstage, and exuded energy, like a roaring furnace. The audience screamed for him. Most of the dancers in the company were not of high quality. I wondered, "Could it be that he doesn't want good dancers around him? Or maybe he's just a lousy teacher, if he teaches them at all." I went back to visit him in his dressing room. Like so many charismatic male dancers, you think they're over six feet onstage, then on meeting them, you find out they're half a foot less than you'd imagined. Chabukiani was short, about fifty-four years old, slim, sinewy, and sort of ugly. He greeted me graciously.

---

* I did my best to become a mixture of two styles: Chabukiani's excessive, grand, powerful gestures, macho, folk-derived; and Vladimiroff's, with gentle ease, tossing off virtuoso steps as if glory was the day-to-day garment he wore, all simplicity. Chabukiani was out there, arms flying, full of bravado. The great Russian dancer Vladimir Vasiliev could swim easily in both styles, but the superb Danish dancer Eric Bruhn would find it hard to be Chabukiani—he was inherently a pure, simple classical dancer. Besides Chabukiani, the other male dancers who inspired me as a boy: Igor Youskevitch, in my memory flying out of the wings in the ballet *Coppélia;* and in every performance of Ballet Society, the art of Todd Bolender, and the smooth bouncing power of William Dollar. When André Eglevsky joined NYCB, he became my mentor and a model for me.

A couple of days later, I saw him dance in his ballet *Othello.* He played the title role in blackface, with some kind of white paste smeared on his teeth, a sort of thick Elmer's Glue. The choreography was full of dramatic histrionics right out of silent movies, often ludicrous and embarrassing, but with moments of riveting theatricality and drama. In one haunting scene, Othello convulses, suffering an epileptic fit at the thought of his wife's adultery. Iago, the diabolical plotter, lurks in the background, relishing his general's anguish, then creeps slowly behind him. At the end of the scene, Iago perches on the prostrate Othello's back, balancing on the one foot he's placed directly between Othello's shoulder blades, crushing him into the earth as if he were a malevolent cassowary growing right out of Othello's spine. Several moments of stillness pass, then Iago raises his beak-like visage to stare at the audience with black, unblinking eyes as the lights fade to darkness—chilling!

At the end of his performance, the entire audience leaped to their feet, and many left their seats to run down the aisles to be as close to the stage as possible. The Tbilisi theater was trapezoidal in shape, with the stage the wider part, and box seats on each side shaped like stacked blocks, rising overlapping, and abutting the edges of the stage. Chabukiani's bows were theatrical marvels, as dramatic as anything I've ever seen.

He entered and stood down center, close to the footlights, with his arms spread into a wide V, then started walking backward until he touched the red velvet curtain behind him. Then, instead of stopping when his back grazed the curtain, he kept going, leaning against the curtain and pushing with his feet, moving the volumes of red velvet slowly back upstage, leaning his weight more and more into the curtain, until he was almost horizontal, as if shoving a locomotive back down the tracks. By now, the audience was clapping rhythmically and stamping while chanting his name. As if a crimson brush was sweeping him slowly toward his fate, Chabukiani allowed the weight of the red velvet to sweep him forward, until it shoved him right to the edge of the footlights. Another inch, and he would have nosedived into the orchestra pit. There, he stopped. Then, this master of theater slowly drew in his outstretched arms, as if gathering every member of the audience and clasping them to his breast, hugging and squeezing them into his body. To top it off, he put a kind of wild, ecstatic expression on his face, his eyes wide as if having a vision, then bent his head forward in a bow. Taking a big breath, as if inhaling every fan, he suddenly looked up with an enormous, jubilant grin beaming like sunlight. During all these shenanigans, he was being pelted with flowers from the screaming fans from the boxes and aisles, even from members of the orchestra.

When it was NYCB's turn to be in that theater, I had Chabukiani's dressing room, and it had its own private toilet. In the middle of a very large concrete room, some twenty by twenty feet, stood a wooden riser of five by five feet, approximately two feet high. Triumphantly, on top of the riser sat the toilet. A single wire with one dim light bulb dangled from the high ceiling, the switch for it on the wall near the door. There was nothing else in the room. I imagined the riser covered a hole in the floor below (I hoped). I sat there on that toilet throne and thought, "Chabukiani sat here!"

As in Leningrad, accompanied by my trusty camera, I went with Balanchine on a tour of Tbilisi. We met up with a tall, imposing man. The pair of them talked in both Russian and Georgian, and then Balanchine introduced me: "This is my brother." I knew Balanchine had a sister, and I'd met his brother Andrei, but knew nothing of another brother. "He is seventy-seven years old. Priest!" Did I hear Balanchine wrong? Did he say "my brother"? Could he have meant brother-in-law? Or brother, as in a religious title? Was there an unknown and secret relative? A mystery never clarified.

"What do you think of Chabukiani?" I asked Balanchine. He twitched a bit and said, "Opening night here, Chabukiani said of us, 'Amateur choreography!' but, you know, years ago, when Chabukiani was touring America, he heard I had told Kopeikine I didn't like him. So you see? He still resents." Balanchine pointed to one of the many posters that covered Tbilisi, showing Chabukiani in *Othello,* and asked, "You see poster? Only his name, Chabukiani, not even Shakespeare. Now, when you look at our poster, you don't even see name Balanchine."*

The dean of critics at the *New York Times,* John Martin, wrote for decades about the world of dance. In his early criticism, he was neither a fan of Lincoln and his dream nor a balletomane in support of Balanchine. However, as time passed and Ballet Society evolved into NYCB, he gradually converted. In 1962, John Martin arranged to accompany us on this historic return of Balanchine to Russia with his NYCB.

* Balanchine insisted that he be listed only as ballet master. "I am not big director. Just ballet master." When you have the power, it makes no difference your title. Stalin was known as the "secretary" of the Communist Party.

For years, in stupid arrogance, I had avoided contact with John or any other critics. If they watched company class or rehearsal, I would ignore them, and elude them if they sought an interview. Over the last decade, I had been the frequent subject of John Martin's reviews, devastating at times, "Dancing like a bull in a china shop," or adulatory, "The most interesting choreographer on the program."

And here I was in Russia, sharing *zakuski* with John Martin. I was courteous but aloof. We made genuine contact on only two occasions on the whole trip, and I was somewhat uncomfortable as, I felt, was he. The first was on the company bus, where we conversed for over an hour, and I recall thinking afterward, "I like this guy." The second was an after-performance party in Balanchine's honor in Tbilisi, where we both got sotted. Georgian parties are like that; your host fills your glass and offers a toast, "To mothers!" If you don't drain your glass, they complain, "What's the matter? Don't you love your mother?" Then comes, "To women, to love, to dance! To art, to friendship! To Georgia! To America!" until the ceilings swirl, legs turn rubbery, and silly smiles plaster faces. Paranoid, I'd think, "Why don't they get drunk? They're emptying their glasses, too! Maybe it's not vodka they're drinking, it's water." Supporting each other, John and I staggered out of that party, holding on to each other and inching down the hill, and it seemed we had a thousand or so kilometers of laughter down the slope to our hotel—old *bonhommes.*

Later that year, he wrote an article for the *Times* calling me the first classical male ballet dancer America had produced, and identifying me as the definitive Apollo. Still, old habits ruled, and I ignored him, until he retired from the *Times.*

Within a week of his retirement, I was on the phone. "John! Let's have a cup of coffee together." I'd operated under the assumption that an artist must have an adversarial relationship with critics. How childish, and now I needed to express regret for failing to acknowledge his importance in my life. Dance journalists attend performances, not just yours, but those of thousands of other artists, matinee and evenings— for years. John was so sweet at our breakfast, mumbling shyly, "You cannot imagine how many times I would try to capture in writing the effect of what I'd seen in a performance. I'd have only thirty or forty minutes to make a deadline. And in the morning, I'd wake up to read what I'd written, and cry out, 'No! That's not what I meant to say! I didn't capture it.' " He told me that most choreographers hounded him before, during, and after the premieres of their works. Jerry Robbins would be at his throat, whether the review was positive or negative. Balanchine, he told me, was the exception; he kept himself removed. But Lincoln made up for it, endlessly cajoling, but more often, intimidating.

A friendship formed at that breakfast, and for years after I visited him in Saratoga, where he had retired to share a home with the choreographer Zachary Solov.

In John Martin's writing, you recognize a superb usage of the English language that is rarely encountered today. So much dance criticism is dumbed-down dross, and petty power gossip, where the reviewer advises the management as well as the reader which corps de ballet dancers should be promoted and what roles they should do. Can you imagine the same presumption in the world of music? "Mr. Levine, your second violinist is so extraordinary, she should be first." Or addressing the brass section, "Your French horn, John Smith, is a standout. Why don't you revive a Mozart horn concerto for him?"

BAKU

November 28 was Shaun's birthday, and we were in the last city of our tour. No rehearsal that day, so, with Felix, our guide, we explored Baku.

We anticipated delight at the Turkish baths. With precognition, Felix sat it out. After a shower, we lay down on a marble tabletop, and a tattooed slab of a masseur pounded us with soap-filled animal bladders. The skins had pinprick vents that released suds. When we were pink and foaming, he ordered us to wash off, and that was it. We paid the fee and left. I'm not good at shopping or sightseeing; wandering around, seemingly without purpose, exhausts me. "Let's go back to the hotel," I suggested. "If you want," Felix ventured, "we could return by another route." "Whichever's the shortest," I requested. Felix was silent, then mumbled, "There may be something interesting to see." "Naw, naw, naw," I dismissed, but Shaun interrupted, "Shut up, Daisy. We're going to follow Felix." The three of us trotted down a narrow side street. Felix seemed to know where he was going. But after ten minutes of walking, I was grumbling. Felix ignored me. "This is a very interesting building," he said, pointing to a nondescript stone structure across the street. "Oh? So what's so interesting?" I grunted. Shaun interrupted, "Felix, what is it?" He whispered to Shaun, "It's a synagogue. There is only one in Baku." "Oh, how nice, Felix, would you like to go in?" How happy Felix was, nodding and smiling, as he left us. He scurried across the street and disappeared into the building. We sat outside on the curb, waiting. "He's Jewish, Daisy, but probably can't admit it to anyone. But with us in tow, he has an excuse to go in. He can claim that he was giving us a tour, and just went in to check out the hours it would be open."

Some twenty minutes later, a beaming Felix emerged from the building, and we continued our walk, through a maze of streets and alleys, back to the hotel. Felix talked a flood—of communism, his life, his family, and how it had been years since he'd visited a synagogue. He trusted us. Shaun had made, in Felix, a friend for life.

A few days earlier, we had tried to mail postcards to our spouses— Shaun, to his love, Cris Alexander; me, to Carrie. We intended to write, "I love you and miss you and thank God! It's over," both in English and Azerbaijani, the language of the country. The concierge and interpreter at the hotel desk nervously announced to us, "There is no such language. We speak and write Russian here." Shaun protested, "But before Russia, there was Azerbaijan, and it wasn't that long ago!" "No! There is no such place. We were always Russian." Shaun's Irish was up. Swelling and red-faced, he puffed, "You're not that ignorant, and you're not that young. There are buildings all around here that are not Russian. They're from another culture. Even your guidebooks speak of Azerbaijan!" "Oh," she stammered, "that may be from ancient times, prehistoric. Nobody remembers that time or what those people spoke."

Our Last Performance of the Tour

. . . was chock-full of drama.

Diary entry, December 1, 1962:

> Very good *Raymonda* at the matinee this afternoon and even better at night. The wind is howling outside. It's said Baku is worse than Chicago in that respect. Mr. B seems happy, and told me he plans to arrange company classes in New York regularly (*he'd been teaching less since Tanny's illness*). We are to leave around 5:45 in the morning for the

airport. Shaun, with Robert Irving, Tony Blum, and Frank Ohman, were almost arrested for taking pictures today.

They had been ambling along making their way to the theater from the hotel, with Shaun taking pictures of whatever spurred his interest. Every building had a superintendent who wore a red armband as a symbol of authority. Their real job was to report to authorities the comings, goings, and utterances of the tenants. As Shaun was filming some street urchins playing after the rain in a puddle of water, a red band noticed him and, spouting a torrent of Russian, tried to seize Shaun's camera. He lifted it as high as he could, as if holding a basketball from opponents' pawing hands, and screamed, "*Nyet, nyet!*" Then he started speed-walking toward the theater, yelling to his trio, "Quick! Let's get to the theater as fast as we can." Irving later reported gleefully, "My dear, we couldn't keep up with him." Red Band #1, calling out an alarm, followed, and other red-banded comrades emerged from buildings along the route, to join the pursuit.

Fortunately, it wasn't long before they reached the theater. Unfortunately, Shaun, his camera still held high, was pursued by a mob now numbering close to two hundred, with Red Band #1 in the lead. A police car pulled up at the same moment the throng arrived at the stage door, and a pair of militiamen jumped out. Red Band #1 waved an accusing finger at Shaun and his camera. Shaun was chanting his familiar mantra, "*Balyet,* Balanchine, NYCB! *Artiste!*" and pointing to the stage door. After listening for a few moments, the senior militiaman ordered his partner to disperse the crowd, and ushered Red Band #1 and several of his cronies, with Shaun and his ballet trio, through the stage door into the vestibule.

The stage doorman stood, open-mouthed, as this motley cast of characters pushed their way past. From the vestibule, a few feet of hall opened onto several wide marble stairs that grandly led down to the theater's buffet, a large dining room where most of the company dancers were lounging around drinking tea, eating yogurt, and slurping down delicious white bread, deliciously slathered with butter and a half inch of caviar. The food available for purchase in the theater buffets of Kiev, Tbilisi, and especially Baku was far better than in the canteens of Moscow or Leningrad.

What a superb entrance Shaun made, elbows raised, left and right hands touching the area over his breasts as if he were Birgit Nilsson or some other divine diva filling her lungs before launching into an ear-splitting aria. "Felix! I've done it again. Felix, where are you? Come save me!" Behind him, spread out as if they were part of his royal robe, were the militiaman, Red Band #1, and his red-banded cronies. Irving, Frank, and Tony fanned out stage right and left and descended to join the rest of the dancers, leaving Shaun in the center spotlight. From the back of the canteen rose Felix, our sole interpreter on these last few days of the tour. He put down his cup of tea and casually approached the militiaman. The militiaman began his report that Red

The company gathers, "GOODBYE TO BAKU!" 1962. At left, Allegra is sitting next to Eddie Bigelow. Blanchine is standing fifth from left. I am standing in the back row on the far right, next fo Felix with his Hitler moustache. Eddie Villela, in a suit and tie,

Band #1 had a complaint against Shaun. Felix raised his hands slowly, palms out, in a "Stop! Hold on a moment" gesture. The militiaman paused midsentence. It was so unlike gentle and timid Felix that the room hushed, as well. Felix reached inside his jacket pocket, ominously pulled out a notebook and pen, and methodically flipped through several pages, as if browsing through a dozen KGB reports. Reaching a blank page and holding his pen ready, he turned his gaze on Red Band #1 and softly intoned, "Name?" Red Band, his eyeballs beginning to move rapidly, right-left, right-left, right-left, stammered out a name. Felix returned to the notebook and slowly wrote the

beaming; Arthur Mitchell smiling in his stripes. Why are we so happy? HOORAY! WE LEAVE TOMORROW!

name. The militiaman removed himself from Red Band's side. Looking up, Felix softly inquired, "Wife?" and, as he wrote down the spouse's name, beads of sweat appeared on Red Band #1's forehead, and his red-banded lackeys faded back and dematerialized. No one moved. Felix continued in his deadpan tone, "Children?" The militiaman finally spoke up. There was a rapid exchange in Russian between him and Red Band #1. Felix slowly nodded his head, and, as if he were a bishop dispelling a blessing, pronounced, *Xhorosho*—good—and closed the notebook. Red Band #1 curled his tail under his backside, and fled. The militiaman backed off and followed just as quickly.

"What did you say, Felix, my savior? Tell us what happened!" Shaun cooed. Felix glowed, now he was in the center spotlight, reenacting the finale in English. "I recommend you drop this complaint and go home," the militiaman had advised Red Band #1. "And keep your mouth shut, for your own good. Quick, quick. Disappear."

Out of the thousands and thousands of performances dancers do in a career, there are certain ones that stick in the mind—good and bad. For me, in dance, *Raymonda* closing night in Baku is one of the good ones; *Tchaikovsky Pas de Deux* in Leningrad and, again later, at the Carter Barron Theatre in Washington, D.C., were also standouts. Etched in my happy memories of great dramatic theater is Felix in the spotlight at the theater canteen on the last day in Baku.*

---

* At the Carter Barron, on its enormous stage, I had to cross 120 feet of space with three cabrioles. It meant making tremendous preparations, trying to eat up space. Melissa, my ballerina, threw herself into dives, flinging herself off a cliff, and trusting me to catch her. Backstage afterward, Shaun gave his imprimatur: "Daisy, you and Milly just gave the performance of a lifetime." That night at the Carter Barron, the humidity remained in the air but the temperature dropped suddenly, so hot bodies literally smoked. Inhaling my own body's steam, I was trembling with joy.

Memorable, but in a negative way, was my first *Apollo* in 1957, where I was so ashamed of my performance, I wanted to quit dance. In a later positive memory, I was on a high, performing *Apollo* at the Staatsoper in Hamburg, in honor of Stravinsky's eightieth birthday, with him conducting. Three nights in a row. Still later, a low that bothers me to this day, again in *Apollo,* dancing the role in the outdoor theater at Ravinia, in Highland Park, Illinois, I cheated myself by not preparing adequately to be at my peak when the curtain rose, and felt my performance reflected it. But that never happened again. There was joy in every *Apollo* after that—in each one, I worked on something different to master. And each performance became a challenge, and an achievement, but never the pinnacle.

LEAVING THE SOVIET UNION

We couldn't *wait* to leave. HOORAY! The plane left Baku on time and made it into Moscow, but as we landed, snow started. The pilot warned that the airport was shutting down. We might have to stay over in Moscow. Our wails filled the plane. Then, a rumor of hope: we were going to try to fly out, the last plane before they closed the runway. "Goodbye, Felix, goodbye! Get off the plane. Hurry!" He looked so sad—like the cartoon character Mutt in *Mutt and Jeff*, the tall one, slightly stooped, only Felix had a moustache. He lingered saying his goodbyes to Shaun.

As the engine started and we pulled away from the terminal, a chant rose, "Go, go, go, go!" When the plane lifted in the air and the landing gear snapped shut, we erupted in cheers and applause.

It's not a long flight to Copenhagen, but a thousand years of contrast. The terminal at Copenhagen—divine. Colors so bright, and so much light! So many goods and luxury items, people happy, actually *smiling*. A few hours later, we boarded an SAS flight to New York.

How heartwarming to be home. Carrie, so relieved. Chris, cute as a button, dashed around trying to get everyone's attention, and George stared at me and cradled the Kremlin tower I'd sent for his birthday. Over the next several days, when I wasn't eating, I slept.

After a few days, I went to take Vladimiroff's class. At the first sight of me, he rushed up. He didn't ask, "How was Russia? Wasn't the Maryinsky Theater beautiful?" or "How did you dance?" His first words were, "Did you go to studio?" "Yes," I said. "Did you do barre at my spot?" "Yes, of course." "Isn't the studio beautiful? Isn't it?" I hemmed and hawed and replied, "Well, it wasn't that special . . . It was okay, actually kind of grungy." He took a step away from me, and his head went down. Then he looked up, got a twinkle in his eye, and said, "But you didn't look up and see it? Years ago, before I left Russia, I leaped twenty feet up and wrote my name on the ceiling before coming down. If you had looked up, you would have seen it."

It cost several hundred bucks, but I had my suitcase full of 16 mm cassettes developed. I set up the projector and screen and eagerly gathered my family around—to discover, with numbing disbelief, that the footage up to Vienna and before Russia was fine, but every cassette taken in the Soviet Union was blank. Not one picture of Balanchine, Lincoln, the company, Shaun, the canteens, the hotel dining rooms, the paper bag, the cities, the streets, the cabbages, the theaters, museums, cathedrals, or Felix and his synagogue. All erased by the police. My price for rooming with Shaun!

And oh yes! There was a letter from Hamburg. The city planned to sue me for injury to their streetcar.

Balanchine's Muses

No single woman in Balanchine's life served as a supreme muse. Rather, a succession of ballerina-muses would rise and fade, like a range of mountain peaks, inspiring him to near-obsessive passion and leading him to create extraordinary ballets. Allegra, one of those muses, commented to me, "From the new girl in the corps to the principal ballerinas, he loved us all . . . in varying degrees."

When I was a child, the ballet world hummed about his breakup with Vera Zorina, and soon after, broke into a chorus over his new star, Maria Tallchief. While married to Maria, it was evident he became drawn to the budding talent of Tanaquil LeClercq, then, over the next thirty years in overlapping sequence, Diana Adams, Allegra Kent, Gelsey Kirkland, Suzanne Farrell, Patricia McBride, Kay Mazzo, Karin von Aroldingen, and, in his final years, Kyra Nichols, Merrill Ashley, and the teenager Darci Kistler. He spoke of Darci's potential to me, with regret that he wouldn't be around to cultivate her. "Nobody should touch her—one could ruin what she has."

As Michelangelo used his genius to release figures from a slab of marble, Balanchine recognized the potential in a ballerina, and sought to mold her and make ballets for her. We heard from his lips, throughout his life, "Ballet is woman." He longed to be the sole sculptor, and resented *his* muse going off to study with other teachers or being influenced by other choreographers, and the ballerinas were uncomfortable having boyfriends or husbands hanging around the theater; it was unspoken, but understood. Balanchine didn't want his favorites running off after performances to another man, husband, or child. No distraction. Only his ballets and him.

One ballerina from NYCB's early days, the worldly Ruth Sobotka,* rebelled. She didn't worry about Balanchine's sensitivities; she flaunted her boyfriends. "Ruth advised us about sex," Carrie said, "'the curse'

---

* Extremely gifted as a designer, Ruth created the costumes for Jerome Robbins's masterpiece *The Cage* in 1951.

[monthly menstrual periods], and how to handle boyfriends. All the corps de ballet girls doted on her. She was rumored to have had the prince of Monaco as a beau [pre–Grace Kelly]." One man in particular she often stashed in the narrow wings at City Center to watch performances. Bearded, disheveled, in an ankle-length overcoat, he reminded us of a homeless bum. We dubbed him "El Stinko." Balanchine didn't like him, and would sniff, "Dirty man with beard!"—as usual, equating men with beards with the distasteful or pornographic, probably stemming from his hatred of Lenin. Eventually, Ruth up and left the world of dance to marry "El Stinko"—Stanley Kubrick.

It disturbed Balanchine, his muses having another man, and motherhood would affect the shape of their bodies and deflect attention from their art, and him. Balanchine's genius fed on the image of the aloof, elusive woman. If she was married or already had children, he felt hobbled. He needed to believe and hope that he could attain the muse, and wooed her through his ballets. If he succeeded, they sometimes wed . . . and it never worked. At home, an ordinary woman was revealed and the spell broken. His creative engine languished, and he soon sought a replacement.

In his domain, he was without peer. But competing with another man in the bed department was a level field. Though he was supremely confident wooing his muse in classes, rehearsals, and through his choreography, in the actual dating and courtship rituals he needed a surrogate—and that surrogate was the male dancing partner. Over the years, I played that part with a variety of muses. Onstage, dancing the pas de deux, I was a stand-in for Balanchine. After performance, at supper, his foil.

A typical scene, from the early days with Tanny:

Balanchine: "Tanny, Jacques, maybe tonight after performance, we go out? What you think?"

At supper, afraid of being turned down or overstepping in direct seduction, he courted his goal with an end run, setting up an environment of courtship by using me. "Tonight, the pas de deux was marvelous, shimmering, more than ordinary. And you, Jacques, you partnered her"—with a sidelong glance to Tanny—"ah, she floated." And then, still addressing me, he'd gesture to Tanny, "She was so beautiful, like angel. I think maybe I want to explore more with . . . you . . . together." He'd conclude, "Tanny . . . with Jacques . . . together, maybe new ballet . . . next season. I have music I like."

"If I'm an angel, it's one with tattered wings! And as for floating around with him," Tanny would gesture to me, "he can only get me off the floor by pinching my waist on the lift."

With every muse, it was a variation on the same script. Allegra's reaction—sitting silently, fiddling with her fingers, she'd widen her eyes and look uncomfortable. Diana would sit, erect and unmoving, serene and glacial. Suzanne would lower her eyes, tilt her head, look modest, and pout a bit. Karin, totally open, would blast out, "Oh! That sounds exciting! Vonderful! Vhat music?" Tanny, self-effacing, would quip, "Come on, George, I'll never be an angel. You must be blind."

Before I was born, Balanchine had been married to Tamara Geva, then Alexandra Danilova (in a common-law arrangement). When I was doing my first pliés at the barre at SAB in the early forties, Vera Zorina was his wife, and we hardly ever saw Mr. B during that time. He was off to Hollywood, Broadway, or Europe, choreographing for Zorina—until they broke up. In 1946, he married Maria Tallchief, and made marvelous ballets for her, but their home life was miserable. "I was very unhappy living with Maria," he reminisced. "It was so difficult. She would play poker with friends from her Ballet Russe days—in our bedroom—til four in the morning. I would have to sleep on cot in hall."

No ballet dancer from the United States had achieved international stature before Maria, and Balanchine, with his ballets, did that for her. The English had their Fonteyn; the French, Chauviré; the Russians, Ulanova; the Cubans, Alonso; and now the U.S. could claim their Tallchief. It helped that Maria was a princess. Her mother, a Scotch-Irish lady, had married a full-blooded Native American chief of the Osage tribe. Maria was grand in every way—the whole company loved it when she would come for company class in the morning, robed in a stunning mink over her practice clothes. As we started our pliés, she'd slip off the mink and, nonchalantly, drop it on the floor, its edge in the rosin box.

When Zorina left him, Balanchine was brokenhearted; when Maria left, he was relieved. In 1951, there were headlines in the New York papers: "Tallchief Leaves Balanchine! Marriage Annulled." The papers quoted Maria explaining, "I wanted to have a baby."

Maria was the company's star, but Balanchine had shifted his passion and attentions elsewhere—to coltish Tanny, and the exquisite Diana Adams, who had recently joined the company. To his chagrin, he

Diana Adams, the Dew Drop in The Nutcracker, *1954. Who could be more perfect?*

needed Maria and continued to create ballets for her, but she had lost her place as primary muse. Maria declared publicly, "I will accept alphabetical billing, but I will not be *treated* alphabetically."* I never saw the two of them more miserable than when he was creating the ballet *Gounod Symphony* (1958). Inventing the pas de deux for Maria and

---

* In 1956, Maria married a sweetheart of a man, Henry Paschen Jr., "Buzzy," a Chicago businessman who had long courted her. They soon had the baby Maria so desired—and named her Elise. That love child evolved into a stunning woman of high intelligence; deeply passionate about poetry, she earned a Ph.D. from Oxford. You may find, while riding the NYC subway and avoiding eye contact with fellow travelers, your gaze wandering to the printed announcements. If lucky, you'll come across short poems among the ads—"Poetry in Motion"—*Elise's* baby.

me in the rehearsal room on the fifth floor of City Center, he was frustrated with every step he devised, and so was Maria. They'd growl at each other, and several times he walked out in the middle of rehearsal—unheard of for him (I had never seen him do it, ever—before or after).

Tanaquil was intelligent, acerbic, witty, beautiful, graceful, and chic. Balanchine choreographed inspired works for her—but I noticed his fascination with Diana Adams immediately. On tour, I once had a dressing room situated so that I could peek across the alley into the girls' dressing room. There were Tanny and Diana, in their bras and panties, sitting around with Balanchine, smoking cigarettes. I was shocked that they didn't cover up. He had it so easy! I had to skulk around, a teenage peeping Tom. Balanchine found himself pulled between these two long-legged beauties. Had Diana been available, I believe he would have chosen her as his next wife, but she was married to a handsome, dramatic ballet star, Hugh Laing, in a bizarre and torturous relationship. Hugh was bisexual, and his lover, Antony Tudor, came with him as a package—into his marriage with Diane and into NYCB as a choreographer. Diana and Hugh were hired as principal dancers. Lincoln was all for it. He had the hots for Hugh, and Tudor enjoyed a brilliant and international reputation.* Laing and Tudor were the price Balanchine paid to have Diana in the company.

Diana was a beauty, aristocratic, with flawless ballet technique. Her milk-white skin and elegant, serene demeanor would make her a lodestone for Balanchine. A Blessed Virgin Mary type—mysterious, small-breasted, seemingly modest and retiring. But married to Hugh, she was decidedly unattainable. So Balanchine married Tanny.

Though he was married to Tanny, Balanchine lavished more and more attention on Diana. When Diana divorced, he would have jumped at the chance to have her, but by then, Tanny and Diana were the best of friends. There were rumors Tanny and Balanchine were going to separate, but before any conflict surfaced, Tanny got polio. Balanchine, traumatized, redevoted himself to her. No matter what any doctor told him, he was determined to get her out of that wheelchair and back

---

* Balanchine admired Tudor, in particular the ballet *Lilac Garden:* "I could never make ballet like this," he commented. "Lucia [Chase, director of Ballet Theatre, later American Ballet Theatre] made mistake. She should have built her company around Tudor and given him everything, to see where his choreography could go." Nevertheless, when Diana divorced Hugh, Balanchine soon got rid of both Tudor and Hugh.

dancing again, if only by the sheer force of his will. Until that occurred, he believed he was no longer free to pursue Diana or anyone else.

Tanny was doomed to spend the rest of her life in a wheelchair, so she adapted. "When I need something, I call the appropriate person to help to run an errand—Eddie Bigelow, he never turns me down—to make a complaint about a failed delivery. I get black Natasha, Natasha Molost-woff, to call them—she has the meanest phone voice!" When Tanny needed someone to take her to a party, I would sometimes get summoned. "Jacques, come pick me up, George is busy." My function? To help her into her chair, to the elevator, and out of the building. "Now go get a cab," she'd order.

"Tanny, you're so brave," I used to say. "There's nothing brave about it, Jacques. You make the best of the way things turn out. I'm in a wheelchair now. And there's some compensation. Before, if I didn't have to dance the matinee, I'd wake up on a Saturday morning and be noshing a danish and slurping coffee, when the phone would ring. 'Patty Wilde is sick. You have to go on in *Swan Lake*.' I'd hang up the phone and go into the bathroom and throw up. Now, I'll never have to be afraid of going onstage as the Swan Queen again."

Tanny was tall and skinny. She didn't want to be the Swan Queen— "I'm not a swan, I'm a crane," she'd protest. But she forced herself to be a Swan for Balanchine. He would push her onstage—literally, he would stand in the wings and shove her, and she'd stumble on for her entrance.

By 1959, Balanchine had given up hope that Tanny would dance again, and his fixation on Diana increased. Look at the works he choreographed for her between 1959 and 1964: *Episodes, Panamerica, Tchaikovsky Pas de Deux, Agon, The Figure in the Carpet, Monumentum pro Gesualdo, Liebeslieder Waltzer, Ragtime, Modern Jazz: Variants, Electronics, A Midsummer Night's Dream, Noah and the Flood,* and *Movements for Piano and Orchestra.** Once, Diana asked me to rehearse *Tchaikovsky Pas de Deux,* but when the time came, I was exhausted, and canceled. The next day, Balanchine ranted at me on the phone, "How dare you cancel a rehearsal with Diana?"

If anyone came close to being the equivalent of what Lew Christensen was for Lincoln, it was Diana Adams for Balanchine. Few realize

---

* Although inspired by and choreographed for her, most of these works were not premiered by Diana, but by replacements. Diana would work out—consciously or unconsciously—something to keep herself off the stage.

the passion he had for her; Diana was arguably the most important in the succession of muses in his life. Much later, Suzanne Farrell came along to become, for a while, an extension of Diana.

After the triumph of his ballet *Illuminations* (1950), Frederick Ashton was invited by Lincoln to do another work. Freddie chose the legendary romance of Tristan and Isolde and called his ballet *Picnic at Tintagel* (1952). Diana Adams would be Isolde, and I was told to show up for rehearsal. Two hours into rehearsal, it finally dawned on me that I was playing Tristan. I complained to Mr. B that night, "I don't think I'm good enough. I'm not even eighteen yet. Do I have to do it?" Unconcerned, he replied, "Of course you have to. Doing is how you become good enough."

His true concern was that *his* Diana was in the hands of another choreographer, and during rehearsals, his jealousy grew. He developed a habit of sending Eddie Bigelow to interrupt us—"Balanchine needs to speak with Diana," or some made-up excuse. Finally, Freddie confronted Balanchine.

Years later, over lunch at the Connaught Hotel in London, Freddie confided, "My dear boy, I will never forget how difficult it was to do *Picnic*. Every time I had you and Diana together, that person, Eddie Bigelow, would come to the door to take Diana away. There was always an excuse, 'She's needed onstage by Balanchine.' Or some such ploy." Finally, Freddie had had it. "I went and told George, 'My dear man, for weeks, I've been trying to finish my ballet, but have not once had my Isolde available for more than an hour. If *I* invited *you* to do a ballet for the Royal, and I didn't like you or your ballet, you would never know it. You would get more than everything you needed—good manners demand it. I'm canceling my ballet and returning to London!'" Freddie said gleefully, "You know how his face twitches! Oh! How he apologized. He gave me everything I needed after that, everything!" *Picnic at Tintagel* premiered February 28, 1952. It was a success.

The following spring, Balanchine started making changes in Freddie's ballet. "You know this red beard you wear? Take it off. It makes you look like man in dirty postcard, where you see, in picture, socks, shoes, beard, and nothing else." So I danced *Picnic* without the beard. Before long, "This ballet is not for Diana. Better for Melissa—she can do anything." If we ever had a dramatic star, a ballerina with the passion and intensity of Eleonora Duse, it was Melissa Hayden. She went right into the role of Isolde; Diana never danced it again. Within a year,

As Tristan, enwrapped with Diana Adams as Isolde, 1952

Balanchine had taken *Picnic at Tintagel* out of the repertoire. It's forgotten now, and what a shame: it's among the best of Freddie's ballets.

During the period between 1956 and 1959, Balanchine was bursting with ballets, and all the juicy roles were Diana's. Outwardly, Diana was born perfect in every way, except that her belief in herself was not equal to what her outer gifts appeared to claim. When people have been gifted beyond others, they're expected to perform beyond others. But if the gifted person is filled with self-doubt, that expectation becomes torment.

As the years went on, Diana wanted out. She kept getting injured, missing performances. Like Tanny and so many others, she wanted to please Balanchine, but deep in her heart, she didn't really love to dance.

Finally, her escape would be to marry and have a child. That would dampen Balanchine's demands. So she married our stage manager, Ronnie Bates, a sweet guy from Tennessee. But Balanchine wouldn't let her slow down or quit; he kept creating ballets for her.

Once, while watching the pope give his Christmas blessing on TV, Michael Tolan, my actor-friend, remarked, "Now there's a job you can't quit! After all, you're chosen by God; the only escape is death!" Michael continued, "You think the pope's saying a prayer? What that old guy on the balcony is really saying is, 'Please, I don-na wanna be pope anymore. I'm-a so tired. I-a wanna quit. I just-a wanna go home and watch TV. *The Nutcracker* is on-na tonight! Please let me go.'"

Over the next six or seven years, Balanchine devoted himself to choreographing for Diana, and some of his most important works came out of that period—the groundbreaking *Agon,* and later *Movements for Piano and Orchestra, Episodes,* and in a burst of genius in early 1960, *Tchaikovsky Pas de Deux* and the gorgeous *Figure in the Carpet.* It became a dice toss to see if Balanchine would have the pleasure of watching Diana premiere the ballets he had created for her. She was either injured, recovering from a miscarriage, or bedridden in anticipation of a birth.

Before our tour of Japan and Australia in 1958, Balanchine secretly had Karinska make a Swan Queen costume for Allegra, because "I can't count on Diana," but insisted that no one tell Diana there was a backup. He didn't want her to think she had a way out. Allegra did perform the Swan Queen to great acclaim, all over Australia. If Diana performed on that tour, it was in less than a handful of performances.

THE FIGURE IN THE CARPET: THE LOST BALLET

It was rare that I had social time with Diana and Balanchine—he had Tanny to go home to, and before long, Diana and Ronnie were paired. Then unattainable Diana, predictably, became even more an inspiration to Balanchine.

Many of the ballets Balanchine created derived from Lincoln's suggestions, and Lincoln was a furnace of ideas. The majority were farfetched, but every once in a while, there would be a spark. "George! What about a ballet about a Persian rug?" So came *The Figure in the Carpet.*

Set to Handel's *Water Music* and *Royal Fireworks Music,* the ballet opens with a vista of dancers, costumed in shades of beige and brown, representing sand in the desert, shifting and weaving in intricate patterns. Balanchine used to suck the thumb of delight looking at the choreography, exclaiming to me, "See? The rhythms of the steps for the corps de ballet—syncopated—and the patterns they move in, are playing with the harmonies in the music. It is so interesting." I nodded, smiled, and acted as if I knew what he was talking about.

During the course of the ballet the movement of the scenery was choreographed as well. A multicolored carpet backdrop is woven—first the frame, and then various wild, exotic birds, flowers, and landscape motifs were added. Once the carpet was fully woven, a grand tapestry is revealed, with a three-dimensional fountain ensconced at its foot, running the length of the stage. Then the spectacle continues with a series of divertissements and a grand pas de deux for the Prince and Princess of Persia. During the finale, the fountain lets loose its watery spray.

That was the concept. It was to be an hour-long ballet, with Diana and me as the Prince and Princess. We were to be dressed in white and crowned with white plumes—Balanchine invented a pas de deux for us, in the style of Louis XIV's French court, with lots of little footwork, glissades, gigues, and sarabandes. I recall countless hours attempting to perfect the footwork in my variation. I never had ideal feet for ballet dancing, so it was daunting and exhausting for me to do the busy steps and look good. I often got calf cramps.

When Balanchine finished the pas de deux, he invited our conductor, Robert Irving, to come in to view the choreography. The pas de deux had been created at a certain tempo. Irving (with stuffy British accent) announced, "Oh no, George! It's way too slow!" Balanchine was peeved—it was awkward to fit the choreography into the faster tempo—but Irving insisted he was right. They got out the metronome and checked the score's time signatures. Balanchine kept muttering, "Well, you know, maybe a *little* slower." Irving put his foot down. "I mean, I grew UP on this, George! I mean, Handel, after all!" The next rehearsal, Balanchine, in a couple of hours, choreographed an entirely new pas de deux for us, to the now faster tempo. Same style, but new steps! And the new version was better!

March 1960. The final weeks of rehearsal for an ambitious spring season. Two new Balanchine ballets were to be premiered, the first on March 29, when we would open with the world premiere of *Tchaikovsky Pas de Deux*. However, the advance buzz vibrated for the second, the world premiere of *Figure in the Carpet.* It was scheduled for April 13, a couple of weeks later. Diana was to star in both ballets, and I was her partner.

Thursday. Balanchine finishes choreographing *Tchaikovsky Pas de Deux* and the finale for *Figure in the Carpet.* Everyone is keyed up. We open in five days.

Friday, bang! Diana is out. A miscarriage. She informs Balanchine that she will have to stop dancing for a while. Fortunately, Violette Verdy has been understudying Diana in *Tchaikovsky,* with Conrad Ludlow covering me; but for *Figure,* there were no understudies. It's four days before we open, and somebody has to replace Diana. Balanchine picks Allegra. "I have to invent new pas de deux, Jacques," an agitated Balanchine announces. "Allegra is not Diana, different." By the end of the afternoon, he had created a new pas de deux for Allegra. Essentially, a third version.

Monday's our day off, and Tuesday is the premiere of *Tchaikovsky Pas de Deux.* "Mr. B, I have a suggestion. I can't fit in the rehearsals I'll need with Violette in time for *Tchaikovsky* on opening night. How about if Conrad dances it with Violette for the opening? And when Melissa gets back from her leave, I'll dance *Tchaikovsky* with her."

Balanchine allows me to skip the premiere of *Tchaikovsky* and devote my time to preparing Allegra for *Figure.* Later, having recovered, Diana returns, but rather than putting her back into the role of the Princess, Balanchine choreographs a brilliant Scotch variation especially for her, and has Karinska, the costume designer, make her the most gorgeous of costumes. "I'll never forget how beautiful Diana looked in that costume," Allegra commented. "Karinska could read Balanchine's mind, and always made the most exquisite costumes for the ballerinas he loved the most."

The whole company was in the midst of rehearsals all day and performances at night. Not two weeks into the season, a few days before the premiere of *Figure,* Allegra (who, the year before, had married the celebrity photographer Bert Stern) announced to Balanchine that she was pregnant and suffering the worst morning sickness! "Mr. Balanchine, I don't think I can dance."* He was devastated, went home in a snit, and pouted.

---

* Months later, Allegra gave birth to her first child, the lovely Trista (meaning sad or sorrowful).

Melissa arrived from Chicago like the cavalry in a Western. "Let Melissa do it," Balanchine grudgingly acquiesced. After the shock of Diana's miscarriage (which Balanchine saw as a betrayal), he had somehow pulled himself together to redo the pas de deux for Allegra, but with her out he gave up—done in by babies! So I was left to coach Milly in everything she would need to know to dance the Princess. It was a lot for her to learn, but Melissa loved nothing more than a challenge, even with the handicap of being Balanchine's reluctant third choice. He left all the rehearsing of Milly to me.

I'm sure Balanchine felt the gods were against him. At dress rehearsal, the fountain in the ballet finally came into play, and it leaked. "We've solved the problem!" Ronnie Bates announced before the premiere. Wrong. During the grand finale, we all slipped on the water that puddled on the stage floor.

In subsequent performances, the fountain stayed, but the water valves were turned off. The ballet, like a mirage, has disappeared. Diana never danced *Tchaikovsky Pas de Deux* or the Princess role in *Figure in the Carpet,* and Balanchine, watching his ballets, could only dream of how Diana would have danced them.

On the Russian tour in 1962, the company was lucky if Diana got onstage at all. She was always injured or sick, and, in everything, Allegra replaced her. "I danced every performance in Russia except one. It was a matinee," Allegra told me. "Balanchine let me take it off."

Allegra was to Diana what Diana had been to Tanny—the muse waiting in the wings. But Allegra kept having babies. Why? Because, according to her, "After my first baby, Trista, was born, all I wanted to do was play with her, but there was never time, with all the rehearsals and performances. I figured the only way to get time away from dancing would be to get pregnant again. Then I would *have* to be home, and could play with Trista. So that's what I did . . . three times!" Susannah and Bret were two and three. She once coyly commented, "I offered the audience a little suspense, because no one knew if I'd appear or not— I didn't know, myself!"

The year 1962 brought a much-heralded dance and music event: Stravinsky composed a ballet score, *Noah and the Flood,* specifically to be premiered on television, with choreography by Balanchine. I was to play Adam to Diana's Eve, and had an added role of Lucifer. As the Dark Angel, I didn't really dance, just posed and floated in the air— eighteen feet off the floor, balanced on a hidden ladder—costumed and transformed into a giant, glittering, winged Azazel. I remember a telling memory of Balanchine, gazing up at me—utterly in his element. He exudes contentment, savoring his creation as if enjoying a delicious lemon drop.

And oh! How Balanchine loved having Diana and me rehearsing. He delighted in playing Adam, partnering Diana the way he wanted me to do.

Drawing of Noah and the Flood

Then I'd replace him, as he rushed over to peek through an imaginary camera and plan the shots. I never saw him happier. All that was missing was his booming voice biblically pronouncing, "And it was Good." Well, it wasn't. Early on, Diana got injured? Miscarried? . . . Whatever. Something! The ballerina Jillana replaced her.

I was in Europe when *Noah* aired on national television, and received a phone call from Balanchine, stuttering with fury, "They have ruined it! Awful commercials! They stopped ballet and music to show Breck—ordinary woman with shampoo! Hair! Breck! Disaster!"

MOVEMENTS FOR PIANO AND ORCHESTRA

Early in 1963, Lincoln won over McNeil Lowry, a power at the Ford Foundation, and wrangled an unprecedented funding coup—millions of dollars to Balanchine's SAB and NYCB. The overall goal was to improve the quality of the teaching of ballet. Across the country, several companies associated with Lincoln and Balanchine received funding. Teachers would be sponsored to come to New York for master classes with Balanchine. He even offered a class on choreography but, after a couple of attempts, dropped it. "You can't teach it," he pronounced. More successfully, he shared his pedagogy—methods he had developed to achieve facility and mastery in ballet techniques.

Additionally, he picked a handful of his NYCB dancers to travel around the country to visit different dance schools; if we saw talent, we were free to invite chosen students for a scholarship at SAB. Diana espe-

Creating the ballet Movements for Piano and Orchestra *with Gloria Govrin and Pat Neary, 1963; Balanchine's quip: "Second position is the natural position for woman."*

cially relished escaping the pressures of New York, and enjoyed the power of granting scholarships to the aspiring. She chose many talented students, among them the teenage Roberta Sue Ficker from Cincinnati (who later caught the virus of name change, and became Suzanne Farrell).

Back in New York, Diana joined me in rehearsals for another Balanchine milestone—Stravinsky's new piece, *Movements for Piano and Orchestra*. When Balanchine did a ballet for one of his muses, he didn't want to be bothered with anyone else. He focused his full attention on the chosen one. But our company's ballet master John Taras had insisted there be understudies, and lobbied for Suzanne Farrell, from the corps de ballet, to understudy Diana. Eventually, during rehearsals, Suzanne showed up, lurking in the back of the room, ignored by Balanchine.

Then Diana delivered another mortar round—"I'm pregnant again, and this time, my doctor insists, 'Bed rest! Flat on your back, no exercise, or you'll risk losing another baby!' "—and Balanchine quit. He stormed out of the studio, ranting to me, "She stabbed me in the back! She didn't have to do this now! She could have waited until after the premiere to get pregnant. There are ways!"

Inconsolable, Balanchine declared, "We'll cancel the premiere!" locked himself in his apartment, and refused to answer the phone.

"We have to do this premiere!" Taras insisted. He asked me, "Do you think the understudy can do it?" "Sure," I said. "I'll teach Suzanne everything we do together, and Diana can teach her the solos." So, the next day, I rolled back the rug in Diana's living room, and Suzanne watched intently as Diana, lying elegantly supine on the couch, demonstrated, with hand gestures, all the necessary toe work.

Taras finally reached Balanchine and convinced him to at least come see the understudy in rehearsal. He did and was enthralled. Within minutes, he was up and rehearsing Suzanne, lifting her leg, molding her gestures, demonstrating to me how I should hold her, using every legitimate excuse to touch her.

"God took away Diana, but sent me Suzanne!" Balanchine gushed. Suzanne was superb in the premiere. We also performed it for a TV premiere at the new Philharmonic Hall at Lincoln Center.

The baby came, and Diana and Ronnie named her Georgina. Balanchine, close to sixty years old, finally gave up the idea of having Diana dance for him. She was relieved. He ensconced her as director at

With Suzanne Farrell in an upside-down lift: Karin von Aroldingen, front right, in a floor split, 1963

the school. Balanchine's unwavering devotion shifted to the nubile Suzanne. She became an extension of Diana, who had been never less than perfect, but always detached and cold. As a relay player passes the baton to the next player, Diana passed Balanchine to Suzanne.

Suzanne was the more interesting dancer. She would throw herself off-balance—her entire body expressing the energy of the movement. Every fiber imbued movement with passion and energy. Standing in the wings or onstage with her, you could see her facial features tense with ferocious concentration, but that look didn't cross the footlights. What did project was the drama—by her body, her every movement, her elegance, her love of gesture, the plié and arabesque, the off-balance dancing, her musical instincts, and her powerful, feminine form. She was a demon of dance. Diana didn't really like to dance, whereas Suzanne didn't like to do anything *but* dance. Balanchine dubbed them both "my alabaster princesses."

Mr. B got his new muse. The ultimate in unattainability, she quietly received everything. He gave her more and more, and she accepted it as if it were her due. I never heard her thank him; she gave him her dancing as his reward. Like Odysseus captivated by the sirens, he seemed helpless to resist her. If she came to class wearing an ace bandage on her knee, he would cut the grand pliés at the beginning of class. "You know, maybe we start today with tendu battements. If you want pliés, you can do yourself, later." When Suzanne took the bandage off, "You know, today, maybe we start with grand pliés."

In a ballet I was choreographing, I ended the adagio with Suzanne lifted over my head. Then, tossing her, I would catch her spinning body, seconds before she touched the ground. Balanchine was horrified. "You must change ending. Too dangerous! Suzanne is too precious. She could be hurt! If you don't want to change step, use someone else! Patricia McBride!"

He offered Suzanne an ultimate gift, the power to choose which ballets would be on the program and who would dance them. The company grumbled, but Melissa was most direct in complaining: "She decides who's going to dance what, and gives herself all the juicy roles. The rest of us get her leavings." In company class, standing with her hands on her hips, Milly announced, "I have to wait until she's injured to get to dance!" In personal relations with Balanchine, Suzanne was the perfect hot and cold faucet—warm, caring, and attentive; then cold, distant, and rejecting, juggling him masterfully between the two.

She never gave him her body, except in dance, and what a body—as a dancer, as a muse, fabulous. He got exactly what he deserved (and probably what he truly wanted)—not a wife or a sexual partner, but a muse to worship through his artistic creations.

Balanchine had a romantic, chivalrous streak—Galahad purified by the suffering he undergoes in striving to win his Holy Grail. Onstage, this romanticism translated to elegant and gorgeous ballets. In life, it made him a "stage door Johnny," waiting outside Suzanne's dressing room. Would she have dinner with him? Could he walk her home? He would sit outside, waiting for her answer, while she took off her makeup, or went back to the stage to practice a step she hadn't been pleased with in performance. On one hand, there was something sweet and boyish about it. On the other, here was the greatest choreographer in the world sitting on a bench, waiting to see if Suzanne would allow him to spend time with her. It's easy to judge the weaknesses of others while minimizing our own. I could see myself sitting on a bench waiting for someone I loved and forgetting about dignity and the rest of the world (witness my stalking of Carrie). But he was Balanchine, a giant with judgment skewed, jeopardizing the architecture of the entire company. Carrie commented, "Who would have ever believed that we could lose respect for Balanchine? But we did." And yet, I thought, how beautiful! He threw away what anyone would think and allowed himself to be entranced. It's mythic: the King, in the suppertime of his life, by a nymph enchanted, who happened to be a goddess of Dance.

DON QUIXOTE

In May 1965, Lincoln told me that I was to play Don Quixote to Suzanne's Dulcinea in Balanchine's new full-length ballet of the same name. Once again, I was to be the surrogate. But it didn't happen; Balanchine decided, for the opening gala and as often as possible, to dance the role himself. The ballet world was agog. It would be a public expression of his devotion for Suzanne. Richard Rapp, a stalwart member of the company, would understudy and be ready to cover for him if needed.*

---

* Richard Rapp did perform the role and superbly, and in later life went on to teach at SAB, and did so masterfully. He truly understood Balanchine's technique and aesthetic.

A man haunted by a beautiful woman, Suzanne Farrell, 1964

Balanchine envisioned Don Q striving for the sublime, his soul enriched by the quest, while society ignores, ridicules, or discounts the nobility of the pursuit. His dedication had a religious flavor. In the book of heaven, Balanchine believed the Don Qs of the world are closest to God. "I throw my pearls before swine." The misunderstood hero, the artist, was the pearl, unrecognized, alone, and on a different plane of existence, fighting windmills. *Don Q* would bring this theme together with another—his idealization and pursuit of Dulcinea, man in service to woman.

Waiting at a bus stand on Sixty-third Street and Broadway, Balanchine told me, "I have gift for you—something special: *Meditation.*" He explained, "You are man, ordinary man, *Jedermann* [Everyman], you see? Walking alone through life, dreaming of her. Haunted—she comes to you, you hold her, strive to keep, but are doomed to lose—she disap-

Christopher d'Amboise in a striped shirt, white socks, and a scared look, 1964

pears, so you walk on, but because of her, you are different! No more ordinary, made better." Balanchine's description of the man in meditation also describes the transforming power of art and is at the heart of what classical ballet is. To participate as a performer or as an audience member makes one better.

Among his hundreds of ballets, there were crowd pleasers featuring superb choreography because he was a consummate master of the craft, and then there were those ballets that touched/explored/illuminated themes precious to him—*Apollo, Concerto Barocco, Serenade, Meditation, Violin Concerto, Movements for Piano and Orchestra,* and *Diamonds* are just a few. It irritated him when an audience didn't know the difference.

Don Quixote was not a success. I thought it great, and my dear friends and balletomanes Drs. Boris and Louise Krynsky felt he had captured Cervantes with a work of genius. "Don Quixote suffered delusions, but without people who have these kinds of delusions, we have no humanity," Louise said. A profound ballet. Balanchine gave it to Suzanne.

In 1964, when I was thirty years old, I started an experimental ballet class for boys on Saturday mornings. My son George was eight years

George d'Amboise armored for Balanchine's prologue in Don Quixote, *1965*

old, and Christopher, close to five, and I wanted them to experience the art and discipline of ballet without having to be the only boys in a class filled with girls. I invited George's classmates at the Collegiate School to give up their Saturday mornings and have ballet class with me. Balanchine was intrigued and delighted when he heard, and, as usual, gave me anything I wanted—in this case, a pianist and a studio at SAB (at the time, located at Broadway and Eighty-third Street). The first Saturday, about half a dozen boys showed up; within a few months, there were close to twenty, many not from Collegiate. Some boys took class in galoshes, and of the eighteen to twenty boys, three went on to professional careers in dance. One boy, Philip Jerry, commuted from Albany. He came in by train on Friday, stayed with a relative, attended class, and Saturday afternoon, headed back home. A producer for *New York Illustrated,* Bernie Morris, developed an award-winning television special about the class, called *Sandlot Ballet,* featuring Philip as narrator.

Balanchine invented a prologue for *Don Quixote,* because he wanted to use the boys in my Saturday class. In the prologue, the seated Don, surrounded by books, dozes and dreams. Thick fog covers the stage, and a tiny damsel enters,* fleeing a coterie of miniature knights—armor-clad, with helmets of horns, rats, and lizard faces. In his fantasy, the Don leaps to his feet, seizes a sword, and, in vigorous battle, defends the frightened damsel. ("He hit with that sword for real!" my boys gushed. They were afraid to get close to him. "He's dangerous!" George complained admiringly. In a later season, when Christopher joined his brother knights on the stage, he described his terror of Balanchine. "When he did the role, I'd try to hide! He would swing his sword with such vigor that sometimes it would slip out of his hand and go clattering across the stage.") At the climax of their battle, the Don

---

* A very young Judy Fugate, who grew to grace the stage in later years as an exquisite ballerina.

Suzanne Farrell in Don Q, *1965*

vanquishes the little knights, saves the damsel, and afterward, exhausted, collapses into his chair. A servant girl, Dulcinea (Suzanne Farrell), comes in with a basin of water to wash his feet and gently dry them with her hair.

Balanchine as the Don, touching the membranes of your heart, was a little pudgy, and, with his one lung, huffed and wheezed his way through the difficult passages of choreography. But to see him on the stage in *Don Q* was one of the great moments in the history of ballet.

Magnificent! Balanchine expressing the beliefs that formed him and were central to his soul.

Toward the end of the ballet, the narrative suspends for a moment and gives way to a fantastic dream sequence. It doesn't necessarily advance the plot; rather, it contributes by raising the magic and atmosphere of the entire production. Exhausted and dejected, the Don crawls to a corner of the stage to collapse into sleep, and dreams. The stage fills with a cascade of beautiful female dancers. Amid their swirling, all action is centered around Dulcinea. In her solo, Suzanne flew all over the stage in the inspired choreography he had built on her gifts. She was so in control of time that she inhabited it, commanding and ordering the space she moved in. At the end of her dance, as if feeling the inevitability of loss, she stopped near his supine body, gasped, ran backward to center stage, and dropped to her knees with her face in her hands. I'd stand in the wings and watch her perform, and think, "What's happened to Suzie? What's inside her? Who's in there transforming her?" Certain dancers become larger than just a dancer doing a role; they seem to channel a greater force. Suzanne danced possessed, as if inhabited by a goddess of dance who was using her as a vent. For me, the effect of her performance in the coda of *Don Quixote* will resonate forever.

Watching my daughter Charlotte dance, I realize she, too, has this gift of being larger than a woman dancing, somehow a window to the force of the art form that uses her as its medium. Other artists as well—the dancing of Maria Tallchief, of course, and the passion and drama of Melissa Hayden in all her roles. Merrill Ashley in the ballet *Ballo della Regina.* And the iridescent Allegra Kent didn't even have to dance—she only had to stand onstage. This gift cannot be taught—it is or it isn't.

Eventually I danced the role. I tried to emulate the vision of Balanchine in the role of Don Quixote. I don't think I was very good.

Don Quixote was some three hours long, and my boys' class of miniature knights performing in the prologue were cast as altar boys in the finale. During the long wait, they were relegated to a holding area in the lower concourse of the New York State Theater. Francis and Paul Sackett, brothers in the company, appeared only in a few scenes,* so

---

* Francis and Paul are highly intelligent and unconventional, with the blood of Spanish caballeros running in their veins.

On my knees with Farrell in Don Q, *1965*

they were assigned to chaperone and keep the boys out of trouble. "We played games, wild! It was bedlam down there in the dressing room! Till we got everyone into their costumes and up to the stage for our final processional." With flames in the background from the burning of books by the Inquisition, the entire cast, in lines, sway past the Don as he lies dying in his bed. Scenes from his life pass before his fevered vision—galley slaves and royalty; bishops, priests, monks, and acolytes; mothers with young children; cripples and beggars; even a herd of pigs—a procession of a life represented by the entire cast moving in a diagonal from upstage right to downstage left.

At one point during the procession, everything stops, and the Don, transfixed by a vision of Dulcinea, floats into the air, reaching for his vision. Abruptly jarred into reality, he plummets back to his mattress and dies, mourned only by Dulcinea and a few handmaidens. (The bed had a crudely engineered lift, and the ascent and descent were seldom smooth.) The processional was a ponderous march, a dirge from the composer, Nicholas Nabokov, one melody repeated over and over again, with various instruments embellishing layer on layer. At home, my son George, gleeful, confessed that Alex Foster, his ten-year-old classmate, who was built like a tiny truck, with a broad head, broad shoulders, and no neck, had invented a song for the altar boys to chant sotto voce during the procession. As they swayed in cadence, the chant spread, a virus first taken up by the Sacketts, then as a pandemic throughout the corps.

> *Oh Santa Claus*
> *Come kiss me*
> *On my little*
> *Tushie, tushie, tushie, tushieeeee . . .*
> *Oh Santa Claus . . .*

Tanny recognized that Balanchine needed to be free to pursue Suzanne, and they divorced. On tour, I would often accompany Suzanne and Balanchine to lunches and dinners—we formed a troika—but back in New York, preoccupied with my family, I rarely had time. Suzanne had taken an interest in a young and talented dancer in the company, Paul Mejia. She brought Paul into the troika, new blood, and you'd often see the three of them together. Then, while Balanchine was away in Europe staging a ballet, Suzanne married Paul.

What a shock to Balanchine! Eventually, he did accept the marriage, but tried to ignore Paul's presence in the company. Suzanne expected to wield the same power as before, selecting the programs and casting. She felt so assured of Balanchine's worship that she pushed further and further, testing to see how far he would bend.

On May 8, 1969, there was to be a gala night. Apparently, all day long, Suzanne and Balanchine had been negotiating, with Eddie Bigelow in the role of a tennis ball, carrying messages from one side to the other. Earlier, Eddie Villella had been cast in the third movement of *Symphony in C,* but opted out. Balanchine replaced him with Deni Lamont instead of Paul Mejia. Both had danced the role. Suzanne demanded that her husband perform at the gala. Balanchine circumvented the problem by replacing *Symphony in C* with *Night Shadow,* a ballet starring Suzanne. Suzanne demanded that *Symphony in C* be restored, or she would refuse to dance at all. They were like two children arguing in a playground. Balanchine wanted to see her dance, so he parried. *Symphony in C* was back, but without the third movement. Bigelow delivered Suzanne's response: "Unless the third movement is in, with Paul dancing, I'm not dancing."

I wasn't on the program, had a free night, and was home with Carrie, my feet on the coffee table, watching TV and chicken curry, and guzzling a beer. Right around the theater's half-hour call (7:30), Balanchine was on the phone. "Can you dance *Stars and Stripes* tonight?" "Of course," I burped. "What happened?" "We're changing program," he barked, and hung up.

Twenty minutes later, stuffed and semi-inebriated, I arrived at the stage door and bumped into Suzanne and Paul. "Balanchine threw us out," Suzanne announced dramatically. Stunned, I sympathized, "Oh no, what happened?" They wanted to talk. But I had to get ready to perform. "I'll call you later," I cried out.

Diary excerpt from the next day:

May 9, 1969

Class with Balanchine. Theatre buzzing over Princess and Consort quitting.* Marnee Morris to do the *Brahms* next week. *Xenakis* is put off. Neary will do *Prodigal*. All others covered. I called the Princess to find out what had occurred exactly. She went on that "he did not consult me on the program changes. He always has before. He isn't talking to me. I never led him on to believe I loved him or would marry him." She said she had danced lots for the company and done them favors, that George owed her lots, that he was ignoring her and she didn't have to take it, that Paul was being punished because of her and that he was so talented, and why should they take it? Because he wasn't put into the third movement of *Symphony in C* on the benefit night, and *Symphony in C* was not done, both she and he would not dance anything with the company. She went on to that effect. When I asked her what she would do now, she said, "Paul has a few irons in the fire. I'm not dancing."

Balanchine never wanted to lose her, but he took her at her word, had the costumes taken out of her dressing room, and replaced her in all her roles. With a helpless gesture, he told me he surrendered to fate— *"Chemu byt' togo ne minovat"* ("What has to be, has to be").

On May 10, the next night, Balanchine and I headed over to the Empire Coffee Shop for a favorite post-performance snack—feta cheese, a dish of Kalamata olives, a hard roll, and a bottle of Beck's beer. On the street at the edge of the stairs leading down to the stage door, Balan-

---

* Shaun and I had dubbed Suzanne "the Princess" because Balanchine had referred to her as "my alabaster princess." We nicknamed Balanchine "Breath" or "the Breath" because, like God, he breathed the essence of life into his dancers.

chine paused in the exact spot where I'd run into Suzanne and Paul leaving the theater a few nights before. "She's a witch inside of me. I've got to get her out!" he declared. The exorcism took years.

During those years, Karin von Aroldingen and Kay Mazzo gave him the inspiration he needed to create, as did Patricia McBride. When Suzanne left, Karin ("von Ding" was her nickname) had a breakthrough in her dancing. A young explosion of a ballerina whom Balanchine had met in Germany a decade before, and, as soon as he could, brought to NYCB, Karin had always danced with energy and gusto, but now she transformed herself. Her technique improved, and she developed an added dimension to her craft, an aura of mystery. From a stein of good German beer to a flute of champagne—without losing an ounce of gusto!

Eventually, Suzanne and Paul left the U.S. for Brussels, to dance for Maurice Béjart and his company.

Balanchine now rolled up his sleeves and threw himself into making ballets, several of them masterpieces. *Duo Concertant,* starring Kay, is a jewel; *Violin Concerto,* created for Karin and Kay in June 1972, remains one of the greatest of Balanchine's works; and his delightful full-length ballet *Coppélia,* for Patty, stands out as well.

Some four years later, Balanchine showed me a letter. "I have letter. Suzanne wants to do *Meditation* in the Béjart company, and wants to know if you could come, stage it, and maybe dance first performance with her." Years before, he had given *Meditation* to Suzanne. "Do you want me to go, Mr. B?" I deferred. He answered, "What do you want?" and, like a pair of comedians, we started a loop. "No, Mr. B, what would you like me to do?" "I don't care . . ." "But, tell me, do you want me to go?" "Well, if you want." Finally, he broke the pattern. "You know, maybe some money for you—you have family, need money. And Brussels has very good cuisine."

Her picture was all over Brussels. And even though male dancers were primary in the Béjart company, she was *the* star, and Maurice catered to her. Paul and Suzanne had made their home in a little apartment, with a closet full of wine, and Suzanne had metamorphosed into a thin, streamlined European sophisticate. She had learned to manipulate her knife and fork in the European style, with exquisite table manners, and elegance.

Paul, a soloist with the company, confessed, "Four years of Europe is

Strutting with Karin von Aroldingen in the ballet Who Cares?, *1970*

enough. We would like to return to the States." I immediately sat down and helped Suzanne couch a letter to Balanchine, and, over the next several days, taught *Meditation* to Jorge Donn, the reigning star, who was marvelous—a superb artist and a honey of a person. I turned down Béjart's invitation to dance the first performance. It would have meant rehearsals, costume fittings, complications with scheduling, and staying longer in Brussels. I staged the ballet, wished Jorge the best of luck, hugged Suzanne and Paul, and left.

On returning, I went straight to Balanchine. "She's better than ever. Her body is sleek, streamlined, and you know, Mr. B, in *Meditation,* where I reach out to embrace her and she folds herself into a little ball under my arms as I enclose the empty air? She's never done it better, Mr. B. They want to come back."

Suzanne and Paul showed up during our summer residency in Saratoga, New York. She was nervous and asked if she could stand next to me at the barre, as had been our wont in the past. Paul did not take class, but after, joined us at a lunch I brokered with Balanchine in a nearby Italian restaurant. At lunch, Paul and Suzanne expressed their desire to return to the company. I feared an awkward moment, but time had healed much. Balanchine accepted Suzanne, but did not take Paul, suggesting, "Maybe dancing is not necessary anymore. You are excellent teacher, and can choreograph. Maria [Tallchief] has company in Chicago, maybe very good for you to teach there. I will talk to her." Paul was exiled, and Suzanne made a spectacular return to NYCB, though she flew regularly to Chicago to make guest appearances. Paul choreographed for the Chicago company, notably an excellent full-length *Cinderella* starring Suzanne.

Balanchine never allowed her to wield the same power over him again. Already, he was seeking another muse, and began to focus attention on young Darci Kistler.

Diary excerpt, September 16, 1980:

On tour in Europe. The bulletin board announced that Darci Kistler would learn the Swan Queen in *Swan Lake.* My last dancing in Paris. Suzanne got picky on me about a lift in our performance of *Movements for Piano and Orchestra,* "the lift should be closer to center." I was smiley and easy going, but replied, "It's always been off center." She then complained to Balanchine, who was standing nearby. "No, dear, it's off center. But, maybe, if you want, we can move center over—for you." It was a put-down. Suzanne followed me to my dressing room and, for fifteen minutes, told me how she had danced the full-length *Swan Lake* after she left NYCB, and had hurt her knee doing it.

September 17, 1980. Balanchine set the original Swan Queen's variation on Darci, and asked me to dance it with her. I protested that I was not up to my variation anymore. "Oh," he answered. "We could do without male variation." I said, "No. I am too old. But I would like to teach Darci the pas de deux." Balanchine remarked to me and Robert Irving, who was standing nearby, "Darci, in two years, maybe one, will be my premiere, replacing the old ones who retire."

In NYCB alone, what fabulous ballerinas Balanchine nurtured—the sweet and delightful Patricia McBride foremost among them. And he was mesmerized by the incandescent talent of Gelsey Kirkland. The beautiful Jillana, with the complexion of a pale, dew-touched lily. She and I joined the company in 1949, and through our teens were teased as a couple, "Jacques and Jill." The petite French ballerina Violette Verdy had won the hearts of every ballet fan in New York City by her brilliance in American Ballet Theatre's production of *Miss Julie.* Balanchine wanted her in his company—and got her. She arrived, and garnished and spiced every role she danced. The gorgeous technique of Patricia Wilde, Mimi Paul and her swan's neck, equal to the heaven-sent extension of her limbs, and the fierce, dramatic intensity of Melissa Hayden—they all graced the company for decades, and Balanchine molded many ballets around their superb gifts. As an honor for Melissa

Ballo della Regina: *Balanchine demonstrating to Robert Weiss how to partner Merrill, and wishing he could perform with her, 1978*

at her retirement, he choreographed a ballet specifically for her, *Cortège Hongrois.* Merrill Ashley's artistry so inspired him, he created two ballets for her—and her performances in them are unforgettable. I watched the premiere of *Ballo della Regina,* the first of the two, and envied her partner, Robert Weiss.* With his slim, beautifully proportioned body, he flew all over the stage. But the ballet was about the Regina, Merrill. She danced like an auburn-haired filly, gamboling and cavorting on the meadow of the stage, inhaling sunlight as well as air, as if she couldn't get enough.

And how Balanchine adored Kyra Nichols. "She's perfect. Uncomplicated—like fresh water." Kay Mazzo, gentle, porcelain-like. "She is china doll. Very precious, delicate. Treat carefully—easily broken," he counseled. Karin von Aroldingen became Balanchine's best friend in the company. At the end of his life, he left most of his ballets to her, and to Tanny.

* Robert Weiss presently runs Carolina Ballet, a company in Raleigh, and is a brilliant choreographer—inventive and tasteful.

Ballo della Regina, *1978*

With the exception of Vera Zorina, I was privileged to partner every one of his muses.

As my career was ending, I was too old to partner the teenage Darci Kistler, but I cast her in several of my ballets and paired her with my son Christopher.

There were ballerinas outside of NYCB who captured Balanchine's eye and heart. In Switzerland, he kept a sort of backup ballet company, the Geneva Ballet. Its artistic director, Patricia Neary, was a favorite of his and had been a greatly admired ballerina while in NYCB. Balanchine often escaped the pressures in New York by visiting Patty and her company. When informed I was performing there as a guest artist, he was excited. "Oh, you will dance with Janie Parker." The star of the Geneva Ballet, Janie was a dancer from Atlanta, Georgia, who Balanchine adored and desperately wanted for New York City Ballet. To his shock, she turned him down, and, when she left Geneva, she accepted a place at the Houston Ballet with its artistic director, Ben Stevenson. In her little-girl voice, Janie said, "I'm uncomfortable in New York City;

Rehearsing with Darci and Chris, early 1980s

it's too fast and too much to handle. At NYCB, I'd have to compete and fight with the other ballerinas for roles."

"Stupid girl!" Balanchine cried out. "She took job with this Stevenson man, when she could have had *Balanchine*. I would have given her everything. Even *Coppélia*."

In the year before his death, I often escorted Balanchine to visit the legendary Dr. James Gould for ear tests. Killing time in the waiting room, I once asked, "Mr. B, in the history of all the ballerinas you've taught and choreographed for—from the earliest days, Toumanova, Baronova, Riabouchinska, all the way up till today—who do you consider the most talented? The most unusual?" He immediately answered: "Allegra. She is the most gifted. She is missing only one element in 'the formula to be perfect.' . . . It's like chemistry in a jar. Energy, lots of it, must be there. That's the soup that everything cooks in. Then you put in ambition and humility. 'Ah, I'm not good enough yet, I can be better.' But, there must be balance—not so much humility that you end up saying, 'I'm not good enough, I'll never be ready.' You must have in the formula pride, but not so much that the dancer says, 'I don't do matinees.' You can be stupid and still dance beautifully, but you can't become great without intelligence . . . Allegra has the right ingredients, but something prevents her from being consistent. I can't count on her. Still, I keep her on salary and tell her, 'When you're ready to dance, come dance. If you dance one ballet a year, it's enough.' She's worth it."

Lincoln

I am a ballet master," Balanchine would say, "a maître de ballet," meaning, "I am a master of all the arts that go into the making of ballets." Lincoln Kirstein never felt he was the master of *any* art, and being around the imperial confidence of Balanchine kept him unbalanced. Lincoln often commented, "George is sinister." The word connotes left-sidedness, as well as evil. Balanchine was in no way evil, but "sinister" also suggests a general or vague feeling of fear or apprehension on the part of the observer. Fearful that Balanchine might disagree any time he made a suggestion or offered an opinion, Lincoln endured relentless suspicions that the "sinister" Balanchine undermined him deliberately. Many ideas he presented to George came back to slap him in the face.

At a City Center dress rehearsal for the ballet *Metamorphoses* in 1952, Lincoln came running onto the stage from out front, excited, as if he'd had a revelation. "George, George!" he panted. "The boys' tights! The color's all wrong. They're terrible! They should be pink! Put all the boys in pink tights!" (We were wearing nut-brown tights.) He was so wild—he'd grab a dancer and pull him over. "Look, George! He should be in pink! It'll save the ballet."

Though Lincoln had interrupted the dress rehearsal and every second was precious, Balanchine patiently turned to the wardrobe master: "Do we have pink tights for boys?" Then, for close to twenty minutes, waited patiently while the boys tried on pink tights, and then returned for a costume parade. We pirouetted, pranced, and posed under the stage lights for several minutes. Then, with everyone waiting expectantly, Balanchine turned to Lincoln, and said two words, "Better brown." Lincoln may have been out front for the premiere, but we didn't see him backstage for the next two weeks.

In spring 1982, we had just completed the second Stravinsky festival, and Balanchine and I were walking down the hall at SAB when Lincoln scurried up to join us, and reported, "George! Beverly Sills called me. She wants to do a production of *Perséphone* for City Opera and our company. I told her there's not a chance we'd do anything with the City Opera or her—she's 'Jewish delicatessen'!"

Awaiting the sniff of approval, he got instead: "You know, Jewish delicatessen not so bad! Big, stuffed sandwiches. Pickle. Maybe we *could* do something with her." Lincoln showed us his heels.

Lincoln was an ants' nest of ideas, and I know his ideas inspired many of Balanchine's works. At times, Lincoln would approach me and others with fascinating suggestions for an artist or a composer whose work he felt would be appropriate for a ballet. Melissa Hayden would say, "Oh, Lincoln with his ideas. Nine times wrong, one time right." But how fantastic to be able to say that out of 100,000 ideas a thousand are fantastic.

In contract negotiations, the dancers often made outlandish demands—for example, threatening to strike if they were not guaranteed electric outlets at every makeup mirror in the New York State Theater and on tour. "We need them so that we can plug in our cassettes and study the music we have to dance to," was their justification. In other words, "Rewire the theater for us."

Balanchine did what he always did when he didn't get what he wanted. He called a company meeting, and while we lounged around in our tights and leotards, a room full of cats in repose, he gave his stock speech. "We have to tour to keep company. This is not the first company Lincoln and I have put together. This is, let me think, one, two, three, four? Yes, fourth, and in between there was nothing. And even here, in this theater, if we don't perform, maybe theater will close down, and I will go to Geneva and start another company." Balanchine loved Switzerland; it was where he got his neat, clean, "everything-works-perfectly" fix. As a cop has a backup piece, Balanchine had Pat Neary and the Geneva Ballet. "Some of you can come with me, if you like. Others can stay." I ran home to tell Carrie, "We may be moving to Geneva!"

It was Lincoln who worried about the theater, the board, the company, and the succession. Balanchine never made arrangements for anything in the future—his apartment, the contents of his closets, his friends, his ballets, anything. He said, "After me, I don't care. I want my cake now to eat." So if there is a New York City Ballet today, it is because of Lincoln Kirstein. But without Balanchine, who would want to come?

Without Balanchine, what would have happened to Lincoln's vision of a uniquely American ballet? We have a little idea through the early companies Lincoln birthed—Ballet Caravan, the American Ballet—where he functioned with more artistic control. Whenever he tried to do something that Balanchine wasn't involved in, it fell apart. Because Lincoln was unpredictable, the edifice trembled under his control. Poor Lincoln was an instigator, not a leader . . . and that awareness was corrosive.

Lincoln worked hard at inventing an image for himself, and an important component of that image was the costume—a navy blue suit, black socks, black shoes, white shirt, thin black or navy blue tie, in winter a Navy pea coat. This uniform—routine, unchanging—was a crutch in his attempt to establish an order, a sense of control in his erratic and frightening mood swings. A manic-depressive and God knows what else. Winds in him had met, conversed, argued, and generated a tornado. Medication, probably lithium, allowed him to function. If his crutch broke, a routine was missed, or a medication forgotten, everyone would know, because he would appear in Army fatigues and combat boots.

Onstage at the New York State Theater, a half hour before an NYCB performance in the late 1970s: Balanchine, alone in his usual place in the first wing on stage right, had propped himself on a stool, tired and pensive. Nearby, I was warming up. The only other person in sight, Ronnie Bates, was preparing for the show. Lincoln appeared, in his camouflage outfit, and he headed straight for Balanchine. There was no doubt that trouble was brewing. Imagining Lincoln was about to strike Balanchine, I prepared to throw myself between them. I saw Ronnie slowly starting to edge toward Lincoln, probably hoping to grab him if the need arose. With saliva spraying out of his mouth, Lincoln bellowed at Balanchine, "YOU'RE FIRED!" I think even dust motes in the theater's atmosphere froze. Slowly, Balanchine leaned back until he was bent like a bow and, tilting his chin upward so he could look down his nose at Lincoln, slowly uttered one word, "Ohhhh." Lincoln fled out the door.

Balanchine sought me out. "I told Lincoln, 'Maybe not be around theater so much anymore. Stay at the school, set up office there, play with little boys, make school secure, and write. You are wonderful writer. Write. That's what you should do, keep out of theater.' " And then, to me, he confided, "Lincoln's judgment is totally destroyed by his homosexuality, and he has no taste. He only sees boys onstage . . . However, nobody can write better about ballet than Lincoln."

Portrait of Lincoln Kirstein by Jamie Wyeth, 1965. Jamie told me, "He was always rushing off somewhere, so I painted his back."

The next time I saw Lincoln was at SAB, and the military togs were gone. "George banished me from the theater," he grunted.

Walking fast was a trademark of Lincoln's—in a hurry, rushing from or to somewhere. Pausing, a momentary halt in his various migrations, seemed to anger him. Jamie Wyeth, the artist, captured Lincoln in a brilliant portrait. His back turned, the hawk-like profile radiating power. "I had to paint him that way," Jamie said. "He wouldn't be still for a portrait. So I painted him the way I remember him—barking over his shoulder, 'I don't have time for you now, Jamie!' "

Lincoln would invite me to his house to parade me around for potential funders, and there would be Jamie Wyeth at the same party. Jamie was a beautiful man, married to Phyllis, who, due to an accident, was wheelchair-bound. Lincoln gushed, "Jamie's a great painter. He's better than his father or grandfather. He's marvelous, I love him! He did my portrait." Lincoln was extremely proud of the portrait, and kept it on his living-room wall. Every time I visited his town house, he'd drag me in front of it. Then one night, his manner changed. "That was his last good painting! He wasted his talent; he's nothing now! Once he sold a painting for one hundred thousand dollars it stopped his creativity cold!" It was Lincoln's usual cycle of praise and denigration.

He had an unpleasant habit of accosting his friends and acquaintances and, without provocation, insulting and denouncing them, leaving them sputtering, crushed, and stunned. He also had a knack for zeroing in on people's insecurities and attacking. The assaults were vicious: "What makes you think you can make a photograph!!? Your photographs are shit!" Snarling and glaring at another victim, "You're an amateur; you think you're doing anything new? You haven't done anything new in your whole life, and you never will!!! You're a NOTHING!" All this, to an artist who, a week before, he had espoused at some party: "I've bought his works, they're fabulous, they're too good for the Museum of Modern Art!" If the recipient of such an attack didn't have a strong belief in himself, he would, forever after, be hoping to get back into Lincoln's good graces, inventing excuses. "He didn't really mean that. He was crazy." Many of the people Lincoln built up, then harshly rejected, continued to seek his imprimatur.

Virgil Thomson had been a classmate of Lincoln's at Harvard, and was the composer of the music for *Filling Station,* the ballet that, in its 1953 revival, launched my career. This giant of the music world became a friend, and quite often we visited together. On every occasion, Virgil brought up Lincoln. "Does he talk about me? We were friends, you know, but he turned against me. You know he treated me terribly. He does that to people. He used me, when he needed me, and then when I thought he'd need me some more, he would insult me instead—in public."

If Lincoln's victims bit back—"You're a horse's ass, Lincoln. You're describing yourself! Fuck off!"—Lincoln would pivot and run.

January 11, 1983. The company was abuzz, "Mary Tyler Moore took morning class!" In the past, Mary had occasionally joined us, and Balanchine welcomed her. He was a fan of her show. A message came to me: "Go to SAB. Lincoln wants to talk to you in his office."

Within a second of my arrival at his office, he leaned over me and snarled, "How dare you bring your show-business friends to take our company class!" as if "show business" would somehow tarnish the purity and loftiness of ballet. I remained calm and replied, "She's taken class before. And I didn't invite her, Balanchine did. And Lincoln, don't you think that Balanchine's 'show business' too?" He stared at me, froze for a moment, then grunted, pushed past me, and disappeared down the hall, leaving me alone in *his* office.

Lincoln could not play his promoting/rejecting game with Balanchine. Instead, Lincoln was the little boy chasing after the heels of genius. When I came along, he expected me to be the new Lew, but I was destined to disappoint him. Lincoln expected Balanchine to be a servant to his vision, but instead Lincoln was in the shadow of Balanchine all his life. He had brought a ballet master to America who turned out to be Mount Everest.

Balanchine described to me how Diaghilev had led him "like little puppy dog" around the great museums of Europe, and then left him sitting on a bench in front of a Piero della Francesca or a Caravaggio, with a command: "Sit in front of this painting and look at it the rest of the afternoon." On several occasions, Lincoln did this same number on me, running me through the Metropolitan Museum. With a gesture, he'd indicate, "This is worthless, don't waste your time," and as I looked around to figure out what painting he was talking about, he'd rush down the hall to another exhibition. I'd scamper after him, only to have the experience repeated. For close to a full minute, he lingered at the giant Assyrian stone friezes from Nimrud—winged, powerful, and hawk-nosed. I thought, "That's Lincoln on those panels!"* Those conflicting forces in him—ambition and compassion, brazen energy, determination and fear, bravado and insecurity/self-loathing/distrust of himself—were two-by-fours bashing him around through life. An enemy to himself, yet somehow, he functioned, and managed to accomplish so much good.

Lincoln and Balanchine came together like two elements in an alchemical reaction, and together, their visions and energies (Lincoln's of a uniquely American, male-dancer-driven ballet inspired by Lew, and Balanchine's of distilled and refined choreography in service to women and the art of ballet) transmuted to make a third body, joined

---

* One painting always stopped him cold. "This is my favorite painting," he'd exclaim. On a giant canvas, it depicted the rear end of an enormous white horse— a horse's ass.

entities, NYCB and SAB, that, for a time, bore the marks of both parents. Their presence remains, diluted today, fading, too.

A MYSTIC CONNECTION

Each could not achieve alone what they accomplished together. Lincoln parlayed this treasure he had—George's artistry—into getting his vision realized. Balanchine parlayed Lincoln's drive and genius into founding a school to develop *his* dancers, a company to use to create *his* ballets, an orchestra of high quality with first-class conductors to play the music *he* chose, and a theater to present *his* ballets—that's all he cared about. Without Balanchine, Lincoln would have done what he always did—build up, lose interest; support an artist, then turn on him; create something to be proud of, then discard it with distaste. He never did achieve his place as tsar of all the arts in America. He did, however, find a place to channel his energies, as a promoter and facilitator for Balanchine.

Without Lincoln's entrepreneurship, Balanchine, unconcerned with legacy or anything that might survive him, might never have found a permanent home. "Me. Here. Now." Balanchine undoubtedly would have found other venues to refine and explore his choreography, but here in NYC he had his own school, ballet company, orchestra, and theater. Plus—Lincoln Kirstein, the buffer, the fund-raiser and public relations man, press agent and marketer extraordinaire.

Balanchine admired Shakespeare, especially *A Midsummer Night's Dream,* and was fond of quoting Bottom: "The eye of man hath not heard, the ear of man hath not seen, man's hand is not able to taste, his tongue to conceive, nor his heart to report, what my dream was" (act 4, scene 1). Then Balanchine would expound about how there are things going on at different levels and we're unaware of them—there are other planes, dreams, invisible worlds, and, maybe, other universes. "We need different kind of access, beyond mind, to imagine these other worlds."*

---

* If Balanchine were alive today, how he would have worshipped Lisa Randall, a gray-eyed, golden beauty whose specialty is exploring ideas of other dimensions and other universes. Today she is a world-class cosmologist and professor at Harvard University.

"We see here, and we think this is what is. But we see only tiny little bit. There are other places. Maybe there's here," Balanchine would gesture the shape of a box, "but there is inside, and we don't see inside. But we know there is an inside. Maybe there is inside an *inside,* like Russian nesting doll . . . We are little, and know very little."

He'd continue, expounding on geometry—dimensions—and a hodgepodge of the teachings of G. I. Gurdjieff, the Armenian mystic. "His follower, Ouspensky, was better," Balanchine claimed. "Everything is now, you see—past, present, future—over and over again—is now. Now, now, now, now, now. Even now is not what you think." I was lost and confused, but I think what he meant was that no matter how fast you could grasp, the present is continually becoming the past. Later, on attempting to read Gurdjieff and Ouspensky, I would get even more confused, and put aside their books, thinking, *"What a lot of mystic hodgepodge."*

Lincoln claimed to be a follower of Gurdjieff. Was it because of Balanchine? Gurdjieff had taught in Moscow and St. Petersburg, and had a school in Tbilisi; maybe Balanchine had first been exposed to him there. Lincoln met Gurdjieff in France in 1927, when Lincoln was twenty years old. Did they ever discuss Gurdjieff together? I doubt it. Throughout their long collaboration, how much did Lincoln influence Balanchine, and how much did Balanchine influence Lincoln?

I suspect Balanchine drew more out of Gurdjieff than Lincoln, who, when he was young, seemed mainly to have wanted a guru in his life who would "shape him up."*

Without Lincoln's invitation in 1933, Balanchine might have tried to wrest back control of the Paris Opéra from Lifar, or gone to opera houses in Denmark, London, Argentina, Milan, or Monte Carlo. But the U.S. was the future, and the right place for Balanchine. Nowhere in the world would Balanchine ever find a patron to equal Lincoln. Besides, with his riotous imagination, extensive connections, knowledge, willpower, and drive, Lincoln had the tenacity to stick it out with the ungovernable genius Balanchine. Thanks to them, SAB and NYCB were born, and my attendance there allows me to claim that this wild, untamed youth learned nobility through art.

* Gurdjieff was many things to many people: mystic, guru, businessman, opportunist, confidence man, health food promoter, and, possibly, crook. And maybe he was all of them at one or another time in his life, or a combination of some of them, when necessary. He died in 1949.

The Years Leading to
Balanchine's Death

When Balanchine was in the hospital in the early 1980s, Carrie brought him soup every day. His favorite was borscht, but not the Russian Tea Room version. "Not enough cabbage!" Balanchine complained. So Carrie prepared borscht of her own, based on a recipe from the artist Robert Indiana.* It called for *wedges* of cabbage, and Balanchine slurped and gulped it down like a starving mouse gobbling cheese. He always ate that way, seeming to inhale food, while his taste buds danced, analyzing every morsel with full attention to the texture, spices, and mixtures of flavors.

He was highly sensitive to scent, and gave his favorite ballerinas perfumes selected to match their personalities. "This one is elegant and gentle. Good for Kay." In the elevator or hallways of NYST, Balanchine would sometimes sample the air, and pronounce, "Patricia Neary just came in," or in class, "Ah! Diana, I knew you were here. I smelled your perfume in the hall."

The same with music: he seemed to sniff the harmonies, and no outside noises or distractions disturbed his concentration. At rehearsal, he would sometimes say to the accompanist, "Play something, invent!" and as the pianist improvised, you could see Balanchine silently asking himself, "What's the music doing? Where is it going, what's the structure?" I believe he paid more attention to the architecture of the music

* From Carrie's scrawled notes: Robert Indiana's Borscht: 1) BROWN 1 lb. BEEF CHUNKS on all sides in oil in skillet; 2) HEAT 2 quarts (8 cups) CHICKEN BROTH in large soup pot; 3) ADD beef chunks; 4 CARROTS, quartered lengthwise and half; 4 TURNIPS, peeled and quartered; 2 ONIONS, peeled and halved; 1/2 bunch CELERY, halved (use upper branches and leaves, reserving lower half for another use); 4) PLACE 1 CABBAGE, cut into 8 wedges (gently place cabbage wedges on top, in a wheel shape); 5) CENTER (on top) 1/2 bunch PARSLEY, 1–2 lb.; 3-oz. can ITALIAN TOMATOES (with half of the liquid); 6) ADD 1 tsp. DRIED DILL, 4 BAY LEAVES, 1 tsp. FINES HERBES, SALT, and PEPPER; 7) SIMMER covered for 2 hours (when reheated, use sour cream dab). SERVES 8.

than to the choreography he was inventing. When I watch dance, a small part of my mind attends to the music. With Balanchine, it was the reverse. He was a musician who choreographed.

In the end, he couldn't listen to music. Carrie brought him headphones, a tape player, and a carton full of tapes. But the music hurt his ears.

One afternoon, he was sitting on the side of the hospital bed, his bare feet dangling off the edge. As I settled next to him, my dance bag brushed his foot, and he recoiled, as if touched by burning coals. "Ah! Ah! Ah! Don't touch! It hurts!"

I thought of Balanchine's mantra: "If you want to choreograph, you have to get on your feet and show. If I couldn't show, I'd be finished."

During his illness, no one knew what was happening to Mr. B:

> [I]t was not until an autopsy was done [on Balanchine] that the disease was identified. Creutzfeldt-Jakob disease is rare and the diagnosis is ordinarily made only by microscopic postmortem examination of tissues. (Francis Mason, ed., *I Remember Balanchine* [Doubleday, 1991], p. 604)

Today, reviewing my diaries with hindsight and an understanding of Creutzfeldt-Jakob (CJD), the human form of mad cow disease, the symptoms all seem clear.

> "Symptoms of CJD include forgetfulness, nervousness, jerky trembling hand movements, unsteady gait, muscle spasms, chronic dementia, balance disorder, and loss of facial expression." (Medical Dictionary on MedicineNet.com)

> Affected individuals also commonly suffer visual loss and early death. (*New England Journal of Medicine* 339, no. 27 [1998])

Balanchine was hospitalized in November of 1982, having fallen and broken his wrist and several ribs. He never left the hospital, gradually deteriorating until, some six months later, he succumbed to the monster that ate away his brain.

Symptoms had cropped up earlier, but appeared unrelated, and I had shuttled him from doctor to doctor, searching for a diagnosis. Almost two years before, on June 20, 1981, Balanchine, worried, confessed to me that he was getting tired and dizzy at odd times. A month later, in Saratoga, after a performance of the pas de deux from *Meditations,* he was ecstatic, heaping praises on Suzanne Farrell and me. When he turned to walk away, I noticed, "He walks like an old guy, staggering, his legs spread and his equilibrium off."

On September 18, 1981, SAB's beloved Felia Dubrovska died. Her funeral at the Russian Orthodox church was punctuated with lots of kneelings, standings, and kneelings. Mr. B and I could hardly manage the ups and downs. Eventually, we resorted to clinging to each other for support. Laughing, Balanchine whispered, "I have an excuse, I'm older."

Aging was on both our minds. After her funeral, I regaled Balanchine with a description of the last time I'd seen Dubrovska. She'd summoned me for tea at her apartment, I think it was in the Ansonia Hotel on Seventy-third Street and Broadway or nearby. As we sipped our brew, Felia rhapsodized about her career, her performances, and what a great artist her husband, Vladimiroff, was. "Pierre loved you," she nodded at me. "You were always his favorite American dancer." With that, she coyly presented me with a box. I opened it to find two oblong circles of foam, backed with adhesive. "Put them on every chance you get, especially at night," she confided. "They keep you from creasing your forehead as you sleep, and you'll look younger longer. I have used them for years."

Balanchine sniffed. "Maybe face-lift would work better."

Watching Merrill Ashley and Sean Lavery in *Swan Lake* one evening, Mr. B and I stood shoulder to shoulder in the wings. Their dancing was so lovely; I was entranced. Balanchine, instead of watching, jabbered urgently into my ear. "I go soon to Switzerland . . . a spa . . . for vitality and health!

"The Swiss," he claimed, "have the best medicine. You can't get these injections anywhere else. They make them . . . from horses and bulls, to give you strength."

Robert D. Wickham, one of Balanchine's doctors, commented,

> Mr. Balanchine was very much concerned about staying as youthful as possible. That preoccupation is common in many men as they age. He once told me that in the past he had obtained "rejuvenation" injections in Switzerland. It is quite possible that he got Creutzfeldt-Jakob disease by way of these injections. Such injections have been available in Euro-

pean health spas and clinics for many years. They oftentimes contain extracts of animal glands such as testicular tissue.

The Saturday boys' class I started in the mid-1960s to introduce George and Chris to ballet, I had let drop. In the fall of 1975, I started teaching classes in several public schools in New York City. Bunches of screaming little panthers garnered from the fourth and fifth grades in elementary schools would meet and we would dance. Carrie discovered our bank account was markedly depleted, as I was paying the musicians and travel costs from our savings. "You could set up a nonprofit organization," she said. "It would help you raise money to hire staff and artists and it will become an institution of its own and not be fly-by-night."

To Lincoln Kirstein I went. "Lincoln, I've been teaching young boys dance." (I knew that would grab him.) "Not ballet, but introducing them to the arts through dance. I do the classes in their schools—hallways, corners of gyms, lunchrooms, even on rooftops. Lincoln, I need a lawyer for a nonprofit company. How do you do it?" He was shocked, had never thought of me forming a company, an institute, something outside of New York City Ballet. He had his plans for me. "Well, you have to get a lawyer. Maybe I can find one for you."

I hastened to proclaim, "I don't have any money, so it has to be pro bono."

Neal Johnston was the chosen one. "Lincoln told me you wanted to speak to me." He was not the Madison Avenue banker type. He looked to me a mumbling, scroungy, kind of seedy-looking guy. I was to discover an amazing, sensitive human being, a legendary litigator defending human rights activists. He adored music, was an accomplished pianist, and worshipped NYCB. It took a while, but by mid-1976, Neal had secured the necessary papers and had a request. "You need a minimum of five people on your board of directors, and, if you want, I'd like to be one." No one else wanted to. We were the first, then I shanghaied our best friend Sue Newhouse, and Carrie. With the addition of an entrepreneur friend, Karen Zehring, we made a handful. It was a start. We called it National Dance Institute.

Within a year, Lincoln joined our board as well, though as I expected, he soon lost interest. After attending one board meeting, where he heard I was teaching children that included those with visual and hearing impairments (that is, that I wouldn't be sending him little boys for SAB—early versions of myself and Eddie Villella), he proclaimed, "It'll appeal to people's guilt, so it will probably be successful."

Soon, it included girls as well as boys. Classes held in New York City schools throughout the year culminated in a spectacle, called the "Event of the Year." No one seemed to enjoy it more than Balanchine. From the beginning, he attended every performance, first at the New York State Theater between matinee and evening performances, then, starting around 1979, at the Felt Forum in Madison Square Garden.* Invariably, the morning after the NDI event, I would receive a phone call. "Balanchine here." Groggily, "Oh, Mr. B!" I'd mumble, and he'd continue, "You know, last night, performance—all the children, with wonderful music and dance, making story and theater, good! And big audience. Very important for children to experience this. Me! As a child, I performed ballets at Maryinsky Theater." Awake by now, I'd be babbling, "Oh, Mr. B! It's six thirty a.m.," and he'd interrupt, "All right. Goodbye." Click.

The year 1976 was a seminal one for Carrie, too. She started an exercise class for a group of her friends, eventually dubbed "Carrie's Mob." They met at the small dance studio we had on the top floor of our town house, and, several times a week, explored vigorous floor exercises, jazz, tap, and ballet. In several of NDI's Event of the Year spectaculars, Carrie's Mob was featured dancing with thousands of New York City children. As these memoirs are being conjured and printed, those classes continue, although more recently in the last of these decades, several of Carrie's Mob have begun attending as spirits.

But at NDI's Event in the spring of 1982, Balanchine was different. The moment the overture started, he clapped his hands over his ears and importuned, "Make it stop! The sound is too loud! It's hurting!" He tore pieces of paper from the program, balled them into plugs, and stuffed them in his ears.

As soon as that Event was completed, I began preparing the next year's theme and plot—a *Guys and Dolls* type of musical, entitled *Fat City.* It would eventually include original music and lyrics by a crew of superb musicians and lyricists—Martin Charnin, Lee Norris, Judy Collins, Arthur Schwartz—and a delightful song, "We Do It for Dia-

* Later the Felt Forum was renamed the Paramount Theatre.

monds," for the gangster chief, Legs Diamond, that my son Christopher concocted. I knew Balanchine would love to be included. "Mr. B, I need a tango. Judy Collins will sing it. This is the scene, do you think you can write me one?" Within a week, Mr. B had the music and lyrics of his song in my hand.

> *It was in early spring of life,*
> *We passed each other,*
> *One step and you were gone,*
> *I went my way alone.*
> *We made our mind to find our future everlasting*
> *That rays of sun would shine upon.*
> *Now spring is gone and roses went to sleep,*
> *No petals left for angry winds to sweep.*
> *Why not I when you were passing by?*
> *Why not you when I was passing through?*
> *Some years went by, why don't we try to find each other,*
> *Our roses still in bloom?*
> *Be mine, I'll be your groom.*
> *I know I loved you then and still I love you now,*
> *And I know you love me too.*

I tendered him a check. "It's a five-hundred-dollar honorarium, Mr. B." He sniffed and tore it up. He was fated never to see his tango performed.

Nineteen days later, on June 11, Balanchine was rehearsing the revival of his ballet *Noah and the Flood,* and I had been assisting him for a couple of weeks. That day, he suddenly became agitated, fluttering around, disoriented. Uncharacteristically, he vented furious anger at the boys in the corps, berating them for the way they were manipulating a giant snake-like prop. Pushing them aside, Balanchine seized the snake and started flaying the stage with it. We all backed away. Just as abruptly, he dropped the snake on the stage and, spotting me watching, open-mouthed, rushed over, clutched my shoulders, put his lips to my ear, and whispered, panic-stricken, "Can you continue? Stage it for me? My doctor is coming, I have to see him." *Him?* (Mr. B's doctor was a woman, Edith Langner.)

Somehow, I continued rehearsal, and with Rosemary Dunleavy's help, plus overtime, we forged on successfully.* Balanchine would pop onto the stage, look around with a vague and distracted gaze, exit into the wings, head toward the elevators, spin around, come back, and stare at us, as if surprised we were there. Sometimes he would rush to Ronnie Bates, the stage manager, mumble something, and disappear, only to reappear a few minutes later. No doctor came and he didn't leave—he just wandered around.

I never considered *Noah* a great ballet, but that evening, it went beautifully, and I was happy. Lincoln, ecstatic, scurried around from one person to another, praising excessively. Only later did I discover that Balanchine had given me credit in the program (revised staging, with Jacques d'Amboise). Unfair! Rosemary deserved the credit; I did very little. I was too distraught.†

June 14, 1982. Balanchine's ears have gotten much worse in the last few days, so I took him again to Dr. Jim Gould. I hung around while he underwent various tests. Later, while waiting for the test results, he spoke about repeating *Noah* next spring, and launched again into a description of his plans for *Birds of America,* a full-length ballet, inspired by Audubon's art, with music by Morton Gould. "I will do ballet, and you will be Audubon, passing through countryside with sketchpad, sketching birds of America. We will see history, and the myths of America."

Audubon would encounter Johnny Appleseed and the entire corps de ballet as various apples; later, crows would represent Salem witches. Traveling north to south, the ballet was to touch on the legends of Pocahontas (rescuing John Smith from being burned at the stake), Daniel Boone, Ohio and Mississippi river boatmen, and end in New Orleans with an octoroon ball presided over by the lost Dauphin of France.

He then described dreams of next year's season that, I believe, we both knew would never happen—Peter Martins and I alternating in teaching company class; then, with Jerry Robbins, making a trio, choreographing *Birds of America.* I ventured, "Mr. B, Lincoln is acting like a madman. He's worried about you." Balanchine replied, "Lincoln

---

* Rosemary was functioning as NYCB's ballet mistress at the time, doing 90 percent of the work in rehearsing and staging the repertoire.

† After his death, Balanchine's assistant Barbara Horgan informed me that Balanchine left *Noah and the Flood* to me.

doesn't know anything," and added that he, Balanchine, had always done what he wanted to do without Lincoln. "He only likes boys and is crazy. He needs his pills." There I was, with the two most important men in my life, one dying and the other crazy.

Switching the subject, he lamented, "All ballerinas make demands. They want *this* role only because someone else does it. Suzanne is envious of Kyra, and you never hear her say Darci's name. I have to be like juggler—everybody wants my attention." Returning home, I found that my teenage daughter Charlotte (already launched in her career on Broadway) had sprained her ankle, and needed love, sympathy, and attention. I don't think I gave her enough.

Balanchine kept his sense of humor. On the way back, he recounted how Kip Houston had asked to be made a soloist, rattling off a number of ballets he would like to dance. Balanchine, with a little smile, proudly told me his reply: "Why don't you make a list of things you want to do . . . and you can add to the list, 'Leave the company!' "*

At every meeting with me, Mr. B was a torrent of ideas for the future, a kaleidoscope of intentions—Chris in *Apollo* with Darci, reviving *Native Dancers,*† wanting me to choreograph for Merrill Ashley. "Merrill never asks for anything," he noted. "She's so dependable." My heart sank. He's dying, and imagining a nonexistent future, cramming it with ideas and plans—as if dreaming of projects will keep him alive. Talking of another song he wrote for the children of NDI, he boasted, "Schirmer‡ wants to put out a book of my songs." Balanchine dreaming reminded me of William Golding's *Pincher Martin,* where a drowning man, in the few seconds preceding his death, lives out in his imagination the thousands of details leading to his survival and rescue.§

Bill Hamilton, at that time the company doctor, told me Balanchine

---

* Kip Houston went on to dance principal roles with NYCB.
† *Native Dancers,* with music by Vittorio Rieti, was a ballet inspired by racehorses, choreographed by Balanchine for Patricia Wilde and me (1959). In the early 1950s, Balanchine had given the music to Jerry Robbins for a possible ballet. Jerry workshopped it with some seventeen members of NYCB whom he manipulated and cajoled into working for him for nothing in the off-season. I was one of them. It was never realized. Several years later, Balanchine called Patricia Wilde and me in for rehearsal on *Native Dancers;* I recognized immediately the music I knew so intimately.
‡ G. Schirmer Inc., well-known publishers of classical music.
§ William Golding, *Pincher Martin: The Two Deaths of Christopher Martin* (Harvest Books, 2002).

was "deteriorating rapidly," and Bill believed it was a hardening of the arteries in the brain. Everyone was speculating, struggling to diagnose Balanchine's symptoms—the falling over, the forgetting, the agitation and fear, the cataracts in the eyes, maybe a tumor on the ears.

Something was eating Balanchine's brain. But what?

On August 20, 1982, Carrie, Christopher, and I were in the Hamptons with our friends Dan and Joanna Rose when Balanchine called. "I am counting on Jim Gould to save me!" How did Balanchine find me at the Roses'? I envisioned him sitting on his bed with the phone in his hand, staring at the life-sized cardboard cutout of Wonder Woman he had pasted on his bedroom door. When we had visited in the past, he had always delighted in displaying her to us. She reminded me of Diana, cold and aloof.

"I am counting on Jim Gould to save me!" he repeated. "Do I have any appointments? Does Dr. Gould understand that I am not right? I'm still having my ear trouble. I only hear high notes, and they come from far away. Maybe hearing aid will fix everything," and then he spoke of contacting his doctor in Switzerland. I assured him that for ear, nose, and throat, Jim Gould was among the best in the world, and promised to go with him again to his next appointment.

Back in New York a few days later, I picked him up at nine thirty a.m., and Mr. B spoke of the demands made on him, how everyone was jockeying for position and asking about their place in the future. He was tormented. "Suzanne was up to see me. She feels I have not done enough for her. I told her there are lots of ballets in the repertoire for her, that you, Jacques, can make good ballets, that Peter can make good ballets, that there is Jerry, and others." He became vitriolic, expressing anger at Suzanne's marriage to Paul.

Like everyone else, I was imagining my own life without Balanchine, so I asked again, "What do *you* want me to do? Do you want me to teach classes? Do you want me to be ballet master and continue to choreograph? I'll try to do whatever you need."

The response was mumbling about positions and titles: "They mean nothing. There is title 'regisseur,' there is 'assistant ballet master' . . . Russian titles, French titles. Rosemary [Dunleavy] is a ballet mistress. There is me, there is Jerry, and then there is . . . uh, uh, uh [like he couldn't remember] . . . Taras. And then, somebody else. I don't remember. Assistant. Or something else." And so on. "I need to find another title, another way of listing all of us, and I haven't found it yet.

Anyway, I don't think title. You *are* ballet master." Frustrated, he continued, "You see where is my name on program? Ballet master. Not big boss, just ballet master. That's what I am—master of putting together ballets. Peter is ballet master, Jerry is ballet master . . . you all know how to put ballets together. We don't need other names for this."

The conversation turned to teaching. "I don't like Stanley Williams smoking his pipe in class," he announced,* and on choreography, "Steps are what makes dance interesting. Dance steps that will last." On choreographers, "Peter is good at inventing steps, and you are good at inventing steps. Jerry doesn't invent them as well. Jerry depends on big lifts and tricks and gimmicks." I nodded but thought to myself, "Baloney. Next to Balanchine, Jerry is the best."

While rehearsing a Mendelssohn ballet, I gave the dancers a five-minute break so I could call a dear friend, Harriet LeBell. It was her birthday, September 15, 1982. She was very ill, and could barely hear me, or talk. To my amazement, a half hour after returning to rehearsal, I burst into tears. All the dancers clustered around, sweetly supportive, but I couldn't stop sobbing. I canceled rehearsal and locked myself in the john. Ordinary, day-to-day function is the best therapy for sorrow. When I peed, I stopped crying. I wrote in my diary:

> Lately, Lincoln doesn't answer me if I address him; he just makes a dirty face. He sent me a note expressing his desire to resign from my NDI board. These days, between us, the pen replaces the tongue. Instead of talking to each other, we send notes.

> September 24, 1982: In dance class, it's difficult to concentrate—my mind is filled with thoughts on the dissolution of the environment Balanchine has created and the fragility of his aesthetic. With Balanchine absent, smoking in rehearsals is heading towards rampant. The sight of Stanley Williams teaching while puffing on his pipe as the accompanist, Lynn, chain-smoked—an ashtray on the piano stacked with butts—sent

---

* Stanley Williams was brought to SAB from Denmark as a teacher. Balanchine was impressed with the dancers' footwork from the Bournonville school of dance and wanted it for his company. Stanley was low-key, unaggressive, and gave a simple, easy, and slow class without too much repetition and no pressure. A cult of NYCB dancers formed around him, in many ways, perhaps, as a relief from the intense pressure, speed, and multiple repetitions of Balanchine's classes.

me fleeing down to the stage to find a solitary corner to do my barre.
When the king is ill, the nobles take liberties at court.

The company buzzed with rumors during our early-October performances in Washington, D.C. "Balanchine was admitted to the
George Washington University Hospital!" Barbara Horgan filled me in
on the details: he had fallen again, hurt his shoulder, and had nausea
and fever. Edith Langner, his doctor, rushed down to Washington to
minister to him. They were testing for a brain tumor.

When I was back in New York and rehearsing all day on the
Mendelssohn,* Lincoln popped in to watch, with hot burning eyes and
loathing on his lips. He sat for five minutes, then stalked out. Nancy
Lassalle passed me in the hall, wearing the same snarl. I thought, "She's
caught Lincoln's virus, beginning to look like him." After class the next
day, Lincoln's dam burst. He yelled at me for being a traitor, and went
on about how Balanchine was dying, and Lincoln always thought I
would be the one to replace him, but instead, I was a deserter and had
gone off to pursue other interests. "You're always doing something
else—your Hollywood, your movies, your Broadway, your theater
stuff—instead of paying attention *here*." He quivered with anger. "Lincoln," I said, "we better just stick to writing each other, not talk."

As Balanchine deteriorated, many around me were questioning and
urging, "Where are you in the equation of succession at NYCB? What
do you plan to do? Do something!"

I had been told since my late teens by Lincoln, "You're going to run
this company someday," and it had been implied by Balanchine for
most of my dancing life.

Occasionally in the mid-1960s, Lincoln would invite me to his
home, where he routinely courted potential funders, wealthy patrons,
and foundation heads. A couple of times Arthur Mitchell was there as
well, as we were part of Lincoln's plan. "This is McNeil Lowry. He's the
Ford Foundation," Lincoln growled. "They're worried—if they're
going to give millions of dollars to Balanchine's company, what happens when he's gone?"

A few years later, in 1972, after a performance of *Tchaikovsky Pas de*

* *Celebration,* January 20, 1983.

Deux, Melissa Hayden and I were taking curtain calls. I had an irritating habit of orchestrating the sequence of bows for my partner and myself. "We'll go together now, Milly," I'd order, "then do solos, and then go together again." I was turning into my mother, the Boss. Ronnie Bates called, "House lights up!" ending the bows before we'd completed my imagined sequence. I bellowed, "NO! NO, Ronnie!! We could have had another bow!! You brought the lights up too soon!" Balanchine marched over to me and said, "Come with me." He then collected Ronnie, and we retreated to a quiet corner offstage. Ronnie stood rigid, his face twitching with anger and embarrassment. Mr. Balanchine wagged his finger at me. "You cannot speak to Ronnie that way! Someday you will be running this company, and you will need him to make you look good. You must apologize." I stared at Ronnie's hot eyes. "Oh my God, Ronnie, I'm so sorry, forgive me." We fell into each other's arms, tearful, willful boys brought together by the father figure.

Then in the spring of 1974, shortly after watching *Saltarelli,* a ballet I was choreographing, Balanchine covered me with flattery: "Your future is choreography and teaching. You have excellent sense of judgment in gesture, and taste in choreography." He continued, "You should not have let so long a time go by without doing work [choreography]."

Sure enough, if one day Balanchine made a statement about something, the next day, you'd hear Lincoln embellishing on it. The next morning, he came to the NYST and got me out of class and, in an alcove off the main rehearsal hall, backed me up against the wall.

Lincoln was his usual erratic self, leapfrogging from one topic to the next. Jerome Robbins's ballet *Dybbuk* had premiered the night before, and this morning Lincoln started off on Robbins. "Jerry has no idea what to do with *Dybbuk.* It's all what has been seen before! The music was marvelous; the set and costumes, terrific; and the dancers not to be faulted, but Jerry's ballet was shit, dreadful, 'sub-Clifford.' "* Lincoln was furious, insisting that if Balanchine were to retire or step down, "JERRY ROBBINS WILL RUN THIS COMPANY OVER MY DEAD BODY!"

Lincoln growled that Jerry had complained that I refused to be in his ballets.[†]

---

* John Clifford, an electrifying dancer in the company and a choreographer.
† I assumed that Jerry had given up trying to use me in his choreography. I still danced *Afternoon of a Faun,* and loved it, but had weaned myself out of his ballet

This enormous man, Lincoln, had me pinned between two bathrooms. "I can't escape," I thought. "If I slip left, I'm stuck in the men's room; right, in the ladies' room . . ."

"George's ability generates hate and envy, and there are a lot of people out to get him!" For years, Lincoln said, the Ford Foundation and the National Endowment for the Arts had been hesitant to donate big money because of uncertainty about a successor. "George and I have to play politics, we need Jerry for the Jewish money, and the press and publicity value of him."

Lincoln's voice continued. Staccato bullets from an Uzi:

"Jerry is insisting that if he does not get more rehearsal for *Dybbuk,* he will pull it out. If he does that, I will go to the press and publicize that it is out of the repertoire because it is NO GOOD . . . and FUCK YOU, JERRY ROBBINS!"

Ranting on: "Balanchine is seventy-two, not seventy, and I am sixty-seven," he confided,* adding that he, Lincoln, planned to devote the rest of his life to securing an artistic successor to run NYCB. As neither he nor his brother or sister had children, Lincoln planned to leave a fortune of "six million dollars to the company! and the Ford Foundation will give eight million dollars as an endowment for an academy of dance," provided there was a clear successor to Balanchine.

Lincoln waved a finger in my face. "George says you can put steps

---

Interplay Years earlier, sitting around during the creation of his ballet *The Concert* (1956), waiting for him to use me, I up and told him, "Jerry, I've read half the contents of the New York Public Library waiting around for you to decide what you want me to do. I'm not coming anymore." That had been decades before. A few days after his triumph with critics and audiences with *Goldberg Variations* (1971), we were riding the NYST elevator with a few fellow dancers. Suddenly, he spun his frame to confront me. "Hen, hen, Jock, hen, hen. I'd like you to learn and dance the role that Helgi's doing. Hen, hen. I'd like to see you dancing it." You know how you sometimes grin with embarrassment? Baring my teeth in a frozen smile, I noticed that both of my hands went up involuntarily and clutched my throat. I stammered, "Jerry, I couldn't do that. I couldn't handle your rehearsals or perform more. I'm too old for that." An anguished, high-pitched "EEEEE-YOU!" issued from him. He balled up a fist and hammered one quick blow to the top of my head. We both stood, stunned and unbelieving. The elevator doors springing open on the ground floor ended our little play. As uncomfortable as he was around me, he loved and lit up like sunlight around Carrie. He admired and cared for both Christopher and Charlotte, and choreographed for both of them brilliantly.

* Where did Lincoln come up with that? Is it true? Most accounts agree that Balanchine was born January 22, 1904, which would have made him seventy years old.

together by virtue of your ability as a dancer, and you have musical and analytical sense." Right then and there, Lincoln gave me carte blanche to create any ballet at any time, on any theme I wanted, and insisted that I must choreograph for the fall of 1974, advising, "Work with John Braden, like George works with Rouben Ter-Arutunian and Karinska. John Braden has taste, painting is not his forte, but he is the ultimate craftsman.

"On the basis of *Saltarelli** and your ability as a dancer, Balanchine wants no one else to run the company. George says you are the only choreographer in the world who can make steps and that you are the one he wants to succeed him. That is what we have always planned, but for the last years, it looks like you didn't have a commitment. Do you? Can we count on you?"

In all the years I'd been with NYCB, I had taken leaves of absence to indulge my whims, and later, when I had a family, to make money. I never asked permission, just announced that I would be unavailable at NYCB. I'd done three major Hollywood movies and two Broadway shows (performed in one and choreographed the other), and had been a visiting professor for a decade at the University of California, Santa Barbara. In addition, between NYCB seasons or on days off, I'd assembled trios and chamber groups of the most talented ballerinas to perform with me in concerts and dance demonstrations all over the U.S.† During the holiday season, I would perform the opening night of *Nutcracker* with whoever was Mr. B's favorite ballerina, then take a couple of weeks off to go down and dance with the Ballet de San Juan in Puerto Rico. One year, I took a few months off and toured Europe headlining Ballet

---

* *Saltarelli* (May 30, 1974), music by Antonio Vivaldi, and scenery and costumes by John Braden.

† When NYCB was spending summers in Saratoga, we had Mondays off. I would ask Elise Ingalls, a lovely ballerina, to join me at a theater in Woodstock, New York, where we would perform various pas de deux and variations from Balanchine's ballets. They paid us maybe a thousand dollars for the performance. One memorable Monday, I introduced the pas de deux from *Swan Lake*. Elise was perhaps nineteen years old, and I had rehearsed and rehearsed her, but she was quivering with nervousness. The music began and she danced *so* exquisitely, a performance full of innocence, tenderness, and fragility, and trembling the whole time. After the final note, the audience, rapt, sat in silence, then burst into applause. After our bows, I announced to the audience, "I have never danced this pas de deux with a ballerina that gave a more moving interpretation than the one Elise just gave you."

A quartet of choreographers: With Jerome Robbins, John Taras, and Balanchine, celebrating the end of the Ravel Festival, May 1975

West, and then another year, with the North Carolina School of the Arts. Then, when I felt like it, I performed as guest artist with various ballet companies—among them, Joffrey, San Francisco Ballet, Pacific Northwest Ballet, the ballet companies in Vancouver, Munich, and Hamburg—never asking permission. One summer I left the company to go direct and choreograph the musical *Roberta* for summer stock, then again the next summer to stage *Lady in the Dark,* and the third year my own production of *Peter Pan* that toured several cities. It was a test to see if I wanted to go into directing. I didn't—the ballet and Balanchine were my center. But I never told Lincoln or Balanchine that. I just went off and did what I wanted. No wonder Lincoln thought I was a traitor, though I know Balanchine didn't. Still, I don't doubt they felt my interest in NYCB was lacking a hundred percent commitment.

Suddenly, Lincoln's avalanche of words slowed. "Whatever errors I did in the past to you and whatever you have done to me by virtue of lack of communicating, it is over, done with, forgotten." Lincoln patted me on the back. "I love you and always have." He spun around, dashed down the nearby stairwell, and left me trembling and wondering if, despite all his distortions, the claim, "This is what George wants!" was true.

Betty Cage told me she had once demanded of Balanchine, "Why do you let Jacques run off and do anything he wants?" and he replied, "Nobody can tell him what to do. He's just like me." He didn't realize his words echoed both Carrie and my mother (the "Nobody can tell him what to do" part).

If they were expecting me to step into more of a leadership role in the company, I was a wild horse. Taking off without thinking of consequences, thoughtless as to who might be affected by my actions, I never considered that Lincoln or Balanchine might feel I was throwing the offer back in their faces.

National Dance Institute would occupy more and more of my time and imagination in ensuing years. Today, NDI is the center of my life, and with affiliate programs all over the U.S. and abroad, we have reached over two million children.

That was over some thirty years ago. Recently, Sue Newhouse mumbled to me guiltily that she'd have to miss the next board meeting. I, who try to miss them every chance I get, loudly exclaimed, "Gee, Sue, I don't believe it! This is the first board meeting you've ever missed!" "No," she confessed, "there was one other you didn't know about." Her loyalty is infinite.

By 1979, I had added to my plate the position as full professor and dean of dance at SUNY Purchase, New York, and managed to function in three full-time jobs—for NYCB, rehearsing, choreographing, and performing; for NDI, teaching and choreographing for several hundred children each week in the public schools; and for SUNY Purchase, supervising the students and faculty, and choreographing works for the entire dance department. Sleeping on my desk, dressing-room floors, and commuter trains, I was putting in 120-hour weeks.

My resistance to Lincoln directing my future went deeper than maverick stubbornness. That 1974 conversation after the premiere of Jerry's *Dybbuk* was intense, but it wasn't the first time Lincoln had told me he expected me to run the company.

My reaction to Lincoln or anyone suggesting that I would be running NYCB had always been, "No, don't say that. I don't know what I'm going to do in the future. Right now, I'm going to dance, and I'll do that, until I can't dance anymore. Or until there's no more joy in it,

David Richardson following me across the room

and *then* I'll decide what I'm going to do." I'd continue, "I'm not going to wait around for my father to die to see if I inherit the farm, especially when I don't know if I want to be a farmer. Besides, Balanchine's shoes are too big, no one can stand in them!"

Not long after that conversation in 1974, Lincoln stormed as usual into company class. Dressed in his perennial navy blue suit with slightly scuffed black shoes, he went straight to the front of class and, without even a nod to Balanchine, sat on a bench in front of the mirror. An aura of intense concentration and danger emanated. Balanchine glanced at him once and never looked again.

The dancers were in the center of the ballet studio, executing dance combinations Balanchine was inventing. Some ten minutes passed, with Lincoln, immobile, staring straight ahead while we danced all over the room. Suddenly, he reached down, untied his shoelaces, took off his shoes, and lined them neatly, side by side, in front of his feet; then he sat, leaned back, and, in his black nylon ankle socks, resumed staring for another ten minutes. We dancers were a symphony of leaves fluttering around, trying desperately not to gaze at the shoes, and definitely not looking at Lincoln, a solid black rock, vibrating madness.

Lincoln Kirstein, right before he took his shoes off

Balanchine just kept teaching, testing us with his combinations. After an eternity, Lincoln stood up and stalked out in his black socks, leaving the shoes behind.

Balanchine loved teaching class. It was his turf, and there, he molded and tested his dancers, and found potential muses. I tried never to miss a Balanchine class, even toe classes for the ballerinas. He would invent steps on the spot, showing precisely how the feet moved to the structure of the music: "I have to take dancer and show them how I want them to move." Other choreographic details, he often left vague (the use of arms and torso, for example), and he rarely staged how you entered or exited. We became his instruments, but, contrary to all the media baloney then and now, we were not mindless, slavish, or without personality.

Frustrated that people didn't understand the techniques he had developed, he would inform us, "I am convinced that if you do these exercises this way, you will achieve strength, speed, precision, and control of time—you will have the facility to dance. Whether anyone wants to *watch* you dance, that's something else." He continued, "Choreography, for me, is teaching, but on a higher level. Some dancers have extra something, God gives. You cannot teach this. People say, 'Balanchine doesn't know how to teach soul.' I answer them, 'How can you teach soul?' What is soul? Emotions? I can't teach emotions. Just do the steps to music. If you do that, you've already achieved success. *Who* is doing the steps makes the difference. Allegra doing this step is so much more interesting than somebody else. Both do the same step, both interesting to look at. But, Allegra—you can't take eyes off her."

Why? Balanchine used to say, "God does this." He said the same about Suzanne. Balanchine had a gift for recognizing those "God does this" qualities in certain dancers. That's why he said, "No one should touch Darci [Kistler]. Don't try to correct her. Leave her alone. Trying to teach her, one could ruin what she has."

I became so attuned to him, I'd anticipate what he would be inventing in the next few bars of music, and have prepared several movement possibilities to present to him. Some combination he had designed for my partner would tell me that in the next section, I should be on the ballerina's right side. So, when he'd turn around and look for me, I'd be standing stage right. And he'd say, delightedly, "You know, now you come from there. Right?" He would demonstrate a step, I'd copy, and then I'd take the movement and play with it, adding arms, enhancing the rhythms, contributing a turn, watching all the time to see his reaction. If he liked what I did, he'd leave it. If not, he would take the time to invent something else. I wasn't the only one who collaborated and played with his choreography this way. We all did it in some way. Suzanne Farrell was great at it. And Tanny was a *master*.

When I saw a young dancer having difficulty in a Balanchine class, I would pull him or her aside, as if I was a teaching assistant and coach to Balanchine. It occurred to me, "Is what I'm doing rude?" Once, I asked, "Mr. Balanchine, do you mind?" "Oh, no, no. I like it, it's fine." He didn't feel I was disrupting his class. He was so assured. "Good. You *know*. You help me."* I was practicing the skills of teaching Balanchine

---

* Today, when I teach at NDI, I'll demonstrate a step for the group, and when a student is having difficulty, I help up to a point—"Come here. Let me show you." If,

technique without any intention or desire to do so in the future, simply because his techniques were so interesting. His teaching and choreography all has to do with music and time. Betty told me Balanchine remarked to her, "Jacques, he knows. He really knows." And I do.

Once again, I approached Lincoln, only this time, to ask for help with fund-raising for NDI. Immediately, he offered, "I know someone who's crazy enough, you'll be able to get money out of her." In 1980, Frances Schreuder had given NYCB money to underwrite and commission Balanchine's new ballet, *Robert Schumann's "Davidsbündlertänze."* So Lincoln brokered a lunch for us, and as we sat together, I thought, "She's creepy. I don't want to have anything to do with her."

With Frances Schreuder, I sensed an unbalance, a turmoil of volcanoes in her.

---

after a minute or two he or she still doesn't get it, I'll say, "Great. Marianne [or some other teaching assistant], could you work with her?" Or sometimes I'll ask another student who knows the step well (a "peer mentor") to help, and they go off into a corner. And then I keep going, and I know that the assistant will be working with the struggler, and out of the corner of my eye, I'm watching. When they return, I'll have the struggler and his teacher demonstrate for the rest of the class. We do that all the time. It's an excellent way to train teachers and, at the same time, make sure no one falls behind in class.

A Close Call with Death

I was not quite seventeen, still a teenager, when Brad and Lobelia came into my life.

New York City Ballet, on a national tour, had stopped for an engagement in Los Angeles. Our performances would be at the Greek Theatre in Griffith Park, set in the middle of a forested glen. The complex held some two thousand green seats, sloping toward a grand stage, framed by a rectangular proscenium.

After opening night, two old friends of André Eglevsky gave a party for the cast at their home in South Pasadena.

Eglevsky had met the Bishops in Los Angeles years before, when he was a young star performing with the Ballet Russe. Lobelia, a devoted ballet fan, persuaded her husband, Bradford, to accompany her to a performance. The moment Eglevsky floated on stage in one of his famous leaps, Bradford was captivated. André seemed to move through the air in slow motion, alighting silently, feathersoft, combining the smooth feline grace of a tiger with the power and masculinity of a young Hercules. Bradford was transformed into a balletomane.

Eglevsky was an international superstar, and was now heading our company. I watched and studied him constantly, and tried to achieve the ease in dancing that was his hallmark. In particular, his multiple pirouettes in slow motion challenged me. He became a mentor and a friend.

At the Bishops' party, André presented me to our hosts as if I were his gift. "Lobelia, Bradford, meet Jacques, the next generation. Reminds me of me when I was his age, only not as smart," André smirked. "He's our next star . . . as long as he takes my advice." He passed me to the Bishops as a relay runner hands off a baton.

In a burst of generosity Lobelia said, "Why pay for a hotel? Come stay with us. We would love to have you."

I moved into the guest bedroom of their home in South Pasadena, and became a participant in their family life. I loved their home, their pool, Lobelia's cooking, and them. They had a teenage son, Brad Jr., who was maybe three years younger than me. We bonded immediately.

Bradford Sr. looked like a Madison Avenue ad agency's dream. Fair-haired and slim, with rugged features and a westerner's melodious voice, his manners were impeccable. Humorous crinkles bracketed his eyes, and one felt warm and safe in his company. His wife, Lobelia, with her broad cheekbones, grand smile, and generous heart, worshipped and doted on her Bradford. Vastly energetic, she was a brown-eyed houri, with an open and optimistic personality. When I arrived at their home after performance, she'd be up and waiting to feed me. In the morning, no matter how early I arose, breakfast would be laid out, Lobelia to keep me company.

Over the years, I stayed with them every time I visited Los Angeles, whether shooting a movie, a television show, or dancing with a ballet company. When I was not in Los Angeles, we communicated regularly—phone calls, letters, and postcards. Lobelia did most of the corresponding, and generally, her news dealt with Bradford. She supported and guarded him, geared the tempos of her life to his.

Bradford was a geologist and a wheeler-dealer in the oil business. An independent, he eschewed working for a corporation. Studying and analyzing various geographical areas, he would option mineral rights from the owners, form a consortium of partners, raise money, and dig a test well. If the well came up dry, millions were lost. If it gushed, hooray! . . . wealth! . . . Until it went dry! Then he would start over again, one day a millionaire, next a debtor.

Lobelia had dreamed of a life as a singer and actress, but instead fell in love with Bradford. Cooking, fussing over him, she made a beautiful home, and shared her passions—opera, ballet, and theater. When Bradford was off in the field, Lobelia channeled her tremendous energy, volunteering for arts organizations and dabbling in educational courses—Italian language, opera, Renaissance art, floral arrangement, and cooking classes.

Brad Jr. was an only child. He had his mother's broad cheekbones and large frame, but his father's fair hair and quiet reserve. His parents adored him, and he seemed to remain unspoiled—super-smart, analytical, and somewhat remote. Except when I was visiting. Playing Daniel Boone and Jim Bowie, we disturbed the drowsy quiet of Orange Grove, Pasadena, with the wild games of a pair of screeching Indians, blood whooping in our veins. I taught him how to throw knives, a skill devel-

Brad Jr. photographs his teacher demonstrating, Pasadena, late 1950s

oped in my days of hiking and camping. I bought a bow and arrow, and we put up a target in the back of the garage, opened its doors, and from the back of the house Robin Hooded our arrows (we hoped) straight into the bull's eye, or at least somewhere near the garage.

You would expect a young boy to be bugging me every time I was around, "Let's go play at throwing knives again!" but that was not the case. It was I who always initiated the games. Gangly, athletic, strong, Brad Jr. was a quick study. When we played chess together, he would clench his jaw and concentrate intensely. In any of our games, he was determined to excel, to win. Though reticent, he was focused.

Four years passed. Brad Jr. and I grew up. When he was eighteen, I was twenty-one, and had just married Carrie. Now my wife and I stayed at the Bishops' when we were in LA, and after our children were born, we all splashed around in the Bishops' pool.

After Brad Jr. finished Yale, Lobelia conveyed to me somewhat mysteriously, "Oh, he's enrolled in a military language school in Carmel, California."

Then, she said, "Oh! He's with military intelligence."

Next, "Oh, he's with the State Department," though what exactly he did there was never mentioned.

One day, all excited and bubbly, Lobelia called me in New York City, full of details about Brad Jr.'s romance. "It's serious, Jacques. He's engaged to Annette, and she's a darling. At his high school, she was a cheerleader when he was on the football team. And she loves the outdoors, Jacques! They're always off bushwhacking in the woods somewhere." And then, not long after, in a letter, "At last, I've got the daughter I always wanted. Annette and Brad Jr. are married!"

Visiting LA for a television special when both Brads were away, I had the most sumptuous meal cooked for me by Annette and Lobelia, twitting and giggling around the kitchen like two beautiful birds. It was remarkable how similar Annette was to Lobelia—the dark hair, broad cheeks, enormous dark eyes, laughter, and vitality.

Annette and Brad Jr. eventually had three children, but, to my regret, I never had occasion to meet them, for, not long after the first was born, Brad Jr. was stationed overseas.

His assignment was Trieste, Italy, where his specialty—the languages and cultures of Serbia, Croatia, Bosnia, and Slovakia—would be invaluable. I remembered Trieste from our New York City Ballet tour there. The riots near the theater, and my guilt in deserting a company full of exhausted and injured dancers to go off to Hollywood.

"That's a volatile area. What's he going to do over there?" I asked, and Lobelia dropped hints, vague mentions of the lives and deaths of "Brad's friends in Communist Yugoslavia." I caught the gist that he was running agents. Brad Jr. was a spy!

Nothing would have torn Lobelia away from her husband, Bradford—except a grandchild. Every moment she could pry away, she visited Brad Jr., Annette, and their baby, Brad III. She was in heaven, and the cherub was not the only reason. In Italy, Lobelia could indulge: the opera at La Scala, the art in Florence, unbelievable Venice, Naples, and Rome, all while delving into Italian cuisine and cuddling her grandchild. She took up shuttling between her home with Bradford Sr. in South Pasadena and Brad Jr.'s family in Italy—which, with Annette's pregnancies, kept growing.

Sometime around 1969, I received a letter from Lobelia that Bradford Sr. was ill. He had a previous heart condition and had developed cancer on top of that. "He's fighting bravely, Jacques, and never complains. But it doesn't look good."

Shortly after I heard of Bradford's illness, I was engaged to perform on *The Ed Sullivan Show* with the ballerina Marnee Morris as my partner. We opened the show and were followed by a rock singer—a seedy-looking, emaciated, and slump-shouldered woman with pockmarked, pale skin: Janis Joplin. Marnee and I had just finished our performance, and Janis was watching from the wings. "Hey, dancer," she said, "I like you, and I like the way you move. The band and I plan to party tonight and I'd love for you to come with us. You too . . ." She gestured toward Marnee. Without waiting for an answer, she went onstage to perform. Marnee couldn't believe it. "She's coming on to you . . . and she's so famous. Let's watch her segment, and then go to the party." Marnee was into that rock and hippie stuff. Not me. She headed for the party and on to a night of drugs with Janis and her band. I headed home to inquire, "Carrie, who's Janis Joplin?"

That same night, Lobelia called me. There's a three-hour time difference between New York and LA, and they had just finished watching *The Ed Sullivan Show.* Bradford was in bed. "Jacques, he forgot his pain and illness during your performance," Lobelia said. "It's the first time in all these months of suffering that I can remember him being happy. He kept saying, 'How I love the ballet.' "

They had made plans for her life after his death, which was imminent—Lobelia would sell the house and go live with Brad Jr., Annette, and their children. Soon Lobelia's letters were coming from Africa. Brad Jr.'s latest assignment was Gaborone, Botswana. It was an exotic place, very different from northern Italy. There, Lobelia planned to play with her now three grandchildren, especially the new baby, Geoff. She hoped to renew her life.

In the mid-1970s, Lobelia informed me, "Brad Jr.'s to be stationed in Washington, D.C. We're coming home! We're finally leaving Africa!" She sounded relieved. "It's time to come back, it's time for the children to learn about America and being American."

They set up house in Bethesda, Maryland, and flung themselves into the middle-class suburban lifestyle with gusto—parents' associations, tennis, bridge clubs, reading circles, involvement with local charities and social organizations. The family adopted a pet dog—a golden retriever named Leo. The children made new friends, and everyone flourished. Articles were written in the local newspaper about them: "The Perfect Family—Mr. and Mrs. America and their kids."

I was over forty by then, and my dancing career was slowing down. Having recuperated from a recent knee operation, I was back to performing, albeit with a doctor's warning that if I continued, he would probably see me in another year for a second operation. I was thrilled just to be able to dance again.

New York City Ballet was headed to the Kennedy Center in Washington, D.C., and I was scheduled to dance in two marvelous roles: *Meditation,* and the last movement of *Brahms-Schoenberg Quartet,* roles choreographed for Suzanne Farrell and me by Balanchine. I was commuting between New York and Washington.

Lobelia wrote to tell me, "We've got our tickets for the ballet, Sunday, February 29 [1976]. The whole family's coming, Jacques." She was thrilled to see me and have her ballet fix. "Brad Jr. wants you to stay with us in Bethesda; it is only a few minutes' drive across the Potomac to the Kennedy Center. You can save on hotels; it'll be like old times, Jacques. And you can meet the grandchildren!"

I called Lobelia: "Carrie's coming down too, and we'll have our bags at the theater so we can go home with you right after the performance."

Making schedules, giving orders, organizing things. I love it. I was excited—Carrie and I would be living with the Bishops again.

Two days before our date with the Bishops, my knee went out onstage, so I called Carrie, saying, "Don't come down. Stay home, I'm coming back." On Saturday morning, depressed, I limped my way back to New York. I didn't want to talk to anyone, just focus on healing and returning to dance. Lobelia, Brad, and their family would come to the performance, find out I was injured, and would surely call Carrie or me in New York.

At the doctor's office the next day, I was told, "No performing for a while."

A dancer's identity is wrapped up in his or her body. If you can't dance, you lose identity. I wandered around New York, lost. Then I would exercise, take a ballet class, reinjure myself, doctors again—therapy, back in dance class—too soon—injured again—and so on. Getting older, but trying to hold on, and putting on a smiling face—eating, drinking, going to parties, and basically marking time, inwardly miserable. Somewhere, a little voice in the brain was saying, "Why didn't Lobelia call to see how I am?"

"Carrie, have you heard from Lobelia?"

I would have thought she'd have been on the phone the morning after they attended the February 29 performance and heard of my injury.

One morning, up early, unable to sleep and wandering the city streets, I spied a headline in "Mystery Family Found, Bodies Burned." It recounted how, on Tuesday, March 2, a ranger on fire watch in North Carolina spotted a tendril of smoke in the valley below, and conscientiously drove down to investigate. The ranger came across a fire in a pit. In the pit, flames crackled amid the swirling smoke of damp wood— the hissing of a demon orchestra feverishly tuning—masking the smoldering bodies of three children and two women. Discarded at the rim of the pit was a shovel, its sharp edges shining among the leaves.

They traced the shovel to a hardware store in Potomac, Maryland, and records revealed that a Brad Bishop Jr. had purchased it.

The authorities tried to reach Brad Jr. by phone. No answer. They called the State Department and were told to call back in the morning.

Further inquiries by the police to the State Department revealed that Brad Jr. had failed to report to work the previous week. "Oh, he left work last Monday, said he was feeling sick." No one remembered seeing Annette or Lobelia that week, and the children had not been in school. At their home, the police found a vacant garage and no response to bells or knocks. They broke in and found an empty house, blood everywhere. The all-American Bishops—including Leo, the dog—were nowhere to be found.

Subsequent investigation confirmed that the bodies in the North Carolina fire pit were Annette, her three children, and Lobelia. Brad Jr. and Leo had disappeared. Brad Jr. was the prime suspect in the murders.

I followed every news development avidly. The authorities believed that the two women and the three children had been bludgeoned. Evidence showed that one of the women had locked herself in the bathroom and was trying to open the window when the door was smashed. All over the bathroom were bloody fingerprints. Lobelia's.

Maybe Brad Jr. had been kidnapped, been killed, and his body left somewhere else. And what about the dog? What happened to Leo?

Carrie and I searched for an answer. Could this have been some monstrous revenge for Brad Jr.'s actions as a spy in Yugoslavia or Africa? Was Brad Jr. forced to watch the death of his family and then taken off to be killed and buried?

The police believed that the murders had taken place Monday, March 1, 1976. We would have been staying at their home. Had Carrie and I been with them, would we have added our blood to the house?

Would we have been in the fire pit? Or would our presence somehow have deflected or deferred the killings?

Investigators reported that Brad Jr.'s credit card had been used at a North Carolina store on March 2. There was a story of a waitress at a diner describing a man "acting strange and nervous." After an altercation with another patron in the diner, he had used Brad Bishop's credit card to pay the bill, and fled. The waitress exclaimed, when shown a picture of Brad Jr., "That's the man!"

I called André Eglevsky on Long Island. He had retired from performing and had started a ballet company there. For months, we were both terrified that Brad Jr. would show up on our doorstep—a fugitive, and mad. Months turned into years, and there were no new developments. The story faded from the papers but remained buzzing ominously in my brain engine.

Amazingly, no one ever came to talk to us. The police must have found the letters we had exchanged, our plans to stay with them that night. A friend of mine at the *Washington Post* informed me that for several years the paper had assigned some of their reporters to do nothing but try to track down Brad Bishop Jr., without success.

In the late 1970s, it was reported that a member of the State Department had gone to the restroom in a restaurant in Italy and, at the urinal, recognized a bearded Brad Bishop Jr. He stared and mumbled, "Brad? Is that you, Brad?" The man fled. "Brad, wait. Brad!"

Some twenty-three years after the murders, in the spring of 1999, Carrie viewed a news item on television. A couple who had worked with him spotted Brad Jr. at a train station in Switzerland. Their train had stopped next to another train, parked on a parallel track, and while gazing out of the window of her compartment, the woman saw, staring back at her through the other train's window, Brad Bishop Jr. She called her husband over, "I think that's Brad? Isn't that Brad?" The two parties stood there, staring, their faces inches away from each other, separated only by the panes of the two train windows. As Brad Bishop's train slowly pulled out of the station, he smirked and held both hands up—a "Don't shoot" gesture—as if he was a bad boy caught with his hand in the cookie jar: a "You got me."

Horror stories—the ones that raise the awful thought that no one is what they seem—forever cling to the dark shadows of the human mind. Dwelling on them, you begin to trust no one—those closest to you?

yourself? Paranoia and madness threaten to crack through the earth and darken your soul. Order and civilization collapse, fly apart. In defense, a door in the brain snaps shut.

I had played and been friends with a boy who grew into manhood to slaughter his entire family.*

---

* The story of the Brad Bishop murders has been featured on a number of television shows, including *America's Most Wanted.* I believe the State Department, CIA, FBI, and police continue their search for Brad Jr. to this day.

The Years Leading to Balanchine's Death, Continued

By 1982, as I approached fifty, my life as a dancer was in a holding pattern, as a plane hovers over Kennedy International Airport, on its way down.

Balanchine's health was steadily declining, and the word "succession" implied his death, something I didn't have the ability to imagine. I'd try, asking myself, "Jacques, what's going to happen with Balanchine gone?" and a black curtain would descend, impeding any thought in that direction. What did Balanchine expect of *me*? I decided to ask.

"Mr. B, what do you think I want to do?" He replied, "Make movies and Broadway shows. Direct, choreograph, teach. You are very good at directing, putting big things together." I realized he was thinking of NDI and our yearly extravaganzas. I ventured, "Do you want me to be part of NYCB?" Blinking, he answered, "Yes, of course, always, but you have to support your family and you need money." I announced, "George is in the Air Force, Chris's career as a dancer is soaring, the twins are eighteen and launched on their careers,* and Carrie is passionately pursuing her art as a photographer. Tell me what you need."

Balanchine rambled, seemed to change the subject. "Lincoln is a homosexual, always for boys, and will destroy everything. He is in love with Joe Duell.† Only I care about women, and woman *is* ballet. Like you have wonderful racehorses, you must treat them well and serve them. Taras, Jerry are not ballet . . . Jerry is Broadway.‡ I am disap-

---

* Charlotte had no doubts that she would be a Broadway star, and Cate, full of doubts, had opted for Denison University and a career in pedagogy.

† Two brothers, Joseph and Dan Duell, joined NYCB and eventually became principals. As a student at SAB, Dan lived with Carrie and me at our home. Joe was the type of dancer that was a magnet to Lincoln—pale white skin, muscled, handsome, quiet, soft-spoken, gentle, serene.

‡ I once asked Balanchine, "Jerry is such a big Broadway star, but he has been willing to work under you for all these years? Why?" His answer: "He wants to be close so he can analyze what makes Balanchine Balanchine—and steal it."

pointed in Ronnie Bates. He cannot see [how to light ballets], and I can see.* No one is around to tell, the clothes are junk [that is, when Balanchine is no longer around, there will be no one to direct the lighting designer and costume designer on how to dress and light the dancers]."

Balanchine continued, "I say, 'The best silk, the best costumes always.' But I need help. I cannot do it all. I never knew you were ready now, yes, good. It has to be, in the future, someone who loves women—not a homosexual—the only two people are you and Peter."

Balanchine rarely *demanded*, but if, when he was in the hospital with no hope of recovering, he had tried to persuade me to direct the company, I would have insisted, "Jerry is the one. Or, if Lincoln balks at Jerry . . . a troika—Tanny, Karin von Aroldingen, and Rosemary Dunleavy."† I wanted to be remembered: "There for Balanchine, gone when he's gone."

Jerry was tormented, like Lincoln. Each had qualities of brilliance, bordering on genius, and each was gifted with wit—marbled with meanness. On their shadow sides, they sometimes behaved like monsters, determined to camouflage any sign of a gentler, sunlit side. But it cropped up. Lincoln once came into my dressing room and proudly showed me a picture of himself marching amid hundreds of African Americans in Selma, Alabama, the only white protester in the picture, carrying a little black boy on his shoulder, like St. Christopher carrying Jesus. And Jerry, underwriting the medical costs for injured dancers, on the condition that the dancers never tell anyone.

Jerry in his choreography, and in his life, was a seeker. He hoped and dreamed of a better world, without prejudice, with races and cultures

* Martha Swope was NYCB's premiere photographer for many years. Each season, Balanchine, while setting the lights for his ballets, would demand, "We need it brighter," and Martha would have to adjust the f-stop on her camera to a lower setting than her records for the previous season indicated (the f-stop controls the size of the iris opening of the camera lens—higher settings create a smaller iris). Those mysterious and murky pools that defined the early lighting plots of Jean Rosenthal were gradually being erased. I knew his eyes had been fading for quite a while. Subsequently, when Carrie became the company photographer, she noticed it, too. "Mr. B's eyesight's going," she said, "but the brighter lights he's demanding are great for taking pictures!"

† When it was announced that Jerry and Peter would share the role of artistic director (they called themselves "ballet masters in chief"), I called Rosemary Dunleavy and suggested, "The company needs you. Jerry and Peter need you. While they need you, make sure you get official recognition. Otherwise, they'll replace you as soon as they can."

in harmony, somehow finding that place despite society's rules, nationalism, fear, hate of other cultures, and divisions of religions or class. His work in the theater and dance are full of these themes. At NYCB, *The Guest, Age of Anxiety,* and *Dances at a Gathering* come to mind. And on Broadway, *West Side Story* was at the apex.

Despite Lincoln's personal animosity toward Jerry, there was no doubt that, next to Balanchine, Jerry was the preeminent choreographer and man of the theater in America. It surprised me that Lincoln allowed his distaste for Jerry to jeopardize in any way the future of the company.

Balanchine never said no to Jerry Robbins, but he never said yes to anybody. Like Louis Quatorze declaring, "I am the state," Balanchine continually declared, "After me, I don't care. It will be different. Something else. Right now, with these people, and this music—that's all I care." When Peter Martins went to Balanchine's hospital bed to receive his imprimatur and be officially installed as his successor, Peter told me Balanchine answered, "You'll have to fight Jerry for it." It was something that Alexander the Great said on his deathbed: "Let the strongest win."

You could always tell where you stood with Lincoln by studying Nancy Lassalle's behavior.* A patron and groupie who dedicated her life to the company and, especially, the school, from its earliest days, she reflected what Lincoln projected. At this time, she was telegraphing Lincoln's disfavor toward me, turning down the corners of her mouth and averting her eyes when she saw me.

He would wander around, come up to dancers, stare at them, saying nothing or, all of a sudden, yelling, "Get out!"

As Balanchine faded, Lincoln's behavior rippled into a Jackson Pollock. One noon, dripping sweat after ballet class, I was gossiping with Carol Sumner† in the hall. Lincoln appeared. Spotting us, he pressed himself against the wall and, like a crab, sidled past as if afraid our bodies might touch. I ventured a nervous, "Hi, Lincoln. You got a moment?" He squeaked out a high-pitched "Yeeeessss!," then, acceler-

---

* She became the single most loyal patron of, and believer in, Lincoln Kirstein's dream, and was a devoted friend to Tanaquil LeClercq.
† Carol Sumner, a very attractive ballerina with NYCB, danced in the company for years, and later became a teacher.

Lincoln Kirstein accosting Suzanne Farrell

ating his crabwalk, slipped through the hall door, and out of sight. "Oh, well. Lincoln's not lucid," I said to an open-mouthed Carol.

That same night, in the dressing room I shared with the elegant Icelandic star Helgi Tomasson, I sat alone, putting on my makeup. The first ballet, *Swan Lake,* had just ended, and I was still haunted by Tchaikovsky's angst-ridden chords. In the adjacent dressing room, Peter Martins was frantically changing out of his Prince costume to prepare for the next ballet, when Lincoln burst into his dressing room. You could hear everything through the doors. "Peter, you're THE ONE," he bellowed. "You have to watch everything George does!

There's no time to waste! Watch all the ballets, over and over. Sit in the balcony, sit on the sides! Watch from the orchestra! Sit in the front row. Analyze it all! Everything onstage! The patterns. The entrances. The exits. Find out how George does it!"

The warning bells were ringing for places onstage. "Sorry, Lincoln, I'm in the next ballet. I have to go!" Peter dashed off. There was no sound of Lincoln exiting, only silence. He didn't shuffle his feet, he didn't move. I didn't move. Was he sitting? Was he standing? It seemed forever. Finally, the sounds of sighs and grunts, then Lincoln exiting the dressing room and going down the hall.

Several minutes later, having donned my woolies, I headed downstairs to warm up, and, on opening the door to the stairwell, froze. A white-faced Joe Duell stood on the landing, pinned with his back to the wall by the looming body of Lincoln. Directly over Joe's head, attached to the wall, was a red fire extinguisher in a glass case, and next to it, a heavy red fire ax hung in brackets. "You're THE ONE, Joe!" Lincoln insisted. "I don't trust Peter. Can I count on you?"

I backed out, eased the door shut, took the elevator to the stage, and, in a corner in the wings, managed a warm-up. In an hour, it would be my turn to go onstage for the ballet *Who Cares?*

As Balanchine was dying, our artistic body seemed eviscerated, bereft of vital organs. His company classes started our days. Without him, we were disconsolate children, coming in for breakfast with no one in the kitchen. Orphans with an unknown future.

Despite the leadership vacuum, the company was dancing beautifully, presenting a positive facade. But with the curtain's descent, dark shadows enveloped. Little groups with glum faces whispered in corners, and no one seemed able to meet another's gaze, and storming about was the terrified and terrifying Lincoln.

Believing that he may have to be prepared to run the company, poor Joe Duell came to me supplicating: "Jacques, when Mr. Balanchine does tendu battements, does he . . . ?," imploring. Or, "You think we could meet in the morning and have a cup of coffee, so we could talk about Balanchine?" My son Chris told me Joe would call him too, asking to meet. "He was crying for help," Chris later commented, "and none of us answered."

After Balanchine died, Joe and a small group of dancers conducted séances on the stage of the NYST. They'd gather in the empty theater and create ceremonies to call on Balanchine and ask what to do. Not long after Balanchine's death, Joe took off all his clothes, did a grand jeté out the window of his apartment, and fell to his death.

I felt guilty that I'd ignored Joe's pleas, discounting him as a wounded psyche that wanted me to indulge him with stroking—and was relieved to hear from Chris that he, too, felt remorse over ignoring Joe's cries in the wilderness. That spread my guilt around. I imagined the secret terror Joe must have felt when Lincoln cornered him, insisting, "You're the one!"

I didn't even realize how much *I* was hurting, and had little patience for anyone else's angst. The world I knew, and was so much a part of me, had faded away. Scarlett O'Hara felt the same way when Atlanta burned down. I was on my last legs as a dancer. Thank God NDI and its programs were filling my hours.

When it appeared Jerry was going to be left out, he threatened to take all his ballets out of the repertoire and go to the press. A stew of egos boiled, intrigue fomented behind the scenes, and, after board meetings galore, a solution evolved. Jerry Robbins and Peter Martins would share the powers of artistic director. Peter would assume responsibility for the day-to-day administration of the repertoire (outside of Jerry's works), and Jerry would enjoy doing whatever he wanted. Lincoln, chewing his tongue at the sound of the name Jerome Robbins, realizing he had no choice, added ulcers to his physical problems.

Peter, kowtowing to Jerry, achieved an amazing feat of diplomacy, dancing carefully around Jerry's periphery and giving him everything he demanded.

Being the curator of the Balanchine museum would doom anyone for life, an Atlas, bound to carry the burden of Balanchine's legacy. I admire Peter for assuming the mantle. Like Atlas, he can never drop it; the weight of the icon that was Balanchine forever hangs over him, the company, and the school. No matter what Peter does, no matter the ballets he (or anyone else, for that matter) choreographs, everything is compared to Balanchine.

The mastery of moving people on- and offstage was long ago achieved by Balanchine, and as he continued to choreograph, he invented and surprised his audiences with new ways of using his materials. (The ballets *Serenade, The Four Temperaments, Ballo della Regina,* and *Liebeslieder Waltzer* are a few examples.)

But the true essence of Balanchine is not in his supreme choreo-

You never knew what you would get if he turned on you.

graphic skills; instead it is found in a subtle and mysterious presence that seems to permeate his ballets and is part of the makeup of the artist himself.

His art was his life. "If I couldn't move, I couldn't choreograph and I would be nothing," was a lament he often voiced.

As a whiff of an exotic perfume transforms an environment, experiencing his ballets seems to enhance the finer qualities in us. Viewing his ballets, we recognize that Balanchine is a person of sensibilities and taste.

There is humanity at work. Harmony is in the company of beauty and not one drop of false sentiment exists. A visual autobiography, his ballets are a description of himself, with morality and spirituality at their core. He knew what mattered, and it had to do with good manners.

Of course he was jealous, at times greedy, devious, and willful. Vindictive, too! Hooray! Human! His life was a roller coaster of success and disappointments, loves and losses; but the center of him was unshakable, not a tremor. He had no doubts. He knew himself. His world sat with him.

It drove Lincoln nuts!

If you can't erase it, use it. So, over the years, Balanchine has been marketed, and turned into a fashionable brand name, claimed by everyone. Playboy bunnies even boast in their résumés, "I was in Balanchine's company."

Balanchine had been dead less than six months. Peter Martins and Jerry Robbins had been installed as co–ballet masters in chief of NYCB. Lincoln was choking with doubts.

"He wants you to come over to his office NOW!" I got the message in the middle of pliés at the barre, so I left class to meet an agitated Lincoln, waiting at SAB. "You failed me!" he roared. "Where were you?! Where *are* you?!!" You know the feeling you get in the principal's office? Numb, but your fingers tingle, and you need to pee? That was me.

Switching to a pathetic high-pitched voice, he wailed, "What's going to happen to the company, Jacques? What's going to happen to the company?"

I couldn't take my eyes off his hands. Not for him, the ordinary biting of nails. He had ripped strips of skin from his cuticles; on each finger, striations of raw flesh radiated toward his knuckles like the spiky crown on the Statue of Liberty. I felt such pity for him. "It's going to be fine, Lincoln. NYCB will go on. You and Balanchine have built a company that supports the livelihoods and careers of hundreds, if not thousands, of people, and you have hundreds of thousands—no, millions—of fans. Besides, there's SAB. Companies come and go, but SAB is a foundation. It's solid. It's all right, Lincoln. It's all right."

My reassurance didn't work. He loomed over me and jabbed his finger at me, rhythmically punctuating every proclamation: "At last, the tyranny of one man is over! Balanchine was never my friend. Do you think he ever asked me out socially? It was always business." Then, in a bizarre switch, he continued in a low voice, as if talking to himself, "We're going to get rid of those titty girls in the corps de ballet! All the boys at the school will wear uniforms, with a silver lyre emblem on the breast!" Then wailing again, "Oh! What's going to happen? What's going to happen?"

I needed to escape. I hugged Lincoln, patting him on the back. "It'll be fine, Lincoln, it'll be fine. It'll take a while, but it will all work out," and stumbled out the door.

"The tyranny of one man is over"? The cankerous sore that never healed in the depths of Lincoln's soul was this realization—Balanchine was not in service to him; Lincoln was in service to Balanchine. If he rebelled, Balanchine would have continued without him, unflappable, unstoppable. Lincoln had spent most of his life raising money and doing public relations for Balanchine. What frustrations over the years had accumulated, with great lakes of resentment dammed up? What a marvelous mess of a man you were, Lincoln!

I loved Balanchine, but I loved Lincoln more. Why? I think it's because Balanchine was unassailable, with no chink in his armor. Lincoln was a wounded giant full of holes in his soul, like the character Lenny in *Of Mice and Men,* only Lincoln was a genius of clashing intelligences. I loved that intelligence, his energy, his wild, skewed, and opinionated statements and ideas, his monumental visions and passions. I imagined I understood his inner terror. Many find his prose hard to read; I relish it. In it, I hear him speaking and understand his mind. Whether or not I agree with him, it's passionate writing, scathingly honest, but because I know him so well, I recognize the manipulation.

Balanchine was the central influence in my life. He defined serenity, a calm heartbeat to Lincoln's crescendos. He rarely exhibited anger, but if he did, it was shocking. An incident that took place on the stage of City Center: I was in my first year in the corps de ballet, my sixteenth birthday yet to be reached. Some union rule had been broken, and a big shot in the stagehand union came onstage and interrupted Balanchine's rehearsal. Balanchine avoided acknowledging him, as if he was a buzzing fly. The union chief called all work to a halt. "Everything's stopping. Get off the stage. If you don't, I'll close you down. You won't even be able to walk in the stage door."

Balanchine became incoherent, spitting inarticulate words; fury distorted and twisted his tongue. We felt embarrassed, yet protective. No one wanted to see him this way. This was not our Mr. B. Eventually, cool heads prevailed. Union rules were addressed, problems solved, and the next day, we were back dancing. Balanchine, the serene master we all knew and loved, reappeared.

The only other time I saw Balanchine vulnerable was in his servile devotion to Suzanne. It was unnerving to witness Balanchine lose his equilibrium, but it humanized him, and made him more lovable, more like us.

"Mr. B, he needs someone with him twenty-four hours a day," Karin told me on November 2, 1982. "He fell and broke ribs, several, and has a hairline fracture in his wrist. He is going into Roosevelt Hospital." When I heard that, I became numb. God! It's happening.

Ronnie Bates ventured, "Our boss looks like he's out of it, so the two of us have to work to hold all the good together, because there is some lousy stuff going on." Ronnie never told me exactly what he meant by "all the good" and "lousy stuff." I assumed he meant Balanchine's legacy, and what would replace it. Feeling isolated, the dancers were closing in on themselves. We were emotional wrecks. Cliques were forming. Whispering groups collected in clusters that would break apart if another dancer walked by. Shaun O'Brien and Frank Moncion joked, "Everyone at SAB will have to learn to speak Danish as a compulsory language to be eligible to join the company!" A virus was loose. Its symptoms—gloom, avoiding eye contact, staring at the floor. Our pervasive furtiveness seemed to lower the wattage of the light bulbs. I was no better, separating myself from everyone, not even confessing to Carrie the depth of my congested spirit. My shaft of light was NDI, spending time with a thousand children who had never heard of Balanchine or NYCB.

At breakfast one morning, Chris challenged me. "Do you want to run this company? Because if you do, you'd better start fighting for it. You're going to have a battle." I thought, "Dear protective Chris, worried about his papa's position and image." I answered, "Chris, dear, the last thing in the world I would want is to open the door to Balanchine's office and call it my own."

Many years later, Peter Martins, who was doing his best to run the company, told me that Suzanne Farrell had demanded that she share with him the artistic direction of the company. He could continue to run the operations, but she would be in charge of Balanchine's repertoire, and Balanchine's office would be hers. They split. Suzanne left the company and eventually formed her own group, the Suzanne Farrell Ballet, based in Washington, D.C., and inspires the dancers in her group by the model she projects.

Despite the lack of hope in NYCB as Balanchine declined, I continued to try to enlist the help of every doctor I knew, trying to diagnose what was wrong with Balanchine. On my visits to him at Roosevelt Hospital, he would speak to me in a mixture of Russian and English, as he oscillated from good days to dreadful ones.

On November 14, he was delightful—he looked good and sounded fine. Proudly, he claimed, "I have four," gesturing to his broken ribs. Lying on the bed in a blue hospital gown and viewing the TV with a young Hispanic nurse next to him, he explained, "Better this morning! The dizziness still, when standing and walking, and a little sometimes when sitting, too. But my ears hear sound underwater." We talked more than an hour. Topics ran the gamut, from advice on choreography to the importance of a costume designer. "You must choreograph, explore new ways to move. Experiment, experiment, then throw away. Everyone must be dressed beautifully. You must find your Karinska." (I mentioned China Machado—the legendary model—and her exquisite taste, knowledge of clothes, and expertise as couturiere. Mr. B seemed to like the idea . . . perhaps it was my description of her beauty.) The conversation went to Petipa vs. Bournonville. I said, "You mean you don't like Bournonville?" "No, I like . . . it's just I think he's a step backward from Petipa." Again, he brought up his script he had given me many months before, his preface to *Nutcracker.* Inspired by the original *Tales of Hoffmann* story, the script explored the early life of the Mouse King. Who was he? Where did he come from? "Maybe you can make big television special. Get your friend, the star, Mary, to do it."*

And, oh, how he waxed on about the talent of the company's dancers, in particular, Darci. He mumbled that maybe in the future, he could still function, supervising revivals and maybe choreographing some easy pas de deux for the company. Then, "No. I am finished. Nothing for me. Now, it is all other people." I reflected on how he lived in the present. The word "now" meant a great deal to Balanchine. He used it often. He made plans for the future, but lived the "now" of the moment.

At the hospital, among the get-well cards on Balanchine's table, I noticed one, collectively signed, "Your stage crew," and another, "Your devoted orchestra." I saw none from "the dancers of NYCB" or "the students of SAB."

November 26, 1982. If Balanchine ever had a best friend, it was Karin von Aroldingen, and Balanchine's fading hit her the hardest. Her relationship with Balanchine was rarest among his multitude of muses—a principal dancer, happily married, and a mother, she was his arm-in-arm confidante. Poor Karin was extremely depressed. Balanchine called on her constantly. She might be onstage performing, but he would phone backstage and demand, "Get her off the stage, I need to see her right now!" Once, after a lengthy visit in the hospital, when Karin and I were leaving, Balanchine lamented, "I'll be here for six months." I replied, "No! You must get out, get back home. Every

_____

* Mary Tyler Moore

morning, do your physical therapy, afternoons, too." With a doleful look, and plaintive voice, he importuned, "Karin, stay awhile." I waited outside in the hall some fifteen minutes until she came out. We walked back to the theater in silence.

Two days later, talking a blue streak, Balanchine announced, "I can go home next week!" We were sitting shoulder to shoulder on the edge of the bed, the phone right on his lap. I believe he was forgetting numbers, not hearing, or pushing the wrong numbers and not getting through. He demanded, "Call theater for me, I need Karin! Call the stage." I dialed the switchboard. "Hi! This is Jacques, can you ring the phone up on the stage?" Impatiently, Balanchine called out, "Tell them it's Balanchine!" as if afraid they had forgotten or discounted him. "Tell them it's Balanchine!" His voice betrayed a flicker of doubt. He had been calling Ronnie Bates to make nonsensical demands and requests—"Go look in the rosin boxes! There's no rosin!" or "The curtain is stuck! Get it fixed!"

Lincoln's secretary, Mary Porter, confirmed that the SAB benefit would feature the Mendelssohn ballet I had been playing around with (Jerry's ballet was definitely not ready, and I heard Peter Martins had refused to do one). I thought to dedicate the ballet to the teachers of SAB, and notes had gone back and forth with Lincoln as to titles. Mary hinted, "Lincoln likes 'Dedication.' " I teased her, "How about calling it 'Progression of Heirs'?" Mary got all twittery, taking me seriously, and nervously squeaked, "Oh! With all the talk and worry now about THE SUCCESSION, that would not be a good title."*

Soon, Lincoln sent a note, saying he didn't like "Dedication" as a title. "It's pretentious and presumptuous." I wrote him back, "Lincoln, I picked that title because Mary Porter said it was your choice." With Lincoln's erratic notes and Balanchine dying, I felt both my parents dismembering.

It was almost a week before Christmas, and Carrie and I made our daily visit to Balanchine. Francis and Paul Sackett, with Vera Zorina, dropped by, and Balanchine hardly acknowledged them. When they left, he stared at Carrie and spoke at length about how lucky I was to have her to take care of me. How he had no one, how he wanted to go home, but was scared and needed help.

---

* There were several attempts to find a title. Eventually the ballet was called *Celebration*. It was thrown on in a hurry and disappeared just as fast.

We all knew he would not be going home. Dr. Bill Hamilton told me they planned to set up an apartment-like room at the hospital for Balanchine, with costs to be covered by Eugenia Doll.* The nurse told me, "Go anytime, they'll let you in. Visiting hours for Balanchine are open." Maria Tallchief's daughter, Elise Paschen, and Suzanne Farrell came by. Suzanne stayed for about twenty minutes and left, announcing dramatically to me in the hall, "I can't bear to see him like this. I'm not coming back. I want to remember him the way he was." Melissa visited, too—heroic, brave, and generous. Nancy Lassalle and Barbara Horgan came as well, bringing the newly published catalog of his works, *Choreography by George Balanchine* (1983).

Lightening the gloom at the NYST was *Nutcracker,* with children dancing joyfully on the stage while families watched gleefully from the audience. Frank Moncion, as Drosselmeyer, fixed his hair to look like a crown roast and played a goofy, doddering figure—delighting all of us onstage and in the wings. Except Jerry, who hated the interpretation and was livid. Lincoln was furious, as well. The rest of the company cheered. Our pent-up sadness needed a release valve.

The day before Christmas, Carrie brought Balanchine a small tree, encrusted with hanging fruits. She remembered him speaking of his struggling Russian childhood, and how they hung fruit from the branches of their trees, as they had no ornaments.

Early in the morning on December 26, the hospital seemed deserted. "Hi, Mr. B. Is this a good time? I'm on my way to class!" He ignored me. His balance unsure and with trembling legs, he shuffled over to the bathroom and went in, leaving the door ajar. I kept jabbering. "Carrie has a new soup for you. Chris danced last night, he was so great. I rehearsed the NDI children in your tango.† You can come see it when you get better!" and so on, an avalanche of blather. More shuffling sounds. "You okay in there, Mr. B?" He was standing over the little aluminum sink, with his false teeth in one hand and a toothbrush in the

---

* Eugenia Doll was an ex–Ballet Russe corps de ballet girl who had married Henri Doll, a multimillionaire.
† Balanchine's song for NDI's 1983 Event of the Year (for which we were, at that point, rehearsing) was eventually performed by my son Christopher and Janet Eilber, along with roughly a thousand New York City schoolchildren and a group of New York City police. The whole show was narrated by the actor Kevin Kline. Bits of this dance are featured in the Academy Award–winning documentary *He Makes Me Feel Like Dancin'* (1983).

other. He couldn't manage to clean them; the teeth kept slipping out of his fingers and falling into the sink. "Here, let me do that for you." Seeming somnambulant, he allowed me to take the teeth and toothbrush. I cleaned, polished, and rinsed his teeth, returned the toothbrush to the plastic cup on the sink, placed his teeth in his hand, turned my back, left the bathroom, leaned against the wall, and wept.

The next day, Tanny in her wheelchair, Carrie, Chris, and I made a quartet in his room. A bit later, the stunning Christine Redpath came by with our chief of wardrobe, Leslie Copeland, aka "Ducky." We tried to be silly and light. Balanchine proclaimed drolly, with a woeful expression, "There's no more cabbage in my soup! What's borscht without cabbage?" We giggled, and debated the virtues of various recipes. "The hell with cabbage, what about beets?" Ducky queried. "They're more 'ealthy," he continued, exaggerating his Cockney accent. Tanny piped up, "The hell with the health and the beets, it's the dollop of sour cream that counts!"

On the way out, Tanny was grim. Angrily, she told Carrie and me, "God should have let George get old, like Churchill or Adenauer. It's so unfair. He survived a lung operation, giving up smoking, cutting down on drink, a triple bypass, and now this! *THIS* is to finish him—defeat him? I feel so betrayed. George is losing the ability to see, hear, and communicate." She speculated that though his illness seemed sudden, several incidents in retrospect made her think that it may have been going on for a long time. "Ten years ago," she recounted, "George was talking to me about plans for his Audubon ballet, describing a section he envisioned for Diana Adams, called 'Lady Skunk,' and described her costume in detail. 'Very chic.' Not long after, when I talked about 'Lady Skunk,' he looked at me as though I was nuts, as if he had no idea what I was talking about."

"Tanny," I commiserated, "it's a tragedy, his mind is shorting out." Tanny shot back, her voice hoarse, "That may be a blessing. He isn't aware that his own legs are worthless. Let's hope he dies off. Who knows how old he really is, he may be lying. We should feed him lots, get him fat so he won't last long, so the next heart attack will work."

In silence, we took the elevator down. I got Tanny out of her wheelchair and into a cab. Carrie and I trudged home.

Returning from her morning visit a few days later, Carrie said, "A rotund, motherly nurse told me in a soft Caribbean accent, 'He was very bad today. Abusive. He calls "Karin, Karin," and can recognize her footsteps in the hall. He counts them, and, when she has to go, doesn't want her to leave.' "

New Year's Eve, 1982. Did my morning class, then over to visit at one thirty p.m. Balanchine alone, talking in Russian, and crying. I held his hand, and petted and stroked his face and head—he kept scratching his own head and stroking it himself, then started pulling the sheets over his mouth and up to his face, as if hiding from something frightening. I too was frightened and shaking and needed to move, so I took him for a tour in his wheelchair, zooming up and down corridors and careening around corners for half an hour. Then we took the elevators, and visited other floors. When we returned, one of the musicians came by to thank Balanchine for the new wooden floor under our orchestra pit (they had all signed another card, "Happy New Year's Day/Get Well"). Eddie Bigelow helped organize a little gathering—Bill Hamilton, Carrie, and a few others, less than ten. Suzanne showed up. I was surprised, remembering her dramatic statement a few weeks earlier. We drank champagne and toasted the New Year, with little hope. Tanny had articulated what we all felt—no elegant exit for him, just a long, undignified end with a wail.

For the next three months, while paddling in the stream of life, there was always an inner cry in my throat, "When will he die? When will he die?" Karin seemed never to leave his side. A great, loving mother, she would sit next to him on the bed, holding his head against her breast, stroking his hair like a child, and softly singing lullabies in German.

> *Guten Abend, gut' Nacht, mit Rosen bedacht,*
> *Mit Näglein besteckt, schlupf unter die Deck'!*
> *Morgen früh, wenn Gott will Wirst du wieder geweckt.*
> *Morgen früh, wenn Gott will Wirst du wieder geweckt.*
>
> *Good evening, good night, with roses adorned,*
> *With carnations covered, slip under the covers.*
> *Early tomorrow, if God wills, you will wake once again.*
> *Early tomorrow, if God wills, you will wake once again.*

Carrie put it beautifully, "She [Karin] received from him lots, but gave back even more and is still giving back." Once, when there seemed to be some improvement, a cute nurse, Ana, from Cali, Colombia, and I each took an arm and walked Balanchine halfway down the hall and back. Because he claimed to have vertigo, he had not walked in weeks. Propped against the wall, he sang a Mexican conga while Ana and I danced for him.

I wrote a note to myself: "Jacques, something is wrong with you. You're too tired and listless—and you have let your body go, it's getting weak and functioning poorly. Balanchine is wasting away. Are you doing the same thing to yourself?"

I went over to see Mr. B on Easter Sunday and found him unconscious, with two nurses feeding him intravenously. "His pneumonia is back," was their grim statement. I stayed only a minute.

April 30 was a glorious, glittering spring day. I was awakened at six a.m. by a phone call from Barbara Horgan, reporting quietly, "Mr. B died around four a.m." "Thank God!" I thought. "He didn't drag on anymore." It was spring renewal, but with tears.

Later that day, at the theater, rehearsing half a hundred children for our coming NDI Event, Shaun told me he was there the night Balanchine died.

> Daisy, there was such a bustle outside his room, with agitated nurses running in and out. One of them said, "He can't see anyone," and shut the door. I stood outside . . . for over an hour. I kind of knew what was happening, but couldn't leave . . . Then, through the closed door, I heard Balanchine calling, "MAMA!"

On April 30, 1983, at the age of seventy-nine, Balanchine died.

Working with NDI children at the State Theater's rehearsal hall, I found myself foggy and disoriented. Balanchine used to hear the dancing feet of NDI children from his office below and come up to watch. Today, it was Lincoln who stuck his head in, stared for a moment, and left—I suspected he wouldn't let us use the theater's studios for our Saturday-morning rehearsals anymore. Outside the theater were the dance critic Jennifer Dunning and a swarm of cameras and paparazzi. "Hey, sir, wait. Don't you want to make a statement?" I didn't answer, pushed my way through.

Late that evening, I met with Gail Papp at the Public Theater to discuss a project, but it was impossible to talk, so Gail and I opened a bottle of champagne, and drank toast after toast to Balanchine.

Balanchine's Burial

Tuesday, May 3, 1983. Balanchine's funeral commenced at nine a.m. The church, located on Ninety-third Street between Madison and Park avenues, has a mouthful of a name: *Cathedral of Our Lady of the Sign, Synod of Bishops, Russian Orthodox Church Outside of Russia.* At Russian Orthodox rites, there are no pews or padded kneeling pillows, so STANDING ROOM ONLY means more than a packed house. By eight a.m., the church was already full, but my family and I squeezed ourselves in, got a candle each, lit them, and by nine o'clock were immovable. A few people fainted standing, unable to fall. Packed together and unaccustomed to standing in place, we undulated in a slow dance, shifting our weight from foot to foot—hot, tense, bereaved, seeking comfort. As I looked up, I'd swear the figures in the icons layered up the walls were rocking too. Hundreds gathered outside the church, blocking the doors.

In the sanctuary, the environment of loss was thick and darker than a shadow's shadow. On my left, almost crushed by the mass of people, was Tusia, the mouse-like Russian seamstress, four feet tall, weighing about fifty pounds. She had been a devoted serf her whole life to the great costume designer Madame Karinska.* As a pagan sorceress or goddess has a familiar to do her bidding (the black cat to a witch, Jiminy Cricket to Pinocchio), so Karinska had her Tusia.

Occasionally, my gaze would meet other pairs of tearful eyes, pause a moment, then sadly move on. Familiar friends nearby received a hug and then a silent separation: Allegra Kent, Merrill Ashley, Kay Mazzo, Tanaquil LeClercq. Across the way stood Alexandra Danilova, the legendary ballerina assoluta (in the ballet world, there is no crown higher). Danilova was known for her gorgeous legs and, at seventy-

---

* Karinska retired in 1977 after designing *Vienna Waltzes.* She died in October 1983, some six months after Balanchine. She was ninety-seven years old. An excerpt from my diary, December 11, 1954: "Karinska told me a friend asked her what she had put in the costumes that made Jacques stay in the air so long? 'Love,' she had answered."

something years old, she was still teaching. At that time, I was taking her class regularly and admired how beautifully those still-elegant legs demonstrated a battement tendu.

She headed a cluster of balletomanes—a White Russian mafia—seamstresses from Karinska's costume shop, teachers and administrative staff from the School of American Ballet, and other Russian friends and cronies, all paying homage to the man who epitomized and carried forward pre-Soviet culture through the art of ballet.

Balanchine had preserved vestiges of another time and culture, and to Danilova and all the Russians, he represented St. Petersburg and the Maryinsky Theater before it became Leningrad and the Kirov. As many present-day Cubans loathe Castro, so the White Russians loathed anything Soviet. Balanchine choked with anger when, at the UN in October 1960, Nikita Khrushchev spoke vehemently about how the Communists would someday crush capitalism. Khrushchev took off his shoe and slammed it into the desk before him repeatedly, and said, "We will bury you!" Though you rarely saw Balanchine lose his cool, he was still choking the next day, complaining, "They're not translating it truthfully! Khrushchev is cursing and using foul language, spewing vulgarities of the most common Russian of the street! Peasant pig talk!"

Over a multitude of heads, I spotted Frances Schreuder, the underwriter of Balanchine's ballet *Davidsbündlertänze,* her back to the wall, her face expressionless. Her son had been convicted of murdering his grandfather, and she was accused of conspiring and instigating the murder. Her trial was scheduled for the fall and she was the only person standing in that church who had space around her.*

Eddie Bigelow was at my shoulder. Stuffed into a tall, bony frame with a surly exterior was the heart of a caring, loving man. I reflected—Eddie was there, in thrall to Balanchine and Lincoln, from the earliest days of Ballet Society in 1946. Eddie performed in anything and everything, and was a lifelong servant to dance and dancers. Eddie—filling in for injured corps de ballet dancers; acting the character roles, the monster roles; holding a banner at the back of the stage in *Firebird;* fixing costumes; running errands; dyeing shoes; carrying injured dancers

---

* She was later convicted of the crime and spent thirteen years in a Utah prison. Several books and television movies have been written about her (among them *Nutcracker* by Shana Alexander, and *At Mother's Request,* by Jonathan Coleman). She died in 2004.

to the hospital—Eddie could always be counted on. If you needed a moving man, Eddie carried your furniture up and down stairs. A chef? He would cook giant pots of spaghetti, supply the vodka, Chianti, or scotch, and argue with you incoherently for hours, rambling off lots of words that sounded like they meant something, but we never could zero in on what his subject was. We loved to play cards together . . . canasta, poker, bridge. God bless him. In service his whole life! Behind the scenes Eddie and the self-effacing Betty Cage gave their love, labors, and most of their lives to the ballet company. They should have their Oscars, along with Balanchine and Lincoln.

Suzanne Farrell, white-faced and sheathed in black, stood near the coffin, holding lilies in her arms, like Albrecht in *Giselle.*

The young, imposing Father Adrian, standing over six feet tall, officiated from the altar. He had been Balanchine's priest. Russian liturgy echoed off the walls, intoned by Father Adrian and answered by the many Russians in the church. The power of ritual, communally shared, is meant to establish an architecture of order and become a road to healing, yet throughout the ceremony all I registered was the murmuring and the subdued sobs of those around me, as if my brain heard only the bass line of an orchestra. The presence of deep sorrow generates loss, fearfulness, and even anger. The only comfortable person present and at peace was the deceased.

In my unease, my mind wandered and focused on Bigelow, imagining him in the role he created in the ballet *La Valse:* cloaked in black velvet, white pancake makeup on his face, black circles under his eyes, a shadow of Death; a timeless presence overlooking Balanchine in his coffin.

The high point in the British 1949 movie of Pushkin's *Queen of Spades* takes place at the funeral for the old Countess Ranevskaya. The army engineer, Hermann, who brought about her death, leans over the open coffin to kiss her forehead, and her eyes pop open!

Then, I heard it. A little sniff. Didn't anyone else hear it? It came from Balanchine. One nostril, a slight twitch. Didn't anyone else see it? I saw it! And then another, and then his mouth twitched. A woman near the coffin began gasping, backing up. Balanchine sitting up! Screams! Bodies paralyzed, frozen with disbelief. Others scrambling to get away. Balanchine was looking around. I pushed my way through the backing multitudes to embrace him. And he announced, "I was sleeping . . ."

The service was reaching its end, and lights faded on the stage. Many of us stayed, lined up to approach Balanchine on his bier. At my turn, I stepped up, touched his hand, petted it, really, tears dripped off my cheek. I leaned over to kiss his forehead. Luckily, I did not drip on his face. What did I expect? Balanchine's forehead to be cold on my lips! It was warm.

Leaving the church, Shaun told me that Danilova didn't cry at Balanchine's funeral because, she claimed, "Makeup and tears don't mix."

Carrie, Chris, and I joined Tanny and her buddy, the boyish-looking Randy Bourscheidt, New York City's deputy commissioner for cultural affairs. We packed ourselves into a limousine, supplied by Nancy Lassalle for Tanny's use, and followed the cortege, a line of black beetles traveling in limbo-land along the right lane of the Grand Central Parkway. We were being drawn toward Oakland Cemetery in Sag Harbor, New York, where Balanchine's plot lay open, calling.

There was no small talk in our vehicle, until . . .

"I don't believe it!" Randy declared. He was looking out the window. In the left lane, hurtling by, was Frances Schreuder, alone in the back of her limousine and desperately determined. She passed our entourage, the Wicked Witch of the West from *The Wizard of Oz* melded with Carabosse from *Sleeping Beauty.*

The cemetery, beautiful with its newborn foliage emerging from winter sleep, was a landscape to rest in. The weather was far from restful, a tumultuous, windswept, gray, watercolored day, but appropriate for the occasion. Lost in grief, we gathered on a knoll a short distance from the roadway. Our small group, less than half a hundred, stood around the coffin—each of us touched in different ways by the monument that Balanchine had been.

A large part of our identities was molded by our association with him. As musical themes introduced in the early movements of a symphony come together in the last movement, so did grief, palpable during the ceremony at the cathedral, unite all of us at the gravesite. Few were without tears. I felt divided—a part of me was separate— watching myself and everyone else in a slow-motion dream. I was playing my part in a silent movie, surrounded by a trio of Balanchine's ex-wives: Tanny, next to me in her wheelchair; Alexandra Danilova; and Maria Tallchief, a few feet away. The set, a vision of tree branches running their fingers through the wind. Grieving nearby were Karin von Aroldingen; her handsome, salt-and-pepper-haired husband, Morty; and their yellow-haired, teenage daughter, Margot.

Balanchine never had a family of his own in the traditional sense, except the one Karin, Morty, and Margot gave him. They opened up their home to him, and he was Margot's godfather. He had a comfortable, homey life with them, the kind where you sit around in your underwear reading the morning paper, or watching TV late at night with your feet up on the coffee table and eating junk food. Years earlier, Karin and Morty had acquired a condo for their family in a development in Southampton, and they had persuaded Balanchine to invest in a small one for himself. He loved it there and would cook scrumptious feasts in his sandals and bathrobe. With Karin, Morty, and Margot, he had a life of the ordinary, a world away from Lincoln Center, the State Theater, and his New York City Ballet. The Sag Harbor cemetery is a few miles away from his condo.

We formed a circle, clustered around the grave. Some of us stood alone, others huddled close, perhaps trying to find solace in one another, but, just as in all death, the solitary is supreme. A quartet of lumpy gravediggers waited on the outskirts, leaning on their shovels, routine for them, since they probably bury half a dozen people a day. Outside our circle, on a solo knoll some twenty-five to thirty yards away, stood Frances Schreuder. Conducting the ceremony, Father Adrian led the prayers, the wind blowing his long, curled hair and belly-warming beard into fluttering black-brown ribbons. After the prayers, one by one we went up to the hole and dropped flowers into it. I pushed Tanny there in her wheelchair, her hands like eagle's claws gripping the chair's arms; it seemed all her life forces centered in those clutching fingers. I split the flowers I had, and we threw them on the casket.

The very bones in Tanny's face seemed to tighten. "Get me out of here," she said. She was on the verge of screaming, so I quickly wheeled her toward the limousines.

"We're supposed to go to Gold and Fizdale's,"* I mumbled, "for the reception."

"I'm going back to New York," she screeched. "I've got to get out!"

It took a while, returning along the dirt road to where the cars were parked. At Tanny's limo, she took command, and in clipped, short sentences, ordered a litany of directions: "Don't forget to lock the wheel-

---

* Arthur Gold and Robert Fizdale were duo pianists, and for decades close friends of Balanchine and Tanny's. They had a home nearby.

chair before you try to lift me out. Now, pick me up carefully. Don't bang my head against the edge of the door."

I'd been her partner for years. I used to tell her what to do. I would fling her in the air, catch her, spin her, and always be in total control. At that moment, I was terrified and could barely move.

"Okay, next, make sure my back is placed tight against the seat. Push that switch to fold the chair up, you can put it in the front seat next to the driver. Then you can go, get out!"

Have you ever noticed how quickly mourners leave the cemetery after a burial? Everyone wants to get back to life, as quickly as possible. When I wended my way back to the grave, only the four gravediggers were in sight. As I got closer, I could see someone else, a girl on her knees. It was sweet, round-faced Margot, sprawled out at the edge of the open grave, sobbing, with her arms reaching down toward Balanchine's casket. The gravediggers stood nearby, uncomfortable, unable to shovel in the dirt.

"Get back, little missy," one of the shovelers said. "It's all over." I put my arms around Margot and lifted her out of the way. Where were Karin and Morty? Tanny had taken the limousine and left. I was at a loss. I didn't know how to get to the reception. I didn't know where Carrie and Chris had gone. Frances Schreuder had vanished, and there I was stuck with a dead body and a sobbing teenager.

There was a car coming up the dirt road! Thank God! Karin and Morty were returning with Carrie and Chris to pick us up. PHEW!

When people are under emotional stress, they're likely to indulge their pleasure centers—go shopping, buy themselves unnecessary gifts, drink, and gorge themselves on food. Or the reverse, they go alone into a dark corner and try to sleep, turn off the world. Everyone was confronting a future without Balanchine. The cemetery crowd gathered at Gold and Fizdale's to party, and food was being gobbled and wine flowed. I headed straight for the biggest table and proceeded to slurp away, trying to sample every delicacy at the ample smorgasbord. Amidst all these people, grieving the loss of the giant of dance, I reflected that aside from his favorite muse at the moment—and, perhaps, Stravinsky—Balanchine never cared much for anybody.

Someone tugged my sleeve. I looked down, and there was Tusia at my elbow. Woeful Tusia. (The tugging reminded me of her once fiddling with my arm at Madame Karinska's studio, where I had been summoned for a costume fitting on my day off. It was a sunny, brilliant

Karin von Aroldingen at Balanchine's grave, 2003

day, and I stood patiently, half-clad in a pin-studded muslin mock-up of a ballet tunic. Under Madame Karinska's eye, Tusia basted the gusset, and mumbled, with great foreboding, "Oh, Jacques, you must be careful today. The sun is out.") Gloom was her nature—she had dark circles under her eyes, even when they weren't there. Today, at Gold and Fizdale's, fussing with my sleeve, she mumbled, "Balanchine is gone, Jacques, and soon Madame will be gone. What do we do now? What do we do?" Through a mouthful of shrimp remoulade, I managed, "What do you mean, what do we do? We do what we always do. We eat and drink and keep going."

Tanny had bolted with the limousine, so, champagne glass in hand, I made the rounds, trying to solicit a ride home. "L'chaim!" I proclaimed with every glass. A Hebrew toast, from a people who have suffered great loss and tragedy—responding with a cry "TO LIFE!" Go on, survive, continue! We had him once a little while, and dance did sport with song, but now no more.

I was reminded of a line from Aeschylus' *The Persians:* "Death is long and without music."

In August 2003, Karin von Aroldingen and I visited Balanchine's grave. Standing on the grass over him, I took Karin in my arms, and we danced a waltz. There was an audience. Across a dirt path, less than ten yards away, stood a single headstone bearing the names of Gold and Fizdale; they were buried beneath, one on top of the other. Around a corner of the path was Alexandra Danilova's grave.

Right around the death of Balanchine, I flippantly mentioned to a friend, Hope Cooke, "After fifty, it's harder to stay in the air."

But National Dance Institute kept my fingerprints on the ceiling, and has allowed me to spend a life playing my games—not so different from the stoop in Washington Heights ("You're going to be pirates!" I'd order my pals from the gang. "I'll be the captain! Here are your swords.") Though at the start, I wanted only to introduce children (boys especially) to the magic of dance and the arts, NDI became my way of interpreting Balanchine and Lincoln's legacy—bringing together the highest caliber of artists from the worlds of music, dance, and the visual arts, in collaborations on the highest level—only applying and evolving this legacy in service to children, and vice versa (children in service to the arts).

National Dance Institute

In the fall of 1982, when I wasn't squiring Balanchine from one doctor to another, a documentary filmmaker, Emile Ardolino, followed me around as I taught dance to children in public schools. Emile was captivated by the idea that a whole section of my Event of the Year featured a song by Balanchine. Emile and I had met through the PBS series *Dance in America,* where he and Merrill Brockway were admired for their brilliance in presenting dance on film. Emile came with Judy Kinberg, roped in to be a producer. (In later years, she became a legend for her productions of dance for PBS.) Emile's film, titled *He Makes Me Feel Like Dancin',* released in the fall of 1983, was a sensation, and immediately won a slew of awards, including an Emmy, a National Education Award, and the 1984 Oscar for best documentary—all thanks to Emile's brilliant direction. It launched his Hollywood career, and his next film, *Dirty Dancing,* followed soon after.

In the early spring of 1984, between taking ballet classes, performing, and choreographing the next Event for NDI, I found myself flying to the Academy Awards with forty schoolchildren selected from our New York City program. I had been commissioned to choreograph a dance to Irene Cara's Oscar-nominated song, "What a Feeling." The Oscar producer had originally planned to film a group of children dancing in the streets of New York City, but decided that flying us out to Los Angeles to perform live would be cheaper. In the midst of our rehearsing the "What a Feeling" dance in New York, Emile popped in and informed me of a wild coincidence: *He Makes Me Feel Like Dancin'* had been nominated for best feature documentary! He would be going to the Oscars too! Wow, a double whammy that became a pair of home runs.

Our NDI dancers performed beautifully to "What a Feeling" and the song won the Oscar. The stage manager and crewmembers told me, "We've never had better-behaved children, in any production of the Academy Awards, than your NDI kids." I thought, maybe in LA they expected our NYC public school children to be thugs. At the end of the

Emile Ardolino defending his Oscar, 1984

show, the children were scheduled to return for a final pose, so they were stationed in a holding area on stage right. Over the speaker system, the presenter, Jack Palance, rasped, "Now for best feature documentary, the winner is—*He Makes Me Feel Like Dancin'*!" The camera cut to Emile, scrambling from the audience to make his way to the podium. He had no sooner touched the golden statue than a horde of shiny-eyed NDI children burst from their holding area, flooding around him with outstretched hands, trying to seize the Oscar. Pinned against the podium, he clutched the statue, then held it aloft and, laughing, managed to struggle through his thank-you speech. In the Academy Awards' carefully scripted evening, that moment was the high point. The incident is often shown in highlights from the Oscars.

A few years before *He Makes Me Feel Like Dancin'* won the Oscar, Carrie remarked, after photographing me in the ballet *Movements for Piano and Orchestra,* "I can't seem to snap a good picture of you during performance. Maybe you should get out of dancing that role." "What do you mean?" I huffed. "Right now, there isn't anybody in the company who could do it better than me!" Carrie quietly responded, "Yes, that may be true, but the way you're dancing now is not as good as the memory of the way you danced it last month." I immediately announced to Mr. B, "I don't think I should dance this role anymore. Who do you want me to teach it to?" Within a few years, I had taken myself out of all but a few ballets.

I think most people talk to themselves. And out loud. At least at some point in their lives. And I know in most cultures we commune with the ancestors. I do it all the time. I talk to the Boss a lot. And at most performances, while waiting to make an entrance, I'd say, "This is for you, Vladimiroff." Or, "Oboukhoff, I never had a chance to watch you do *Swan Lake,* but watch the one I am about to do. It's for you." Do I believe there is communication? No. Yes. It focuses and enriches the ritual that is, night after night, the art of performance, and it pays the necessary recognition to our teachers.

In February of 1984, with Balanchine not yet gone a year, I found myself waiting for my final entrance in his ballet *Davidsbündlertänze,* overwhelmed with the realization that, for the first time in my life, I didn't want to go onstage. From that eight-year-old dancing Puck to the man now approaching fifty, I had relished every performance, the rehearsals, the millions of tendus, the varied artists and great ballerinas I'd shared the stage with, and, best of all, the constant striving to make each performance better than its predecessor. I thought, "It's over!" and then out loud, "Boss, it's been great. Thank you, Seda. Thank you, my teachers." There was only that final pas de deux left, with my ballerina, Suzanne, our dance ending with a slow lift, floating her off the stage, into the dark shadows of the wings. So I went on to dance, whispering to the stage, "Okay, Mr. B, here we go, the last of the wine."

A few years back, the executive producer for Video Artists International, Ernie Gilbert, contacted me for an interview. He had tracked down several television shows from the 1950s and '60s, where I partnered, among others, Tanaquil LeClercq, Diana Adams, Melissa Hayden, and Lupe Serrano. In those days, we danced on floors of cement in tiny television studios, and the broadcast was live. If you fell, millions of viewers went "ouch" for you. No chance to fix goofs. Today, when I watch myself dancing on those clips, it's as if it's somebody else. As when gazing at your baby pictures, you think, "I was cute then. What's happened to me?"

Each performance had always been an opening night as well as a closing night—I tried to treat every moment on the stage as if it was my first, as well as last. To be onstage now was a gift; to dance tomorrow was a hope. Melissa summed it best when a fan inquired, "Miss Hayden, what's your favorite ballet to dance?" "Honey," she answered, "tonight, if I dance on the stage, that's my favorite ballet." Balanchine would say, "Why are you holding back? Give everything now. What are

The last of the wine, 1984

you saving it for, when you're too old?" That night I answered, "Yes. I'm too old. I've nothing left to give."

That season was "Goodbye, NYCB." I would still derive joy from doing a ballet barre, but only as exercise. By then, I had already dabbled with several careers, playing around in academia as dean of dance at SUNY Purchase and visiting professor at UC Santa Barbara, and my NDI, in its eighth year, was exploding with possibilities. Now I could throw myself 100 percent into NDI, seeding programs in other cities, developing international exchanges, and stretching staff and purse strings, continuing to invent extravaganzas of dance and theater, while cajoling and garnering every acquaintance, celebrity, superstar, and musician I met to participate.

Through NDI, I found a chance to play the game of dance on a much grander stage, and this second chapter brought something more fulfilling than my career as an individual performer. Today, when I see the quality of NDI teachers at work all over the country, I think, "Look what came from holding that child's hand and teaching him how to lift his leg and how to place it." It's global. I know those NDI teaching artists—the Ellens, the Tracys, the Emilys, the Kays, the Arthurs, the Catherines, the Neals, the Tims, Biancas, Dufftins, Marys, and Jerrys—are transforming another generation, inspiring through the arts, and better than I did. So far, over two million children have been affected by our program, and there's a ripple effect that keeps going. We have alumni who went through the program as children—on our board as well as teaching in our program. And alumni whose children are in our programs.

When in public—buses, trains, on the street, restaurants, airplanes—I am often addressed by people. "Oh, I saw you dance at City Center when I was growing up!" or "I'll never forget you in the NYCB." That's one subject they bring up. The other is, "Oh! You're the guy who works with children. I love what you do." Or, "My son (daughter) was in your program. He's in college now, and still talks about it." "Are you still working with children? I have a granddaughter . . ."

Once, on a packed number 6 subway train going north from SoHo, I became aware of a space opening up around me. Staring at me was a ferocious toughie. As eye contact is something to avoid in the subway, my fellow passengers had inched away nervously. The thug spoke up, "I was a tomato." Everyone froze, but I got it, right away. "You must have been in our 1989 show," I said, "*Meilleurs Amis. Tomates à la Provençale!* P.S. 40, right? You were vegetables dancing with Frogs' Legs in the French Bistro—" "Hey," he answered, "you remember! It was great. But I ain't dancing now. I'm a musician." The train pulled into the station. "This is Fourteenth Street, I'm getting off here. Goodbye! Good luck!" and, battling the crop of commuters barreling in, he shoved his way out the door. Meanwhile, my fellow passengers, smiling now, "Hey, you got a dancing school? Can I send you my kid?"

NDI spread—nationally and internationally. Artistically, in inspiring children through the arts, we are the engine in the front of the train; moneywise, we're way at the back, trying to catch up to the caboose. Not exactly the way the Ford Foundation and corporations would applaud.

But so what? If I had spent my time, energy, and imagination raising money, I would maybe be a wealthy competitor to George Soros, and never have had the time to hold the hand of a child and say, "Try this step."

Each time I can use dance to help a child discover that he or she can control the way they move, I am filled with joy. At P.S. 199 in Manhattan, there was one boy who couldn't get from his right foot to his left. Everyone was watching. He was terrified. And what he had to do was so simple: take a step with his left foot on a precise note of music.

He kept trying, but he kept falling, until finally, he was frozen, unable to move at all. I put my arm around him and said, "Let's do it together. We'll do it, moving forward, in slow motion." We did. Then I said, "Now do it alone, and fast." With his face twisted in concentration, he slammed his left foot down, directly in front of him, smack on the musical note.

The whole class applauded. He was so excited. He was on the way to discovering he could take control of his body, and from that he can learn to take control of his life.

Dance is an art of communication that expresses emotions by controlling and ordering movement, as well as tempo, and molding and defining space. That's what our universe is about. We can hardly speak without signifying some expression of distance, place, or time. "See you later." "Meet you at the corner in five minutes." Even "Where are you going?" implies space and time. Every time you shake hands in greeting or raise a glass in a toast, you're participating in a dance.

The art of dance chooses and choreographs what movement will take place and where, in what kind of space, and for how long, in how much time, how fast or slow. And those selections determine the emotions experienced by the viewer, as well as the performer.

As a performing art, dance has to be taught, and it's best to set up an environment where student and teacher discover together.

Demand precision, be clear and absolutely truthful. Never teach something you don't love and believe in. When I have a new group of young students, I use Madame Seda's technique. I make up a test. "All one hundred of you have exactly thirty seconds to get out of your seats and move to the stage. When you arrive, spread out and hold still. But—no noise, like ghosts." And I whisper, "Go . . . ," and start a countdown. Usually, they run, yelling and giggling, and arrive with several seconds to spare. "You failed the test. There was noise, and most of you got there too soon. I said, 'exactly thirty seconds'—not six or eight or eleven. Go back and do it again. And if you don't get it, again until you do."

They usually get it the second time. Never have I had to do it more than three.

Congratulate and thank them on the extraordinary control they have just exhibited. Once the children see that we are having a class of precision, order, and respect, they are relieved. It's the beginning of dance. Precision and exactness are steps toward truth.

I've taught dance to Russian children, Australian children, Indian children, Chinese children, fat children, skinny children, handicapped children, teenage triathletes, New York City police, ninety-year-olds, and two- and three-year-olds—even a crawling baby. The technique is the same everywhere, although there are cultural differences.

Teaching in China in 1985, I said to the children, "Move closer, so you can see what I am going to do." In New York, everyone would have jostled in, to press around me. But, to my surprise, the Chinese students all backed away. In China, that crowded country, they had discovered the way for a mass of people to see what a teacher demonstrates—not "Move closer," but "Open up"!

As there are cultural differences, there are also differences among individuals. In any group of dancers, some excel more than others. There are many reasons—genetic, environmental, the teachers they've had. Learning curves vary. People blossom at different times. But whatever the differences, someone admiring you, encouraging you, works better than the reverse. "You can do it, that was wonderful, can you show us again? Hooray! The second time was even better!" is superior to "That's no good. You've got to try harder." That may work, but it doesn't seed a love for the subject. YES is better than NO. There is a Hafiz poem that translates something like this:

> *The God who knows only four words*
> *Not the word NO!*
> *Not the word DON'T!*
> *Not the words that cause disorder or conflict.*

Teaching a dance class in any space available. We added girls, 1978.

*The God who knows only four words
Keeps repeating them—*

*COME DANCE WITH ME
COME DANCE WITH ME
COME DANCE WITH ME . . .*

I don't believe there are any untalented children. But I fear there are many whose talents never get to flower. Perhaps they were never encouraged. Or no one took time to find out how to engage them.

However, the single most terrible thing we are doing to our children, I believe, is polluting them. I don't mean just with smog and crack, but by not teaching them the civilizing things we have taken thousands of years to develop. You cannot have a successful dance class without good manners, without respect. Dance can teach those things.

I think of each person as if they had a trunk up in the attic. What are you going to put in your trunk? Are you going to put in machine guns, loud noises, foul language, violence, greed, and ignorance, commercials full of lies? Because if you do, that's what is going to be left after you, that's what your children are going to have, and that will determine the world of the future. Or are you going to fill that trunk with music, dance, poetry, literature, science, discovery, generosity, caring, magic, good manners, respect, sharing, and loving friends?

Fill your trunk with the best that is available from the wealth and variety of human culture. Those treasures will nourish you and your children.

That's what Balanchine liked about NDI. He would always say, "It's so important, what you do. Children, onstage, dancing to music, with costumes and storytelling. Like me, as little boy, in Russia." It made me realize why many of his ballets included children.

"How the hell did you ever start NDI?" is a common question.

"Without thinking," I respond. "I'd go to the principal of a school and say, 'Do you want a dance class for free? Starting with boys only. Not during lunch, not after school, and it shouldn't interfere with their play if they do sports, gym, or recess. Give me any place—a hallway, a corner of a gym, a lunchroom, or the roof." Or outside on the sidewalk.

I paid for my own pianist and a drummer with a full set of drums (which meant two cabs there and back for every school). Initially, there were four schools and a community center out in Bedford-Stuyvesant. The first performance, in May 1977, was at the New York State Theater between matinee and evening. A composer friend, Lee Norris,* put some musician pals together: "Come on, we'll make some music, only I can't pay you!" The stage crew left the lights on for me; a couple of usherettes volunteered to work extra to seat parents and friends out front. Only about thirty of the eighty or so boys I was teaching showed up for the performance. The director John Avildsen† came with a film crew (all volunteers too).

---

* Lee Norris I knew through Michael Tolan, the actor I had met when I was directing and choreographing *Lady in the Dark*. Lee became musical director and composer for NDI for the next twelve years. I think he's a genius.

† John Avildsen and I worked together with John Travolta on *Saturday Night Fever*. Avildsen was the director and I was the choreographer. I spent several months disco dancing with Travolta, working on moves. Using the studio on the top floor of our house, with Carrie filling in for the love interest (not cast yet), we experimented on a pas de deux. Avildsen, after winning his Oscar for *Rocky,* got into an altercation with Robert Stigwood, the producer of *Saturday Night Fever,* and was replaced by another director. Even though I was assured by Stigwood and Travolta that they wanted me to stay on as choreographer, I quit, feeling loyal to John Avildsen, as well as holding the belief that the new director should pick his own choreographer. A friendship was forged with Avildsen that continues to this day.

The show was a little over a half hour, starting with a teaching demonstration and improvisation, ending with maybe five minutes of a choreographed dance. The little film John made, *Dance on a May Day,* I took to the Ford Foundation, and Marcia Thompson, a ballet aficionado, helped me secure a $25,000 grant. I was supposed to use the money to hire an executive director/bookkeeper. Instead, I used all of the money to pay more dance teachers and musicians and expand the program into more schools. The following year, the Ford Foundation gave me—I think it was $17,000—stipulating, "You must use this money to hire an executive director." I didn't.

To the rescue came Sam Montgomery, a corporate psychologist and balletomane. "You need help," Sam announced. "I'll throw a lunch for NDI, and I'll invite two of my clients, Celanese Corporation and McKinsey and Co." Celanese Corporation came in with money, always welcome. Then, at lunch, Sam questioned the McKinsey executive, Pam Bronk, "What are YOU going to do for NDI?" Surprised but cool, Pam responded, "I'll see what I can do." She persuaded her company to underwrite a study: "What Does NDI Need?" Ultimately McKinsey paid for Pam to serve as NDI's first executive director to help us organize and create a true institution, while she conducted a search for her replacement. Within a year, she joined our board of directors. Sam also persuaded a friend, Jean Schumacher, head of a public relations firm, to work for NDI pro bono.

We have always had great music. Every dance class in every school we partner is graced by a superb pianist or percussionist, and live music is central to every one of our events. Stellar musicians, singers, and narrators abound. From 1979 to 1989, our Events of the Year were held at the six-thousand-seat Felt Forum at Madison Square Garden. For that decade, Lee composed and orchestrated hundreds of compositions for our Events, and conducted them all. Galt MacDermot (best known as composer of the musical *Hair*) composed and conducted a sensational score for one of our Events, *The Shooting of Dan McGrew,* based on the poetry of Robert Service. Subsequently, Jed Distler, Neal Kirkwood, Peter Mansfield, Dave Marck, Tim Harrison, and, today, our musical director, Jerry Korman, have waved the baton and given NDI the best in musicianship.

The internationally admired composer and eccentric genius David Amram composed and conducted several shows for us, and no one was more fun. David is a farmer (a real farmer). He kept his chickens, goats, and vegetables clustered on a few acres in New York State, a couple of hours north of Manhattan. A world traveler, David didn't need to know languages; he'd play music—any instrument from any culture. Around his neck, he wore a necklace of whistles, shakers, and sound-producing goo-gads. I never saw him without it, even in black tie. Collaborating on a score for an NDI show about India, we were hosted for a week by Howard Gilman at his White Oak plantation. A nine-thousand-acre spread on the border between Georgia and Florida, White Oak is home to a menagerie of animals, endangered species, strange birds, and thoroughbred horses. While staff members saddled up a couple horses for David and me to ride, David spotted a huge collection of varied hunting horns displayed on a nearby wall. One after another, he began to play the horns. Dogs all over the nine thousand acres began to bark. Horses in their stalls whinnied and reared. Snarling cheetahs ran in circles; rhinos snorted and stamped; giraffes quivered; and the herd of zebras stampeded. Birds all over flew in panic. The phones in the stable clamored, "Stop him, stop him!" Oblivious, David was transported—composing symphonies, in his mind, for thousands of horns playing in zoos throughout the globe. That's my kind of guy. Even though he named his prize donkey Jacques.

Celebrity songwriters have been inspired by NDI, and gifted us with original lyrics and music—Martin Charnin, Arthur Schwartz, Jule Styne, John Kander, Dick Hyman, Morton Gould, and Judy Collins have all come through with original songs for NDI over and over again. Even Chris, my son, came up with a honey of a song titled "Legs Diamond." Josh Logan wrote me songs and lyrics, as did Balanchine, who wrote me several and saw every NDI Event from the front row until the year he died.

Visual artists have responded to my request to create backdrops, donate art, or otherwise participate in NDI—from the early days, I list just a few: Red Grooms, David Levine, Alex Katz, April Gornik, Eric Fischl, and, more recently, Robert Mitchell, John Alexander, Ann McCoy, Leo Meyer, Robert Rauschenberg, and his brilliant disciple and superb artist Darryl Pottorf.

Our international exchanges started with China, in 1985–86. Fifty children from Beijing and seven children from the Shanghai Conservatory of Music who played ancient instruments came to perform with more than fifteen hundred New York City schoolchildren. Twenty-five artists, choreographers, and dignitaries, including Deputy Mayor Bei, from Beijing, came to the U.S. for a month.

They brought a silk drop the length of a city block, depicting an abstracted version of the Great Wall of China. The Chinese government wanted to spread the effect of this exchange, so the drop was painted by 150 children from three different cities in China—fifty each, from Shanghai, Xian, and Beijing. We used it for the first act.

Alex Katz designed the scenery and props for our second act, and a bevy of American stars came to perform—Ann Reinking, Cloris Leachman, Mary Tyler Moore. My children Chris and Charlotte (stars themselves now) performed to music Morton Gould composed specifically for them. There were dozens of tiny ballerinas I chose from children's classes at SAB and Joffrey Ballet School to dance to *Beijing in the Mist,* a haunting composition by the composer Chou Wen-Chung. Dr. Chou was a professor at Columbia University, and passionate about using the arts to develop positive connections between China and the U.S. Without him, our China-America program would not have succeeded. Judy Collins's song "The Other Side of My World," written for the occasion, has become NDI's signature song. She graced us by premiering it as part of the *China Dig* performance.

THE OTHER SIDE OF MY WORLD
(music & lyrics by Judy Collins)

When I was young, I thought that the world was something I held in my hand.
The stars were my view of the heavens,
The ocean was mine to set sail on.
When the rain fell, I danced in its drops and knew
Somewhere the sun would be shining;
When the moon rose on the mountain,
I knew somewhere day would be dawning.
On the other side of my world,
I dreamed that there was some little child just like me.
We might be as different as day and night,
But we would meet alright
And put our worlds together—someday.
I grew so fast and soon I was tall;
I put all my dreaming aside.
Paradise vanished for pleasure,

And I never walked in the rain.
I had my life on this side of the earth
And you had your life on the other.
Sometimes I'd wake from my sleep,
And I would remember the promise.
On the other side of my world,
I knew there must be some grown-up child just like me.
We might be as different as day and night,
But we would meet alright
And put our worlds together—someday.
Suddenly now, you hold out your hand,
And in it I see my own heaven.
My world and yours are as one;
I know I never was dreaming.
Come take my hand and we'll walk in the sun,
And we'll dance in the raindrops together.
We live in one world at last—I am so glad that I found you.
On the other side of your world,
I am the grown-up child just like you.
We might be as different as day and night,
But we have met alright
And put our worlds together—today.

You cannot imagine the roar that rose from the audience of six thousand when, at the end of the first act, some twenty New York City police officers danced onto the stage—crowd control as the 42nd Street Construction Team started the "dig to China." The idea sprang from Carrie. "When I was a little girl in Highland Park, Texas, I started digging a hole in my backyard, and believed that if I could keep it up, I would have a tea party in China."

In 1985, China had barely opened to the West. At a dinner party, a fellow guest, Dr. Robert Ruben from the Einstein School of Medicine, mentioned that many Chinese students were coming to the U.S. to study Western medicine. His comments added fuel to Carrie's idea. I mused, "Maybe we *could* do something with children and China . . ."

Our Chinese guests were housed in New York at the 92nd Street Y, gratis. The flag of China hung next to the Stars and Stripes outside the Jewish Y, even though I was told that China at that time had not recognized Israel as a nation.

Several of our staff lived at the 92nd Street Y to facilitate and assist our Chinese guests, among them Jennifer Jacobson, who was inspired to learn Chinese. She ended up teaching English in Hangzhou until the government's violent response to the 1989 student protests at Tiananmen Square forced her out. Seventeen years after the original exchange, my daughter Charlotte and her husband, Terrence Mann, adopted a baby girl from China, and named her Josephine. "Dancing with all those Chinese children in 1986 rubbed off on me," Charlotte explained.

In 2003, we received an official return invitation from the Chinese government. "Come to China. Bring children and artists, and work with our children and artists, in Shanghai." The extraordinary entrepreneur Shirley Young, who had been on the NDI board during our first exchange, arranged, underwrote, and mothered our NDI team from the time we left New York in August 2003 until our return a month later. Born in Shanghai and raised in the United States, this brilliant, persuasive woman has devoted her life to engendering positive exchanges between the United States and China, particularly in the arts. "It's been a long time coming, this invitation," Shirley remarked. "The Chinese didn't feel their country was ready for guests before—but they do now. And you can meet and work with Dou Dou Huang, the premier dancing star in China." Several of the 1986 *China Dig* children, in 2003 chic and elegant adults, came from Beijing to join us for our performance at the Shanghai Grand Theater, as did Michelle Vosper and Miss Yu, our interpreters from the first collaboration. For several nights, we feasted together in Shanghai, and laughed about the 1986 exchange and their return trip to China.*

It seems that after their three-week stay in New York City, Deputy Mayor Bei insisted that on the way back, the Chinese delegation make a stopover in Hollywood. He wanted to visit Disneyland, and he got his wish. "We were all standing around outside the Magic Mountain ride," Michelle chortled, "over fifty bright-eyed Chinese children eagerly lined up, ready to go." Deputy Mayor Bei announced, "I go first to test. See if it is safe." He came out of the Magic Mountain tunnel shaking, white-faced, and gasping, "No Magic Mountain! NO. NO. NO!"

* In the summer of 2010, NDI's artistic director Ellen Weinstein and NDI teacher Kaye Gaynor flew to China to collaborate with Dou Dou Huang and dancers from the Children's Palace in Shanghai. They invented a beautiful dance to a Chinese take, *The Red Thread*. The work had its premiere that summer with the Shanghai children coming to America to dance with our New York City dancers.

.   .   .

Over the next years, I did my best to bring the world our NDI children in New York City. "Think globally, act locally," was the mantra, and NDI fostered thrilling international exchanges with Australia, Israel, Ireland, Russia, Indonesia, Africa, Mexico, and India. In our perform- ances, we explored the themes, stories, and cultures of those magnifi- cent lands. In organizing these exchanges, Carrie traveled with me to all the countries, photographing and keeping diaries. We didn't dance together anymore, just toured. Except once.

Leaving Moscow to go to Leningrad (setting up an exchange with children from the then Soviet Union), we were dropped off at the Moscow train station, and went out to the platform early. The wide expanse of the empty platform stretched into gray non-horizon. A few shafts of light came from above, a stage set waiting for action. A Rus- sian locomotive, twice the size of others in the world, stood idling in the station, hissing clouds of steam. It began to snow. I took Carrie in my arms, and we waltzed up and down the platform, in and out of steam clouds while snowflakes, little wet kisses, covered our faces and hands.

The idea of getting Soviet children to come and dance in New York was sparked by the original production of *The Shooting of Dan McGrew.* The original, and precursor, to our Soviet production originated in 1985 at P.S. 29 in Brooklyn, at the corner of Baltic and Henry streets.

In the spring of 1983, Joseph Papp and I were collaborating on a proj- ect, a revival of the musical *Roberta,* when he suddenly queried, "Is there anything else you'd like to do?" "Sure," I replied, "I always wanted to do the poem 'The Shooting of Dan McGrew,' by Robert Service, and utilize an entire school as the cast. How does that grab you?" "What's it gonna cost?" "I don't know, Joe, it'll take about fifty thousand bucks and most of a school year." He sat down and wrote the check.

The school I picked in Brooklyn, P.S. 29, had a principal, Mrs. Zagami. Unfazed when I explained that I wanted to take over her whole school for a month, she responded, "Are you kidding? I'm from Italy! Calabria! I can handle anything!" In the production, she performed as a blunderbuss, with her kindergarteners and first graders (tiny tots) as her buckshot. Some four hundred second, third, fourth, and fifth graders were snow, wolves, reindeer, miners, dance-hall girls, piano notes, and assorted Alaskan riffraff. The teaching staff, I dressed in sandwich boards marked "Whiskey," "Vodka," "Rot Gut"—bottles lin- ing the bar. But, in their scene, the tiny tots stole the show. A miner has

Rehearsal for The Shooting of Dan McGrew *on the roof of P.S.29, 1985*

caught Dan McGrew, played by the superb artist Donlin Foreman, cheating at cards, and in the ensuing confrontation, McGrew maneuvers his accuser so that Mrs. Zagami has a clear shot. She fires her weapon, the blunderbuss (constructed from a French horn on a stick), and blows the victim away—and for close to a minute, streams of buckshot (tiny tots dressed in gray jumpsuits with silver football helmets) gallop over his prone body, gleefully treading on him as the audience howls with glee.

Joe had produced the original production of *Hair* at his Public Theater, and put me in touch with its composer, Galt MacDermot. Galt's thrilling score used lyrics from "Dan McGrew" and various other Service poems, and he conducted the orchestra and singers for performances that took place on the playground behind the school. An audience of one thousand filled the playground each evening for a week. Seated on portable bleachers, they cheered and cheered, as did family members crowding the windows in buildings abutting the playground.

So successful was P.S. 29's Event that we revived it in 1990, at the Brooklyn Academy of Music Majestic Theater (now called the Harvey Theater).

In that revival, I added twenty little ballerinas to dance as ice crystals in an arctic blizzard. Scattered among them were eight visually impaired dancers who had taken classes in ballet with me for several months (two had been born without sight). All danced exquisitely. One prominent lady complained, "Well, where are the blind children? I can't tell them from the others. How does anyone know there are blind kids up there dancing? You should announce it."

I needed to fill out the show, and decided to add a scene with bears, which immediately brought Russia to mind. The poem "Dan McGrew" takes place in the Yukon during the Gold Rush. Russians had explored and settled the region, colonizing the indigenous population. When Secretary of State William Henry Seward convinced President Andrew Johnson to purchase Alaska from Russia for the U.S. (reportedly for over $7 million), the venture was labeled "Seward's Folly." The gist of the ridicule from the critics of the day: "Idiots! You just bought mountains of ice!"

In 1990, perestroika was shattering the ice that had been the Soviet Union. Barriers were breaking, and the Iron Curtain cracked. I thought, "Why not bring over Russian children to guest star as bears?" An ambitious gambit, but, as portents of possibility, two more Georges came into my life—George Kennan and George Soros. I met them both at the home of Sue Railley, a dear friend with a genius for putting people together for mutual benefit. Kennan was the most admired American statesman in Russia, and probably globally. With his connections, all doors in Russia opened. "You are a friend of George Kennan? How can I help you?" was heard anytime I mentioned his name. His daughter Grace had been born in Riga, Latvia, loved Russia, was equally connected, and was a balletomane. She became my interpreter. George Soros, with his generosity in underwriting all of our airfares, relieved me of having to dip into my own bank account.

My back-and-forths to Russia to make this happen reconnected me with some of the great Russian dancers who were my peers and friends. Best of all, in Moscow, I met Gregory Nersesyan, a man who would become my artistic brother. He looked like a small bear himself, slightly comical with an ironic, wry sense of humor. A lover of literature and theater, fluent in English, Grisha translated plays in Russian and English, but his favorite occupations (besides family) were good friends, vodka, and conversation. His wife, Marina, a beauty, always acted as though she had difficulty with English, but she understood and

George Kennan in the center of a doughnut of children, 1990

could speak it quite well, if Grisha ever let her have a chance. Marina's mother was a rehearsal pianist at the Bolshoi, and the world of ballet accompanied that of poetry and drama in their home. Their two children, Nelly and Kyril, were to become entwined with our family. In later years, Kyril danced with NDI in New York, winning friends wherever he bounced his energetic frame.

And so I returned to Russia, not as a performer with NYCB, but as promoter, director, and choreographer for NDI. In Moscow, it was Grisha who found the choreographer, the studios, the musicians, and the children; Grisha who got us in and out of museums, restaurants, and all around Moscow, at times paying for a car and driver. Grisha anticipated every problem, then moved ahead, and solved it before it materialized. In addition to the dancers, he arranged for three children—musicians from the Prokofiev Conservatory of Music—to compose and play an original piece that would premiere in Brooklyn. The success of this Russian exchange was a direct flowering of Grisha's efforts.

Our first Russian exchange was a sensation. The dancing Russian bears and precocious musicians were hosted by families of our New York City children, and the true success of this exchange happened backstage and outside the theater, where bonds formed among children. Unforgettable was the scene of the Soviet children's departure, when their newfound friends from American host families surrounded the bus, all in tears, at parting. Little Russian fingers waved from windows as the bus pulled away. "Don't forget me!" they wept. "I'll never forget you!"

Despite being in his late eighties, George Kennan made the trip from his home in Princeton to Brooklyn for our premiere. After the show, Kennan sat on a fire escape backstage, talking and laughing, smothered in Russian children.

For one Event, *A Day in the Life of Coney Island,* thanks to a conversation at a party, Jim Wolfensohn agreed to underwrite the cost of bringing close to twenty lifeguards from Bondi Beach, Australia, to spend several weeks in New York, to dance and star with over a thousand children. The youngest Aussie was a seventeen-year-old knee-dissolving nymph; the oldest, a leathery, muscled forty-year-old man. They were all triathletes and beautiful. When they'd walk in their surf club uniforms to our rehearsal hall, pedestrians gawked and cars stopped. The cast on our theatrical beach included Penelope Hope, a four-year-old Shirley Temple type from East Hampton, Long Island, and a whole community of senior citizens from Chinatown, led by a ninety-year-old Chinese tai chi master. My sister, Ninette, joined them in their dance. Jim Wolfensohn became a dear friend and has supported NDI ever since. In an Event in 1989, Jim's daughter, Sarah, a superb pianist, played the harpsichord in a scene from the French court where Cardinal Richelieu presided, a hundred secret agents (children dressed as rats) as his spies. The court jester? Nobel Prize winner Arno Penzias, head of Bell Labs, whose discoveries were such as to seriously support the theory of the big bang. As in all our shows, there were dancers—so-called challenged—who performed alongside all the other stars. Dancers in wheelchairs and children with hearing and visual challenges have always graced our stage.

And then there was our India Event. Ted Tannen, from the Indo-U.S. Subcommission, and Richard Lanier, from the Asian Cultural Council, said to me, "Don't you want to do something with India? We may be able to find some funds to help." Over the next two years, Carrie and I traveled to several places in India, mostly southern. We arranged for our New York teachers to tour, as well, and brought Indian artists over to work with our children. It all came together in a mystical performance at the Majestic Theater, performed over two weeks. Red Grooms designed an extraordinary set, and, with Tom Burkhardt and Andy Yoder (his assistants) using electric knives, turkey slicers, carved out of foam a moveable Indian temple, then painted the entire temple in garish colors. Bob Mitchell, one of theater's great scenic artists, designed and had built a golden staircase, rising up to a chakra of the sun. Great artists from India came over to perform with us, headed by Mallika Sarabhai. Michael Moschen, who had just won a MacArthur "genius award," mesmerized cast and audience as Hanuman, the Monkey King. There were beautiful children from the Dhananjayan Academy of Dance in Madras. The music was a mixture of Western and Indian, under the baton of David Amram.

By far, *Rosebud's Song* was the most complex production ever attempted by NDI. Named for Rosebud Yellow Robe, the great-great-grandniece of Sitting Bull, *Rosebud's Song* theatricalized humanity's relationship with nature and the environment on a global scale. Two thousand New York City children represented sunlight and water, as well as varied life forms from land, sea, and air. I needed representatives to portray every human culture on earth. How to do it?

I solved it by seeking children from cultures that live in earth's most extreme conditions—highest, lowest, coldest, hottest, driest, and wettest—and thereby encompass the globe. Carrie packed her camera. She had been the photo chronicler of NDI from its first days, and there is nobody who is a better traveling companion. She traveled with bags of films, lenses, cameras, a case of bottled water, her suitcase, which encloses, among necessities: travel books, diaries to be filled, mosquito netting, vitamin pills, baby wipes, boxes of crackers, jars of peanut butter, and Kaopectate—she's always prepared. We've had to use them all. As joyful and scintillating as she was as a dancer on the stage, Carrie more than equals her performing career as a photographer and diarist. Her charm and wisdom many times saved my blundering and chutzpah in dealing diplomatically with the many cultures we danced across.

The highest place on earth is Mount Everest, which is shared by the countries of Tibet and Nepal. We happened to meet a couple in Santa Fe, John and Carroll Kelly. A photographer and a social worker, respectively, they knew, worked in, and loved Nepal, and told us about a private elementary school, the Mount Kailash School in Katmandu, and its principal, Jampa Lama Wangdu. "Jampa will help you find the children you seek." His parents were old friends of the Dalai Lama, and still lived in a village at sixteen thousand feet, except at the height of winter, when his mama comes down to Katmandu to see her Jampa.

The grand lady of Texas, Lupe Murchison, heard about our quest.

Always serious Divas, 1992

Always smiling Tsering, 1992

"What's it gonna cost to bring children from Nepal for your event?" she queried. "About twenty-five thousand dollars, counting everything," I threw out. "Well, you've got the money, honey." She wrote a check, and Carrie and I flew off to the Himalayas.

Nepal, like India, is best defined as the extreme not only of altitude, but of every human condition there is—from fat to thin, from opulent to destitute. We were housed at the upper economic level, thanks to a wealthy Chicagoan, Tom Pritzker. Tom had lived in Katmandu as a hippie in the sixties, and maintained a home there, which he graciously loaned us. The house and grounds are above the Bagmatic River, and perhaps the most famous of all Hindu shrines, Pashupatinath. Tom's Tibetan staff coddled and fed us sumptuously. "Oh, the pancakes," Carrie sang, "so thin and heaven-sent!" to my accompaniment, "More! Could we have more?"

The American ambassador to Nepal, Julia Chang Bloch, was a dynamic powerhouse of intelligence and charm. She adopted us and our project. When I wasn't dancing with the children at the Mount Kailash School, Carrie and I were treated to parties, hikes, and picnics by Julia. Carrie reflected, "It is nice to know that every once in a while, our government puts the right person in the right place . . . probably by mistake." One trek in particular ended with a culinary extravaganza Julia held on a mountainside terrace. It's in our memory, up there in the "Pantheon of Great Outdoor Feasts."

Throughout our auditions at Mount Kailash, two children

excelled—Divas, a boy of nine years, and Tsering, a girl not yet eight. On their entrance in *Rosebud's Song,* the Mount Kailash children would announce, "We represent the peoples from the highest places on earth, and have come to dance for you."

Jampa revealed that he had been a dancer in his early days and demonstrated simple movements from Tibetan folk dances—heavy and clomping. Over the next several days, we formulated the choreography for the two children, and Jampa handed me tapes of Tibetan music for our New York musicians to use as inspiration. The quality of Jampa and the Mount Kailash School was so impressive that Carrie and I decided to underwrite a portion of tuition for two girls to attend school for the next decade.

Next, from Nepal to the Dead Sea, the lowest place on earth. As the Dead Sea lies thirteen hundred feet below sea level, there could be no argument it was the lowest. Israel and Jordan share that deep valley, and at Israel's Ein Gedi kibbutz, on the edge of that sea of salt, we danced for days. Carrie and I took a day off to float around in the waters of the Dead Sea. Impossible to swim underwater. I closed my eyes tight to keep the salt from stinging, took a lungful of air, and managed to force myself under for a second, then relaxed, and was immediately shoved back up to the surface, as if on an express elevator. You can, however, float for days, as those salt deposits buoy you up. Unfortunately they dry and preserve you as well.

From the moment we set foot in Tel Aviv, this trip to Israel was heartwarming for Carrie and me. Old friends from Denmark, Herbert and Suzie Pundak and their son, Ron, facilitated. How the hell did Ron have time to do it?* He was one of the architects of the Oslo peace accord, and those negotiations were going on concurrently. Yet he found time to take care of Carrie's and

Tamara Annau and Ilana Frank, my Israeli white doves, 1993

* Today Ron Pundak is the general director of the Penes Center for Peace.

my needs, and Suzie accompanied us the whole time, adding her vote in the audition process.

We had other connections who paved our way with velvet carpets. Gracing the NDI board is Nili de Rothschild. Her father is revered in Israel, and I had only to mention their names and Israelis would run blindfolded through traffic to help. Isaac Stern and his then wife, Vera, beloved in Israel, were supporters as well.

After days of auditions, I finally chose two darling girls, Ilana Frank and Tamara Annau, who would later reveal themselves as nurturers. They had caught Suzie Pundak's virus, Jewish mama to all humanity. Their dance was inspired by a pair of white doves flitting among salt deposits. They would be the ones to announce, "We represent those that live in the low places on earth, and have come to dance for you."

To my surprise, the wettest place on earth is part of the United States—the island of Kauai, in the Hawaiian chain. This time, I decided to bring a teenager from our NDI summer program as my assistant: Marie Lanier, a fifteen-year-old gamboling filly, who had a streak of serenity out of place for her age. We were hosted by Benedict Twigg-Smith and her husband, David, in their home on Coconut Avenue in Honolulu. Carrie glowed. "You can dip your toes in the ocean where Diamond Head meets the Pacific." From our bed, one could roll out and slip down into the ocean for a pre-breakfast swim with multicolored fish and green turtles.

Our contact in Hawaii was the legendary dancer Jean Erdman. She

Sandra leads her classmates, August 1993

was never without her red beret, so you could find her in a crowd, whether on a bustling street in New York or the beach in Honolulu. Widow of that guru of culture and myth, Joseph Campbell, Jean put us together with the singer and Hawaiian celebrity Jimmy Kaina. He decided who we should meet, what dance schools we should visit, and in what order. One dance class in a school near Pearl Harbor was conducted by a superb teacher, Olana, and a tiny goddess undulating in the midst of her classmates was revealed—Sondra Toth. She had the type of talent that cannot be hidden. Bury her in the back, and her glow would take center stage. Her parents came from the island of Kauai, but lived in Honolulu. Ideally, we were seeking children who lived on Kauai, so, before choosing Sondra, we decided to fly there and audition locally. In Kauai, my young assistant, Marie, and I danced with dozens and dozens of children, and eventually chose Nalei and Tammy. Carrie took thousands of photographs, and when all the arrangements had been made with the parents, our feastings and visits over, we said goodbye—"See you in New York!"—and returned to Honolulu for a couple of days of R & R.

Marie was going back a day earlier than we, and at the airport, just as she was boarding, I was paged on the intercom. Thunder striking me could not have been more disturbing. It was a phone call from Kauai.

Raul and Daniella in their backyard, November 1993

Nalei and Tammy's parents had changed their minds. I sputtered out, "Why? What's happened?" and received an answer, delivered as though it had been rehearsed, "Our parents and grandparents are from Kauai. Our children were born here. If they travel to New York, later on they may not want to settle and stay on our island. It's better if they don't go." I turned and mumbled to Carrie, "Do you think it's too late to ask Sondra Toth to come?" Marie, who had barely spoken the whole trip, and had paused instead of boarding her plane, walked over to us and quietly piped up: "You lucked out. It worked the way it should have, from the beginning. Sondra should have always been the first choice. She was the best, and isn't NDI about the best?"

During the performances of *Rosebud's Song* in New York, Sondra stole the show. Her heart-encompassing smile, swaying hips, and gentle fluttering hands in her Hawaiian dance, represented all who live near water. Her dance was the key segue into our finale, danced by thousands of children to the music and lyrics written for us by Judy Collins.

The driest as well as coldest places on earth are found in Antarctica, but for where people have established cultures, Antarctica does not fit—except for frozen scientists and explorers.

The driest *inhabited* place on earth is the Atacama Desert on the western coast of South America. Archaeological digs have found beautifully preserved mummies from 10,000 years BCE. In the Atacama, there are places so dry that for hundreds of years, there are no records of anyone ever seeing a plant or an animal.

In the barren desert, in a field on the outskirts of San Pedro de Atacama, we held our auditions. Local children danced for us, and others came from settlements hours away. As we were dancing together, dust devils would appear. These miniature swirling tornados, from two or three to eight feet high, would materialize like ghosts out of nowhere, spin, wave in slow motion at us, then dematerialize. Minutes later, haunting us, another would appear, form, then shift and wave for half a minute, and just as you released your held-in breath and exclaimed, "Look! Oh my God!" they were gone. Carrie tried to capture one with her camera, but failed. I don't think they liked being impressed permanently on anything. The next day, we chose gentle and beautiful Daniella and Raul to represent this arid and eerie landscape of the Atacama. The dust devils did not protest.

For our coldest extreme, outside of Antarctica, Siberia and the town of Yakutsk won out. It is not uncommon for temperatures to drop as low as -80 to -90 degrees Fahrenheit. Most of the town consists of concrete buildings held six to eight feet off the ground by stilts sunk deep into the frozen earth. Giant insulated pipes go from one building to another in a topsy-turvy maze. They bring steam and hot water, while others carry waste and sewage. Telephone poles are crooked, leaning at different angles due to the heaving of the earth.

There are still a handful of charming wooden homes, though none are original. With thick walls, double doors, and triple-paned windows draped with quilted curtains, they are heated by wood- or coke-burning stoves; gradually, the warmth melts the permafrost they're built on. The Polish journalist Ryszard Kapuściński describes the plight of these houses in his book *Imperium:*

> Released from the grip of the cold, the houses become limp and slide deep into the earth. For many years they have been standing considerably below street level; that is because they were built on permafrost and the warmth they have radiated over time has hollowed out niches for them in the icy soil, and with each year they sink into these more and more. Each little house stands in a separate and increasingly deep hole.
>
> Now the wave of April warmth hits . . . and its lopsided, poor little houses twist, grow misshapen, sprawl, and squat ever closer to the earth. The entire neighborhood shrinks, diminishes, sinks in such a way that in some places only the roofs are visible—as if a great fleet of submarines were gradually submerging into the sea.*

They are tough in Yakutsk; schools stay open unless temperatures drop below -58 degrees. Try to expectorate outdoors in that temperature, and your spit will explode as it exits your mouth, and be ice before it hits the ground. I tried to imagine what would happen to the smoke and soot when it froze coming out of chimneys. Again, Kapuściński explains:

> The smoke and soot spewed from the chimneys, freezes in the frigid air, and if there is an atmospheric inversion preventing any wind, the atmosphere becomes so thick that a child bundled up on his way to school can recognize the imprint of his teacher who had walked through the thick soup several minutes before.

* Ryszard Kapuściński, *Imperium* (New York: Vintage, 1994).

Yuli Markov and Lisa Roandall pose on a hot day in May 1993

We were there in mid-May, and bundled in furs. Once again, George Kennan's daughter Grace came as our interpreter, and Grisha made all the necessary connections, through friends in the Ministry of Culture for the city of Yakutsk. He got us from the domestic airport in Moscow, and it took him six hours in that hideous, chaotic, and thug-filled hangar to get us to our plane. We sat on the tarmac for another three, and then we flew through six time zones to the city of Yakutsk. Joining Grace was her friend Evgeny,* a cameraman and journalist, who was recording our adventures for a future television news story.

In Yakutsk at two thirty in the morning, the sun was up and so were the people. Yuri Sheikin, the deputy minister of Yakutsk, was our host, along with a compatriot—a woman named Galina. She was from northern Yakutsk and would be the key facilitator. For the next several days we auditioned and danced with close to a hundred of the most adorable children. Every girl in pigtails, and most of them had training in dance.

For meals, we ate on massive aluminum plates, heaped with mountains of buckwheat groats—kasha. Ladles of boiling fat were poured on the heap, and on a separate plate, what appeared to be slices of Wonder Bread were actually slabs of solid fat. You could opt to wash this down with flavorless sticky sweet soda, beer—or vodka. A whiff of their prize vodka caused brain cells to wither, so I stuck to soda and beer. They claimed the vodka was 400 proof, whatever that means. To touch your lips to that brew caused a third-degree burn. What would it do to the esophagus or stomach lining? Maybe nothing—grease-soaked kasha and fat slabs make superb insulation.

---

* Recently, Grace told me Evgeny burned to death in his country home. A Michael Moore–type of journalist, Evgeny was a gadfly, calling governments and the powerful to transparency and accountability, and was not one to bow to the Russian version of a mafioso threat: "Desist, or we will make you very unhappy." Grace is convinced it was arson.

The local ballet company was performing the ballet *Don Quixote,* and Yuri Sheikin arranged our tickets. The superb training given in the Moscow and Leningrad ballet schools somehow extended all the way out to Yakutsk. The dancers were very good, especially the two principals. This company put most American regional companies to shame.

On our final day of auditions, mothers and fathers filled the doorways of the studio. Of the places we visited, choosing here was the most difficult. There were dozens of boys and girls of equal ability and charm. We paired up combinations, and Liza Lazareva, an eight-year-old Audrey Hepburn lookalike, was a perfect match for our handsome ten-year-old hero, Yuli Markov. Galina recommended the choreographer Lyubov Bogdana Nikitina, and we had many meetings with her before we left. As with other choreographers, it was not carte blanche, there were guidelines. I knew approximately the small area of the space they would dance in, maybe fifteen by twenty feet, and each dance was limited to approximately three minutes. Lyubov would be responsible for the dance movement and choice of music. "I think the musician should be shaman," she proposed. "Whatever you choose," I responded, "just let us know as soon as possible, as passports and visas have to be arranged."

A year later, at the first rehearsal in New York City, our American musicians were in awe of the sounds that came from the shaman. His two-inch fingernails tapped a small round drum, alternating with beats from a thin stick with one end carved into a small ball, sort of like a musical quarter-note with a twelve-inch stem. His rhythms supplied background to bizarre magic conjured by his voice—bird coos, crows, hisses, howls, and grunts—plus the whistling vibrations from a Jew's harp tucked in his mouth. The range of pitch, at times, soared so high ears screeched, and in lower registers the shaman's rumblings caused your stomach depths to quiver.

Traversing the globe, experiencing the extremes of landscape, Carrie and I were amazed by the people. How they hold on to life, clutching at their habitat, no matter how inhospitable, surviving and developing roots and culture in unforgiving conditions. The beauty and awe-inspiring tenacity are a hymn to the imagination and intelligence of the human being.

To top the thermometer for blasting heat, the Danakil Desert in the Horn of Africa claims the crown. Nomads wander the Danakil, African versions of Native American Comanche and Apache—fearsome warriors. The Afar tribe is legendary. They would share with us three

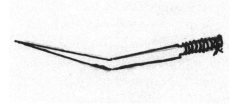

Drawing of an Afar warrior's knife

of their extraordinary children—Osis (eleven years old), Zahra (ten), and Hussan (nine)—none of whom had been in an automobile before, much less flown in a jumbo jet to the Big Apple.

We pulled it off, but did we have help. To get to the hottest place on earth, you start in Addis Ababa, Ethiopia. There, the United States Information Agency, a branch of the State Department, came to our aid, along with assorted NGOs and personal friends. Addis Ababa—"new flower"—the capital of Ethiopia, is an up-and-down town on the side of a mountain. We arrived the day after Ethiopian Christmas, January 8, chock-full of vaccines, yellow fever shots, and malaria pills, and were handed a printed State Department directive: "Visitors shouldn't drive outside of Addis Ababa, the countryside is riddled with explosive mines, and violence and banditry are rampant." On arrival at the airport, a jazzed-up version of "God Rest Ye Merry, Gentlemen" blared from the loudspeakers. Carrie laughed, "Do I hear castanets in that music?" A gentleman from the USIA, Dell Hood, met and mentored us, and introduced us to a bevy of people. Aside from Dell, Isaac Russell, who just arrived from the States, was to be a star on our project. Isaac had been a lawyer in municipal bonds based in Hartford, Connecticut. In his mid-fifties, after putting his youngest child through college, he passed the Foreign Service exam and started a new career. Isaac traveled with us to the Awash region of the Danakil, where a contingent of the Afar were reputed to be encamped. He insisted we carry our own saline solution, because, if needed, a transfusion in a local clinic would most likely kill you.

A charming woman, Tision, representative of the government and assistant to the minister of the arts, was our guide. Aside from our driver, we had a cameraman, Mateos, and hopefully on arrival we would be met by two interpreters, Sisay and Abdu. They had left several days ahead of us to seek out the Afar. We traveled in a Land Rover, first to a town called Nazareth for an overnight. "When the sun goes down, we don't travel," Isaac cautioned us. "If you drive after dark you can be in big trouble, or dead. Bandits put barricades across the road, steal the car and its contents, and kill the occupants." After fitful dreams of mayhem, at dawn we continued on our way.

Our three winners, Zahra, Hussan, and Osis, January 1994

Our destination was a station (outpost) called Melkased, and, despite no visible roads, we eventually found it. It took us some five hours before we spotted a handful of trees and a few thatched huts. And the Afar—with Sisay and Abdu standing among them, beaming. The warriors were wrapped in white robes, and each had a Kalashnikov draped over his shoulder. Their long stork-like legs and pancake-flat feet were shod in thick leather sandals, and they carried wicked-looking knives shaped as if a straight blade had been bent slightly in the middle, a crook in an elbow. These sinister blades in their scabbards swung groin high, draped on cords from the warriors' necks. Behind the huts, we spotted some sixteen children waiting. These eight-to-twelve-year-old youngsters auditioned with trepidation. I kept them jumping, bouncing, spinning, switching feet, and spiraling à la Martha Graham. Carrie, with her eye rarely leaving the camera's viewfinder, was in heaven. Luckily we'd brought a drum with us, and within the first five minutes I zeroed in on the most awkward dancer in the group, and made him "KING DRUMMER."

Little by little, as I eliminated, I would add to the "King's orchestra," instructing new members, "You, clap . . . you, whistle . . . you, hiss! Take these sticks and beat them together. Here's a stone and a pot!" My percussive and vocal group grew and sounds, thuds, whistles, clicks, clatters, and swishes accompanied the dancers, until the musical ensemble had reached thirteen. By then, my orchestra was jamming, and I had zeroed in on the last three dancers—two boys and a girl. I called an end; we had danced nonstop for three hours.

Their chieftain had spent this entire time observing us, then commanded, "Wait!" and disappeared. We didn't know what to think; perhaps he was consulting with the other tribal members and the parents? While we all sat and waited for the chief to give his imprimatur, yea or nay, Carrie grabbed the three—Zahra, Hussan, and Osis—and took off for a photo op. In late afternoon the chief returned with the three children's parents and, with a slow nod of his head, solemnly announced the Afar word for "yes," then demanded the interpreters inform us, "Do you know why we let you take our children from their homes? Because the way they will behave while in your land will show you our honor, and the whole world will know that we Afar are God-fearing people." Mythic, grand—and, as it turned out, prophetic.

In the late spring of 1994, our varied groups from the earth's geographic extremes gathered in New York City. As with the Chinese delegation in 1986, the 92nd Street Y housed our guests during their stay. NDI staff stayed with them, but I knew the two Ein Gedi kibbutz girls, Ilana and Tamara, would become the leaders, worrying and fussing over the other children. I could even imagine them reading bedtime stories to the others and tucking them in. "Has everyone gotten enough to eat?" "Anyone need help with anything?" And, sure enough, when I was harsh during rehearsal to Zahra or Tsering, or any of the other children, those two white doves from the Dead Sea would coo and flutter around them, commiserating and stroking hurt feelings. In a kibbutz, everyone has to share and care and be responsible for their duties. In the midst of bedlam, trying to stage dances for two thousand children as the orchestra rehearses, scenery is being hung, and lighting plots created, I noticed, out of the corner of my eye, Ilana and Tamara practicing. They wanted to be perfect, and they were. When they weren't polishing their own dances, they were helping the others with theirs.

Besides the children from the extremes of the globe, I had gathered all my production elements together and finally chosen the star. Alexandra Rosen, a nine-year-old girl from a public school in New York City, won my heart with her simplicity, bright smile, dancing energy, and innate modesty. She would be my Rosebud, the girl-child plucked from a hole in the earth and presented to the sun at the climax of the show. She would weave, from the earth's myriad life forms, a blanket—a rainbow cloak for all the earth to wear on a trip to the stars.

I don't believe it would be possible today to recreate what *Rosebud's Song* became. Not with millions of dollars and a high-powered team could Disney come close. Almost one thousand Native American children in the U.S. painted their faces on canvas and sent them to us to hang as part of our scenic backdrop.

Hundreds of Native Americans from dozens of reservations drove across the country to attend our Event, and Clinton Elliott, from the Ojibwa tribe, was our narrator. We featured Native American singers and drummers, Broadway dancers and musicians, and some thirty string players from the Mannes College of Music. For our final act, they played excerpts from Stravinsky's *Apollo*. Judy Collins wrote the most exquisite song to grace our finale.

On opening night, directors, choreographers, and producers all cede power to the performers. I sat out front, became a member of the audience, and waited to experience the unfolding of what I had envisioned, choreographed, and produced. It didn't happen quite that way. The bear-sized Clinton Elliott, who was programmed to commence with an opening speech, departed from anything I'd written or directed. He started chanting in his Native American language, reaching into a pouch he had slung around his waist. He took out handfuls of tobacco, crumbling and scattering them over the stage floor, as he walked in circles and back and forth across the stage. Blessing the space, he continued his chant, calling on all participants, audience included, to

The entire cast, wearing a rainbow-colored blanket, 1994

celebrate and take part in the ritual about to unfold. My hair stood on end, one of the great moments in theater, and it lifted us right out of the Paramount Theater at Madison Square Garden and into a sacred, timeless arena.

Leading to the climax of the performance, the Woman of the West (my daughter Charlotte, dressed as a Native American woman) refuses to bring the child, Rosebud, from the hole in the ground. "I must wait till all are here," she announces. On cue, the two thousand New York City children streamed onto the stage, dressed as fish, birds, flowers, insects, plants, rocks, and trees. The dancers representing water were the last to arrive, streaming down the aisles of the theater and breaking onto stage, and when in place, the entire cast called out, "Show us the child!" The Woman of the West answered, "But now we must wait for the people to come."

Two thousand children parted, backed away from the audience, and sat, as Tsering and Divas arrived. "We have come from the highest place to dance for you and see the child," and the clumping Tibetan choreography Jampa and I had choreographed almost a year before began. The two thousand New York City children sitting in a semicircle watched, open-mouthed, without stirring or moving as the succession of guest children from the extremes of the earth gave us their dances. The only moment to equal the mythic power of Clinton's opening chant was the sound and vocalizations made by the shaman from Yakutsk. Had Joseph Campbell been alive, he would have cried out from the audience, "That's what I've been writing about all my life!"—being connected to the metaphysical, the collective, the essence and ancientness of it all. The rapture of it. And what a varied, gorgeous mosaic of the human family was represented by the array on that stage, the beauty of those faces—the Afar, the white doves. Daniella and Raul in their Chilean folk dance. Dear Sondra Toth, with her lilting water dance, the last of the "people" to dance.

Satisfied that all had assembled, the Woman of the West conjured Rosebud up from under the stage floor to stand high on a platform at the back. Rosebud appeared holding a circular drum in her arms, and as she beat, the entire cast responded, as if the stage floor itself was in the throes of an earthquake. She danced to the rhythms of her drum, causing two thousand multi-costumed children to respond in patterns across the floor until a rainbow-colored quilt had been formed. Rosebud was carried, as a floating form, above the dancers, threading through and among them, accompanied by Judy Collins's song:

ROSEBUD'S SONG
(music and lyrics by Judy Collins)

Let us weave a blanket together today
Threads made out of silver and gold.
A blanket that will warm us
And keep us from the cold,
A blanket that will stretch from pole to pole
Let the cold stand with the snow.
With garnets that are pink and sapphires that are blue
Add the strands of opals and emeralds too.
Tapestry of wonder, tapestry of light
Tapestry to stretch from day to night.
Let the rocks chant to the waters
And the flowers to the trees!
Semiprecious jewels, rainbow-colored light.
My oceans and rivers flowing day and night.
Many-colored landscapes every form and hill
Make a bridge that carries me to you.
Let the fish and birds and insects
Every one of them embrace!
When the north greets the south
And the west goes to the east.
Let the highest touch the lowest!
Let the hot know the cold!
And the day returns to night.
All our threads of silver and multicolored bars
Now we have a tapestry that is ours.
Underneath our blanket, safe at peace we are
Ready for our journey to the stars.
Underneath our blanket, safe at peace we are
Ready for our journey to the stars.

Rosebud arrived center stage during the last few lines of Judy's song. Then, the entire cast swayed, a giant blanket undulating, and the strings from the orchestra swelled into the sublime chords of Stravinsky's *Apollo.* A giant glowing sun rose from the back of the stage, the entire cast pivoted to face the back, and two thousand hands reached for the sun. As the stage lights faded, we saw a sea of silhouetted hands reaching toward the golden globe. Except for Rosebud. On the darkened stage, she continued to face front, and slowly reached her hand above the audience as a pinspot faded on her face.

I lost touch with Alexandra (Allie) Rosen until March 2007, when the following letter arrived. It answers beautifully a question often asked of me: "How many children who pass through NDI go on to have a professional career in dance?" I answer, "I have no idea, and I don't worry about it. NDI is so much more." Allie's letter expresses this better than I, or anyone, ever could.

Dear Jacques,

I need not remind myself, or anyone else for that matter, that it has been over ten years since I played Rosebud at the Paramount Theatre at Madison Square Garden. When I turned 23 in January of this year, I remember thinking how I remember exactly how I felt the moment the stage lights hit my face for the first time when I was 9 years old. I was terrified, yet incredibly energized—knowing that I was the luckiest nine-year-old on the face of the earth.

Not a day goes by when I'm alone that I don't think about what my life would be like now if you had not pulled me aside on that Saturday back in 1994 and said, "You are going to play Rosebud."

You obviously don't need another reminder from someone about how you changed their life. If you had a penny for every child's life you've impacted, I know you would be a millionaire. The other day I was telling my boyfriend of two years how I had never thanked the man who is responsible for my self-confidence, and most of who I am today. So, Jacques, I want to thank you for everything you have done for my life. I currently live in Charlottesville, VA. I am an Executive Marketing Assistant for a small management company here.

Unfortunately, my dancing days are over. After I graduated the dance program at LaGuardia High School back in 2002, I decided that being a "Prima Ballerina" wasn't exactly in the cards for me. Plus, I loved food too much, and my teachers said I didn't have pretty feet. Lucky for me, I was smart enough to earn a 3.8 GPA in college, and graduate "cum laude." That's that.

I'm not sure when you will get this, as I am sure you're busy changing the lives of unsuspecting children. However, I wanted to let you know that you are always in my heart, and will continue to be the most amazing mentor!

Be sweet, Jacques!

Much love,

Alexandra Rosen, NDI Class of '99

On a day off, NDI took all the visiting guests—children and adults—on a trip to the Bronx Zoo. At a cage where five leopards were dozing, one of the Afar children, Hussan, slipped loose from our group and squeezed his head through the bars of the cage and started singing. The cats' ears twitched, their eyes flashed, their noses tested, and the five of them padded straight to Hussan. We rushed to him as well, but then stood frozen, afraid to breathe—in half a second, any one of those cats could have ripped out his eyes. Crowds began to gather. "Hey, Mabel!! Come quick, bring the camera! The kid's singing to the cats!" Hussan sang on, with five pairs of unblinking feral eyes inches from his nose. Suddenly, he paused, several silent seconds, and then made a god-awful sound from the back of his throat, grating and guttural. The cats hissed, bared their teeth, spun, and fled. Hussan pulled his head out from the bars, turned around, and, beaming power, chuckled, "Heh, heh, heh, heh, heh." I demanded of the interpreters, "Ask him what the hell he was doing!" Eventually, they gave me Hussan's answer: "First I did my calling song for the big cats, and when they were ready to listen, I scolded them because they had eaten my goat!"

The interpreters clarified: "You see, the Afar believe if you speak to one rock you will be addressing all rocks; one tree, all trees; one leopard, all leopards. Especially the leopard back home in the Danakil that ate his goat."

A few days later, I sought out the Afar children. "Come join me for lunch." We ended up at a pasta place on Columbus Avenue. Carrie was in the darkroom, so it was just the three Afar children, two interpreters, and me. It's hard to make conversation when English words and concepts have to go through Amharic to Afar and then back, but we managed. "Here's a test for you," I announced. "What is the biggest thing there is? Just absolutely the biggest thing you can think of?" After much discussion among the three, the answer came, "Buildings." "No, no," I said, "buildings are only the biggest things around here. I mean the biggest thing you can think of." I knew I had even the interpreters engaged; I could see them trying to guess what I had in mind. If you asked most college students or professors this question, eventually most arrive at the universe or the cosmos. I sat there smugly, thinking of how I would announce that infinity and eternity are the biggest things there are.

The three children had made their choices. Osis answered, "Human beings"; Zahra, "The world"; and Hussan, "My mother." Well, I started my questioning. "Tell me, Hussan, why is your mother the biggest thing there is?" His answer: "I feel my biggest when feelings and emotions are so huge inside me that I am exploding from the inside out. That is how I feel when I think of my mother." "Zahra, you next, why did you pick the world?" "Because, if I could walk from now until I was old, maybe I could walk around it. But, maybe it is too big and I would die before I could." "Okay, Osis, now you. Why human beings?" He floored me. "Human beings are the biggest thing there is because human beings can *think* of BIGGER THAN BIG IS." Infinity and eternity are concepts coming from the imagination of the human mind. From an eleven-year-old illiterate nomad of the desert? WOW. "Human beings can think of BIGGER THAN BIG IS."

After *Rosebud's Song* had its week of performances and the visiting children were due to return to their cultures, we gathered the children from the geographic extremes of the world, their choreographers, the musicians, the interpreters, and our staff—and took a vote. It was unanimous: the Afar children were the most interesting. They had mesmerized us all.

When it was time to say goodbye, we had a party at Tavern on the Green, hosted by its generous owner, Warner LeRoy. I wondered if I would ever see these children again. Perhaps Ilana and Tamara.

Each of the children received a gift of five hundred American dollars, and returned home with those bills entrusted to the hands of their interpreters and chaperones. I have my doubts regarding the Afar children. I was naive; their dollars probably submerged into the pockets of the adults and never reached their tribe or family. Today, with wars and genocide ripping the area of the Danakil, I fear Hussan, Osis, and Zahra are no longer alive.

A decade earlier, I had taken off my costume and put away my ballet shoes. I rarely attended any ballet. But the ghost of Balanchine permeated so much of my teaching and choreography. Within a few years, it would be Lincoln's ghost, too.

Death of Lincoln

He ended up a recluse, sequestered in his bedroom. I heard he'd died on January 5, 1996, and I missed his funeral but attended his memorial at the State Theater. I don't know how he died—his heart and energies gave out, I guess—and I'm not sure why, but I miss him more than Balanchine. Maybe it's because my relationship with Balanchine was clear, complete, solidly set in grooves. Like an old couple, it needed no further development, and had nowhere to go—whereas my relationship with Lincoln remains unfinished. I shared the years of Balanchine's deterioration and his death, seeing him practically every day. Not the same with Lincoln. For over a decade, I had little contact with him.

Soon after Balanchine's death, Lincoln wrote and requested that he be taken off the NDI board. I wrote back, "You don't have to request. Just resign if you want, but I wish you wouldn't, because having your name is of great value." Several months later, he issued another communication, officially leaving the board. Somewhere along the way, he sent me a check for NDI, I think in the range of $3,000, with the statement "Now I don't owe you anything."

On every pathway in arts and culture, as well as many other fields, a person walking will stumble across the footprints of Lincoln Kirstein. Omnipresent, he had been there, and off the pathways, too. His Napoleonic ambition to be decision maker of all the arts and culture in the country was at odds with never-ending doubts about his own taste. Often, in a discussion with me about ballet, a book, or music, he would bellow, "GOOD TASTE IS MY TASTE!," bolstering himself, posing as the pope pointing a finger, only his fingers had chewed-up nails.

Eric Hoffer, my longshoreman philosopher friend, tried to understand what generates creativity. He eventually said he couldn't figure it out, but imagined that it had something to do with tremendous inner conflicts spawning energy that seeks outlets: tectonic plates scraping abrasively and generating inner volcanoes, earthquakes, and mountains. Eric would have loved Lincoln.

397

Lincoln had wished to be a supreme artist—in particular, a world-class painter, poet, or novelist—but he held himself up to those arts' highest models, and could not find within himself the belief that he could equal them. So instead he turned to support others whom he felt had talent and potential. But like a juggler tossing objects or a light switch flipping, his impulsive belief and support for the chosen ones would turn on and off. Lincoln rarely remained a fan of anything.

Occasionally, at Lincoln's command, I would be summoned to his home in Gramercy Park. He envisioned me a component, some clay for a sperm-of-the-moment plan he had conjured. Lincoln's wife, Fidelma, was an artist and painter, and sister to the more renowned artist Paul Cadmus. Paul was one of the rare few I never heard Lincoln disparage, and I suspected they had been lovers.

At times, Fidelma would make an appearance. Large, brown eyes, rounded, hers were deepened by dark circles, as if she hadn't slept. Staring at you or downcast, she always seemed about to tear. Her lips were dry and cracked, but her voice was soft and tentative, mumbling, as if in her attempt to verbalize, she imagined being clobbered down or ignored. Slim and graceful, Fidelma found it unbearable to be stared at or judged. She became a shade seeking out shadows. Fidelma liked me, and managed to tell me so, perhaps realizing I was not another male inhabitant of their home to whom Lincoln had taken a fancy. I thought he would probably berate me to her after I left. "What's there to like about *him?* He's just an athletic street kid who has become a dancer. All he cares about is applause and show business."

Fidelma never stayed around long, slipping off to another room, I imagined a bedroom full of cats. She and Lincoln, incompatible in so many ways, adored the feline. Fidelma and Lincoln loved and respected each other in tormented ways (love does have a way of finding expression in roller-coaster shapes—look at the Boss and my father, and, for that matter, Carrie and me). As Yeats wrote so beautifully:

> *O love is the crooked thing,*
> *There is nobody wise enough*
> *To find out all that is in it,*
> *For he would be thinking of love*
> *Till the stars had run away*
> *And the shadows eaten the moon.*

With Kyra Blank in class

Fidelma died before Lincoln. Diminished away in a home some-where, I was told Connecticut, I believe unhappy that her life never had its own independent purpose, separate from her brother and Lincoln.

And poor Lincoln, chewing himself up all his life. I imagined him in gloom declining, his doubts in ascendancy like a poisoning perfume. By contrast, Willam Christensen died at over ninety years old, bellow-ing and protesting that he couldn't be in the forefront of the doers any-more. "My time has passed!" Lincoln handled "my time has passed" by hiding in a room, shrinking into darkness. Energy dripping away, he kept his room dark (I hear), and the mattress, his pillow, his clothes, became extensions of his depression. Eddie Bigelow was there while Lincoln's ashes were spread on a pond near his home in Connecticut.

Months after his death, I was informed, "Lincoln left you something in his will." A package arrived, a painting of me from the early 1940s, as an eight-year-old in Kyra Blank's class. It was painted by Fidelma, and I know it was early September in the painting, as my hair is reddish from a summer in the sun. Standing first at the barre, I'm looking ador-ingly at Kyra Blank, with two stolid-faced, grim would-be ballerinas in tutus behind me. It hangs in my office, where I point it out proudly to every unfortunate who enters.

Cris Alexander and Shaun O'Brien's contribution to the above

Balanchine and Lincoln left the legacy of the New York City Ballet and the School of American Ballet—two edifices that I believe may outlive the memories of themselves. Balanchine wanted a place for himself so that he could indulge his art with music and the dancers he admired. After, he didn't give a damn.

Lincoln wanted it to last forever. So one of them got their wish—or maybe both . . .

How many dancers know or care who started, for example, the ballet school of the Paris Opéra, the Maryinsky ballet school in St. Petersburg, the Bolshoi Ballet? Royal Danish? The Royal Ballet in England? Maybe Wikipedia knows.

Death of Milly

She would come into class and head for her favorite place at the barre. Uh-oh, some innocent dancer had taken it. "Hi!" Milly would blurt in a high-pitched grate. "You're new, aren't you? Well, welcome to the company. You're in my spot." Cowed, the new member of the corps (we'll call her Harriet) would slink away to another place, only to be summoned back. "It's okay, you can stand here, but not too near, or on the grand battements, I'll kick you!" We all knew Harriet would soon be adopted. Milly would coach her about her toe shoes—"I like Capezios"—her makeup and hair: "Use a light base, honey, and let me fix your hair." "Where is she? Where's Harriet? Where's my girl?"

When Milly finally retired and stored her toe shoes away, she took to teaching. First she had a school in Saratoga, and, later, one in NYC,

Saratoga Racetrack—Milly would dance anywhere, 1973

eventually becoming a legendary teacher at the North Carolina School of the Arts in Winston-Salem. Anyone who has ever taken a class with her will never forget it. She brought the same integrity, generosity, and compassion to teaching that she had to dancing, plus the blunt talk.

Don Coleman, her husband, dedicated his life to supporting the woman he had married, and she managed an amazing career, while birthing and nurturing their two children, Stuart and Jennifer.

Another of the multitude who changed their names, she was born Mildred Herman. Up until fifteen years of age, she was a top-notch swimmer with dreams of serious competition. Her first ballet class awakened dreams of another stage. She came to New York, got a job dancing at Radio City Music Hall. Got herself into the corps of American Ballet Theatre. Then as a soloist in the Alicia Alonso Company, and finally as a principal in NYCB. We were partners on the stage and in the rehearsal studio for the next several decades.

August 2006. I'm walking up Columbus Avenue. Around Sixty-eighth Street, a couple of patrons eating lunch at a sidewalk café called out, "Jacques d'Amboise! Did you hear about Milly?" I stopped. "You mean Melissa Hayden?," and prepared my public-persona smile, ready to answer, "Oh, I'm delighted you liked my dancing back then," or "Yes, my work with children, thank you." Instead, I was stunned dumb by their next words, "She's dying!" Further up the avenue, I ran into the dancer Suki Schorer, bouncing and gamboling down the street fresh from a tango lesson. "Did you hear? Melissa's got pancreatic cancer." Columbus Avenue was "Bad News Avenue."

That evening, Richard Dryden from NYCB called. "I've got bad news," he intoned, in his singsong voice. "I know, I know," I barked out, "Melissa's dying."

I had not been in touch with Milly (except for an occasional phone call) in almost twenty years, and now I'm getting all these messages? "Go see her!" I thought.

I purchased a plane ticket to Greensboro, North Carolina, rented a car, and drove to Wake Forest Hospital. Milly's daughter, Jennifer, was on the same flight. When we got to the hospital room, Don, who is partially deaf and suffering from diabetes, was slumped dejectedly in a chair. Melissa, weighing some sixty-seven pounds, lay in bed with an enormous oxygen mask that seemed larger than her tiny head. She had patches of straggly hair, dyed jet-black, that looked like strands of seaweed on her sweaty forehead. She looked simian, and the band that held the oxygen mask in place irritated her scalp, so she was continually fiddling with it.

Milly looked up at me, took a few gulps of oxygen from the mask, pulled it from her mouth, and said, "Jacques? Oh my God, Jacques! You came down for my last dance." Back she went for more oxygen, then continued. "Don! Jenny! Is he staying overnight? If he is, there's a pot roast in the freezer." Puff, puff. "Just put it in the microwave!" Puff, puff. We all made small talk, reminiscing about ballet, fellow dancers, and grandchildren.

Shortly, a drained Milly announced to me, "I've always loved you—you were my best friend. I loved you first." Don, slouching in his chair, snapped to the vertical, eyeballs popping. Milly continued, "My husband was second."

I quickly corrected, "Second to your husband! Don was always leading the pack." She stared at me for almost a minute, puff, puff, off went the mask, and she declared, "That's not what I said." Later, Carrie commented, "Of course, she was right. You *knew* her over five years before she ever met Don. That's what she's saying."

On July 28, 1950, we were gathering on the stage of the Royal Opera House in London for morning class when someone announced that it was my birthday. "Hey everybody, Jacques just turned sixteen." "Oh!" Melissa cried out. "Sweet sixteen! I bet he's never been kissed. Well, come here, honey, I'm going to show you how it's done. And, as your birthday present, I'm going to kiss you every day for a whole year!" I got that first kiss, and at the next morning's class, awaited the second with passion. Well, the morning kisses lasted less than a week. On the sixth day, she grabbed my face, covered it with kisses, including my ears, and announced, "All right, honey, that's it, and it's gonna have to last you for the year!" With the entire company laughing, she delivered the coup de grâce, "When you're seventeen, maybe I'll have something else for you!" I became Milly's pet—she said I was like her Saint Bernard, hanging around, waiting.

In her hospital room that August of 2006, I leaned over her to say goodbye, kissing her wet, plastered forehead, then sat for a moment on the edge of her bed. "Milly, this is goodbye. I guess I won't see you again."

She answered, "Well, it's a mystery, and I'm going to go find out. You know all this bullshit about the afterlife? Well, there is one. It's what's left behind, from the way you lived. We did a good job. Goodbye."

NDI Goes On

I took the example of the Sturm und Drang surrounding Balan-chine's demise as to who would lead NYCB in the future, and thought about NDI: "Don't wait. Set up your replacement." So I asked Ellen Weinstein if she would share with me the responsibility to run NDI, and if she wanted, to take over. That was almost two decades ago, and one of the few times in my life I showed any wisdom.

Ellen had been a student of mine when I was dean of dance at SUNY Purchase and then went off for a career as a dancer. Several years later, she popped up in New York. "I'd like to try teaching a little bit. Do you think I could?" Then, a little bit later, "I'll teach, but I won't choreograph. I don't know how." Then came, "I'll choreograph, but I won't direct. I don't know how." Then, "Okay, I'll direct, but I'll need help." Every step Ellen took, she overwhelmed her doubts, and today she guides NDI into its future.

The program started in New Mexico I passed on to Catherine Oppenheimer. Catherine had been at SAB with my twins, and had gone on to perform with NYCB. After Balanchine's death, she danced with the Twyla Tharp company, left and joined NDI. In New Mexico she has made a superb NDI model and a huge success. One of our earliest and most loyal board members, Val Diker, funded and guided that New Mexico program until it was stable and healthy.

Lori Klinger was responsible for seeding a program in Ohio, and in Richmond, Virginia, called Minds in Motion. Lori is artistic director for Rosie O'Donnell's musical theater program, Rosie's Broadway Kids. And there is Tracy Straus, a teacher-choreographer of sunlit ability; she brings joy with dance like a female Johnny Appleseed, birthing NDI babies wherever she goes. From coast to coast, there are NDI programs.

Ballet rarely interests me now. No more can I make love—through coaching, partnering, dancing with and sharing the stage—with those beautiful ballerinas and artists that grace the ballet. When I'm in the audience and I see a ballerina of such incandescence, I yearn to dance with her, to touch and lift, to manipulate and feel the heft of her, and the magic of her movement. Impossible now, for this older guy with bad feet and knee replacements, daydreaming in the audience of rolling the Russian star Diana Vishneva in my arms!

Dénouement

In 1989, I wrote an article for *Parade* magazine, the insert used in Sunday papers nationwide. In it, I spoke of how Madame Seda put my hand on the ballet barre and conjured a love of dance, then passed me on to Balanchine. She didn't have any boys in class, and my sister really was superior to the other girls. Seda gave us up and sent us to the School of American Ballet. It was her expression of love, not so much to us, but to dance.

A few months after the article was published, I received a letter from Madame Seda. I had not seen or been in touch with her for decades. She was in her mid-eighties and had been retired for several years.

> Dear Jacques,
>
> Ex-pupils of mine from all over the country have been sending me copies of your *Parade* article. Your words made me so excited about teaching that I'm thinking of going back and starting again. Thank you, dear Jacques, for writing so well of me, I who did so little for you.

Her letter touched my heart. I saved it, planning to visit her.

In New York City, I cram more into my schedule in one day than I do in a week anywhere else. I dash frantically from one appointment to another. I put off the impulse to visit Madame Seda. Shelved, it lapsed.

One morning, months later, Seda suddenly popped into my head and kept repopping. I wondered, "Has she started teaching again? I should call her." The next morning, Seda again, "Oh, I forgot to call you, Seda. I bet you're teaching class right now, and in your blood-red skirt. Tomorrow," I told myself, "I'll reschedule everything, I'll go out and visit her." This went on for a week. Then one morning, I couldn't stand her repoppings; so I headed for the car, following a road map, to her home in Stony Brook, New York.

Her driveway was full of parked cars. It was an ordinary suburban house, but all the doors were open. Outside the house, balloons and banners attached to trees swayed in the breeze and music waltzed out

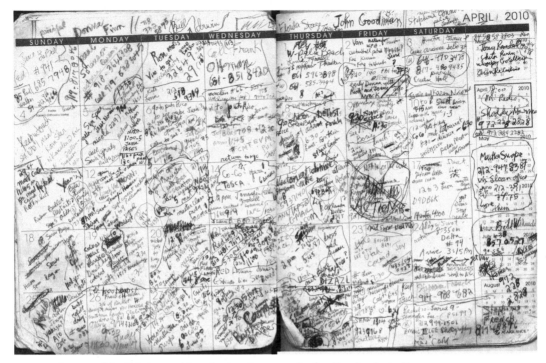

Jacques d'Amboise's monthly calendar. An example of a disordered mind!

the windows. "Ah, there's a party," I thought. "I'm glad I came." It wasn't, and it was. She had died, and it was her wake.

The house was packed with ex-pupils, relatives, and friends. Videos of her teaching were being shown in several rooms. In the living room, the last video taken before her death showed her triumphant. She sat proud, under a gaudy red and gold canopy, playing a portable organ while singing an old sentimental Russian song. In the lyrics, I recognized the words *"Das vidanya." "Das vidanya"*—goodbye.

Seda's training was in Russian classical ballet, but she was Armenian, and folk art was in her soul. Armenians are energetic, passionate, and colorful people. Costumes she made were everywhere, over the curtains in the windows, hanging on the backs of chairs, draped on hangers, hooked to doorjambs and picture frames. Colors that would clash in a painting swirled in harmony here, overlapping figures advancing in a polonaise. Each costume had received Seda's exquisite attention to detail—embroidered with buttons, jewels, crystals, and sequins clustered in a variety of patterns, proclaiming rainbows and a world-class seamstress. I don't recall a bland outfit among them. Tiaras, headpieces, feathers, and plumes graced tabletops and bookshelves. Hundreds of thousands of hours she labored, so her students could become royalty in her theatrical productions. A crown for every princess, a doublet for every prince.

I couldn't rest my elbow anywhere. On every surface, where there wasn't a costume, headpiece, or dance program, sat platters of food and glasses of wine. The air was warm, throbbing with a pungent feeling, accompanied by a constant ebb and flow of voices and music, punctuated by the occasional soloist. As I wandered from room to room, a high-pitched voice exclaimed, "Hey, there's my costume on the wall." Someone pointed at the video. "Look. That's me in the back, the one in the yellow." Another voice, "Oh, that dance—she had us all on toe. God, it hurt!" Food-stuffed mouths, glasses emptied and refilled. Everyone moving, talking, gesturing, a community in a slow dance embraced in good cheer. "Oh, Jacques"—someone I didn't recognize grabbed my elbow—"I'm so glad you're here." I was led around. "This is Jacques d'Amboise. He used to study with Seda." Another high-pitched voice burst in, "Hey, I remember you. How's your sister?" Memory-drenched, I called out, "Thank you, dear Madame Seda, for first putting my feet in fifth position."

I can trace back a direct line from those first classes with Seda and her teaching techniques through over six decades of my career and the formation and success of NDI. I have hundreds of thousands of children and teaching and performing artists who I'm connected to—a community, an extended family, a tribe, united through the DNA of dance and music.

GEORGE

A therapist once said to Carrie, "You can trust your children." When I heard that, I blurted, "What does she mean? Of course we trust our children! How could you not?" "Just read the news," Carrie answered. So that brings me around to our quartet.

Number one son, George, over fifty, lives in the jock capital of America, Boulder, Colorado, and manages a store when he's not skiing, hiking, snowboarding, cooking, and wine tasting. He's a people lover, always finding the right thing to say, the thoughtful action to help anyone who seems wounded. He's a healer.

Balanchine flanked by father and son d'Amboise and bracketed by a quartet of pussycats

And he loves to play. Fairy tales and myths are the ocean he swims in. Children circle, gravitate to him, and climb on him. Our grandchildren live waiting for George. Imagination, off-the-wall, and vibrating, with cuddly love, is George. Carrie and I continue to refer to him as "the Miracle."

CHRIS

Christopher was made for the performing arts. Talent, oodles of it, and he is gifted with perfect pitch, supporting an amazing memory for sound and dialogue. As a boy, he'd watch a television show, gather the family together, and have us howling with laughter as he recreated the dialogue, complete with background music and sound effects. In NYCB, when not starring onstage, he'd go to the orchestra pit, sit next to the clarinetists, and, within a few months, play the repertoire. Besides piano and clarinet, he decided to learn the trumpet, and occasionally played in clubs with jazz bands.

A principal dancer with NYCB, he danced most of the repertoire, and starred in works created for him by Balanchine, Robbins, and Peter

Martins. He tried everything, even a stint on Broadway, costarring with Bernadette Peters in *Song and Dance*. Bernadette the song. Chris the dance.

A voracious reader and an excellent writer—*Leap Year,* his teenage autobiography, was published early in his twenties, with Jacqueline Kennedy Onassis as his editor. The poet Yeats wrote plays where music and dance are necessary to the presentation. And Chris's play, *The Studio,* could be called a ballet with music, dance, and words. It's a study of a choreographer and a pair of dancers, and is to the ballet world what *A Chorus Line* is to musical theater. Anyone who has ever worked in the performing arts will immediately understand the line from his play, "Everything happens here—in the studio."

The play is packed with incidents recounted by Carrie, me, and the family around the dining-room table. I recognized, in the role of the older man, a hodge-podge of choreographers: Antony Tudor, Jerome Robbins, and Balanchine. In the female role, a combination of burning talent and ambition—Melissa Hayden, Merrill Ashley, and Suzanne Farrell. And, in the role of the young male, the ambivalent and ambiguous nature of practically every danseur noble that ever graced the stage.

Perceptive Chris—just as, from a chord played in another room, he can hear a note that is out of tune, he spots falseness in people, and analyzes them constantly, their behavior, as well as his own. George has that gift too. Chris has little tolerance for things that waste time. Once he has accomplished something, he bounces off to something else. His closet shelves are overloaded. But today he shares them with a dream of a dancer, Kelly Crandall. "Like Carrie," a touch of Texas and a charmer. They married the summer of 2008 in Taos, New Mexico, and as they danced the sacred skies applauded in thunder and blessed the ceremony with the most precious gift of the desert, a deluge.

CATHERINE (CATE)

After Charlotte's birth, Carrie's doctor said, "Oh, there's another!" Twenty minutes later, Cate came out, and forever after spent her time trying to please. I'd complain, "Carrie, I can't find my shoes, where the hell are they?" A flash of child in my periphery, Cate was out and back in the room in half a second, beaming, "Here they are, Daddy! They were under a towel in the bathroom."

Karinska gave us a gift of a woolen blanket woven from the wool of sheep she had at her farm and announced, "When your girls can do their first position, bring them to me. I will make them beautiful tutus."

In her last year of high school at the Calhoun School in Manhattan, Cate starred in the musical *Cabaret,* and was superb. Everyone in the audience buzzed: "Is she getting an agent?" "What are her plans?" That night, Cate climbed into our bed and confessed, "I don't want to take a chance with a life in the theater. I can't stand the tension and stress of auditions, and being rejected. Ben, my costar, has no doubts or fears. He told me, 'I'm going to be an actor.' Maybe I should try college." Ben Stiller was her

Getting their tutus at Karinska's costume shop, twins never agree, late 1960s

costar. Years later, at the fiftieth anniversary of Joe Papp's Public Theater, I saw Ben. The first thing he said was, "How's Cate?"

After graduating from Denison University, she became a specialist in early childhood development, married, moved to Santa Fe, New Mexico, and delivered to the world two fabulous children, Shane and Sam. They have their father's, Peter Brill's, strength and tenacity, and Cate's sweetness and champagne sense of humor. She is loved by everyone. Lucky friends of Cate, and lucky Santa Fe. Kay Gayner, who knows Cate well, gushed, "Cate d'Amboise is one of the greatest humans I've ever known." If a parent has a child in a class with Cate, that child is with joy.

CHARLOTTE AND *A CHORUS LINE*

I became a groupie to my daughter. The symptoms started when she did the national tour of *Cats.* I followed her to several cities. In *Jerome Robbins's Broadway,* I saw her starring as Peter Pan and as Anita in *West Side Story* at least a dozen times. Subsequently, there came a succession of roles on Broadway—*Song and Dance;* Lola in *Damn Yankees;* followed by a quartet of "C's"—*Company, Chicago, Contact,* and *A Chorus Line.* I kept count of the number of times I watched her as Roxie Hart in *Chicago:* one hundred sixty. The cast would spot my white hair in the audience, and one would quip, "Guess who's out front again?" And the chorus would answer, "Charlotte's dad—who else?" There was a short but dramatic stint starring in *Sweet Charity,* when the designated star, Christina Applegate, broke her ankle and Charlotte saved the day, stepping in to do the show in Boston and the previews on Broadway.

Decades ago, I had seen the musical *A Chorus Line.* The plot revolves around an audition. It didn't grab me, perhaps because I'd never had to audition for anything. Now, having seen the revival, I find that every moment in that show speaks directly to the heart of the dancer. And to me, particularly when the character Paul recounts how he overheard his father say to the company director, "Take care of my son," and Paul confesses, "I never heard him say those words to me, 'my son.'" The scene wets my eyes. Pop never used the word "son" or "my son" to me or, as far as I remember, to either of my brothers. The Boss, of course, made up for it effusively, to me and everyone else—"My son, Jacques, my son Jacques . . . ," "*Mon petit coco,*" "*Mon chouchou,*" "*Mon petit carrot.*" All vegetables!

Paul gets injured later in the show. He screams and clutches his knee, falls to the ground, and time suspends. Then, as most of the dancers run to him and cluster, a few back away, the implications too painful. "Is it broken?" Suggestions ring out, "No, it's his cartilage! Don't move your leg! No, he should try to straighten it!" With someone already calling a doctor, Paul tries to cover up the pain, wincing as he is carefully picked up and carried off to the emergency room.

Riveting truths are in that scene. First, "Where's his dance bag? Get his dance bag! Don't forget his dance bag." The dancer with a dance bag. I haven't performed in over twenty-six years, and I still carry my dance bag every day, even to black-tie affairs. When Paul's dance bag is gone, so is he.

Another moment of truth is the scene after Paul is carried out. The dancers wander, shuffling, feeling alone. Unable to make eye contact, retreating inside themselves. Until the character Zach, the director, breaks the silence. "All right, that's it, let's continue. Places. Come on, we're going on." Paul is erased from the land of the living. He can't dance anymore. Who is he? We know who *we* are: we're dancers.

Unyielding dedication, discipline, and pain is the crucible that transforms a person who dances into a dancer.

That's why I told Balanchine from the hospital bed after my first knee operation, "Of course I'm ready. Schedule me!" Six weeks *before* the doctor told me I could start dancing again, I was on that stage performing the final movement of the ballet *Brahms-Schoenberg.* OH GOD, was it exhilarating! A sort of pseudo-Hungarian ballet/folk dance Balanchine had choreographed for Suzanne Farrell and me. I wore soft, knee-high boots, and it wasn't until I was going up the stairs to my dressing room after the curtain calls that I noticed a squishy sound—my right boot was ankle deep in blood. During the performance all the stitches had ripped open.

I believe it's the same on the playing field, the tennis court, the baseball diamond, the track, or the gymnastic balance beam—the whole world is the now. The past recedes; everything is in the present. The space you inhabit and the art you're engaged in is all there is. That's what it meant to me every time the curtain went up and I made an entrance. Home, loved ones, parents, children, eating, drinking, taxes, birth, death were unimportant. Dance, the music, and the moment are the universe.

Once, and I don't know how it happened, but in the late afternoon I stubbed my toe so badly, the toenail loosened on the big toe of my left foot and came off, leaving raw flesh. I was supposed to dance *Apollo* that night, so I called up Dr. Louise Krynski, a Russian-Polish friend and spouse to another doctor, Boris Krynski. Louise squeaked out in her tiny voice, "Oh, maybe Boris can help you." At half hour, Boris showed up in my dressing room with an enormous syringe and injected a numbing drug into the toe. I put on my costume and ballet shoes, and went onstage. I don't think Boris stayed to see the performance. I had *Apollo* to dance. He had a gallbladder to remove.

Shortly after Paul is carried out of the audition in *A Chorus Line,* the character Diana Morales answers the choreographer's question "What would you do if you couldn't dance anymore?" Her answer. An exquisite song "What I Did for Love." Listening in the audience, I am visited by a stream of ghosts. Maria Tallchief with her feet so beat up from a lifetime in toe shoes, she needs a wheelchair to get around. Visiting Leon Danielian in his hospital bed, he pulled up the sheets to show me mangled dancer's feet, the toes twisted around each other; one seemed upside down. I took off my shoes and socks, hopped in bed next to him, and we put our feet together, compared deformities, laughed, and proudly showed them to the nurses. "See ladies, what we did for love? Now vote, which are the worst?" Leon won. The ballerina Patricia Neary, Miss Extrovert herself, teaching a ballet class. "Hey, all of you, look at this!" She pulls out the set of X-rays she carries in her dance bag: "See the metal bars in my hips and bones? Well, with all that metal, I can still do fouettés, so why the hell can't you?"—and then she knocks off half a dozen. Suzanne Farrell, coaching young dancers so elegantly, wearing her own bars of metal. Eddie Villella, because of the wear and tear on his joints, ended his career early. A few years ago, at the Kennedy Center Honors, he confessed to me, "I've got to do the hips again, Jack. They wear out after twenty years." Today, I have two artificial knees. Recently, visiting Shaun O'Brien and Cris Alexander at their home in Saratoga, Cris declared, beaming, "Daisy, Shaun and I have been together longer than you and Carrie." Older than Shaun, Cris was standing tall and erect, and next to him, bent over, was Shaun shuffling, with twisted toes like Leon's. What we did for love.

Most heartrending was courageous and determined Merrill Ashley, her face drawn with pain, limping down the street and into the stage door to prepare to dance. A few hours later on that stage, managing to flow smoothly and beautifully. The audience never realized she was in conflict with her body, ignoring its messages, knowing only that she loved the dance so much; she wanted to stay onstage forever.

So many great dancers in my years with New York City Ballet elevated the audience with their individual artistry. The two Johns, John Prinz and John Clifford, thrilling and stimulating in everything they did, stay in my mind, as does Mimi Paul, bringing beauty to every gesture. Marnee Morris spinning all over the stage. Suki Schorer, perking up every performance. Dramatic Nichol Hlinka, small in stature, giant in talent. Whenever Heather Watts performed the ballet *The Cage*, I would go to the wings or out front to watch. I loved viewing Conrad Ludlow, too, and the poetry he brought to a pas de deux. Any time I see a ballet that has in it a role that Eddie Villella, Violette Verdy, or Patricia McBride danced I am haunted by the memory of how great they were. I would need another book to list the names of the dancing artists who ennobled my performing life. In the corps de ballet, among the soloists and principals, everyone found their voice, and Balanchine nurtured and cared for all. As Francis Sackett put it beautifully, "We were

Sharing the stage with Merrill Ashley, 1970

so lucky to be able to grab hold of the tail end of the comet that was Balanchine."

At the fiftieth reunion of NYCB, they posted big placards, designating decades—dancers of the '40s, '50s, '60s, '70s, '80s—I fit them all, and I wandered around, greeting my compatriots. Among those of the first three decades, a quarter of them had joint replacements; by far, the majority were hips. What we did for love.

My memoirs are not filled with angst. There hasn't been horror. My son George didn't die. My brother John did, but he was close to eighty, and I was lucky to be at his bedside with his wife, Mary, his daughter Maureen, and especially my sister, Ninette, who held his hand and sat with him, murmuring praise, "What a great brother you've been, John, what a good man you are," and singing lullabies and Irish ditties, past his final exhale.

A wild, untamed youth learns nobility through art, 1962

I love hanging out with Ninette, a diligent transformer of NYC vacant lots into garden oases, and I got her to perform with NDI. Brother Paul and his wife, Kathleen, for many years came to New York to help out at NDI. Occasionally I pop up to visit their fiefdom in Maine, where they preside over their enormous family. Cate's two children, Shane and Sam, are seizing life with passion and grace, and have performed with NDI New Mexico. Charlotte and her actor husband,

Terrence Mann, are raising their two girls—Shelby and Josephine—
and I have already wheedled the four of them to perform with NDI.

I don't know if anyone reading these memoirs will be disappointed
that there was no revelation of drugs and childhood abuse. I've always
been happy. In Staten Island, I escaped untouched by the man in the
shadows of the barn, I survived the streetcar, never was sued by the city
of Hamburg, and didn't get polio when poor Tanny did. I hugged her
that night in Cologne in 1956, and flew home to my bed in New York;
she flew to Copenhagen, to recline in an iron lung. Dear Tanny, bravery
and humor sat with you in your wheelchair for almost fifty years. Fate
could have had me sitting in its mate, but I can still walk. The Cuban
missile crisis did not escalate into war, so I never had to do pliés in a
Siberian gulag; and Carrie and I weren't at the Bishops' the night of the
slaughter.

Everything was given to me, by the best and of their best.

Twentieth century born, and trying to understand the twenty-first;
I have become a proselytizer for the importance of the arts and learning.
But, above all, and central to everything, I was a dancer.

As Milly said to me, and I often say to Carrie, "We did a good job.
Goodbye."

Appendix: The Novena

In writing these memories, I implored several friends from the old days to set me straight on the exact structure of the Novena. Each person had a different version. I've reprinted one here. (Maybe you can figure it out.)

ORIGIN AND METHOD

This devotion, which the author has called the "Rosary Novena to Our Lady," is of comparatively recent origin.

"In an apparition of Our Lady of Pompeii, which occurred in 1884 at Naples, in the house of Commander Agrelli, the heavenly Mother deigned to make known the manner in which she desires to be invoked.

"For thirteen months Fortuna Agrelli, the daughter of the Commander, had endured dreadful sufferings and torturous cramps; she had been given up by the most celebrated physicians. On February 16, 1884, the afflicted girl and her relatives commenced a Novena of Rosaries. The Queen of the Holy Rosary favored her with an apparition on March 3rd. Mary, sitting upon a high throne, surrounded by luminous figures, held the divine Child on her lap, and in her hand a Rosary. The Virgin Mother and the holy Infant were clad in gold-embroidered garments. They were accompanied by St. Dominic and St. Catherine of Siena. The throne was profusely decorated with flowers; the beauty of Our Lady was marvelous.

"Mary looked upon the sufferer with maternal tenderness, and the patient saluted her with the words: 'Queen of the Holy Rosary, be gracious to me; restore me to health! I have already prayed to thee in a Novena, O Mary, but have not yet experienced thy aid. I am so anxious to be cured!'

" 'Child,' responded the Blessed Virgin, 'thou hast invoked me by various titles and has always obtained favors from me. Now, since thou hast called me by that title so pleasing to me, "Queen of the Holy Rosary," I can no longer refuse the favor thou dost petition; for this name is most precious and dear to me. Make three Novenas, and thou shalt obtain all.'

"Once more the Queen of the Holy Rosary appeared to her and said, 'Whoever desires to obtain favors from me should make three Novenas of the prayers of the Rosary, and three Novenas in thanksgiving.'

"This miracle of the Rosary made a very deep impression on Pope Leo XIII, and greatly contributed to the fact that in so many circular letters he urged all Christians to love the Rosary and say it fervently."—The Rosary, My Treasure, Benedictine Convent, Clyde, Mo.

The Novena consists of five decades of the Rosary each day for twenty-seven days in petition; then immediately five decades each day for twenty-seven days in thanksgiving, whether or not the request has been granted.

The meditations vary from day to day. On the first day meditate on the Joyful Mysteries; on the second day, the Sorrowful Mysteries; on the third day, the Glorious Mysteries; on the fourth day, meditate again on the Joyful Mysteries; and so on throughout the fifty-four days.

A laborious Novena, but a Novena of Love. You who are sincere will not find it too difficult, if you really wish to obtain your request.

Should you not obtain the favor you seek, be assured that the Rosary Queen, who knows what each one stands most in need of, has heard your prayer. You will not have prayed in vain. No prayer ever went unheard. And Our Blessed Lady has never been known to fail.

Look upon each Hail Mary as a rare and beautiful rose which you lay at Mary's feet.

These spiritual roses, bound in a wreath with Spiritual Communions, will be a most pleasing and acceptable gift to her, and will bring down upon you special graces.

If you would reach the innermost recesses of her heart, lavishly bedeck your wreath with spiritual diamonds—holy communions. Then her joy will be unbounded, and she will open wide the channel of her choicest graces to you.

NOTE: In obedience to the decree of Pope Urban VIII and of other Supreme Pontiffs, the author begs to state that, in regard to what is herein narrated, no higher authority is claimed than that which is due to all authentic human testimony.

PROMISES

Made by the Blessed Virgin to St. Dominic and Blessed Alanus.

1. To all those who will recite my Rosary devoutly, I promise my special protection and very great graces.
2. Those who will persevere in the recitation of my Rosary shall receive some signal grace.
3. The Rosary shall be a very powerful armor against hell; it shall destroy vice, deliver from sin, and shall dispel heresy.
4. The Rosary shall make virtue and good works flourish, and shall obtain for souls the most abundant divine mercies; it shall substitute in hearts love of God for love of the world, elevate them to desire heavenly and eternal goods. Oh, that souls would sanctify themselves by this means!
5. Those who trust themselves to me through the Rosary, shall not perish.
6. Those who will recite my Rosary piously, considering its Mysteries, shall not be overwhelmed by misfortune nor die a bad death. The sinner shall be converted; the just shall grow in grace and become worthy of eternal life.
7. Those truly devoted to my Rosary shall not die without the consolations of the Church, or without grace.

8. Those who will recite my Rosary shall find during their life and at their death the light of God, the fulness of His grace, and shall share in the merits of the blessed.
9. I will deliver very promptly from purgatory the souls devoted to my Rosary.
10. The true children of my Rosary shall enjoy great glory in heaven.
11. What you ask through my Rosary, you shall obtain.

Those who propagate my Rosary shall obtain through me aid in all their necessities.

Index

Page numbers in *italics* refer to illustrations.

A NOTE ON THE TYPE

The text of this book was set in Garamond No. 3. It is
not a true copy of any of the designs of Claude Garamond
(ca. 1480–1561), but an adaptation of his types, which set the
European standard for two centuries. This particular version
is based on an adaptation by Morris Fuller Benton.

COMPOSED BY *North Market Street Graphics, Lancaster, Pennsylvania*

PRINTED AND BOUND BY *Berryville Graphics, Berryville, Virginia*

DESIGNED BY *Iris Weinstein*